The Psychology of Teaching and Learning in the Primary School

Primary school education is in a period of controversy and change. Currently raging debates include the best ways of teaching children to read and gain confidence in mathematics; assessment; ways of dealing with emotional and behavioural problems and how to guide children towards good citizenship. This book reviews recent work in psychology which sheds welcome new light on these important areas of concern to primary school teachers and provides clear, up-to-date guidelines for good practice.

After an initial chapter concerned with the nature of classroom teaching expertise, the remainder of the book is divided into three sections:

- organising the learning environment
- teaching the curriculum
- educating all children

The first section includes chapters concerned with the physical environment of the classroom, managing teacher–pupil communication, developing group work and children's motivation. The second addresses assessment; teaching reading and numeracy; an teaching children to remember, understand, think, reason, solve problems and be creative. The final section is concerned with responding to children as individuals, providing equal opportunities, and teaching children with emotional, behavioural and learning difficulties.

This book will be invaluable for tutors and students on courses of initial teacher training, and teachers involved in professional development. At the same time, it is written in a refreshingly accessible style, ideal for the non-specialist, and is well illustrated with practical classroom examples and suggestions for further reading. It offers an up-to-date review of the best available evidence from psychological research, much of which has radical and important implications for teaching primary school children.

David Whitebread is Senior Lecturer in Education at Homerton College, Cambridge. He is the author of the highly successful textbook *Teaching and Learning in the Early Years*, also published by Routledge.

The Psychology of Teaching and Learning in the Primary School

Edited by
David Whitebread

London and New York

First published 2000 by RoutledgeFalmer 11 New Fetter Lane,
London EC4P 4EE

Simultaneously published in the USA and Canada by
RoutledgeFalmer 29 West 35th Street, New York, NY 10001

RoutledgeFalmer is an imprint of the Taylor & Francis Group

Typeset in Baskerville by Bookcraft Ltd, Stroud, Gloucestershire
Printed and bound in Great Britain by Biddles Ltd, Guildford and
Kings Lynn

British Library Cataloguing in Publication Data
A catalogue record for this book is available from the British Library

Library of Congress Cataloging in Publication Data
The psychology of teaching and learning in the primary school /
edited by David Whitebread
    p. cm.
  Includes bibliographical references and index.
  ISBN 0–415–21404–1 (alk. paper) – ISBN 0–415–21405–X (pbk. :
alk. paper)
    1. Elementary school teaching–Psychological aspects. 2. Learning,
Psychology of. 3. Educational psychology. I Whitebread, David, 1948–

LB1555 .P83 2000
372.21'0941–dc21   00-030594

ISBN 0–415–21405–X (pbk)
ISBN 0–415–21404–1 (hbk)

Contents

Figures

Tables

Acknowledgements

The author wishes to thank the following for permission to reproduce material: Heather Elkington, Headteacher, Letchmore Infants' and Nursery School, Stevenage (Figures 5.2, 6.1 and 10.1); James Hickish, Headteacher, The Spinney School, Cambridge (Figures 3.2, 4.1, 5.1, 8.6, 9.1 and 11.1); Simon Hoad, Headteacher, Stapleford Community Primary School, Cambridge (Figures 1.1, 3.2, 4.1 and 16.1); Chris Ingham, Headteacher, John Falkner Infant School, Cambridge (Figures 2.3 and 7.2); L.J. Mitchell, Headteacher, Southfields Infant School, Peterborough (Figure 2.1); Zoë Rhydderch-Evans, Education Consultant, Newton St Cyres (Figure 10.2); Henry Weir, Headteacher, Debden C. of E. Primary School, Saffron Walden (Figures 2.4, 3.1 and 8.5); Jan Wright, Headteacher, Holywell C.E. (C.) School, Huntingdon (Figure 2.2).

Figure 7.3 appeared as Figure 1 in *Developmental Psychology* (1983) 19, 29–39 by M.T.H. Chi and R.D. Koeske, © 1983 by the American Psychological Association. Figure 8.2 appeared in *Children's Minds* by Margaret Donaldson, Fontana, 1978, p. 21. Figure 8.3 is adapted from *The Psychology of Reasoning* by P.C. Wason and P.N. Johnson-Laird, Batsford, 1972. Figure 8.4 appeared in *Studies in Cognitive Growth* by J.S. Bruner, R.R. Olver and P.M. Greenfield, J. Wiley and Sons, 1966, p. 156. Figure 8.7 appeared as 'Bicycle–8' in *Children Solve Problems* by Edward de Bono, Allen Lane The Penguin Press, 1972, p. 185; © 1972 The Cognitive Trust. Figure 8.8 appeared as Figure 4 in Chapter 2 of *Teaching Children to Think* by R. Fisher, Stanley Thornes Publishers, 1990. Figure 11.2 appeared in 'Models of teacher assessment among primary school teachers in England', by C. Gipps, B. MacCallum and M. Brown, *The Curriculum Journal*, 7, 2, 167–83, 1997. The questionnaire on principles of assessment in the Activities section of Chapter 11 appeared in *Making Assessment Work: values and principles in assessing young children's learning*, edited by M.J. Drummond, D. Rouse and G. Pugh, NES Arnold/National Children's Bureau, 1992. All are reprinted or adapted with permission.

Chapter 10 first appeared, in a slightly modified form, as 'Emergent Mathematics, or How to help Young Children become confident Mathematicians' in *Children's Mathematical Thinking in the Primary Years* edited by Julia Anghileri, Cassell, 1995. It is reprinted here with the permission of the original publishers.

Contributors

Roland Chaplain is a Chartered Psychologist and currently works as a Senior Lecturer in Psychology and Education at Homerton College. He worked in a number of schools in England and has experience as a class teacher, headteacher and as head of psychological services. He is currently Project Director of a study sponsored by the NEBP and DFEE examining pupils' self-efficacy, academic performance and school effectiveness.

Colin Conner is a lecturer at the University of Cambridge School of Education, where he teaches on a variety of Advanced Studies courses related to the contribution of psychology to the development of teachers' thinking. He has been actively researching the implementation of National Curriculum assessment since its introduction in 1988. A major element of this has been a series of inter-related projects in cooperation with the local authorities in the Eastern Region of the UK.

Ruth Kershner is a Senior Lecturer in Psychology and Education at Homerton College, University of Cambridge. She has previously worked as a learning support teacher, Primary teacher and child care worker. Her current research interests are in the areas of teaching children with learning difficulties and using information and communications technology in Primary schools.

Peter Kutnick is a Professor of Education (Research) in the Faculty of Education and Sport at the University of Brighton. His primary research and teaching concerns include the development and promotion of social relationships amongst Primary school-aged children. He is currently working on large-scale research projects exploring the nature and use of pupil groups within classrooms.

Donald McIntyre is Professor of Education and Head of the School of Education at the University of Cambridge. He has been researching and writing about teachers and teaching for some thirty-five years. He has a particular interest in Initial Teacher Education, and played a major part in the development of the pioneering Oxford Internship Scheme.

Iain Manson has worked as a part-time lecturer in human development and early schooling while undertaking research to complete his PhD. His research concerns the development and evaluation of a social relational programme for the development of co-operation among Primary school children.

John Robertson is an educational consultant, writer and lecturer, specialising in effective teaching skills and managing classroom behaviour. He has a wide experience in education, having previously taught in schools, worked as an educational psychologist and as a lecturer in teacher training at Homerton College. He now lectures nationally on initial teacher training and INSET courses on classroom behaviour management.

Isobel Urquhart is a Senior Lecturer in Education at Homerton College, working mainly in the Psychology and Language Departments. Before coming to Homerton, she was an SEN Projects Teacher in Essex, having taught for about fifteen years. She has recently worked in Africa and India on the development and evaluation of Primary literacy programmes, and school and staff development. Currently, her research activities continue to reflect her interest in qualitative research methods, narrative and psychoanalytical contributions to learning and teaching.

David Whitebread is a Senior Lecturer in Psychology and Education at Homerton College. Before coming to Homerton he taught KS1 and KS2 classes in several Primary schools, mostly in Leicestershire, for about twelve years. He works with a number of local and national organisations concerned with Early Years education. His research interests focus on children's learning and problem-solving in relation to a range of applied areas, including mathematics, ICT and road safety. Currently he is carrying out research concerned with the development of children's abilities as independent learners.

Joan M. Whitehead is a lecturer in Psychology at the University of Cambridge School of Education. One of her main areas of teaching and research is in gender studies, particularly the impact of gender identity and attitude to sex roles on educational achievement and decision-making. She is currently involved in research concerned with the differences between academically successful and unsuccessful schoolboys.

Preface

Many Primary school teachers will recall attending Psychology of Education courses during their initial training and, although possibly finding some of the material presented quite interesting, never being very clear as to its relevance to the everyday practicalities of teaching young children to read, write, add up, paint, sing, make models and get along with one another. A whole range of research and ideas developing within psychology and education during the last twenty years or so, however, have transformed this situation. Dry and inadequate theories of learning and motivation, derived largely from studying the behaviour of hungry rats, pigeons, monkeys, etc. in mazes, boxes with levers and so on are now properly consigned to the dusty bowels of academic libraries.

This book is written in the belief that, in their place, there is now a genuinely useful body of research and theory which can help Primary school teachers to understand children, their development and learning. In turn, these insights can help practitioners to develop more effective approaches to many aspects of the enormously challenging, complex and endlessly fascinating job of teaching young children.

The book is written largely by members of the Psychology team at Homerton, with contributions from colleagues in the University of Cambridge School of Education and elsewhere. The contents have emerged from courses taught in the college's initial teacher training programmes and have, therefore, been developed and honed through the highly articulate, perceptive and constructively critical appraisal of a vast number of trainee teachers (for whom we are eternally and genuinely grateful!). As such, the book attempts to address important aspects of the work of Primary school teachers and significant bodies of research and theory within developmental and educational psychology which have practical relevance to these issues.

We are wedded to the belief that teachers will be more effective in their practice if they are reflective, analytical in their thinking and in a position to make well-founded and informed judgements. That learning is an active process is, clearly, a major theme of the book. In order to help readers engage practically with the material, ideas and issues addressed, we have provided activities at the end of each chapter which involve private reflection, discussion with colleagues, tasks to carry out with children and so on. Many of these activities are ones which we have used ourselves within our courses and which have proved helpful. Recommended further reading, together with a full list of references, is also provided with each chapter. We hope that trainee and practising teachers, together with teacher trainers and educators will find these useful in developing their own thinking and understanding in relation to the issues addressed.

I should make one other point about the structure of the book. Dividing up the complex and completely interwoven fabric of the day-to-day realities of working with young children into separate topics is inevitably rather artificial, and we have been conscious in writing each of our separate chapters of the myriad ways in which each area or issue relates so closely to all the others. We have refrained, however, except where it was completely necessary, from constantly cross-referring between chapters, as this could have become extremely tedious for the reader. In reading the book, however, it is hoped that readers will become aware of the important links which exist between areas, and without which a complete understanding would not be achieved.

It simply remains for me to thank the colleagues who have contributed to the book for their patience and perseverance, and to appreciate them and other colleagues at Homerton who have contributed in all kinds of ways over the years to the development of my own thinking about young children and their education.

I must also particularly thank the following colleagues who, either as trainees or as school mentors, have provided, or agreed to appear in, the various photographs in the book: Sarah Cameron, Susan Cox, Hannah Curtis, Sue Gardner, Jayne Greenwood, Kimberley Hayden, James Hickish, Melanie Houlder, Manjit Klair, Katie Kowalska, Jude Laidlaw, Holly Linklater and Suzanne Stokes. Thanks, too, to Dianne Conway (and Becky) for the delightful illustration in Chapter 16.

I also, of course, must thank all the children with whom I have worked (some of whom grace the cover and insides of the book!) and who have been a constant delight, mostly in their refusal to behave the way that books say they do.

David Whitebread
Homerton College, Cambridge
February 2000

1 The nature of classroom teaching expertise

Donald McIntyre

EDITOR'S SUMMARY

By way of introduction, this opening chapter explores the evidence about the essential prerequisites for effective Primary school teaching. In doing so, it explodes some of the common myths. It emerges that there is no ideal personality for a teacher; people with very different personalities can be excellent teachers. There is also no one best style of teaching. The best teachers use a repertoire of various styles and strategies; it is not the strategies they use that make the difference, but the skill with which they use them. Being a person (rather than a machine) turns out to be vital. Good teaching is complex and relies upon the sensitivity and empathy of which only a person is capable. It is the capacity for fluent, insightful, almost instantaneous, only half-conscious intuitive judgement, like that of the artist or highly skilled craftsman, which is most characteristic of the highly experienced and expert classroom teacher.

Introduction

What is 'teaching'? Teaching can be the most exciting and challenging of all human enterprises, or it can be soul-destroying drudgery. Which it is depends on how one interprets the task. At its worst, teaching is the communication to learners of what A. N. Whitehead (1929) memorably described as 'inert ideas', slabs of knowledge which the learners are asked to accept and to remember without questioning it and without using it for any purposes of their own. But teaching can be more positively seen in many different ways.

One splendid tradition of teaching stems from the classical Greek philosopher Socrates, who thought of teaching as the art of asking good questions, and apparently practised it that way. On one hand, Socrates believed that by being asked to consider successive good questions, any learners could be brought to reveal the truth to themselves. Plato, in the Dialogue *Meno*, represents Socrates as, for example, teaching Pythagoras' Theorem to a slave boy solely by asking him questions. But Socrates' 'good questions' were not simply aimed at getting people to learn: they were aimed at leading people to search for the truth, a potentially unpopular activity in any society; and so it proved for Socrates, since in the end he was condemned to death for 'corrupting the youth of Athens'. A modern example of this excellent tradition is the book by Postman and Weingartner (1971), *Teaching as a Subversive Activity*, in which they urge schoolteachers to replace the teaching of inert ideas by the teaching of such skills as 'crap-detecting'.

Another very valuable tradition of teaching was first clearly articulated in the eighteenth century by the French philosopher Jean-Jacques Rousseau. Rousseau described how he would 'teach' his pupil Emile until late adolescence entirely through Emile's learning from experience and from the 'natural' consequences of his actions. One vivid model which he used was that of Robinson Crusoe on his desert island: Emile, like Robinson Crusoe, was to discover for himself what he needed and how he could best meet his needs. In this same tradition are the nineteenth-century theorists, Pestalozzi and Froebel, with their emphasis on natural development, on the natural learning of children from their mothers as the model for at least the early stages of schooling, and on learning through play.

Probably the person whose ideas about teaching are currently most influential is the psychologist Vygotsky (1962, 1978), whose pioneering work in the Soviet Union in the nineteen-twenties and thirties became well-known in the west only during the eighties. For Vygotsky, human learning is inherently a social process, and happens most effectively when the learner is jointly engaged with others, such as a teacher, notably on tasks which he or she understands and can usefully engage on in that collaborative setting, but would not be able to cope with on his or her own. Vygotsky talked about these tasks as being in the individual's *zone of proximal development*, which is not only of course specific to the individual learner but also constantly changing. In articulating this powerful idea, Vygotsky thus not only gives us valuable guidance but also reminds us how challenging the task of teaching is.

What is the common element across such different ideas about teaching? Little more, perhaps, than the common goal of helping others to learn as effectively as possible. Teaching is one of the most pervasive of human enterprises, encompassing as it does any activity designed to facilitate learning. Teaching is done in many ways, for example through explaining ideas, through showing people how tasks can be done, through making and enforcing rules, through giving people the opportunity to see things for themselves, or to discover patterns, or to suffer the consequences of their actions, or through commenting informatively on people's performances. Similarly, we are all teachers, in that we all at one time or another try to help others to learn: parents, brothers and sisters, friends, colleagues, officials in every context that is new for us (e.g. transport systems, places of entertainment, government offices) and even casual acquaintances are among those who teach us; and in the same way we teach diverse others in different kinds of contexts. It is quite an interesting exercise to reflect on whether *any* valid generalisations can be made about 'teaching' across the whole enormous range of things that are taught, of people who are taught, and contexts in which teaching occurs. It is difficult to think of any beyond the definition: what we *mean* by 'teaching' is *acting so as to facilitate learning*.

In most societies, however, there have been people, the holders of certain positions, who have had a formal position as teachers of what has been viewed as especially important knowledge. Often these people have been priests or occupants of other religious positions. There have too been *professional* teachers in many societies: in Europe, for example, the history of professional teaching goes back for over two and a half millennia. (It is worth noting that almost universally most teaching has been done by parents and other family members, but that this teaching has generally been taken for granted: it is the additional specialist teaching that is formally recognised.) Even professional teaching, however, has been very diverse in its purposes, its content, its methods, the contexts in which it has been carried out, and also in the nature of the people taught, although on the whole these have been relatively young people.

It is only relatively recently – during the last two centuries – that what we are currently accustomed to has become the norm. Aspects of this norm include the development of national education systems, the assumption that education in these systems will be through attendance at schools, and the aspiration that almost all young people should attend these schools for a number of years. For our purposes, an even more fundamental and striking feature of this recently established norm is that young people (pupils) are organised in classes and that the teaching of these classes is conducted in classrooms. That classroom teaching has become the norm makes it a little easier for us to generalise about professional teaching in schools: it seems likely that classroom teaching expertise has much in common across different contemporary education systems. Yet it is also important to remember that classroom teaching *is* a historical phenomenon: it will not last for ever; indeed it may quite possibly give way, even during the careers of some of those currently learning to teach, to other and possibly better ways of organising teaching and learning in schools.

Classroom teaching and the expertise required

This chapter is concerned with the nature of the expertise required for good classroom teaching. Gaining a general understanding of the nature of that expertise seems an important first step for those who wish to acquire it.

Classroom teaching is a complex and very demanding professional activity (see Figure 1.1), but it is also almost unique among professional activities in

Figure 1.1 Teaching a class of Primary school children is a complex and demanding activity requiring human sensitivity and empathy

that everyone spends a lot of time as a child in classrooms with teachers. In particular, those who wish to become teachers have already spent many years in what has been called an 'apprenticeship of observation' (Lortie 1975); and this apprenticeship of observation seems likely to have exercised a major influence on most people's decisions to become teachers and on their pre-conceptions about what teaching will involve. In many respects this must be helpful: beginning teachers have a better idea of what they are letting themselves in for than do entrants to most professions. On the other hand, there is a danger that prospective teachers (like other members of society) may be inclined to take the expertise involved in classroom teaching too much for granted. Because one is so familiar with it, what teachers need to do may seem obvious, whereas in fact it is much more complex than is apparent to the observer. Here as in other contexts, skilled performances tend to look simple to observers, just because they are so skilled.

This chapter will examine several different views of the nature of class-room teaching expertise, all of which have some claim to plausibility.

Personality

'Teachers are born not made'; 'She's a natural teacher'; 'It's all a matter of personality'. Statements like this are common whenever classroom expertise is being discussed, in school staffrooms as much as anywhere else. There would therefore seem to be good grounds for taking this view seriously. Is it the case then that being a good teacher is a matter primarily of the kind of person one is? The question is one that has intrigued many educational researchers, and still does, but the answer was pretty well established many years ago. Such authoritative reviews as that by Getzels and Jackson (1963) of the extensive research in the area already published then concluded that:

- teachers vary in personality about as much as the whole population does
- effectiveness of teaching (however measured) is unrelated to personality.

More recent research has not led to any different conclusions. There are among classroom teachers those who are extroverts and those who are introverts, those primarily interested in abstract ideas, or in people, or in concrete things, those who tend to be anxious and those who tend to be happy-go-lucky, and all can be excellent teachers. Why then does the idea persist that personality is so important?

Partly, no doubt, the answer is that the kind of person one is certainly tends to be reflected in the kind of classroom teacher one is. And of course some observers will find certain kinds of personality and the related kinds of teaching more or less attractive. Different people certainly teach in different ways, but there are no good reasons for believing that the quality of teaching is related to teacher personality.

A more fundamental reason for the persistence of the belief that personality is important is that it is undoubtedly true that *people* are important as teachers. The fact that as a classroom teacher one is a person matters greatly in at least three ways.

- Drawing on one's personal experience is often very important in making things interesting and comprehensible to one's pupils; more generally, being able to understand and empathise with one's pupils' experiences is crucial in helping them to make sense of things.
- Sensitivity to emotional aspects of learning is also important: the frustrations, efforts, successes and excitements of pupils need to be recognised and sympathised with.
- Human intelligence is important in working out what's happening in a classroom and in deciding what to do.

What matters, then, is not the kind of person that one is, but rather the fact that one is a person with experiences of one's own, with feelings and capacity to empathise, and the ability to think intelligently and creatively about what one is doing. These are fundamental to classroom teaching.

It is important that beginning teachers should not believe that in order to become good teachers they have to become a certain kind of person. On the other hand, they should believe and remember that the full range of their humanity, all their experiences, all their sensitivity, all their talents and all their intelligence can and should be drawn upon appropriately to enhance the quality of their teaching.

Styles of teaching

Anyone who follows the educational controversies pursued in the British press knows that the important questions are about what general styles of teaching are best. Is it whole-class teaching or collaborative groupwork or individualised teaching that is best? Is it best to teach in a topic- or project-based way or to teach subjects? Is it best to emphasise practical activities or to concentrate on the ideas themselves?

Unfortunately the British press is wrong. These are not the important questions. Extensive research has failed to establish consistent patterns of superiority for any one kind of approach over another. Teaching is simply not that simple. For example, two highly publicised studies of teaching styles in English primary schools were those of Bennett (1976) and Galton and Simon (1980). One thing that became apparent from these studies was how difficult it is in practice to categorise teachers in terms of their teaching styles: Bennett found he needed eleven different categories to take account of the main differences. A second finding was that, if there were differences in effectiveness, these differences were very subtle: among the teachers studied by Bennett, it seemed that those who used more 'traditional' styles tended to be slightly more effective, although the most effective of them all was a teacher whose style was 'progressive'; and when Bennett later analysed the data in a slightly different way, it was those who used the more 'progressive' styles who generally seemed to be more effective. Thirdly, as the more careful and sophisticated Galton study found, in so far as styles made a difference at all, different styles were better for achieving different things. From all the research on teaching styles, we can conclude three main things.

- Effectiveness seems to depend much more on the skilfulness with which an approach is used than on which approach is used.
- In so far as approaches do differ in their effectiveness, different approaches are more or less effective for achieving different kinds of learning goals, and to some extent for different learners and for different kinds of context.
- Because that is so, and because variety is itself an important contributor to effective teaching, competent teachers have wide repertoires of approaches to teaching, repertoires which they draw on according to what is needed for each particular occasion.

Knowledge of subject

A third widely suggested idea about what really matters in a teacher is that it is the teacher's knowledge of what she or he is teaching that is crucial.

In its positive aspect, this is an assertion which can hardly be questioned and which indeed is profoundly important: the fuller, the deeper, the more wide-ranging, the more questioning, the more refined one's knowledge of what one is teaching, the more one has to offer, and the wider the range of options one has in choosing ways of teaching effectively. Teachers' lack of knowledge about the subjects they teach is a major reason for lack of effectiveness.

The problem, however, is that while a deep understanding of what one is teaching is a necessary condition for effective teaching, it is far from being sufficient. Teaching, it was suggested earlier, can best be defined as the facilitation of learning. Understanding a subject well should certainly help one to facilitate learning in others; but there's a lot else that one has to do. At a minimum, one has to explain the subject in a way that is clear not just to oneself but also to one's pupils. Furthermore, one cannot assume that most pupils will be at all interested in the subject, or motivated in any way to learn it, nor even that they will attend to what one says to them. Most of all, their learning of the subject will depend on them being able to connect it up with what they do know and care about, with what makes sense to them. So the teacher not only has to have all kinds of skills for motivating and communicating; even more fundamentally, the teacher has to identify imaginatively with the learners, to see the world from their perspective. Basil Bernstein said that:

> If the culture of the teacher is to become part of the consciousness of the child, then the culture of the child must first be in the consciousness of the teacher.
>
> (Bernstein 1970:115).

And of course, not only are the cultures of the children the cultures of some very diverse social groups, but also individual learners interpret and draw upon cultures in their own individual ways.

So anyone who thinks that a good knowledge of the subject that they are going to teach is the only important element in teacher expertise, and that the rest is just common sense, hasn't really thought about teaching very carefully. As noted earlier, the fact that everyone, having had extensive experience of classrooms, 'knows about teaching' can mislead some people into the thoughtless belief that 'the rest' is just common sense. This is a point of view especially common among university lecturers (e.g. Lawlor 1990) who are rightly conscious of the importance of the subject knowledge, but who are misled because their own practice has generally been to leave to their students the whole responsibility for their learning. They have therefore failed to recognise that what they teach may well not be learned, and that in such a case the teaching – however accurate and coherent the presentation of the subject – is not effective. Yet the irritating thoughtlessness and lack of respect of such people for classroom teachers should not lead us to forget that the importance they place on subject knowledge is entirely justified.

Acting in appropriate ways

The way in which most student teachers are inclined, very reasonably, to think of good teaching, is to see it as a skilled performance that one has to learn.

'Tell me' they sensibly ask their mentors, 'how do you get the pupils to participate in classroom discussion so enthusiastically and yet in such an orderly way.
Tell me, because I want to be able to do that.' Mentors, asked that kind of question, often find it almost impossible to answer. What they are being asked for is
the recipe to be used to achieve the particular outcome. And it seems that if
they have such recipes, they are not conscious of what they are. It does, however, seem sensible to believe that they must have such recipes.

So around the 1970s, most classroom research was aimed at answering that
kind of question, that is looking for a generalised answer about what kind of
teacher activity is generally effective in achieving some desired kind of outcome. And this kind of research produced, and continues to produce, a lot
of useful findings which every classroom teacher ought to know about.

For example, what does research of this kind tell us about ways in which
learning is facilitated by the ways in which teachers present information? An
authoritative review of research (Brophy and Good 1986) summarises some
aspects of the relevant research as follows:

> *Structuring* Achievement is maximised when teachers not only actively
> present material, but structure it by beginning with overviews, advance
> organisers, or review of objectives; outlining the content and signalling
> transitions between lesson parts; calling attention to main ideas; sum-
> marising subparts of the lesson as it proceeds; and reviewing main ideas
> at the end. Organising concepts and analogies help learners link the
> new to the already familiar. Overviews and outlines help them to de-
> velop learning sets to use in assimilating the content as it unfolds. Rule-
> example-rule patterns and internal summaries tie specific information
> items to integrative concepts. Summary reviews integrate and reinforce
> the learning of major points. Taken together, these structuring ele-
> ments not only facilitate memory for the information but also allow for
> its apprehension as an integrated whole with recognition of the rela-
> tionship between parts.
>
> *Redundancy/Sequencing* Achievement is higher when information is pre-
> sented with a degree of redundancy, particularly in the form of repeat-
> ing and reviewing general rules and key concepts.... In general,
> structuring, redundancy and sequencing affect what is learned from lis-
> tening to verbal presentations, even though they are not powerful de-
> terminants of learning from reading text.
>
> *Clarity* Clarity of presentation is a consistent correlate of achievement,
> whether measured by high-inference ratings or low-inference indicators
> such as absence of 'vagueness terms' or 'mazes'. Knowledge about factors
> that detract from clarity needs to be supplemented with knowledge about
> positive factors that enhance clarity (for example, what kinds of analogies

and examples facilitate learning, and why) but in any case, students learn more from clear presentations than from unclear ones.

(Brophy and Good 1986:362)

These are very useful research-based guidelines which merit a good deal of reflection and cultivation. So is that not a proper basis for developing teaching expertise? There are some who would say that it is precisely such research-based knowledge that teachers should rely upon to guide their classroom practice:

Specifically, I believe we need to:
1   Develop the technology of teaching by more research, in order to give us the teacher behaviours that are appropriate for children of different ages, subjects, catchment areas and districts ...
2   We need to ensure that all preservice teachers receive the technology of their profession, as would any other group of professionals. ... All teachers must practise these effective methods or the consequences are disastrous.

(Reynolds 1998:28)

Certainly, we need much more of this kind of research and we need to pay much more attention to what we find from it; but is teaching expertise best understood as the disciplined application of 'the technology of teaching'? There are very good reasons for believing that *not* to be the case.

Most obviously, the consequences of any given pattern of behaviour are not entirely predictable. We can, through extensive research, develop an increasing understanding of what kinds of teacher behaviour are likely to be conducive of desired effects in different kinds of circumstances; but these patterns are entirely dependent on pupils' interpretations of, and reactions to, teachers' behaviour; and at best we can only predict with a degree of probability what these interpretations and reactions will be.

To take just one example of this, one of the strongest research findings about teacher behaviour, in the context of science teaching, is that pupils' achievements tend to be higher if, after asking questions, teachers wait for three seconds (rather than the more common one second) to give pupils time to think before asking one of them to respond. Yet this is not the case in every classroom. It appears that if the classroom atmosphere is more severe than average, the effect of the extra wait-time – repeated according to the prescribed recipe – can be to increase the tension in the classroom in a debilitating way rather than to enhance the quality of thinking as intended. As experienced teachers know, the effects of their behaviour are far from being entirely predictable.

What is being looked for in such research are standard recipes, of increasingly sophisticated kinds, just as beginning teachers quite rightly seek standard recipes for doing things, at least to begin with. There's nothing wrong with that except that it doesn't always work. What works with one topic, or one class, or one occasion, may well not work for another. So experienced teachers maintain the same concerns about what they want to achieve, but are ready to use different approaches according to the circumstances. That's why they often have difficulty in giving a generalised answer about how to do things. So beginning teachers learn one way of doing something and then another and gradually increase their repertoires, learning increasingly complex recipes about which approach to use on which occasion; and eventually – perhaps after some years – the knowledge-in-use becomes so sophisticated as not to be recipe knowledge at all, but something rather different. There remains a proper tension, however, between experienced teachers' dependence on their own sophisticated readings of what is needed in each specific classroom context and, on the other hand, the guidance from research about what is generally likely to be effective for facilitating the desired learning.

Rational planning

Good teaching then is not simply a matter of learning the appropriate ways to act in order to get things done. It's at least equally a matter of learning how to *decide* what to do. Is it then appropriate to think about teaching expertise as a matter of very careful and rational planning for each particular course, for each unit within it, and for each particular lesson? Through such rational planning one could build on previous experience and take account of the distinctive problems and possibilities for the specific topic, class and occasion.

The answer to that question must very nearly be 'yes, that's what good classroom teaching is like'; but unfortunately it must also be 'no, expert classroom teaching isn't at all like that'. The reason for such a two-faced answer is that this is indeed what teaching at its best is like for beginners, but it is not quite what the expert teaching of experienced teachers is like. The difference is important, but it is not always easy for beginners to accept.

Student teachers often get frustrated by demands on them, and generally also their own felt need, to spend long hours in planning lessons, but finding that experienced teachers tend to spend relatively little time on lesson planning. It's not just that they don't have the time, although that is true. Often they seem to be able to teach very well without spending time on planning. Why shouldn't beginning teachers copy them?

It should be said that the best teachers, however experienced they are, always take some time to plan each lesson. But it is much less time than beginning teachers need. There seem to be four main reasons for this (cf. Clark and Peterson 1986):

1   Experienced teachers build up repertoires of successful lesson plans for particular topics.
2   When they first meet their classes, experienced teachers teach them how they want things done in their classrooms, and devote considerable time

to teaching their pupils the routine procedures for their classrooms. Each lesson can then take these routines for granted.

3   Experienced teachers tend to concentrate their planning energies on larger units – whole courses and sections of these courses – so that particular lessons are approached as elements within the larger plans.

4   Most important, experienced teachers (like other experienced professional workers, cf. Dreyfus and Dreyfus 1986) learn to make very complex decisions intuitively at great speed while engaged in active teaching. This means that they can have much more flexibility in their teaching than can be achieved with predetermined plans. Beginning teachers, not being able to make complex decisions at speed, have to rely on well worked out plans, including some contingency planning. Gradually the planning and then the teaching itself will become more fluent.

Careful, informed, rational planning is a very important element in skilled teaching. For the beginner, it is virtually all-important. For the experienced teacher it remains important, both for lessons and for longer units, but it increasingly becomes complemented by other kinds of expertise that are more difficult to describe or even to observe.

The professional craft of classroom teaching

It is perhaps the capacity for fluent, insightful, almost instantaneous, only half-conscious intuitive judgement, like that of the artist or highly skilled craftsman, which is most characteristic of the highly experienced and expert classroom teacher. It is also the aspect of classroom teaching expertise that is most difficult to describe or to understand.

At the centre of this capacity for intuitive judgement appear to be complex mental maps of classrooms in general, of different kinds of classroom situations, and of various kinds of desirable classroom states of affairs. A vast amount of information is assimilated to these maps, but it is nonetheless information of which account is taken in highly selective ways: the expert teacher knows what to look for, because he or she knows how to use the information attended to. So the experienced teacher seems constantly to be recognising situations as similar to previously encountered situations, to be taking account of particular significant features of these nonetheless unique situations, deciding what she or he wants to be happening, and deciding too how to bring that about in the light of all the information attended to.

In many respects, as already noted, expert teachers in their dependence on complex intuitive judgements are quite similar to experienced practitioners of other professions. One way in which teachers seem to be distinctive, however, is in their normal pattern of working each in their own classrooms, and in the consequent lack of need for them to articulate their perceptions, their decision-making or their judgements. When, therefore, they do try to communicate what is involved in their teaching, for example to beginning teachers, they generally find this quite difficult and are likely to offer only rather simplified accounts of their practice unless they are encouraged to try hard to reveal its full complexity.

While they are teaching in classrooms, teachers seem to focus on quite short-term goals, and especially on what they see as appropriate kinds of pupil activity for a given kind of lesson or for a particular phase of that kind of lesson. Other goals are mainly concerned with progress of one kind or another, such as the completion of tasks and pupils improving in their ways of working. Each teacher seems to have his or her own way of thinking about such short-term goals, but each seems to have a rich repertoire of ways of achieving these goals and to take account of a great deal of information about the class, the content of the lesson and many other factors in determining which way to choose on each particular occasion. All of this happens astonishingly quickly and in ways that are invisible to pupils or to observers (cf. Brown and McIntyre 1993; Cooper and McIntyre 1996).

Ongoing learning

It would be quite wrong, however, to project a picture of expert classroom teachers as people who have 'cracked it', who after some years of learning have reached a plateau of understanding and intuitive expertise whereby they engage effectively in their daily teaching. Classroom teaching is not like that: one never, it seems, has it all worked out. Expert teachers seem instead to engage routinely in reviewing what has happened in the day's or the week's teaching, considering how it went, what progress each group or individual has made, wondering why this pupil was so disruptive and that one so disengaged and what could be done to get them more interested or at least on task. They 'tinker with their classrooms' (Huberman 1992), with their grouping of pupils, with the amount of time devoted to different kinds of activity, with the extent and nature of the demands they make on pupils and, in the following year, with the way they teach the same topics to the next class. The process of questioning of their practice and of tentative new learning seems unending.

That seems to be the case even in that increasingly unusual situation for teachers, a stable state of affairs, undisturbed by external forces. New opportunities, such as having classroom assistants working with one in the classroom or an increased number of computers available, and new demands, such as curriculum changes or the headteacher's concern that there should be greater continuity of practice among the successive teachers by whom a class is taught, can lead to more fundamental rethinking. Cooper and McIntyre (1996), for example, found that teachers confronted by the National Curriculum for the first time were unusually explicit in their accounts of how their new classroom practice related to their long-term plans for pupils' learning. Under the influence of this major innovation, they seemed to have reverted to rather less intuitive decision-making, at least for some aspects of their teaching. Even the expert teacher, then, is also a perpetual learner.

A complex socially and intellectually skilled activity

Finally, then, by looking at various contrasting ways of characterising teaching, and finding that most have something useful to tell us but that none of them on their own are totally satisfactory, we have to conclude that teaching expertise involves a complex amalgam of some very different kinds of human abilities. It depends on:

- one's capacity for sensitively understanding others, for dealing intelligently with a great deal of complex information, constantly changing, and for making creative decisions about how to act
- developing a rich repertoire of approaches to teaching and the capacity to decide among them on particular occasions
- an understanding in depth of what one is teaching
- readiness and ability to get inside the minds and the cultures of those one is teaching
- knowledge, based on the experience and the research of others, of patterns of teacher activity which have been identified as important in facilitating learning in classrooms, and development of the practical ability to put that knowledge into practice
- very careful and thoughtful planning which will gradually be complemented by an increasingly fluent capacity for intuitive judgement
- readiness to re-examine one's practices constantly and to explore new ways of doing things.

Classroom teaching is a sophisticated, complex, intellectually and socially demanding profession: it needs to be all that if it is to cater for all the diverse learning needs of a class of pupils.

Further reading

Alexander, R. (1995) *Versions of Primary Education*, London: Routledge.

Croll, P. and Hastings, N. (eds) (1996) *Effective Primary Teaching: research-based classroom strategies*, London: David Fulton.

Duckworth, E. (1997) *Teacher to Teacher Learning from Each Other*, New York: Teachers College Press.

Galton, M., Hargreaves, L., Comber, C., Wall, D. and Pell, T. (1999) Changes in Patterns of Teacher Interaction in Primary Classrooms: 1976–96, *British Educational Research Journal*, 25, 1, 23–37.

Joyce, B., Calhoun, E. and Hopkins, D. (1997) *Models of Learning: tools for teaching*, Buckingham: Open University Press.

Mortimore, P., Sammons, P., Stoll. L., Lewis, D. and Ecob, R. (1988) *School Matters: the junior years*, Wells: Open Books.

Pollard, A., Broadfoot, P., Croll, P., Osborn, M. and Abbott, D. (1994) *Changing English Primary Schools*, London: Cassell.

References

Bennett, N. (1976) *Teaching Styles and Pupil Progress*, London: Open Books.

Bernstein, B. (1970) 'Education cannot compensate for society', in D. Rubinstein and C. Stoneman (eds) *Education for Democracy*, Harmondsworth: Penguin.

Brophy, J.E. and Good, T.L. (1986) 'Teacher Behaviour and Student Achievement', in M. Wittrock (ed.) *Handbook of Research on Teaching, Third Edition,* New York: Macmillan.

Brown, S. and McIntyre, D. (1993) *Making Sense of Teaching* , Buckingham: Open University Press.

Clark, C.M. and Peterson, P.L. (1986) 'Teachers' Thought Processes', in M. Wittrock (ed.) *Handbook of Research on Teaching,* Third Edition, New York: Macmillan.

Cooper, P. and McIntyre, D. (1996) *Effective Teaching and Learning: Teachers' and Students' Perspectives* , Buckingham: Open University Press.

Dreyfus, H.L. and Dreyfus, S. E. (1986) *Mind over Machine: The Power of Human Intuition and Expertise in the Era of the Computer,* Oxford: Blackwell.

Galton, M. and Simon, B. (1980) *Progress and Performance in the Primary Classroom,* London: Routledge & Kegan Paul.

Getzels, J.W. and Jackson, P.W. (1963) 'The Teacher's Personality and Characteristics', in N.L. Gage (ed.) *Handbook of Research on Teaching,* Chicago: Rand McNally.

Huberman, M. (1992) 'Teacher development and instructional mastery', in A. Hargreaves and M.G. Fullan (eds) *Understanding Teacher Development,* Cassell/Teachers College Press.

Lawlor, S. (1990) *Teachers Mistaught,* Policy Study No. 116, Centre for Policy Studies.

Lortie, D.C. (1975) *Schoolteacher: A Sociological Study,* Chicago: University of Chicago Press.

Postman, N. and Weingartner, C. (1971) *Teaching as a subversive activity,* Harmondsworth: Penguin.

Reynolds, D. (1998) 'Teacher Effectiveness: Better Teachers, Better Schools' TTA Lecture reproduced in *Research Intelligence,* No. 66.

Vygotsky, L.S. (1962) *Thought and Language,* Cambridge, Mass: MIT Press.

Vygotsky, L.S. (1978) *Mind in Society,* Cambridge, Mass: Harvard University Press.

Whitehead, A.N. (1929) *The Aims of Education,* London: Macmillan.

Part I

Organising the learning environment

2 Organising the physical environment of the classroom to support children's learning

Ruth Kershner

EDITOR'S SUMMARY

One of the first tasks for the Primary teacher at the beginning of each school year is to organise the physical layout of the classroom. Often this will be reviewed and altered as the year develops. The decisions that teachers make about the classroom environment reflect their approach to teaching and affect the quality of the children's learning. This chapter reviews the issues that teachers need to consider when making these decisions and the evidence about the characteristics of effective classrooms, including issues relating to children's emotional and social development and children with special behavioural, emotional, physical and intellectual needs. The importance of taking on board the children's perspectives of the classroom environment and involving them in decisions is also emphasised.

Here are some Year 6 pupils talking about their classroom area in an open plan Primary school.

> It brightens you when you are down, it cheers you up and it has radiators to keep us warm; and all of you stay together, you are not split up – you stay as one big class; and it is really open so you can hear everyone talk. ... Sometimes I like to sit near the window – you can feel the breeze coming and that gets you working. ... Sometimes I like where I'm sitting over there, in the middle of the classroom, because when you look around you can see every single person working.

> It's got a lot of people in it because we have 39 people in our class, and it's a bit stuffy and hot in here.

> It's open, because all the rooms are joined together and there ain't no doors to close it in, to close you in.

> It's nice ... it just looks nice ... all around the sides are all pictures and models.... It's nice and warm and it's got a carpet on the floor so it's softer in case someone falls over and hurts themselves.

Classrooms are very evocative places. Think of all the colours, smells, noises and general 'busyness' of a Nursery or Primary classroom. A visit to school raises memories for any adult who has ever been a pupil, and, as we see above, children have their own impressions and feelings about the environment where they are expected to work and learn each day.

There are many different influences on school and classroom design, including the differing values and expectations of the communities, society and culture in which they are located. James *et al.* (1998) discuss the sociological argument that schools in general are built for surveillance, discipline and control of children, and that this is the framework in which children do or do not become successful pupils, future workers and citizens in modern Western societies. Issues of equality, power and social behaviour in schools must be recognised in any discussion of classroom organisation. In practical terms, this is evident in teachers' debates about the allocation of limited resources like computers and the representation of different cultures in classroom display. We also see these issues arising when teachers direct children to move from place to place in the classroom in response to their behaviour (e.g. away from their friends, or nearer to the teacher's desk).

This chapter is concerned with how the Primary classroom works as a physical context for children's learning and development. One of the key points is that the organisation of the classroom represents the teacher's thinking and, as such, it has the potential to influence and support children's learning in the teacher's absence. In many British Primary classrooms it is now common for teachers to remind children to look at a display of previously discussed story writing guidelines, for example, before coming to ask for personal help.

Classroom organisation: the complexity of decision-making and evaluation

Class teachers usually have some freedom to implement their ideas about the organisation of furniture, resources, display and other environmental features in the classroom areas, hall spaces, corridors and gardens. Yet decision-making about classroom organisation is complicated because the classroom environment has to serve different functions relating to the multiple goals for children's education, socialization and individual psychological development (Rivlin and Weinstein 1995). The school building can support or restrict Primary teachers' organisational decisions. Moreover, specific decisions about 'what should go where' in the classroom and school setting can be affected not only by educational principles and building design, but also by factors like financial limitations, aesthetic beliefs, 'cleanability', and the motivation to change a setting which has become familiar and manageable. Each of these factors will vary in importance for different members of a school staff team.

Teachers may have different educational goals in mind when they make decisions about classroom organisation, as shown by these contrasting explanations from two Year 6 teachers about why they arrange the classroom so that children may move around.

> I think the position of the resources in the classroom encourages the children to be autonomous. They need to be able to go and get their resources as and when they are required rather than having them on tables. ... If resources are set to one side of the classroom then the children have got to make the decision for themselves when they are going to get them.

> > I'm not certain how much the environment influences how the children work. I think space is important, but that's the main thing. ... I don't think children of this age can sustain sitting down for long periods of time. They will when they have to do SATs [i.e. the national tests] and things like that, but it's not their natural thing. They need to be able to get up and move around.

Neither of these teachers wants the classroom to be unduly restrictive, but while the first expresses this in terms of her aims for the children's developing sense of autonomy, the second teacher's concerns are that the classroom environment should be responsive to children's need for physical activity. Here, the two teachers' goals are complementary in accepting and encouraging children's movement, but it is common for teachers to have to manage competing or conflicting aims and set priorities for a classroom organisation which works best for individual pupils and the whole class in the given circumstances.

Given this complexity, there are relatively few general principles about how Primary classrooms *should* be organised, except for issues of health and safety and for certain special needs. However, some basic questions may be asked in evaluating the decisions that are made:

Does classroom organisation respond to children's needs?

As suggested above, teachers commonly make organisational decisions with children's developmental and educational needs in mind. Weinstein (1987) discusses the many ways in which the design of the physical environment of the classroom can facilitate or hinder the activity and social interaction which underpins young children's social, personal and intellectual development. Some examples will be given later in this chapter.

Does classroom organisation match and support expectations about learning and teaching?

One of the findings from research on classroom organisation is that there should be an authentic match with the processes of teaching and learning in that setting. So a classroom set up with the tables permanently in groups, for example, does not work very well if the children are consistently expected to work individually (Alexander 1992; Hastings *et al.* 1996).

Does classroom organisation accommodate changing needs and priorities?

Most teachers' aims and priorities will change from time to time during a school year, and even within individual lessons. The physical environment of the classroom should ideally be flexible enough to allow teachers' various, multi-layered beliefs and intentions for children's development and learning to be realised and visible.

Are the children sufficiently involved in decision-making about classroom organisation?

Children are keenly aware of their surroundings from an early age, as we see below in the information given by 5- and 6-year-old children who prepared a booklet for the 3-year-olds who were about to join them in their pre-school in Italy. The children show their understanding of what the environment allows them to do, following their interests and imagination.

> Doors are all glass doors, so you can say 'hi' to your teacher from the outside, and to your dad from the inside.

> When we were three, we wanted so much to go into the other classrooms, and we used to say, 'How nice they are!' There were better, because we had already seen our classrooms and knew everything of them.

> In the spring trees bloom and form sort of rooms made of hedges, and also some secret passages through the hedge, and you can catch a glimpse of some treasure.

> (Children of Reggio Emilia 1993)

It is clear that classrooms do not simply provide a neutral physical space for teaching and learning. The classroom tells the children something about what is offered and expected of them as pupils, although we cannot, of course, assume that children understand fully or correctly what the teacher may intend. This is one of the reasons why it is important to ask children about what it is like to learn in school, and what their own preferences would be for classroom organisation. Some ideas about how to do this are included later in the chapter.

Making decisions about the physical organisation of the classroom: some relevant factors

Teachers may start the school year with a bare classroom area to equip and organise, but it is more common to be in a position where the area has to be adapted or rearranged for a new class of children. This is also the case when it is necessary to incorporate new resources like computers, or when there is a significant change to the curriculum. For example, the National Numeracy Strategy implemented in England and Wales in the late 1990s incorporated suggestions for organising the classroom to accommodate whole-class and groupwork, including the setting up of 'U-shaped' seating arrangements to help children to participate in the lesson (DfEE 1999, Section 1, p. 29).

In making organisational decisions, the teacher has the challenge of considering several different factors which relate to teaching and learning in the school and classroom setting. These include:

- the processes of children's development and learning
- educational values such as inclusion
- the nature and demands of the curriculum
- the teaching strategies and learning resources in use
- the perceptions or images of the classroom which are held by teachers and children.

Some examples are given next.

Factors relating to children's development and learning in an inclusive classroom setting: general considerations and special needs

General considerations

In introducing a wide-ranging discussion of the physical context of children's development, David and Weinstein (1987:8) argue that any built environment for children should:

- foster personal identity
- encourage the development of competence
- provide opportunities for growth, in terms of cognitive, social and motor development
- promote a sense of security and trust
- allow both social interaction and privacy.

Weinstein (1987) and Weinstein and Mignano (1997) provide many examples of how the physical environment in Primary and preschool settings can enhance children's self-esteem, self-control, pro-social behaviour, gender identity, symbolic expression, logical thinking, creativity and problem-solving abilities, attention span and task involvement. These include:

- the promotion of children's psychological security by providing materials

Figure 2.1 Trainee teachers with their displays, stimulating children's interest and celebrating their achievements

which are 'soft' and responsive, and by using flexible furniture arrangements to provide privacy, calm and comfort for those who need it

- the use of display to personalize the classroom setting so that it represents the children and adults who work there in all their diversity (see Figure 2.1)
- the enhancement of self-esteem by ensuring that the environment reflects the presence of individual children and that it is accessible and comprehensible to them
- the facilitation of social interaction between the children by providing appropriate and sufficient materials to support group activities in spaces which minimize the possibility of conflict
- the development of symbolic thinking and expression with the provision of opportunities for role-play, the availability of unstructured materials for exploration, and the use of print, artefacts and imagery in the classroom environment
- the promotion of motor development through the use of equipment which allows large and small movements, which is adjustable for different sizes, abilities and confidence and which allows children to evaluate and extend their skills and progress
- the support of children's engagement in their work by making materials accessible, by planning 'pathways' through the room to reduce distractions, and by separating incompatible activities.

These examples are not only directed towards enhancing children's individual development and learning. They also underpin the education of the class group as a whole by providing a supportive, differentiated environment which enhances social interaction, tolerance and self-regulation as well as learning. This is the basis for developing an inclusive learning environment in school which is representative of and responsive to children's different needs and interests.

Individual differences and special needs

In addition to making the whole environment more welcoming, accessible and differentiated for pupils, teachers and visitors, there is also a need to respond to the individual needs of specific children and adults in school. The clearest examples of this aspect of inclusion relate to people with physical and sensory impairments. Sometimes it is only when one is placed in the position of having restricted mobility or impaired hearing or vision that the environmental obstacles become evident, and this is the argument for offering people training in 'disability awareness' with the help of aids which simulate the experience, if only temporarily.

PHYSICAL AND SENSORY IMPAIRMENT AND SENSITIVITY

The environmental needs of children with physical impairments could include access for wheelchair users, specially adjusted furniture, the provision of technological aids for learning and private areas for therapy and health care. Issues for children with hearing impairments include the management of background noise and reverberation, positioning to allow speech-reading, inclusion in class discussions, and the integration of signing, visual materials and speech in classroom communication (Watson *et al.* 1999); and for children with visual impairments in mainstream settings, Arter (1999) explains the need to consider the child's seating position, the teacher's position in the classroom, lighting, use of the blackboard or whiteboard, adjustable furniture, storage, displays and the organisation of technological aids.

Wilkins (1995) also writes about the visual aspects of classroom settings, but in relation to 'visual stress' rather than visual impairment. He refers to research on the ways in which certain visual stimuli may provoke epileptic seizures, headaches and visual discomfort. This is the basis for his argument about the need to consider the impact on certain people of factors such as lighting, electronic displays, design features (e.g. stripes), and colour (e.g. coloured lenses and overlays to facilitate the reading of black and white text). There is also a need to consider the auditory effects on individuals of excessive noise in classrooms, given the findings from psychological research that loud, unpredictable noise which is perceived as out of our personal control can have a negative effect on health, mood, task performance and social behaviour (Cave 1998:46). McSporran (1997) suggests that amplification of the teacher's voice could help to deal with the specific problems of noise, distance and reverberation in classrooms, where children commonly have to distinguish the teacher's speech from general background sounds.

DIFFICULTIES IN LEARNING AND SELF-MANAGEMENT

Children with difficulties in learning are a diverse group, but common factors can include problems with independence, self-management and general awareness and use of appropriate strategies for learning in school. Children with specific difficulties in learning and organising skilled movements (sometimes called 'dyspraxia' or 'developmental co-ordination disorder') may also have difficulties in using standard classroom equipment and finding their way around the different areas of school comfortably and effectively.

Many children identified in this way will be given additional resources to support their learning (e.g. computers, individualised books, adapted writing materials, etc.), and some will be accompanied in certain lessons by a learning support assistant. For these children it is important to consider factors like the positioning of the learning support assistant in the classroom, the storing and labelling of any special learning resources and, especially, the access to resources and equipment which supports the children in becoming more independent and responsible in choosing the materials they need for the task in hand (Byers 1996:183).

EMOTIONAL AND BEHAVIOURAL DIFFICULTIES

With regard to children with emotional and behavioural difficulties, factors relating to psychological security, social contact, identity and the development of competence can be particularly problematic in the typically busy, distracting and fast-moving Primary classroom. Certain children will need 'time out' of the ordinary classroom when they cannot cope and this may become a short-term solution. In some schools, the recognition of children's emotional needs has been the basis for setting up separate 'nurture groups' to provide a secure environment in which children can develop attachments and trust as a basis for learning: the class sizes are small and an effort is often made to include features which aim to create a physical and emotional sense of 'home' – such as pets, comfortable furniture, cooking facilities and shared mealtimes. There may also be special features like a full-length mirror, which is intended as a tool to help the children to gain self-awareness and associated self-control as part of their emotional development (Bennathan and Boxall 1996). In some ordinary classrooms, particularly in the early years, many of these features are incorporated to help all the children to develop the sense of security, personal identity and motivation which enables them to learn in the initially unfamiliar context of school.

THE IMPORTANCE OF CONTINUING ASSESSMENT AND RESEARCH ON CHILDREN'S NEEDS

In spite of the examples given above, it is important to avoid making general assumptions about the environmental implications of certain 'types' of individual differences and special needs. As a general principle, organisational decisions would best be linked to knowledge of children's actual difficulties rather than to general beliefs, probabilities or simple convenience (e.g. always grouping children with sensory impairments together with children with learning difficulties to sit at a table near the teacher).

Factors relating to the curriculum, teaching strategies and learning resources in use

The different subjects of the Primary curriculum have intrinsic implications for organising the classroom and school environment, not just in relation to specific initiatives like the Numeracy Strategy mentioned earlier. For example, drama requires an empty, safe space in which to work; physical education requires space and special equipment for active movement; the practical aspects of art, music and science call for resources and working arrangements which allow experimentation and creativity; story-telling needs arrangements for talking and listening with groups of children and individuals, often with the use of props, pictures and actions.

There are also environmental implications which relate to different ways of helping children learn across the curriculum. Teachers may choose:

- to group children in different ways
- to use a range of teaching and learning strategies, such as discussion, demonstration, explanation, investigation and play
- to offer a variety of learning resources, such as audio-visual aids (see Figure 2.2), artefacts, displays, computers, music and visual images.

Each of these approaches has implications for arranging furniture, for the positioning of the teacher and the children, for the use of 2D and 3D display, for the separation of incompatible activities and for the organisation of materials.

The classroom environment has to allow teaching and learning to take place in practical terms. However, organisational decisions may also acknowledge that the classroom conveys messages to the children about the curriculum, educational values and the expectations a teacher has for them as learners. For example, Bearne (1998) discusses the value of setting up a writing area in the classroom, with different types of paper, writing equipment, texts and display space.

> A writing area that is seen as an important part of the classroom environment, and is well-equipped and integrated into everyday classroom work, gives very powerful messages about the value you place on writing. … It is intended as an area where the pupils have some independence

Figure 2.2 Effective classrooms provide opportunities for a variety of ways of learning

and responsibility. It gives them the space to choose their own writing activities. ... It is one way in which classroom experience of writing can most closely replicate home uses of writing.

(Bearne 1998:91)

This is a good example of the integration of thinking about the curriculum, the classroom environment and the children's development and learning.

Another example of the need for integrated thinking relates to the environmental impact of the increasing use of computers in school. Many of the basic organisational issues relating to the use of computers apply across all phases of education, including the location and sharing of resources (hardware and software), technical support, health and safety, security, lighting, furniture and access for use by individuals and class groups (Taylor 1997). Desk-top computers may be classroom-based, mobile or permanently based in a central location. There is also an increasing use of individual lap-tops by pupils. In their discussion of approaches to managing computers in school, Collins *et al.* (1997:108) comment that teachers' organisational strategies tend to be based on a principle of maximum use by pupils balanced with a principle of equitable access for pupils. Decision-making has also to take account of any practical limitations in school, such as stairs, which limit the possibilities. Yet decisions about how to organise computers are not entirely predictable on the basis of systematic evaluations of the costs and benefits.

Sanger *et al.* (1997:35) point out that in many cases teachers' negative attitudes to computers and their relative inexperience in using new technologies have led them to marginalize computers in the classroom or corridor, or to place the keyboards and monitors at an inappropriate level for children's comfort.

Crook's (1994) discussion of the various ways in which computers may help children to learn draws attention to the physical aspects of organising computer use in school. He argues that children do not only interact *with* computers, as when the software provides instructions and feedback for game-playing, word-processing or data handling. Children also interact with each other and the teacher while they are working collaboratively *at* the computer, and, more generally, while working *around* computers even if they are not all working on the same task. Further, children and teachers may interact *in relation to* computers, when they discuss the work they have been doing or when they make a display based on a computer activity. Children may also interact *through* networked computers, and in this case the technology itself provides the medium of communication between children in different environments, often at a great distance. It is worth imagining how a classroom can accommodate these different interactions *with, at, around, in relation to* and *through* computers which lead to learning. For example:

- seating would need to allow individual, paired, grouped or whole-class work
- displays would include some representations of computer software and other relevant imagery as well as work produced by children at the computer (Crook's own research suggests that this wider classroom presence could be an important factor in learning (Crook 1994:105))
- technological resources would be set up to allow large screens for group and class work, and networking for communication beyond the classroom
- noise levels would have to accommodate talking as part of collaborative activity and the use of sound in multimedia work on the computer, while also being monitored for the distractions to other pupils engaged in other classroom activities.

Factors relating to people's perceptions and images of the classroom

In addition to the factors discussed above, it is also important to be aware of the ways in which classrooms are perceived and interpreted by teachers and pupils. The *image* of the classroom can have a significant effect on decision-making about features in the environment and on evaluations of its success. Is the classroom seen as a 'supermarket' with lots of knowledge on offer, or a 'garden' where children's development is cultivated, or an office, a workshop, a theatre, a playroom or simply a meeting place? Such images have implications for how the classroom is set up and how it is evaluated. For example, an 'office' may emphasise the production of work in an efficient but relatively impersonal setting, while a 'playroom' may call for the flexible provision of materials and opportunities for exploration and social interaction.

Clandinin (1986) describes how one American teacher thinks of her classroom as 'home', an image which has immediate implications for the types of interaction, the sense of community, comfort and general atmosphere – factors which are important for teacher and pupils:

> Home … is a group of people interacting together and cooperating together. … I spend as much time here as I do in my own home … and you should be comfortable here. … Environment and atmosphere have always been very important to me because we're living here, it's a living, learning experience. … It's not a dead room, this room comes alive as soon as we all come in here. … It breathes again and lives again.
>
> (Clandinin 1986:107–108)

Yet real homes are very different from each other in social, cultural, psychological and physical terms. What is familiar and comfortable for one child may be alien to another living in different home circumstances; what is allowed for certain children at home may be very clearly forbidden at school – even in an atmosphere with other home-like features. It is important to distinguish the emotional qualities of this teacher's image of 'home' from the specific routines, rules and decorative features which may have very different meanings for individual children and adults, overlain with differences in cultural experience and values.

We need to recognise how the symbolic attributes of the classroom may be perceived differently by teachers and pupils. This is not just a case of understanding different attitudes to certain objects (e.g. positive or negative feelings about computers). There are other cognitive process to consider as well. For example, objects in the classroom are sometimes intended to represent their 'real' versions (e.g. food packaging used for mathematical calculations) while in other cases the same objects may be intended to stand for something else as a stimulus to the imagination (e.g. food packaging used for making models or costumes). The teacher can easily switch between these modes of thinking, but it cannot be assumed that young children will perceive familiar objects so flexibly. Children will not necessarily see clear boundaries between different classroom activities and curriculum areas, especially when the same materials are in use. So building a castle with the maths resources will make sense to the children, although it may not match the teacher's perceptions or intentions for what should be happening at that time. Any problems arising in this way may, of course, be offset with the creative advantages of seeing familiar objects in a new light.

How can psychological theory and research inform decision-making about classroom organisation?

Some of the most relevant principles for classroom organisation emerge from psychological research in the areas of sociocultural views of learning and environmental psychology.

Sociocultural views of learning and 'distributed intelligence'

Within the sociocultural view of learning, it is argued that the individual person and the environment cannot be separated for analysis. Knowledge is seen to be 'out there' in the classroom setting, shared and expressed jointly by children and teachers using the cultural tools of learning, such as speech and writing (Bruner 1996). The sociocultural perspective suggests that the physical classroom environment can both embody and support children's learning. For example, Moll *et al.* (1993) show how sociocultural principles can be evident in the ways in which the teacher organises the classroom for collaborative and individual work and uses displays to represent the children's knowledge and developing ideas:

> There are several large tables in the room that, along with the ample carpeted floor area, provide work space for the children and adults. ... Classroom rules, agreed upon and signed dramatically by the children and teachers, are posted near the door. ... The products of children's thinking are displayed on the walls in the forms of charts and other public documents, such as webs representing brainstorming sessions, data collected during math and science experimentation, ongoing records of thematically organized activities, and lists of questions the children are actively engaged in answering.
>
> (Moll *et al.* 1996:149–150)

This approach to understanding knowledge and classroom learning connects with a view of intelligence as something that is distributed between people participating in joint activities rather than something which indicates an individual child's fixed potential for learning (Salomon 1993). With this perspective, intelligent behaviour in classrooms involves not only the use of language and other mental activity, but also physical tools, artefacts, texts and other aspects of the learning environment (Pea 1993). Examples could include the activities of collaborative problem-solving, reading or building in which it is impossible to identify a child's personal contribution without taking into account the materials which are used and the help and guidance they receive. The point is that children's learning is supported by various forms of technology as well as by cognitive activity and social interaction. The social and physical context is seen to be integral to children's learning and intellectual development. This does not mean that the context 'causes' a child to be more or less intelligent. Salomon (1993) describes a *reciprocal interaction* in the way that activities both incorporate and develop individual children's intellectual abilities. Children's intellectual skills and strategies will be defined in relation to the activities in which they are involved in particular contexts.

Psychological models of intelligence now commonly refer to the environment as well as to people's individual mental activity. For example, in developing his triarchic theory of intelligence, Sternberg asks:

- which behaviours are seen to be intelligent in certain contexts? and how does a child focus on, adapt to and shape relevant aspects of the real life environment?
- when is behaviour intelligent for different individuals in relation to the novelty of the activity, or the degree to which the required mental skill has become automatic?
- how is intelligent behaviour generated through mental activity, the growth of knowledge, and the child's developing awareness and control of learning strategies?

(Sternberg 1985:xi-xii)

Sternberg's response to these questions refers to the demands of the external world, to the internal mental activity of each individual and to the personal experience which mediates between them. With this in mind, we might seek to make schools and classrooms more 'intelligent' in the way that social and physical factors support and extend children's thinking and learning.

Environmental psychology

Research in environmental psychology is extensive, and there are many connections to other disciplines such as geography, architecture, design, ergonomics, sociology, anthropology, epidemiology and ecology. Over the years, environmental psychologists have focused variously on people's perceptions and understanding of the physical environment, people's behaviour in certain physical settings, the impact of people's behaviour on the environment, and the general relevance for development of the physical and social situations in which people spend their lives. (See reviews in Bonnes and Secchiaroli 1995; Cave 1998; Spencer 1998.)

Designing environments for participation and learning

One of the ways for teachers to use principles of environmental psychology in organising the physical environment of the classroom is through the concept of design. Norman (1998) draws on Gibson's (1979) concept of affordances in his discussion of the ways in which the use of everyday objects like taps, doors and computers can be either facilitated or hindered by the signs and clues which they offer through their appearance, controls and instructions. Norman (1998:84) extends this view to identify the constraints of objects as not only physical but also semantic, cultural and logical. So in building a toy motorcycle, for example, there are not only the physical constraints of how the pieces fit together, but also an understanding of which way the toy driver should face and whether all the pieces in the kit should be used to complete the model. The argument is that people use their powers of reasoning and their social and cultural understanding to act in the physical environment. Yet the design of objects and systems may nevertheless hinder people in their actions, and in school we know that children can be faced with systems of storage, display, seating and movement which are not easily understandable or very efficient.

Norman advises any designer to ensure that people know what to do with objects and systems in the setting where they are in use. He says that design should:

- make it easy to determine what actions are possible at any moment
- make things visible, including the conceptual model of the system, the alternative actions, and the results of actions
- make it easy to evaluate the current state of the system
- follow natural mappings between intentions and the required actions; between actions and the resulting effect; and between the information that is visible and the interpretation of the system state.

(Norman 1998:188)

This type of language about system and product design is relatively unfamiliar in education, but the principles can be translated and applied to Primary classrooms where there is so much potential for teachers and pupils to misunderstand each other's views about why they are there and what they are able and allowed to do in that context. A good teacher-designer would look for ways to help children to understand the classroom environment. This would involve:

- avoiding unnecessary complexity in the tasks children have to undertake
- providing children with visible memory aids and feedback
- developing automatic routines
- using appropriate technologies with a critical eye for gains and losses
- maintaining elements of control in the details of actions as well as the overall direction of the task or project of learning
- planning flexibly enough to allow errors and learning from errors.

(Norman 1998:189–200).

This approach rests on the belief that teachers can be strategic, reflective and creative in finding ways to enable children to become active learners in the school environment. One way to justify and guide this work is to look for clear links between design, social participation and learning. Blamires (1999:10) refers to the principles of *universal design* (CAST 1999) which can

Figure 2.3 An interactive display supporting children's learning through observation

be used to underpin classroom strategies for including pupils in all their diversity:

Principle one: provide multiple representations of content
(text, images, sound, models, etc.)

Principle two: provide multiple options for expression and control
(the tools of writing, art, photography, drama, music, computer technology, etc.)

Principle three: provide multiple options for engagement and motivation
(through interest, purpose, challenge, variety, scaffolding and feedback)

Blamires and his co-authors focus on the ways in which information and communications technology can follow these principles and contribute to the inclusion of children with special educational needs. It is also possible to see the general classroom implications for extending the content of displays, for providing children with access to a variety of learning resources, for making arrangements which facilitate interactions between teachers and pupils, and for ensuring that the classroom properly represents the learning that is going on. There is an increasing tendency in Primary classrooms to include displays which support the *processes* of learning to complement the more familiar displays which present the *results* of children's artwork and topic-related investigations (see Figure 2.3).

Weinstein (1987) points out that research on the impact of the school environment is particularly valuable when it includes a measure of children's developmental progress. She cites Nash (1981:175) as 'the first empirical evidence that logico-mathematical knowledge can be supported by class-room design'. In this study, Nash compared 4–5-year-old children in differ-ent settings: 'spatially planned' classrooms in which activities and materials were grouped in relation to learning objectives for different areas of the cur-riculum, and 'randomly arranged' classrooms in which the same types and quantities of equipment were placed in accordance with 'housekeeping' cri-teria like the reduction of noise and mess, or simply arranged randomly (see Figure 2.4). The timetables and teacher-child interactions were broadly simi-lar in the different settings. Nash found that after one year the children in the spatially planned classrooms:

- engaged in more manipulative activities
- became more skilful, confident and creative when combining materials in their constructions
- produced more complex shape, colour and number patterns
- showed earlier understandings of number concepts and Piagetian 'con-servation' of volume
- showed a lower incidence of conflict which they could not resolve by themselves

The implication is that the physical organisation of the classroom actively supported these aspects of children's learning.

This research example brings us to the final section of this chapter, which is about the importance of continuing research in this area, not just by psy-chologists but by teachers and children.

Developing the classroom environment: the importance of ongoing school-based research and consultation

The previous sections have suggested that we can try to 'read' and evaluate classrooms in terms of the educational and psychological principles they embody, and that these principles can in turn be used to make the environ-ment more supportive to children's learning. Yet it was also argued early in this chapter that there are no standard recipes for a good classroom environ-ment. This ambivalent situation can be resolved through ongoing research and consultation between teachers and pupils about classroom organisation. This is not just a matter of reading relevant research literature and trying to implement the findings from large-scale investigations and reviews by educa-tional researchers, useful though they are (e.g. Gump (1987) provides an extensive review of research on environmental factors like the use of space in schools, seating arrangements, learning materials and pupil numbers). Some of the most intriguing and useful findings can emerge from small-scale action research projects by teachers in their own classrooms. Here are two examples.

Figure 2.4 Spatially planned classrooms, in which activities and materials are grouped in relation to different areas of the curriculum, and mutually incompatible activities are separated, appear to enhance children's learning

The effect of background music on children's behaviour in class

Savan (1998), a comprehensive school science teacher, working with a class of Year 7 (11- and 12-year-old) students whose behaviour was extremely difficult in her lessons, carried out a study in which she tried playing classical music (usually Mozart) during science lessons over a period of five months. She found that the children's behaviour and learning improved, with some indications from physiological tests of associated reductions in factors like blood pressure and pulse rate. Savan is appropriately cautious in interpreting her findings from this small study, but her research had immediate value in its own context and in its published form it contributes to the growing psychological and educational literature on the effects of environmental factors such as background music on behaviour and learning (Hallam and Price 1998; Kliewer 1999; Brighouse and Woods 1999). Many Primary teachers already use music at key points in the school day to establish a calm and focused atmosphere for learning and for routine activities like tidying up.

The effect of classroom layout on children's behaviour and motivation

Wheeler (1995) describes a study in a Year 1 and 2 classroom (5–7-year-olds) carried out over two terms in collaboration with the class teacher. Initial observations had shown some areas of conflict caused by the inefficient use of space and resources. The children were involved in designing new class-room layouts and evaluating the effects in terms of criteria like ease of move-ment and the placement of resources. It was found in this study that the new layout had positive effects in reducing conflicts and in improving the chil-dren's working strategies. The key point was how this project – involving the children throughout – increased their sense of responsibility and their pleasure and excitement about being listened to and involved in classroom decision-making. As with Savan above, this case example is not only practi-cally useful in its own terms, but it can be added to the extensive literature on the effects of seating arrangements on children's behaviour, motivation and learning (Hastings *et al.* 1996).

Consulting with children

Once we begin to think about involving children in research and decision-making about classroom organisation it becomes clear that in doing so we are actually doing something very powerful and significant in listening to children's opinions and giving them some responsibility for their working environment. Children have their own perceptions and preferences about classrooms and schools, and Schratz and Steiner-Löffler (1998) provide a good example of a project designed to give insight into their views. In this study, teams of children in a Viennese Primary school took photographs of their school environment and through discussion they established a consen-sus of the places in school they liked and disliked. The authors argue that involving children in this 'photo-evaluation' activity offers a starting point for constructive change in school, provided that the children's ideas are taken seriously.

Teachers in England who have taken steps to consult children about the classroom and school environment have found it helpful to work in a net-work of school-based research projects focusing on learning and motivation (Flutter *et al.* 1998). For example, teachers in an East Anglian Infants school worked with Reception (4–5 years) and Year 1 (5–6 years) children to gather their views of social and physical aspects of the classroom environment as a basis for making improvements in the areas of display, seating arrangements and grouping. To initiate this research, the children took photographs of different areas in school which were later used as prompts for group discus-sions. The results showed that the children found interactive displays help-ful and useful and they had clear preferences about sitting with friends. These findings prompted the teachers to ask the children for further sugges-tions about classroom display and to look for ways to make more of use friendship groupings in class. In another study in this research network, teachers in a secondary school carried out a questionnaire survey with their students to find out their views on the physical environment specifically in order to inform budget spending on school maintenance, decoration and resources.

Once the decision has been made to seek children's views as a basis for school-based research on the classroom environment then the methods for gathering data need some thought. It is worth providing several different options for expressing ideas so that children can be included whatever their levels of literacy and self-confidence. For example:

- interviews with individuals, pairs or groups of children (which may be prompted by photographs of different classroom environments)
- group and class discussion (e.g. in 'circle time')
- the production by the children of photographs and drawings accompanied by captions or verbal comments
- written questionnaires and rating scales relating to specific environmental features
- extended writing (e.g. about 'The classroom I'd like' (Blishen 1969))
- design and modelling with construction materials or on the computer.

Remember that the children can also be involved in the planning and analysis of research about the classroom environment. This type of investigation can be an exercise in data handling as well as in personal and social development, environmental education and citizenship. Further, discussion of different classroom layouts as part of an action research project can be a very useful and concrete way for teachers to share their ideas with colleagues about children's learning and development.

In conclusion

We can recognise that the Primary classroom comes into being as a result of many decisions and constraints, and it changes as the school year continues. Some decisions are in the hands of individual class teachers, while others may follow a school policy on factors such as resources and display. In addition to deciding how best to organise the physical environment of the classroom, we need to ask about the future of education in schools as they are at the moment. There is a growing interest in the possibilities of educating children out of traditional school buildings – an idea which is driven by factors like the increasing use of information and communications technology, the recognition of the fact that parents and other people in the local community have a lot to offer as educators, and the continuing concerns about the pressures on individual children of busy school routines in crowded and sometimes forbidding school buildings. So we need to question the school environment, not take it for granted, and teachers have to work out how to set up Primary classrooms to provide a good context for children's learning in a situation where perceptions and opinions about the quality of the learning environment are varied and financial resources are limited. Involvement in thinking about the classroom environment can both call on and enhance the critical awareness and self-understanding of children and teachers. One of the main conclusions is, therefore, that the physical environment of the classroom should be a focus for ongoing action research by teachers, involving consultation with the children who work and learn there each day.

Activities

A classroom audit

Bearne (1996:250) suggests that '… (a)n audit of the classroom might start with the simple question "What messages about diversity does my classroom give?"'

Write a list of specific questions you would want to ask to see whether your classroom is 'hospitable to diversity' and supportive of children's inclusion. You might consider factors such as display, the use of different languages, the variety of resources and the organisation of space, for example, together with evidence about how the children and visitors respond. When you have the opportunity, spend some time in the classroom with the aim of answering your questions and identifying areas which need development.

Educational aims and organisational arrangements

Write down a list of 5–6 educational aims which you hold for children. Then identify the organisational arrangements which would support these aims. For example, if you want children to engage in creative arts activities then what are the implications for the organisation of working areas, seating, materials, noise and light levels, etc.? Now try to use this understanding of the links between educational aims and organisational arrangements to evaluate specific organisational strategies that you have used or observed. Why do certain aspects of classroom organisation give the immediate impression of being examples of 'good practice' or otherwise?

The purpose and use of displays

Look at a selection of classroom displays. What do you like and dislike about them? To what extent do they reflect the children's presence in the classroom? How do they represent the learning that is going on?

If possible, spend some time in the classroom and observe how children use the displays. Ask the children what they like and dislike about the displays, and whether any particular displays help them to learn.

Does this exercise give you any new ideas about the different types of display you would want to develop in school?

> **Involving children in research and improvement**
>
> Ask a class of children to write about their current classroom and their
> ideal classroom, or try one the other methods suggested in this chapter
> for seeking children's views. Then ask a group of children to look at the
> results and make a list of the ideas and preferences which emerge.
> Work with the children to identify 2–3 priorities for immediate change
> in the classroom. Discuss with them how these changes could be imple-
> mented and evaluated, then try them out in practice over a period of
> about half a term.
>   What are the advantages and disadvantages of involving children in
> this way?

Further reading

Cooper, H., Hegarty, P., Hegarty, P. and Simco, N. (1996) *Display in the Classroom: Principles, Practice and Learning Theory*, London: Fulton.

Dudek, M. (1996) *Kindergarten Architecture: Space for the imagination*, London: E. and F.N. Spon (Chapman and Hall).

Hastings, N., Schwieso, J. and Wheldall, K. (1996) 'A Place for Learning', in P. Croll and N. Hastings (eds) *Effective Primary Teaching: research-based classroom strategies*, London: Fulton.

Spencer, C. (1998) 'Environmental Psychology', in P. Scott and C. Spencer (eds) *Psychology: A Contemporary Introduction*, Oxford: Blackwell.

Weinstein, C.S. and David, T.G. (eds) (1987) *Spaces for Children: The Built Environment and Child Development*, NY: Plenum Press.

Wragg, E.C. (1999) *An Introduction to Classroom Observation*, 2nd edition, London: Routledge.

References

Alexander, R. (1992) *Policy and Practice in Primary Education*, London: Routledge.

Arter, C. (1999) 'Environmental issues', in C. Arter, H.L. Mason, S. McCall, M. McLinden and J. Stone (1999) *Children with Visual Impairment in Mainstream Settings*, London: Fulton.

Bearne, E. (ed.) (1996) *Differentiation and Diversity in the Primary School*, London: Routledge.

Bearne, E. (1998) *Making Progress in Primary English*, London: Routledge.

Bennathan, M. and Boxall, M. (1996) *Effective Intervention in Primary Schools: Nurture Groups*, London: Fulton.

Blamires, M. (ed.) (1999) *Enabling Technology for Inclusion*, London: Paul Chapman Publishing /SAGE.

Blishen, E. (ed.) (1969) *The School that I'd Like*, Harmondsworth: Penguin Education.

Bonnes, M. and Secchiaroli, G. (1995) *Environmental Psychology: A Psycho-social Introduction*, London: Sage.

Brighouse, T. and Woods, D. (1999) *How to Improve Your School*, London: Routledge.

Bruner, J. (1996) 'Culture, Mind and Education', in *The Culture of Education*, Cambridge, MA: Harvard University Press.

Byers, R. (1996) 'Classroom Processes', in B. Carpenter, R. Ashdown and K. Bovair (eds) *Enabling Access: Effective Teaching and Learning for Pupils with Learning Difficulties*, London: Fulton.

CAST (Center for Applied Special Technology) (1999) *http://www.cast.org/*

Cave, S. (1998) *Applying Psychology to the Environment*, London: Hodder and Stoughton.

Children of Reggio Emilia (1993) 'Children in Reggio Emilia Look at Their School', *Children's Environments*, 10, 2, 126–9.

Clandinin, D.J. (1986) *Classroom Practice: Teacher Images in Action*, London: Falmer Press.

Collins, J., Hammond, M. and Wellington, J. (1997) *Teaching and Learning with Multimedia*, London: Routledge.

Crook, C. (1994) *Computers and the Collaborative Experience of Learning*, London: Routledge.

David, T.G. and Weinstein, C.S. (1987) 'The Built Environment and Children's Development', in C.S. Weinstein and T.G. David (eds) *Spaces for Children: The Built Environment and Child Development*, NY: Plenum Press.

DfEE (Department for Education and Employment) (1999) *The National Numeracy Strategy: Framework for teaching mathematics from Reception to Year 6*, London: DfEE.

Flutter, J., Kershner, R. and Rudduck, J. (1998) *Thinking about Learning, Talking about Learning*. Report of the Effective Learning Project, Phase 1, supplemented by Flutter, J. (1998) Phase 2 Report Summary, Cambridge: Homerton College/ Cambridgeshire County Council.

Gibson, J.J. (1979) *The Ecological Approach to Visual Perception*, Boston: Houghton-Mifflin.

Gump, P.V. (1987) 'School and Classroom Environments', in D. Stokols and I. Altman (eds) *Handbook of Environmental Psychology*, Vol. 1, NY: J. Wiley and Sons.

Hallam, S. and Price, J. (1998) 'Can the use of background music improve the behaviour and academic performance of children with emotional and behavioural difficulties?', *British Journal of Special Education*, 25 (2), 88–91.

Hastings, N., Schwieso, J. and Wheldall, K. (1996) 'A Place for Learning', in P. Croll and N. Hastings (eds) *Effective Primary Teaching: research-based classroom strategies*, London: Fulton.

James, A., Jenks, C. and Prout, A. (1998) *Theorizing Childhood*, Cambridge: Polity Press.

Kliewer, G. (1999) 'The Mozart Effect', *New Scientist*, No. 2211, 6 November, 34–37.

McSporran, E. (1997) 'Towards better listening and learning in the classroom', *Educational Review*, 49 (1), 13–20.

Moll, L.C., Tapia, J. and Whitmore, K.F. (1993) 'Living knowledge: the social distribution of cultural resources for thinking', in G. Salomon (ed.) *Distributed Cognitions: Psychological and educational considerations*, Cambridge: Cambridge University Press.

Nash, B.C. (1981) 'The effects of classroom spatial organisation on four- and five-year-old children's learning', *British Journal of Educational Psychology*, 51, 144–55.

Norman, D.A. (1998) *The Design of Everyday Things*, London: MIT Press (originally published as *The Psychology of Everyday Things*, NY: Basic Books 1988).

Pea, R.D. (1993) 'Practices of distributed intelligence and designs for education', in G. Salomon (ed.) *Distributed Cognitions: Psychological and educational considerations*, Cambridge: Cambridge University Press.

Rivlin, L.G. and Weinstein, C.S. (1995) 'Educational Issues, School Settings and Environmental Psychology', in C. Spencer (ed.) *Readings in Environmental Psychology: The Child's Environment*, London: Academic Press.

Salomon, G. (1993) 'No distribution without individuals' cognition: a dynamic interactional view', in G. Salomon (ed.) *Distributed Cognitions: Psychological and educational considerations*, Cambridge: Cambridge University Press.

Sanger, J. with Willson, J., Davies, B. and Whittaker, R. (1997) *Young Children, Videos and Computer Games: Issues for teachers and parents*, London: Falmer Press.

Savan, A. (1998) 'A study of the effect of background music on the behaviour and physiological responses of children with special educational needs', *Psychology of Education Review*, 22 (1), 32–35.

Schratz, M. and Steiner-Löffler, U. (1998) 'Pupils using photographs in school self-evaluation', in J. Prosser (ed.) *Image-based Research: A sourcebook for qualitative researchers*, London: Falmer Press.

Spencer, C. (1998) 'Environmental Psychology', in P. Scott and C. Spencer (eds) *Psychology: A Contemporary Introduction*, Oxford: Blackwell.

Sternberg, R.J. (1985) *Beyond IQ: A triarchic theory of human intelligence*, Cambridge: Cambridge University Press.

Taylor, C. (1997) 'Organising IT resources in educational institutions', in B. Somekh and N. Davis (eds) *Using Information Technology Effectively in Teaching and Learning: Studies in pre-service and in-service teacher education*, London: Routledge.

Watson, L., Gregory, S. and Powers, S. (1999) *Deaf and Hearing Impaired Pupils in Mainstream Schools*, London: Fulton.

Weinstein, C.S. (1987) 'Designing Preschool Classrooms to Support Development: research and reflection', in C.S. Weinstein and T.G. David (eds) *Spaces for Children: The Built Environment and Child Development*, NY: Plenum Press.

Weinstein, C.S. and Mignano Jr., A.J. (1997) *Elementary Classroom Management: Lessons from research and practice*, 2nd.ed., NY: McGraw-Hill.

Wheeler, S. (1995) 'The right environment', *Research in Education*, 52 (3), 93–9.

Wilkins, A. (1995) *Visual Stress*, Oxford: Oxford University Press.

3 Managing face-to-face communication in the classroom

John Robertson

EDITOR'S SUMMARY

This chapter focuses on the ways in which verbal and non-verbal communications between teachers and children affect the quality of behaviour and learning in the classroom. Issues discussed include ways of ensuring children are paying attention, the impact of different seating arrangements, establishing turn-taking, managing classroom rules and establishing authority. Techniques to engage children's interest in tasks and to establish the right emotional tone are also explored.

The focus of this chapter is on face-to-face communication between teachers and pupils. This obviously concerns the verbal information contained in the meanings of the words and sentences they use when they speak to one another but in addition, the vocal variations in pitch, timing and volume convey a second level of meaning concerned with the emotional nature of the message. Is the speaker bored or excited, calm or angry, curious or disinterested? Facial expressions, gestures and posture contribute to this form of information which, even though the meaning is sometimes ambiguous and certainly less verifiable than words, plays a major part in the way listeners react.

A third less apparent message or signal which is conveyed when people communicate is concerned with the nature of the relationship they claim to have with each other. Is this a meeting between people who consider themselves equal or who believe they differ in status? Are they strangers or do they know one another intimately? People may deliberately or unconsciously convey 'who they think they are' in relation to each other, a fact which has particular significance for teacher–pupil relationships. It is not, therefore, simply what is said and how it is said that is significant, but who is saying it, or more precisely, what relationship we believe we have to the speaker.

An instruction, question or statement from a teacher to a pupil will therefore simultaneously convey meanings concerned with ideas, feelings, attitudes and relationships, as will the pupil's response, and this will be discussed in more detail later in this chapter. However, it is the overriding responsibility of the teacher to ensure that face-to-face communication can take place in an orderly manner and it is this which will be dealt with first.

Controlling communication

Are you receiving me?

How do we know whether pupils are listening to the teacher? (see Figure 3.1). It is not possible ever to be sure without subsequently checking, but one can be fairly safe in assuming they are not paying attention if they themselves are talking to each other. However, some teachers seem prepared to talk to the backs of children's heads, raise their voices over the ambient chattering and ignore those who continue to walk around the room, in spite of the fact that they are far more likely to be listening if they are quiet, still and looking at the teacher. This might seem impossible to achieve with some children but there will never be a better opportunity than in the first encounter with the class when the teacher establishes what she expects from the pupils and what they can expect of her. Failure to assert the right to control communication from the outset will only make it more difficult to do so later, as the pupils quickly learn that with this particular teacher they can choose when and if they will attend.

Consider this brief episode which lasted no more that twenty seconds, transcribed from video tape. A new supply teacher has lined up her class outside the classroom, making sure they are reasonably quiet before letting them enter.

TEACHER: Right, lead in quietly. (*The teacher remains outside the door and as the pupils enter they begin to talk noisily but not in an unruly way. When most have entered she follows, picking her way through those who are removing jackets, getting out books and chatting. As she does so, she repeats her instructions above their noise.*)

TEACHER: Can you sit down please ... OK sit down please. (*Before reaching her table at the front of the room she turns towards the main body of the class.*)

TEACHER: Would you please sit down and would you please take your jackets off because you're going to be (*she turns and walks to the front*) you're going to be too hot otherwise. (*She continues to her table and looks around the room.*)

Throughout the whole episode, the pupils were talking, some calling across the room, as they settled into their places. Few even looked at the teacher when she spoke. The pattern of communication, and to some extent the nature of the relationship with this teacher, were being established. Her

Figure 3.1 To be effective, the teacher must have the children's attention

'instructions' simply added to the background noise and general air of hustle and bustle and she unwittingly contributed to the disorderly atmosphere. Had she, instead, stood inside the room as the pupils entered, to keep an eye on what was happening, then calmly made her way to her table, allowing time for them to settle, she could then have called for attention, and not continued until she achieved it. The first instruction, or 'contact signal' might have to have been given in a raised voice above the level of noise and repeated as necessary until all the pupils were quiet and attending, in the following manner:

TEACHER: Right, could I have everyone's attention? Thanks. (*Waits a few seconds.*)

TEACHER: Everyone's attention. (*Looking in the direction of those not attending.*)

And for any who still persist,

TEACHER: I need *everyone's* attention … thanks.

Rogers (1994) suggests that 'thanks' implies you expect the students to comply and is therefore more definite than 'please', but whichever is used it must not be said in an uncertain or pleading manner. Ideally one should achieve attention simply by looking at the pupils in a manner which shows one is waiting to begin, but with some groups a more active approach might be necessary (see Robertson 1996, for a more detailed analysis of this behaviour).

The teacher would thereby begin to establish that when she calls for attention she expects to receive it. Of course in the longer term such things as the quality of teaching, the consistency of practice and the consequences for non-compliance will influence whether they continue to attend, but initially they are likely to comply as they will not yet have learned to ignore the teacher.

In a similar respect, when one addresses an individual pupil in the class it is important first to establish eye contact before giving the message. Calling a pupil's attention, preferably by name, and continuing only when he or she is looking makes sure the message is being received.

A frequent problem for teachers is controlling the build-up of noise when children are working in pairs or small groups. One should be aware that a rising pitch is not a good sign and probably indicates that they are getting too excited and off-task. It can be helpful to agree appropriate 'voice levels' with the children before any activity and then to remind them when they 'forget'. The most commonly used level will be 'partner voice' where only their partner should hear what is being said (Robertson and Webb 1995). Instead of complaining that 'It's getting too noisy' the teacher can be more specific and positive, reminding the group, 'Remember we should be using our partner voices'. Those who still fail to comply can be brought back for a 'practice' session during the lunch hour, as was the case with five young girls. The teacher told them they had ten minutes to practise their partner voices so that she would be able to hear that they were talking but not what they were saying. She returned to her table but in a few minutes one of the girls approached her. 'Miss ... I can't think of anything to say.'

Are you sitting comfortably?

It will not come as a surprise to experienced teachers to learn that the way pupils are seated in a room will affect the patterns of communication and consequently their behaviour (see Figure 3.2). When seated around tables they are in face-to-face contact with each other and at any given time some will have their backs to the teacher. Such arrangements are essential for collaborative activities or small group discussions because they facilitate interaction, but when pupils are required to work largely independently on a task or to attend to the teacher, they encourage distraction. As is the case with adults, much of the talk that children engage in is of a social nature; sharing experiences and expressing attitudes and opinions. Talking about the films they have seen, the latest gossip or their favourite pop and sports stars gives them a sense of identity and belonging with their peers and is an essential social activity. However, during most lessons social talk is often inappropriate and simply distracts others from concentrating on their work. Casual remarks and questions such as 'Are you going out tonight?' require someone else to comment or answer and can very quickly lead a whole table of pupils off-task for some time. Hastings and Schweiso (1995) showed that

Figure 3.2 An effective classroom will offer a variety of seating arrangements; how children are seated will affect their level of concentration and their opportunities for social interaction

in the two Primary classes they studied, more time was spent on-task when the pupils worked in rows rather than around tables, and in a further study time spent on-task by three disruptive pupils 'increased dramatically' when two were seated in rows and one on his own.

Some children are very easily distracted and can distract others and it therefore makes no sense to seat them in social groupings when they are expected to work independently. There is no reason, space permitting, why the seating should not be arranged to suit the type of activity undertaken, and moving the furniture could be part of the lesson just as it is with equipment and apparatus in Physical Education. As a general guideline, for teacher-led whole-class activities or when pupils' behaviour is in question, they should be seated facing the teacher in rows or on separate tables around the room if space permits. For independent working some may even concentrate better when seated facing a wall, but for collaborative activities social groupings are required. The recent recommendations for the Numeracy Hour (DfEE 1999) require the pupils to be seated in a horse-shoe arrangement which is often used by modern language teachers in secondary schools as this facilitates communication between any one individual and the rest of the class.

Flexibility in seating arrangements to suit the nature of the activity and the attitudes of the pupils should be one's aim. but rather than simply imposing these on the pupils it is preferable to discuss one's reasons with them beforehand. However, it is usually safer to start with more formal arrangements with a new class and introduce social groupings when a good cooperative working atmosphere has been achieved.

One at a time, thanks

When a small group of people are talking informally together, the conversation is regulated by unwritten 'rules'. Evidence summarised by Argyle (1991) shows that turn-taking can be quite well established by the age of 12 months and even appear as early as 12–18 weeks. By 18 months children also look at the listener during or after their utterance, which is a feature of adult communication, probably to collect feedback. Turn-taking can flow very smoothly between adults with pauses sometimes as short as one-fifth of a second and is mediated by various cues such as the speaker using a 'terminal gaze' at the listener, returning to a resting position after gesturing, ending with a fall in pitch and completing a sentence. The speaker can expect to be looked at by the listeners and will watch and listen for signs that someone else wishes to speak, such as an audible intake of breath and an upward movement of the head.

When a class of pupils is facing the teacher they are inevitably less aware of each other's cues for turn-taking and unless the teacher is careful to order their contributions some will quickly learn that 'he who blares, wins'. In such large group sessions the teacher should indicate who has the floor by naming and remaining looking directly at that pupil, probably with raised eyebrows, which is a sign of attention. If the teacher even glances at any pupils who interrupt prematurely this will encourage them to continue, whereas a raised palm in their direction while sustaining gaze with the nominated pupil, or a quick aside such as 'Hang on a sec, Paul', are unambiguous signals for them to wait. If the teacher looks at those who call out or, worse still, replies to them and fails to resist interruptions, some pupils quickly begin to comment directly to one another, sometimes shouting across the room without reference to the teacher. At the first sign of any unruly 'cross-talk' between pupils the teacher must interrupt and restore order as such situations can quickly degenerate into chaos. It is helpful to have a few ready-made comments for such occasions such as 'Let's keep it orderly', 'One at a time thanks' or 'Hands up if you have a comment'.

Corrective consequences

In a survey of 117 students aged 15–17 years, Langford *et al.* (1994) concluded that rules which guaranteed the right of others to learn were overwhelmingly supported, making the case for negotiating rather than imposing such rules. There were, however, a small minority who rejected such rules on the bases of general hostility to teachers.

Negotiating sensible classroom rules with younger pupils gives them a sense of ownership over their own behaviour but, nevertheless, some will still not comply with those rules even though they fully understand the reasons for them. If teachers respond with punitive measures aimed at deterrence this may well help to produce the sort of hostile attitudes found in Langford's survey of older students. It might not always be possible to improve a pupil's attitudes and behaviour but we should be careful not to make them worse. When pupils fail to respond to private low-key reminders or to follow clear directions they should be given choices about the consequences rather than threats. Compare a teacher who aims to deter with the publicly delivered threat 'Mark! If I see you fooling around again you're coming out the front and sitting on your own!', with one whose aim is to inform by privately telling the pupil 'You can choose either to get on with your work sensibly or you'll have to sit on your own at the front. It's up to you, Mark'. Consequences should always be predictable so that pupils have the opportunity to make informed choices about their behaviour. They should, when possible, be given privately to avoid humiliating pupils in front of their peers and delivered in a calm and mildly regretful manner or at least in a neutral fashion, avoiding at all costs any show of personal satisfaction or revenge; such attitudes are likely to escalate the conflict and evoke hostile responses from pupils. A 'detention' (e.g. keeping in at lunchtime) should be used to try to work with the pupil to 'fix the problem' and build a better relationship rather than to punish and deter.

Every teacher must assert his or her right to control communication from the outset by:

- establishing contact before delivering messages
- resisting interruptions to themselves or others
- quickly restoring order when necessary
- ensuring fair consequences for persistent offenders.

If the teacher does not take control, then the more dominant and outspoken pupils will.

Cognitive communication

Given that teachers are able to create the right conditions, they will obviously try to impart the prescribed facts, comprehension and skills to their pupils. It is an old cliché, but teaching is not about filling empty vessels but about lighting fires and the way the teacher presents a subject and interacts with the pupils will influence the motivation with which the work is undertaken and the extent to which learning takes place. In this respect the work must present some challenge to the pupils so that, with effort, they can achieve success. Success without effort will not give a sense of achievement; failure in spite of considerable effort is disheartening. It is essential, therefore, that all children understand and can manage the basic work and activities but that more challenging material is always available for those able to tackle it. When a child has worked quickly and successfully through the task set and clearly has a good understanding of the concepts, the words one should not hear from the teacher are 'If you've finished you can draw a picture about it' or 'Now you can colour in the drawings'. These are time-filling activities which do nothing to increase motivation or a sense of achievement.

The need for Primary teachers to adopt more whole-class teaching and to ask challenging questions, more recently advocated by OFSTED inspectors (OFSTED 1994), had emerged from earlier research into successful teaching (e.g. Mortimore *et al.* 1988; Galton 1989; Alexander 1991) but knowing the right questions to ask is largely a function of one's knowledge of the subject. This places considerable demands on the knowledge of the generalist teacher and a case can be made for increasing the extent to which Primary school teachers specialise as some already do in music, physical education and, to a lesser extent, mathematics (Richards 1994).

I once observed a Year 6 group working on a topic about the wheel. Several had brought in various small wheels and one boy was aimlessly spinning a cog from a clock and he commented to his companion that it was spinning backwards. They both watched for a moment as the cog appeared to spin in the reverse direction but they soon lost interest, so I asked them if it really had been spinning backwards. They knew this was not the case but did not know why, so I suggested they tried to find out. After spinning other wheels made of different materials they eliminated surface reflections as the cause of the illusion but then found that the effect was not produced near the window so deduced it was something to do with the electric light in the room. The problem then was how to explain the stroboscopic effect to them, a difficult concept even for able children. I therefore asked five other pupils to sit in a circular arrangement around a table and let the two boys stand at the side to observe. The task was for the seated pupils to pass an object around the table from one pupil to another but the observers could only look when I said they could. The object started at pupil A, which the boys observed before closing their eyes. It was then quietly passed from A to B to C to D in a clockwise direction. I stopped them at E and let the boys see where the object was before they again closed their eyes. This process was repeated and on subsequent clockwise revolutions I let the boys observe the object at D, C, B and A. When I asked them which way round the object had been passed they both thought it was anti-clockwise, having only seen it 'move' in that direction. With very able pupils one might have left them to speculate on how this effect could 'shed light' on the spinning cog illusion, but I decided then to explain that the electric light was in fact a series of rapid flashes allowing them fifty glimpses of the cog every second, in the same way that they had only 'glimpsed' the object being passed round the table. Most appeared to grasp at least the rudiments of this explanation and all seemed interested, but without some specialist knowledge it would have been difficult for me first to notice the opportunity, the brief 'spark' when the pupils noticed the illusion, and then to engage them in exploring the effect in the hope of kindling a fire.

Motivating pupils with challenging questions and activities are essential aspects of successful teaching. In the previous example the pupils were engaged by the unexpected response when the boys believed the object had been passed in the opposite direction and a similar approach was used by a student teacher in a lesson I observed. The aim of the session was to teach the main ideas involved in the water cycle: evaporation, warm air rising, condensation, rainfall and so on. I had previously seen this explained by another student who had used a clear, well labelled diagram showing lakes, evaporation, clouds and hills, and it had seemed quite successful. However, this student gathered all the children around her on the carpet and produced a mirror from her handbag. 'Now, hands up, can anybody tell me what you think will happen if I huff on this mirror?' The question was asked in an intriguing 'I wonder if anybody knows' manner and was greeted with a host of straining arms held aloft. They knew it would go misty and several were allowed to try and watch the mirror first cloud over then slowly clear. They guessed that the mist was water and a short discussion about evaporation followed. She then produced another mirror and asked the children to watch carefully when she huffed on it. To their evident surprise, nothing happened. Why didn't it turn misty even when they were allowed to huff on it? They speculated that it was a special glass or had been coated with 'anti-water' material, but when she let them touch it they realised it was, in fact, quite hot as she had kept it next to a hot water bottle in her bag. In order for the water to condense from their breath it had to meet the cooler surface of the first mirror. The discussion went on to misty bedroom windows on cold mornings and hence to the general principles involved in the water cycle. This student had:

- produced the unexpected
- related to their personal experience
- involved them in the activity
- asked questions in an intriguing manner
- reacted positively to their suggestions

and had thereby ensured that the main ideas would be far more memorable for the children than had she simply told them.

Good teaching is about capturing children's interest so that they are keen to learn and participate. Before sowing the seed prepare the ground.

Affective communication

The teacher is leading a class discussion in a Personal and Social Education session.

TEACHER: There are many groups of people in the world who suffer. Can you think of any groups of people in the world who suffer?
P(1): (*Calling out*) Homosexuals, black people, witches, black magic people. Anyone who's different.
TEACHER: (*While pupil giving his answer*) Homosexuals, yes, mmm.
P(2): (*Sitting beside the first pupil and leaning back on his chair*) And people, like fat people and stuff.
P(1): (*Smiling*) Fat people?
P(2): (*Laughing*) Yeah!
P(1): (*Laughing*) No.
TEACHER: Can you turn to the next page …

One can see in this brief extract the teacher failing to keep the discussion orderly by accepting the calling out and the subsequent cross-talk between pupils, as dealt with earlier. Though this does not necessarily lead to disorder, with some groups it might. However, there are other aspects of the communication which should certainly concern the teacher. Although the answer given by the first pupil was correct and he was clearly thinking about the question as shown by his reflection 'anyone who's different', the attitude expressed by the pupils was entirely inappropriate. The topic was serious – people who suffer – and a major aim for the session should have been to get the pupils to treat it seriously. The first pupil gave his answer in a dismissive way as if he were reciting a shopping list and he subsequently ridiculed his neighbour's contribution, which led to the casual joking disagreement. Though teachers may not be able to control the prevailing mood in a group they have a responsibility to try to influence it.

On this occasion a serious attitude was called for but on others a teacher may need to calm a lively group or try to generate enthusiasm in uninterested pupils. Emotions are predominantly conveyed by non-verbal behaviour: vocal variations, facial expressions, posture and gestures. Think of the numerous ways in which an everyday greeting such as 'Hello, nice to see you' can be expressed to communicate dislike, embarrassment, pleasure, ridicule and so on. We believe the truth lies not in the meaning of the words but in the manner in which they are expressed. Whereas we understand the words people use by decoding the sentences to gain the meaning, emotions are directly experienced from others. We may not even be aware of the behaviours which are conveying the feelings any more than the sender may be conscious of using them. Quite simply, we 'catch' feelings from others so that when they are expressing grief, seriousness, calmness or excitement, to some extent we also experience those emotions.

If we can first gain the listener's full attention they will in some respects experience any emotion which we express with authenticity and integrity. In the extract above the teacher was far too passive, accepting the attitudes which the pupils imparted to the subject rather than attempting to convey feelings of concern and seriousness. Had he instead interrupted in the following way it might have encouraged them to treat the subject seriously:

TEACHER: There are many groups in the world who suffer. Can you think of any groups in the world who suffer?
PUPIL: (*Calling out*) Homosexuals, black people, lesbians, witches …
TEACHER: (*Holding hand up, palm facing pupil*) Just a second … (*scanning class to make sure they are all attending.*) Adrian's got some good suggestions. … (*Looks back at Adrian with a curious, almost puzzled expression*) In what ways do homosexuals suffer in our society?

Valuing the pupil's answer would encourage him to think more deeply about the question and if the rest of the class were confronted with a teacher who looked serious and interested in their contributions rather than passive, they would be far less likely to treat the subject in a flippant manner. Anyone who continued to do so might be given a direct reminder such as, 'Mark … (*waiting for eye contact*) … we need to treat this subject seriously'. In contrast, if the teacher had smiled in response to the original joking between the pupils, the flippant attitude would have been encouraged.

Experienced teachers are continually influencing the prevailing mood in the class, sensing when it is appropriate to share a joke or to be serious, to be calming or enthusiastic, to encourage or disapprove.

Communicating relationships

When people meet one can infer aspects of their relationship by the way they behave towards one another. Good friends treat one another differently from total strangers; managers behave differently towards their subordinates than to their superiors. These two dimensions, sometimes referred to as 'intimacy' and 'status', have been widely researched and many subtle behaviours have been shown to reveal the nature of the relationship being claimed (e.g Mehrabian 1972; Robertson 1996).

Both intimacy and status will feature strongly in teacher–pupil relationships. When first meeting a new class of pupils, intimacy is low; the teacher has yet to learn the pupils' names and find out about their abilities, temperaments and interests, but by the end of the year she may well have met their parents and know many personal details about their private and domestic circumstances. In turn, the pupils may have found out such things as the teacher's first name, her birthday, her likes and dislikes and her taste in clothes. This knowledge represents a growth in the intimacy of the relationship between the teacher and her pupils and she is likely to treat them far less formally than at the beginning of the year, enjoying more social exchanges and jokes, and generally being much more friendly and accessible. To foster such relationships it is worth trying to make time during breaks, lunch times or the transitions between activities to make informal contacts with pupils by passing friendly remarks such as 'Looking smart today Karl', 'Good work you did yesterday Janet' or 'Great haircut Mark', but it is a mistake to 'court friendship' by trying too hard to be liked. Good relationships based on trust and respect take time to develop.

In contrast, when a teacher first meets her new class she has the task of immediately establishing and consolidating her authority, one aspect of which being the right to control communication, which was dealt with earlier. In early face-to-face meetings a teacher's behaviour towards the pupils is more formal and focused primarily on the tasks in hand. In turn, the pupils will be more wary of the teacher, not knowing what to expect of her, and are therefore likely to behave in subordinate ways towards her such as facing, using formal forms of address and adopting upright postures. In the previous transcribed extract, the second pupil, Mark, was rocking back in his chair when he called out to the teacher, from which one can infer probable features not only about his attitude but also about the relationship he claimed to have with the teacher. Subordinates tend to adopt upright postures in face-to-face meetings with superordinates, particularly in formal situations, whereas the latter can remain relaxed. A more tense, upright position is associated with alertness or readiness to act and might once have functioned as a 'fight or flight' reaction in the face of a threat. It is now widely recognised as a sign of attention with connotations of respect rather than fear, and pupils who deliberately resist 'standing up straight', avoid eye contact and display sullen expressions are rightly judged as conveying disrespectful attitudes. In Mark's case his demeanour was not hostile, but from his relaxed position one could probably infer that he was not conscious of the teacher's status as it is far less likely that he would have behaved in that way had he been speaking to someone whose authority was more significant for him, such as the headteacher.

Teachers initially should claim the right to behave in ways towards their pupils which are essential to the performance of their role, taking initiatives such as calling pupils over, asking questions and giving instructions, and should expect pupils to forgo those rights thereby expressing the status difference in the relationship (see Robertson 1996). In the early meetings particularly they must therefore discourage actions from pupils which prematurely claim to assert their own status relative to the teacher and must themselves express their authority by controlling communication and movement, setting the agenda and taking initiatives.

When good working habits are established and more informal relationships begin to develop, the teacher can rely on the pupils to act responsibly and will be able to relate to them on a more equal basis in the knowledge that they will not 'overstep the mark'. If all goes well, relationships will become friendly and informal and the teacher will then only occasionally need to assert her authority.

In summary, face-to-face communication in the classroom is a complex process. Successful teachers simultaneously create conditions in which orderly communication can take place; they can impart facts, concepts and skills, generate motivation, regulate the emotional climate in their classrooms and build appropriate relationships with their pupils. In addition to all this they make it look easy, which it isn't, and enjoyable, which it is.

Activities

Face-to-face impressions

Imagine you are meeting your Year 1 class for the first time. How would you introduce yourself and what would you be trying to achieve?

- What would you say?
- How would you say it?
- Where would you look?
- Would you ask any questions?
- Would you smile?
- How would you stand or would you sit?

Would you vary the way you presented yourself and what you said in the following contexts? What would you be trying to achieve?

- Introducing yourself to your new Year 6 class some of whom, in previous years, have developed the reputation for being difficult to manage.
- Introducing yourself to a tutor and a group of fellow teachers from other schools with whom you will be studying on a course.

Conveying attitudes

You will need to try this with a partner or small group of colleagues.

The way we ask questions and respond to answers can reveal how we feel about what we are doing and why we are doing it. Question your partner or the group briefly on aspects of an everyday subject on which they would have some knowledge or opinions, such as school rules, e.g.:

- Why should you put your hand up to ask a question?
- Why do we need a rule about walking in the school building?
- Why should you turn up for lessons on time?

Choose one of the following and try to convey the attitude described in the ways in which you ask the questions and respond to the answers:

- I expect everyone to know these answers and I am testing to make sure that they do.
- I am very critical of this group and fed up with their casual attitude (e.g.: the way they disregard the rules).
- I am really interested to know the group's views as I always find their ideas valuable.
- I am bored with the subject of school rules and feeling tired, but I have to do it.

When you have finished discuss how your partner/s felt about you and their involvement in the activity or subject being discussed.

Creating interest

How do you manage to get your pupils interested in your lessons? Think of a successful lesson you have developed and consider in what ways you attempted to capture their interest. Can you think of examples you have used or seen of the following?

- *Apparent incongruity*: showing something where the results are surprising and go against the pupils' expectations.
- *Challenge*: presenting a perceptual, intellectual or physical problem.
- *Dramatisation*: enacting or role-playing a scene or incident. Storytelling.
- *Involving pupils*: using pupils actively to illustrate points, demonstrate, brainstorm ideas as a class or in small 'buzz groups'.
- *Competition*: setting teams to work competitively on a given task or compete in a game.
- *Personal experience*: relating the subject to your own or the pupils' personal experience, e.g.: a popular TV programme, a news item or a human emotion.
- *First hand/real material*: objects, sound recordings, videos, documents.
- *Public commitment*: getting pupils to declare their views or opinions ('Hands up how many of you think that ...). Acting as devil's advocate.

- *Novelty*: doing something different, unusual, surprising or out of character.

Can you think of other ways of capturing children's interest?

Seating arrangements

Look at Figure 3.3 (page 56) which shows various seating arrangements and complete the following tasks:

- Draw arrows on each to describe the pattern of communication which you think would be likely to occur in each arrangement.
- Rank the diagrams in terms of the formality of the arrangements. What factors do you take into account in these decisions? Do you require additional information?
- State one advantage and one disadvantage of each arrangement.

Further reading

Neill, S. and Caswell, C. (1993) *Body Language for Competent Teachers*, London: Routledge.

Robertson, J. (1996) *Effective Classroom Control: Understanding teacher-student relationships*, London: Hodder & Stoughton.

Robertson, J. (1997) *No Need to Shout*, Heinemann.

Rogers, B. (1997) *You Know the Fair Rule*. 2nd edition, Pearson.

References

Alexander, R. (1991) *Primary Education in Leeds*, University of Leeds.

Argyle, M. (1991) *Co-operation: The Basis of Sociability*, London: Routledge.

DfEE (Department for Education and Employment) (1999) *The National Numeracy Strategy: Framework for teaching mathematics from Reception to Year 6*, London: DfEE.

Galton, M. (1989) *Teaching in the primary school*, London: Fulton.

Hastings, N. and Schweiso, J. (1995) 'Tasks and tables: the effects of seating arrangements on task engagement in primary classrooms', *Educational Research* 37, 3, 279–91.

Langford, P.E *et al.* (1994) Do senior secondary students possess the moral maturity to negotiate class rules? *Journal of Moral Education*, 23, 4, 387–407.

Mehrabian, A. (1972) *Non-verbal Communication*, Aldine Atherton.

Mortimore, P. *et al.* (1988) *School matters: the junior years*, Open Books.

OFSTED (1994) *Primary Matters: A discussion on teaching and learning in primary schools*, OFSTED publications centre.

Richards, C. (1994) 'Subject Expertise and its deployment in primary schools: A discussion paper', *Education 3–13*, March, 40–43.

Robertson, J. (1996) *Effective Classroom Control: Understanding teacher–student relationships*, London: Hodder & Stoughton.

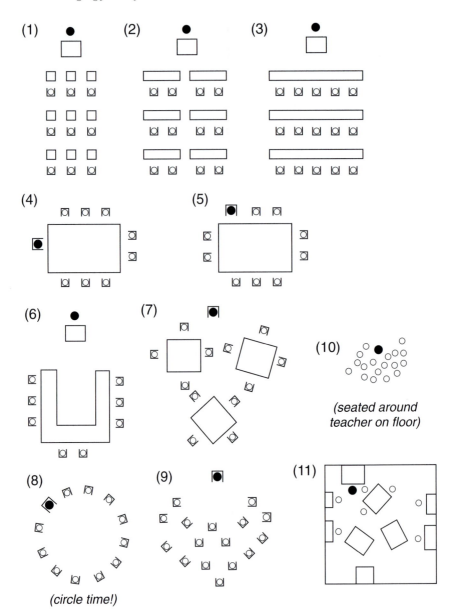

Figure 3.3 Seating arrangements

Robertson, J. and Webb, N. (1995) 'Rainbow Shades to Tone it Down', *Times Education Supplement* June 30.

Rogers, B. (1994) *The Language of Discipline*, Northcote House.

4 Communicating well with children

Isobel Urquhart

EDITOR'S SUMMARY

Being a good communicator is fundamental to being a good teacher. However, there are structural features of classroom life which make effective communication difficult. This chapter explores the ways in which social interactionist theory, derived from the work of Vygotsky, can help us to understand what factors contribute to the effectiveness of teachers' communications with children. Learning is seen to be enhanced when teachers successfully 'scaffold' children's performance on tasks within their 'zone of proximal development' i.e. on tasks which they can manage with help, but couldn't manage on their own. Successful scaffolding involves maintaining children's attention on the task, subdividing the task, if necessary, into more manageable parts, directing attention to relevant features, modelling the processes involved in completing the task and so on. It also involves the skilful use of a repertoire of verbal strategies including instructing, questioning and cognitive structuring. Finally, the chapter discusses issues relating to discontinuities between the communicative environments of the home and the school for some children, about which teachers need to be aware.

Introduction

As teachers, we spend a lot of time talking, and listening, to children, and so there is an obvious sense in which it is important to make sure that our communications help children think and learn effectively. Indeed, teaching should involve a profound understanding of the way in which the communication going on in the classroom *is* the learning, not just a neutral medium through which knowledge is transmitted from one mind to another.

Where does knowledge come from?

As with so many psychologically-framed questions, the answers to this question tend to raise the dualistic nature–nurture debate once again: is the development of children's minds determined by innate pre-set capacities? Or do children's minds develop in a cultural environment that shapes, in particular ways, what it means to know and understand? Over the century, psychologists have framed this question in ways that have influenced their research – either exploring the evidence for innate predispositions, or describing and analysing the interactions with the environment that promote thinking and learning. However, current thinking within psychology adopts a 'social interactionist' approach that avoids simple either/or explanations. We undoubtedly do possess extraordinarily extensive and flexible neural networks which are biologically structured. These predispose us to perceive and organise our world in response to our cultural environment (Papousek and Papousek,1987; Trevarthen *et al.* 1996). That is, our given genetic make-up acts – albeit with great flexibility – to constrain the limit and range of actions and reactions we can make to our environment. On the other hand, the quality and quantity of the environments we find ourselves in, the cultural and social conditions and affective relationships we experience, encourage and facilitate the capacity of our innate dispositions to make meaning at all, and will most certainly affect the kinds of meanings we make, the ways of knowing ourselves and the world and the ways of learning that our culture recognises and permits (Garton 1992).

Social interaction

In this chapter, the focus will be on the way current social interactionist theories explain how social and cultural contexts contribute to the development of children's minds. A social interactionist approach typically examines how the process of communication develops, and how it contributes to children's thinking (Rogoff 1990). In particular, the chapter considers how these explanations help us to understand what factors contribute to the effectiveness of teachers' communications with children. However, it is important to realise that early communications between adults and children usually involve social interactions in which children *jointly* construct meaning and understanding in and through their communications with adult, more expert members of their culture (Garton 1992; Wood, Wood and Middleton 1978). This collaborative communication process is, therefore, very different from seeing the child as the classic *tabula rasa* (i.e. as a blank sheet) onto which adults inscribe their own abstract, mental representations of knowledge. On the contrary, 'abstract' mental representations of knowledge or skill are so called because they are abstracted from activities that take place in the empirical world, the world of material objects and social interactions. Children are actively making sense of these practical contexts, participating in constructing the meaning of the events and experiences that occur. More-over, in these practical contexts, children are often engaged in talk, either to themselves or in dialogue with parents and other expert speakers.

Early communications

Social interaction begins very early. Children are born into social situations with many opportunities to become skilled communicators right from birth. Importantly, therefore, evidence shows that care-givers engage their infant children as active collaborators in the communicative process, not simply as recipients of others' transmissions. Evidence shows mothers engaging in face-to-face social interactions with babies, e.g. peek-a-boo games, turn taking games where the mother leaves silences for the baby to make a response, and then responds herself, which are claimed to lay the basis for later conversational turn taking (Snow 1972:86). In these early interactions, which Trevarthen *et al.* (1996) famously termed 'proto-conversations', moth-ers respond to their babies as much as babies respond to their mothers, and this process continues as babies grow. As they become able to move away from their mothers, infants and young children also develop language as a way of maintaining relationship over distance. These conversations eventu-ally become child-initiated, and at that point represent the child's entry into social communicative exchanges, responded to by further talk from the mother.

Language in use

Theorists such as Bruner (1983) and Halliday (1978) have observed that chil-dren do not learn language as a thing in itself. It is not that the child is anx-ious to speak and sets about learning language from its parents and siblings. The child learns language because language is useful in communicating his or her feelings, wishes, desires and so on. It involves learning how to produce and understand utterances in a wide variety of contexts, learning to use lan-guage as a resource for communicating with other people. Language invari-ably occurs, for young children, in a context of joint meaning-making between themselves and adults (or more experienced peers); the child wants the adult to bring something, or wants to share her interest in the birds in the garden, or needs to know more about something the adult is doing, etc. That is, as Wells (1986) describes it, children's learning to talk depends on inter-actions where the child is a participant in a conversation, which acts as the site where a child's hypotheses about how to construct their representation of language and the construction of meaning embedded within it can be tested. The feedback from the adult – elaborating the topic of conversation, asking for clarification, fetching the stuffed animal from behind the radia-tor, etc. – confirms or challenges the child's hypotheses and provides the stimulus for further language development.

If thinking depends on the kinds of active, jointly constructed processes we have suggested, with individuals predisposed to make sense of themselves, other people and the environment around them through and in their verbal communications with others, then it is important to ask ourselves how learning can be optimally developed through the help provided by other people in the environment. By observing in detail how social facilitation provided by more skilled participants contributes to children's learning and leads it in certain directions, we may find principles of learning that will be helpful to us as teachers in developing effective ways of communicating with children in classrooms.

The contribution of Vygotsky

A major theoretical explanation for the importance of the social context in cognitive development is to be found in the work of the Russian psychologist Lev Vygotsky. It was Vygotsky who suggested that the very early cognitive development of children is greatly transformed by the use and internalisation of cultural tools, such as language. Many studies show very young children and their parents in social interaction, usually involving a spoken dialogue of some kind, in which both participants mutually make sense of each other's actions and reciprocate in construing meaning from the shared context (Edwards 1997). In Vygotsky's terms, the 'expert' (parent, teacher, older child) can be described as using a mechanism, a tool, that conveys or mediates his or her understanding so that a task can be accomplished, just as a physical tool is the means by which physical tasks are accomplished. Vygotsky described a range of such intellectual tools:

> Examples of psychological tools and their complex systems may be a language, different forms of numeration and arithmetics, mnemotechnic aids, algebraic symbols, works of art, writing, charts, diagrams, maps, figures, all possible kinds of conventional signs.
>
> (Wertsch 1991)

The main mediating mechanism, the main tool, that humans use to share a common culturally constructed understanding, is communication through talk.

In this extract from Wells (1986) we can see how Mark's mother uses strategies to keep a conversation going; she adopts the child's perspective and in her next contribution to the conversation, tries to include something of what the child has just said, and extends it, or encourages the child to do so:

MARK: (*Looking out of the window at the birds in the garden*) Look at that. Birds, Mummy.
MOTHER: Mm.
MARK: Jubs [birds].
MOTHER: (*Inviting Mark to extend his own meaning*) What are they doing?

MARK: Jubs bread. [Birds eating bread]

MOTHER: (*Extending Mark's meaning*) Oh look! They're eating the berries, aren't they?

MARK: Yeah.

MOTHER: (*Extending and paraphrasing*) That's their food. They have berries for dinner.

(Wells 1989: 47–8)

By experiencing and participating in the use of such cultural tools with other, more skilled users, children eventually internalise them. In the process of internalisation, these social tools or mechanisms are transformed into what Vygotsky called 'higher' mental processes, such as attention, memory, the ability to plan, to reason, etc.; the components, as cognitive psychologists have traditionally studied them, of thought and mind.

One of the main attractions of Vygotsky's theories of cognitive development for teachers, therefore, is that he believed that the contribution of a more advanced tutor was central to the cognitive developmental process, and thus he saw instruction and teachers as performing a crucial and essential role in children's development.

How children learn from more knowledgeable others

In any social interaction, therefore, children learn the *means* through which a society expresses and communicates its collective and evolved knowledge, as well as the content of the communication. A child takes in, that is, *internalises*, ways of structuring and making sense of the world through his or her collaboration in social activities, and this includes the talk that occurs between skilled and less skilled participants. What is spoken to a child is later said by the child to herself or himself, and is later further abbreviated and transformed into the silent speech of the child's thoughts (Tharp and Gallimore 1988).

Over time, what is initially expressed in an external symbolic form (for example through spoken dialogue) is transformed, through the process of internalisation, into mental representations which can be thought. This capacity to develop what Vygotsky called 'inner speech' allows children to organise their perceptions, understanding and voluntary actions in mental structures which are already embedded in the language they have been hearing and exchanging with more experienced members of their cultural communities.

Vygotsky argued that we can observe this process of internalisation when we overhear young children talking out loud to themselves (for example, when trying to make a model, or play out a fantasy game with toy people, or when remembering something) and that this stage is eventually superseded by internal thought which he hypothesised would be a kind of abbreviated talk.

Katharine Nelson (1989, 1996), extending Vygotsky's ideas, has recorded and examined in detail the monologues of a child as she lay in bed just before going to sleep or on waking, and similarly argued that this activity was an important aspect of learning to think and to remember. Interestingly, she points to the importance of storying and narrative structure in the development of a child's mental life. She confirms that the models and conversational supports provided by parents are highly influential in the child's structuring of events. The ability of the mother to model and support coherent whole-narrative structures is paralleled in children's structuring of their memories.

We can say, therefore, that in the conversations and dialogues that make up the verbal interactions between individuals, minds meet each other in and through the talk expressed, and are mutually influenced by the encounter. Children learn the ways our culture constructs, organises and expresses its knowledge and experience. Thus children learn *how* to think as well as *what* to think, through learning their language and through participating in other symbolic and communicative exchanges.

The encounter is also intersubjective; that is, both participants are mutually responsive to each other's communications. A skilled tutor sensitively adjusts his or her assistance in the collaboration to the needs of the learner, receiving feedback all the time as to whether his or her communications have been helpful or not. In order to fine-tune his or her helpful responses, the tutor adapts his or her communication in the light of the response from the less experienced learner. There is also some evidence to suggest that the tutor's own understanding of the learning context is further developed and refined by having to reformulate his or her understanding in language adapted to the needs of another learner.

Guided participation

In Vygotsky's theory, the child learner is thought of as acquiring the knowledge and skills valued by her culture through a form of 'apprenticeship' or 'guided participation' in cultural competence, where what was first experienced as a social interaction becomes the individual's personal and internalised mental process. Vygotsky argued that children's minds develop best in situations where their own attempts to solve a problem are guided by an adult who structures and models an appropriate response or solution to the problem. Vygotsky described it thus:

> Any function in the child's cultural development appears twice, or on two planes. First it appears on the social plane, and then on the psychological plane.
>
> (Wertsch 1980:26)

Wertsch *et al.* (1980) investigated Vygotsky's claim that the emergence of any new function is first social and then psychological. Mothers with children aged two, three or four years old completed a construction task together. They had to build a replica of a model of a truck, using a set of different shapes and different colours. In order to build the truck successfully, it was necessary at certain times to consult the model, e.g. in order to copy exactly the layout of different coloured squares representing the cargo in the truck. Wertsch noticed that there was a difference between the youngest and oldest children during these moments. Whenever the mother looked at the model, the child looked too. This occurred in ninety per cent of the times when the mother looked at the model. He concluded that very young children were able to understand that the mother's gaze was meaningful and used this to interpret the situation and make an appropriate response, i.e. look at the model themselves. However, as children got older, the number of mother-guided looks by children declined, and Wertsch concluded that this demonstrated, as Vygotsky had suggested, that there had been a shift from tutor-regulated activity to self-regulated activity. Older children seemed to be more efficient at extracting the relevant information from maternal looks and had internalised the strategic usefulness of looking at the model from information mediated by an adult.

Social interaction with more competent others would, therefore, appear to be an important component in cognitive development. Our minds are both individual and social, developed both through and for our engagement in cultural life.

The zone of proximal development

Teachers and parents know that children who seem unable to solve problems, complete tasks successfully, or remember things when left to do them on their own, will often be more successful when they are helped by an adult. The adult is able to judge the needs of the child and transfer his or her understanding of the task to the child. Gradually, the child seems to be able to take on more and more of the task until they can do it independently, and use the skills in other contexts. In order to describe the process of transfer of responsibility for successful learning from the adult to the child learner, Vygotsky thought of individual learners as possessing a 'zone of proximal development' in which the transfer took place. This rather clanking phrase has become something of a cliché in educational discussion. Like all clichés, it is in danger of losing its freshness and ability to capture our imagination, yet it remains an extremely helpful idea for teachers trying to understand how their communications can help children learn.

The zone of proximal development refers to the gap that exists for any individual between what he or she can do alone, and what he or she can do with help or guidance from someone who is more knowledgeable or skilled. It also describes the point in a learning situation when an individual is most sensitively disposed to benefit from guidance from a more competent person. i.e. the point where an individual is not quite able to manage the next stage of the task on his or her own, the place where we can identify the proximal 'next step' needed for the individual's developing understanding or skill. In this zone, the skilled tutor can facilitate the individual's level of independent achievement to new levels of skill and comprehension.

Within the zone of proximal development, the more expert learner uses various means to communicate his or her understanding of the task and how to successfully accomplish it in order to help a less experienced learner. In applying this idea to working with children, in jointly working on a problem, the child's individual mental capacities develop through experience of the use of mental tools by the more competent person. It is hard to overstate the importance of the tool that is language in communicating the knowledge and skills of the skilled tutor to the inexperienced learner, who will internalise the language in which thought processes needed to understand and carry out the task successfully are organised and mediated.

Scaffolding

The means by which adults assist young or inexperienced learners have come to be described as a form of 'scaffolding' that skilled tutors provide, that structures the task and supports the learner (see Figure 4.1). Like real scaffolding, the tutor gradually removes structure and support as the inexperienced learner's independent capacity develops. In Vygotskyan terms, the scaffolding moves from being a social, external communication to becoming part of the internalised and individual thought process, contributing to the development of metacognition, the ability to know how we think, and to choose effective strategies for thinking through tasks, and solving problems, etc.

Scaffolding, therefore, refers to ways in which social assistance is provided to young learners. It relates to the means of assistance provided in the zone of proximal development, for example by structuring the task into small, understandable steps and communicating instruction in this form in order for a child to achieve success. The skilled tutor sensitively adjusts the level of instruction to the needs of the learner in a collaborative task, ascertaining as she goes along whether her level of instruction is sensitive to both the actual and potential levels of development which form the limits of that zone.

Bruner (1983) had originally identified this contingent teaching, the sensitive adjustment of instruction to the needs of the learner, as part of the way that mothers help children learn to talk, but subsequently also noticed how it formed part of how mothers assist children in problem-solving activities. This was investigated in a series of studies of teaching and learning interactions between mothers and their children (Wood, Bruner and Ross 1976). Here the researchers asked mothers to teach their 4–5-year-old children how to put together some blocks to assemble a pyramid construction. The model

Figure 4.1 A trainee teacher and a headteacher 'scaffolding' a child's learning

was not available for children or mothers to look at during the activity – all the help had to come from the mother.

The options available to a mother were identified as follows. She could:

- make suggestions (e.g. 'Why don't you try to put some blocks together?')
- add to her words by touching or pointing to some of the blocks
- suggest that they both try to put the blocks together
- structure the task further by arranging the blocks in the order in which they needed to be put together
- show the child how to put some or all of the blocks together while the child watches her.

The researchers classified these instructional options in a hierarchy of adult intervention. Notice how the amount or specificity of instruction increases, while the degree of responsibility on the child for what happens next, decreases.

In a longitudinal study (Moss 1992), some further characteristics of mothers' scaffolding techniques were identified. In particular, Moss noted that mothers worked continuously to 'nudge' children forward in their ability to accomplish problem-solving tasks.

- Mothers tended to stay 'one step ahead' of the child, introducing new skills that the child would not actually be able to manage unaided for some time.
- Mothers consolidated useful tactics that the child had already demonstrated.
- Mothers inhibited actions they considered developmentally immature (e.g. they encouraged children to verbally identify the shape and colour of some wooden blocks rather than simply point to them or pick them up).

Scaffolding, therefore, is a metaphorical term that describes a process of instruction which is specific to the actual learning context, is task-directed and helps to focus the child's attention to the relevant aspects of the task. This last feature is very important. Children are, as we have emphasised, actively trying to make sense of the situations in which they find themselves. However, because of their lack of experience, they do not necessarily know what are the salient features of the context which will help them to understand the situation correctly. We have seen some experimental examples of how mothers help their children by directing their attention to salient features of the task. Here is a more naturalistic example of how two children tried to solve a problem without adult assistance in identifying the salient features of the problem.

> Thomas and Andrew were about 5 and 6 years old when they came across a cat stuck on top of a roof, mewing pathetically but appearing unable to jump down. They were most upset for the cat and tried to think of a way to solve the problem. There were no adults around at the time so they tried to find a solution by themselves. They construed the problem as how to persuade the cat to jump down from the roof and decided, on the basis of their experience of the world and of cats in particular, that if they drew a picture of a bird on the pavement, the cat would want to catch the bird and would jump down from the roof.
>
> (personal anecdote)

As adults, of course, we can see that Thomas and Andrew made a number of misconstruals of the situation based on their lack of experience. The roof was too high for the cat to jump down, and Thomas and Andrew also assumed cats could perceive a symbolic representation of a bird as a bird, and further assumed that a cat could be deceived into thinking a symbolic representation of a bird is a real bird, that as cats hunt birds, this cat would automatically want to pounce on the drawing, and so on. However, it is an ingenious and illustrative example of children actively trying to make sense of a situation and solve a real and pressing problem. What is missing from their version, however, is a knowledge and understanding of the salient features of the situation. The presence of adults would have guided Thomas and Andrew towards the 'right considerations' (Light 1983) that might have led to more effective solutions.

The lesson for us as teachers is that our ability to point learners to the salient features of a task is most important. We learn that what appears to be effective is not so much giving children the right answer and expecting them to memorise it, as orienting young learners towards those 'right considerations' so that they can internalise the appropriate ways of thinking about the problem and own the understanding themselves. This capacity in experts to identify and focus children's attention on the salient features of a problem has also been identified as centrally important by Reuven Feuerstein (Sharon 1987), in his description of how adults mediate 'thinking skills' to children. Feuerstein became famous for the very successful Instrumental Enrichment programmes he invented that enabled many individuals identified as having learning difficulties to achieve real gains in their thinking and learning. Indeed, the process of making explicit through language some of the salient features of a task or how to go about solving a problem is one of the most powerful aspects of what we mean by education. It pervades our teaching, informing, for example, how we select which aspects of learning to draw children's attention to when we plan lessons and set up activities and tasks for children, and how we then communicate our explanations and instructions, ask questions and give verbal feedback.

Scaffolding, therefore, is identifiable as part of the means by which adults enlist children into the social and cultural knowledge of their community, in naturalistic settings, such as mothers and children talking and solving practical problems together. It is also identifiable in communities where children are gradually included in learning adult skills such as bronze making or weaving (Rogoff 1990). According to Vygotsky's theory and Bruner's applications of that theory, much of this knowledge is communicated through 'language in use', talk in a practical or social context, and is internalised and comes to form the mental representations and structures of thought and memory. The talk of the tutor in these contexts is adapted to the needs and developmental capacity of the child in sensitive and flexible ways, constantly challenging and simultaneously supporting the child at the edge of his or her learning, as described by the model of the zone of proximal development. Clearly, such a powerful process throws light on the nature of effective communication and instruction in general, and therefore how it should be applied in the context of school learning. It is those teaching procedures that we now look at in the light of effective communications in school.

Differences between home and school interactions

Unfortunately, the evidence is that effective scaffolding of children's learning through productive talk is not as common a feature of the Primary school classroom as might at first be thought. Consideration of the different social and linguistic contexts of the home and the classroom throw light on the reasons why this appears to be the case.

We have seen that, in interactions with their parents, children are active learners busily making sense of their experience. Most of children's learning in the home occurs spontaneously in the context of problems and events that arise in everyday social contexts, which are resolved and talked about with the help of an adult who provides an additional resource. Children are encouraged and supported in participating in conversation, with adults allowing children to initiate many interactions, and providing conversational 'bridges' that respond to the child's previous utterance and inviting him or her to talk some more, and tend to make verbal references to the child's or joint activities when they contribute themselves. Adults also respond to children's utterances by extending, elaborating on the child's contribution, which shows the child that his utterance is acceptable and understandable, or by seeking clarification. In general, therefore, children are engaged in conversations, which are necessarily collaborative (Wells 1986).

However, when children move into a school environment, they encounter a new kind of social interaction where collaborative language exchanges with adults are very different. Far from offering a richer language environment than children have experienced in the home, there are some significant ways in which children's use of talk can become more limited. Wells found that children tended to play a much less active role in verbal exchanges: they initiated fewer interactions and exchanges, asked fewer questions and made fewer requests. They used language forms which were simpler than those which they were prepared to try out at home – they used simpler grammar, they chose a more restricted range of subjects, and did not use language for more speculative and imaginative purposes, tending to remain within the here-and-now uses of language. Indeed, in school, children's language was frequently used simply to make minimal responses to requests to display their knowledge and understanding. Unlike parents, teachers tended to dominate the conversations with children. They initiated most of the interactions and exchanges by making requests, asking questions and asking children to display their knowledge. Unlike parents, teachers tended to expand on their own meanings rather than extend the meanings contributed by children. In general, therefore, children seemed to experience a reduced opportunity to learn through talk with adults, and their contributions tended to be positively valued only when they reproduced the teacher's own line of thought and the language in which the teacher produced it.

The means of assisting performance

If, as teachers, we are to avoid falling into this kind of relatively impoverished linguistic and communicative pattern, it is important that we consider how language is being used in our classrooms and how it could be developed to enhance children's learning. In this respect, research on scaffolding in classroom contexts could potentially be enormously helpful. Tharp and Gallimore (1988), for example, have derived from their studies of classroom language a list of six means of assistance used in school contexts. They caution the reader, however, that this list includes means of assistance that do not necessarily depend on the internalisation of language but extend to the internalisation of other symbolic representations such as images. Some of the means of assistance they include, such as contingency management (the use of rewards and punishments) and feedback (the giving of evaluative commentary on performance), derive from other schools of psychological thought, such as behaviourism, social learning theory and cognitive science. They describe three specifically linguistic means of assistance.

Instructing

The importance of instructing and giving explanations is that the instructing and explaining voice of the teacher becomes the self-instructing and self-explaining voice of the learner as he or she makes the transition from apprentice to autonomous learner. Tharp and Gallimore (1988) argue that avoiding direct instruction may deny learners the most important outcome of teaching interactions: 'that heard, regulating voice, a gradually internalised voice, then becomes the pupil's own self-regulating, "still, small" instructor.'

What then are the essential characteristics of good instruction? We can look back at some of the principles of scaffolding and the importance of contingent learning to provide the kind of flexible and sensitive awareness of the learner's needs that will help us to adapt our language and the way we structure the task appropriately. However, scaffolding can be misapplied if it leads to rigidly specifying a structured set of teaching steps which requires all pupils to progress in a predetermined sequence towards a predetermined goal. What will have been lost is the collaborative, participatory aspect of learning that we have seen is so influential in the home context, and also the positive drive, within the skilled tutor's use of scaffolding approaches, towards the ever-increasing autonomy of the learner. Teachers should try to ensure that direct instruction pays attention to what individual pupils can already bring to the tasks they are required to perform, and allow children to be actively involved in making meaning, by letting them initiate talk about the topic, ask questions and express their opinions. By using talk to express their own understanding, they can begin to internalise and 'own' the learning. If we respond to children's contributions with interest, answer their questions, and encourage and challenge them to elaborate and extend their utterances, then our instruction and our explanations are likely to be more meaningful than if we simply tell children what we think they need to know and then check that they can remember what they were told.

Questioning

It is somewhat ironic that while parents will often complain about the number of questions that children expect them to answer, the opposite is true of schools. In schools, it is the teachers who ask the questions, and children who are expected to provide the answers. However, the functions of questions children are asked in school can be very unlike those that questioning performs in their everyday lives. This can be clearly seen in Table 4.1, where questions including display questions made up 34.4 per cent of the teachers' spoken language in the classroom in Wells' study.

Teachers ask questions, often seeking a display of information they already know, (e.g. 'What does this word say?'), making requests that do not have the right of refusal implicit in them (e.g. 'Could you stop talking now?'), and seeking information about individuals that might normally be regarded as private and personal (e.g. 'Could you tell us about your weekend, Tom?') The most typical interaction in teacher–pupil discourse is described as a Question–Answer–Acknowledgement exchange (also known as the Initiation– Response–Feedback exchange). Watson (1995), in a small-scale study, described categories of teacher talk and ranked them by frequency of use. She found the kinds of teacher talk likely to develop children's capacity for metacognitive reflection were rarely used. This included the use of questions as a means to prompt children to reflect on their own metacognitive reflection.

When questions are used for learning (as opposed to requests to display knowledge or for assessment), they are a central and powerful device, partly because they encourage children to listen and think (Blank, Rose and Berlin 1978 in Wood 1988), and partly because they expect a spoken reply. This latter demand evokes in children the need to convert thoughts into explicit language and thus to assist thinking, as they try to formulate their thoughts in speech, for instance by reasoning out loud, stating their own views, expressing uncertainties or reaching for explanations, as well as narrating stories or recounting an event or describing a process. Questions that assist learning provoke in the child a way of thinking that he or she is not able to produce alone and are thus part of how we assist children in their zone of proximal development. Wood reminds us that, just like the sensitive mothers' contingent help, teachers formulate questions which are at the appropriate level of need for different individuals and are of the appropriate kind. They can be thought of as prompts or cues we offer about how to think about a topic. As we ask questions, we model a linguistic structure that, internalised, helps children organise their thinking about the task, and to know how to think about school topics as well as what content to remember. However, poor questioning leads children to restrict their thinking and avoid taking risks, seeking confirming experiences of correctness, rather than the kind of cognitive conflict that helps move thinking on to a more advanced stage of development. Good questions are therefore an important part of scaffolding.

Table 4.1 Children's experience of language at home and school (Wells 1986)

Features of language use (absolute values)	Home	School
No. of child utterances to an adult	122.0*	45.0*
No. of adult utterances to the child	153.0	129.0
No. of child speaking turns per conversation	4.1*	2.5*
No. of diff. types of meaning expressed by child	15.5*	7.9
No. of grammatical constituents per child/speech	3.1*	2.4*
Proportions (Child)	%	%
Initiates conversation	63.6*	23.0*
Questions	12.7*	4.0*
Requests	14.3*	10.4*
Elliptical utterances, fragments	29.4*	49.4*
References to non-present events	9.1*	6.4*
Proportions (Adult)	%	%
Questions	14.3*	20.2*
Display questions	2.1*	14.2*
Requests	22.5*	34.1*
Extends child's meaning	33.5*	17.1*
Develops adult's meanings	19.1*	38.6*

Source: Wells 1986:86

Notes: Figures are averaged over all 32 children in the study
    * Statistically significant differences

Open and closed questions

Closed questions are very specific and are often used by teachers to ascertain whether or not a child knows something or not; they usually require children to give restricted, terse answers which can only be right or wrong. 'What happened when Harry Potter put on the hat?', 'What's the name we give to the hot rocks that come out of the volcano?' To ask children questions which have correct, factual answers is not wrong, but where this kind of questioning predominates, it is using a powerful learning device in a very limited way, and can discourage children from seeing a question as an invitation to thought, a challenge to their thinking, an opportunity to persist in their thinking and learning. Closed questions often force children into the position of having to work out what answer the teacher is thinking of, and if the question is too hard, the teacher ends up having to answer her own question.

> A teacher once asked her class: 'What is a frog?' Getting no answer she progressively answered the question herself, giving parts of the words as cues but getting no response: 'An ... a ... am ... amph ... amphib ... amphibian!'

> (Fisher 1990:19)

Open questions on the other hand have more varied purposes: they encourage children to reason, to infer, to evaluate, to express opinions and to argue a case, drawing on evidence and justification, or they may invite children to make a personal and reflective, imaginative response.

Children asking questions

Fisher (1990) quotes a story that Isidor Rabi, a Nobel Prize winning nuclear physicist, told about his mother. When he used to come home from school, she did not ask the usual question: 'So what did you learn today?' She asked instead: 'Izzy, did you ask a good question today?' What we are asked to learn from this is the importance of encouraging children to ask more questions. Look again at Wells' study of questions at home and school. Children at home ask questions all the time, led by their powerful curiosity. Where does that curiosity go in school? It must still be there, and teachers can unleash it through encouraging children to ask questions. A student teacher, depressed about the dullness of her work on the Egyptians, complained that the children seemed bored. She had worked long into the night researching everything she could about the Egyptians, had read all the books, had sorted out the information into themes, but the lessons were flat and uninteresting. The trouble was the children had quickly realised that she had all the answers, that they had nothing to do but receive the information from her. When she realised this, she turned the whole thing round. What did the children know about the burial habits of the Egyptians? What did *they* want to find out about them? Was there anything that particularly interested or puzzled *them*? The classroom began to buzz – children began to turn to the information books on the display table, asked to go to the library, brought in their Dads' precious history books with pictures, brought in models of the pyramids and souvenirs from holidays. Their use of websites became more focused as they asked more specific questions; they learned to evaluate sources as they read contradictory information in different texts. The ability to ask a powerful question is a key skill in effective learning, but we learn it through practice, and so we must both model questioning for children and provide them with opportunities for asking and answering their own questions.

Another key skill in asking questions is giving more thinking time for answering. One of the most frustrating experiences of my teaching career was when I supported children with special educational needs in lessons. They rarely attempted to answer public questions because they expected to be wrong, but when they did, they often needed a lot of thinking time to formulate their answers in words, lots of time to get lost, muddled up, and find their way again, prompted and supported by a sensitive teacher. Instead, teachers, anxious not to prolong the child's perceived discomfort, would interrupt them, assuming they were going to get the answer wrong, or would gloss their answer with their own version of the response. And yet, for all learners, but for unconfident learners above all, the opportunity to think aloud is vital to their cognitive development.

Cognitive structuring

One of the ways in which skilled tutors can assist children's learning through communication is by providing a mental framework within which specific kinds of learning can be understood. These frames of reference can involve sharing with children the set of rules about how to play a team game or conduct a discussion, for example, or exploring the set of beliefs that make sense of religious activities.

Currently, there has been a great deal of interest in the ways in which different frames of knowing are linguistically differentiated, so that learning the genre characteristics of different kinds of knowledge – the way history, as it is expressed in a specific 'set' of language choices, is in fact the creation of history itself. Some theorists go so far as to claim that it is impossible to grasp the ways of understanding that make up knowing a subject without being able to join in the discourse (language in use) of that subject (Christie 1998; Sheeran and Barnes 1991). If this is so, then we have to ensure that children are given opportunities to do so, because Christie argues that school failure can be described precisely in terms of a failure to master the genres of schooling: the essay, the scientific report, the argument.

In practice, cognitive restructuring involves teachers in encouraging children to organise their learning experiences within the often arbitrary and rarely articulated 'ground rules' or expectations of the topic or subject. This involves, as has been emphasised before, the making explicit of those ground rules by teachers, the sharing with children of the salient features of the topic. Teachers help children to use, as well as simply to recognise, the linguistic features of the subject to the point that they are able to use these frames independently to organise their knowledge and experience, and also to recognise new examples of existing cognitive structures. In order for children to internalise these frameworks, we have to provide for them meaningful opportunities in which to try out and internalise those frames. This essentially requires children to be given collaborative and participatory opportunities, in which they can talk to each other and write their understanding, using the generic features of different kinds of register and writing styles to which they have been introduced.

School language and cultural variations

When examining psychological arguments and evidence in favour of a particular theory, it is important to be alert to the possibility that what is being claimed as a common or even universal characteristic of children's development may, in fact, only reflect the experience of the most commonly studied cultural group. Many key psychological studies in the past will have been carried out on middle class children within typically white, male, western cultural contexts. More recent studies, however, take a great deal of interest in looking at how differences between social communities can create differences in ways of knowing and understanding, and that these can have a deleterious or positive effect on how successfully children from different communities enter into school ways of communicating understanding. Recent interests range from studies that look at different social classes and cultural communities within one nationality (Heath 1983) or comparing communities from very different nationalities (Rogoff, *et al.* 1991). Psychologists share this interest with sociologists and anthropologists and there are interesting challenges for all concerned in how to explain and make use of our different ways of understanding cultural differences.

The means by which cultures mediate their knowledge and skills to their young vary, and this variation has enormous implications for how children learn in the particular social context of school. Schools have a particular set of preferred mediational tools that reflect the existing social interactions of some communities and not others. There is abundant evidence that it is characteristic of education in the developed world to emphasise certain ways of communicating the shared knowledge of the culture. In particular, schools favour conveying meaning through making, and encouraging children to make, explicit, declarative statements which include giving verbal explanations, making a reasoned argument to support an opinion, expressing a point of view, asking appropriate questions, and, in general, construing education as largely the capacity not only to understand something implicitly, but also the ability to *make explicit*, in talk and in writing, the nature of our understanding, an argumentative structure behind what we know and can do implicitly.

As teachers, we should be aware, therefore, that some kinds of school communication will be unfamiliar and alienating for some children, and it is our obligation, as skilled tutors, to manage the dilemma. On the one hand, in order to succeed at school and beyond, children have to internalise the communication processes in which knowledge and understanding are embedded in public life – in order to be a historian or scientist, they need to be able to communicate their understanding in the particular linguistic genres of talking and writing like a historian or scientist; on the other hand, tutors have to find the means by which they can adapt their talk so that the kind of contingent learning described above will draw the child through the zone of proximal development into further autonomous levels of understanding and skill, as defined by school learning.

Barnes (1976) observed that teachers often failed to see that children had in fact learned what had been taught. Teachers seemed unable to recognise the learning unless couched in the technical language of their own level of understanding. Similarly, they were often unaware of the difficulties and ambiguities in their own use of abstract forms of talk, in which they themselves understood their subject, and that these often confused children and alienated them from the subject.

If we are unable to build effectively on the different cultural experiences of some learners, however, the danger is that we then contribute to an educational disadvantage that helps perpetuate social inequalities for some cultural communities. Furthermore, we need to recognise the ways in which schools marginalise other ways of communicating understanding so that we overlook and ignore evidence of understanding when it is not conveyed in linguistic forms we recognise.

We should also be aware that, despite the emphasis on verbal communication in this chapter, language is only one of the symbolic means through which we represent our external, socially mediated experience as internal, mental thought. Non-verbal forms of communication – the capacity to represent experience visually or emotionally, for example – should also be considered, although in our kinds of educational context which rely heavily on verbal and written explicit demonstrations of knowledge for evaluative purposes, we may find it harder to justify this kind of implicit knowledge.

Finally, it is not part of this chapter to talk about the emotional conditions in which effective communication can take place. Suffice it to say that when children are confused, nervous or anxious, or are demoralised or despondent about their ability to participate or achieve satisfactorily, or are bored and alienated by tasks and activities that have no relation to their own experiences, then effective communication will not occur. One of the assumptions of effective communication between adults and children is the presence of a benign relationship between tutor and learner (Durkin 1995). This does not always occur, but where children are hostile or anxious, we can be sure that the dialogue and participatory talk so necessary to learning will be impaired.

76 *Communicating well with children*

Activities

Questioning

Think of a topic that you are interested in teaching.
What challenging questions could you ask?
How could you encourage children to generate questions and
 evaluate which are the most interesting?
How could your questioning be more inclusive?

Scaffolding

Observe a teacher or trainee teacher instructing a group of children in
a new skill or concept. Make notes of your observations, detailing:

- how the expert scaffolds the task for his or her learners
- what techniques of instructing, questioning and cognitive restructuring the teacher uses
- the use of participatory talk

Further reading

Donaldson, M. (1978) *Children's Minds*, Harmondsworth: Penguin.
Garton, A.F. (1992) *Social Interaction and the Development of Language and Cognition*, Essays in Developmental Psychology, Hillsdale: Erlbaum.
Rogoff, B. (1990) *Apprenticeship in Thinking: Cognitive Development in Social Context*, Oxford: Oxford University Press.
Wertsch, J.V. (ed.) (1985) *Culture, Communication and Cognition: Vygotskian Perspectives*, Cambridge: Cambridge University Press.
Wood, D. (1988) *How children think and learn*, Oxford: Blackwell.

References

Barnes, D. (1976) *From communication to curriculum*, Harmondsworth: Penguin.
Bruner, J.S. (1983) *Child Talk*, Oxford: Oxford University Press.
Christie, F. (1998) *Literacy and Schooling*, London: Routledge.
Durkin, K. (1995) *Developmental Social Psychology*, Oxford: Blackwell.
Edwards, D. (1997) *Discourse and Cognition*, London: Sage.
Fisher, R. (1990) *Teaching Children to Think*, New York: Simon & Schuster.
Garton, A.F. (1992) *Social Interaction and the Development of Language and Cognition: essays in developmental psychology*, Hillsdale: Lawrence Erlbaum.
Halliday , M. (1978) *Language and Social Semiotic*, London: Edward Arnold.
Heath, S.B. (1983) *Ways with Words*, Cambridge: Cambridge University Press.
Light, P. (1983) 'Social interaction and cognitive development: a review of post-Piagetian research', in S. Meadows, (ed.) *Developing Thinking*, London: Methuen.

Moss, E. (1992) 'The socioaffective context of joint cognitive activity', in L.T. Winegar and J. Valsiner (eds) *Children's Development within a Social Context*, Vol.2. Hillsdale: Erlbaum.

Nelson, K. (1989) *Narratives from the Crib*, Cambridge MA: Harvard University Press.

Nelson, K. (1996) *Language in Cognitive Development. The Emergence of the Mediated Mind*, Cambridge: Cambridge University Press.

Papousek, H. and Papousek, M. (1987) 'Intuitive parenting: A dialectic counterpart to the infant's integrative competence', in Osofsky, J. D. (ed.) *Handbook of Infant Development*, 2nd Edition. New York: Wiley.

Rogoff, B. (1990) *Apprenticeship in Thinking: Cognitive Development in Social Context*, Oxford: Oxford University Press.

Rogoff, B., Mistry, J., Goncu, A. and Mosier, C. (1991) 'Cultural variation in the role relations of toddlers and their families', in M.H. Bornstein (ed.) *Cultural Approaches to Parenting*, Hillsdale: Erlbaum.

Sheeran, Y. and Barnes, D. (1991) *School Writing*, Milton Keynes: Open University Press.

Sharon, H. (1987) *Changing Children's Minds. Feuerstein's revolution in the teaching of intelligence*, London: Souvenir Press.

Snow, C.E. (1972) 'Mothers' speech to children learning language', *Child Development*, 43, pp. 549–65

Snow. C.E. (1986) 'Conversations with children', in P. Fletcher and M. Garman (eds) *Language Acquisition*, 2nd edition. Cambridge: Cambridge University Press.

Tharp, R. and Gallimore, R. (1988). *Rousing Minds to Life*, Cambridge: Cambridge University Press

Trevarthen, C., Aitken, K., Papoudi, D. and Robarts, J. (1996) *Children with Autism: diagnosis and interventions to meet their needs*, London: Jessica Kingsley.

Watson, J. (1995) 'Teacher talk and pupil thought', *Educational Psychology*, 15, 1.

Wells, G. (1986) *The Meaning Makers*, London: Routledge.

Wertsch J.V. *et al.* (1980) 'The adult-child dyad as a problem-solving system', *Child Development*, 51, 1215–21.

Wertsch, J.V. (1991) *Voices of the Mind: a sociocultural approach to mediated action*, London: Harvester Wheatsheaf.

Wood D. (1988) *How children think and learn*, Oxford: Blackwell.

Wood, D., Bruner J. and Ross, G. (1976) 'The role of tutoring in problem solving', in *Journal of Child Psychology and Psychiatry*, 17, pp. 89–100.

Wood, D., Wood, H.A. and Middleton, D.J. (1978) 'An experimental evaluation of four face-to-face teaching strategies', *International Journal of Behavioral Development*, 1, pp. 131–47.

Wyer, R.S. (ed.) (1995) *Knowledge and Memory: the real story. Advances in Social Cognition*, Vol. 3. Lawrence Erlbaum Associates.

5   Enabling children to learn in groups

Peter Kutnick and Iain Manson

EDITOR'S SUMMARY

Despite clear evidence from psychological research that children can often learn more effectively through collaborative groupwork, this teaching strategy is not widely used with any success in Primary classrooms. This chapter analyses the reasons why this is the case and argues that a vital ingredient has been missing in the approach. For children to learn effectively in groups they need to learn social competence and be able to form and sustain close relationships. A programme of classroom activities which have been shown to facilitate these abilities is outlined.

Introduction

Over the last twenty years, there have been two main types of study concerning the use of groups in Primary school classrooms: those showing that a particular method can enhance classroom learning (e.g. co-operative or collaborative learning); and those showing that the groups in which children are seated are unlikely to produce the interaction (generally through talk) that promotes classroom learning. While readers may agree about the importance of co-operation and collaboration in the Primary classroom, rarely are children found actively co-operating in class. The most successful examples of co-operation and collaboration are found in the research literature where a teacher/researcher has 'experimentally' structured a co-operative/collaborative exercise. The contradiction that experimental methods can enhance learning while naturally occurring classroom groups may inhibit learning sets the background for this chapter. Within the chapter, we consider what is problematic about the effective use of groups for classroom

Figure 5.1 Groupwork in classrooms can enhance children's learning, but it must be genuinely collaborative

learning, why these problems exist and what can be done about them. In short, we ask the question: how can classroom groups encourage and support learning?

Where do the problems lie with regard to the effective use of groups in primary school classrooms?

Primary school classrooms of the late 1990s look very different from those of the early 1970s and before. The change in 'look' has been described by Maurice Galton (Galton and Williamson 1992 and elsewhere), and identifies that the traditional physical layout of a classroom evolved from rows of individual desks with a teacher's desk at the front of the room, to children sitting around (small) tables. While the traditional layout of classrooms has changed, we should be cautioned not to be lulled into a false sense of security and think that sitting around small tables actually allows children to learn in a 'child-centred' manner or that children will use these seating groups to enhance their learning. There are two key research studies in the UK that show that seating groups do not support interaction and learning in infant and junior school classrooms.

Infant based

Bennett *et al.* (1984) noted that many teachers organised their classrooms to allow children to sit around tables but, for the most part, the children pursued individualised courses of work. This individualised work left children dependent on their teachers for support (when pupils lacked understanding) and approval (when the child had completed her/his work). Due to the individual nature of the work assigned, children were unable to ask their peers to help or clarify their questions and, correspondingly, children did not develop a range of skills to support their peers.

Junior based

Galton and colleagues (e.g. Galton and Williamson 1992) found a dramatic contrast between the amount of time that children were asked to sit around tables (referred to as seating groups) and the amount of time that these children worked collaboratively in classrooms. Galton and Williamson noted that children were placed in seating groups for nearly 60 per cent of classroom time but asked to work as a group for 5 per cent of their tasks. In contrast, children sat as individuals for 8 per cent of the time but asked to work as individuals for 80 per cent of their tasks. Underlying the contrast between seating and working arrangements are two main points: first, teachers may not plan for the relationship between seating and work, thus offering an ambiguous approach to group work for their pupils. Second, children receive a mixed message; they are held accountable for individual learning efforts and their group seating may inhibit their real learning. Interviews with these children found that:

- pupils were unsure about working with other children when the teacher did not provide direct support for this interaction
- pupils were afraid to open themselves (and their thinking) to the group because other group members did not have the support and encouragement skills displayed by their teachers
- peers may be very competitive rather than co-operative.

A third study provides a focus on the importance of group skills for children in the Primary school. In Tizard and Hughes' (1984) comparison of learning interactions at home and at school, the researchers noted that any individual child is also a member of a class with twenty to thirty other children. Pupils have to compete with one another for teacher attention while spending a large amount of their time in the presence of their peers. Much teacher time was spent controlling competition between children and talking to individual children. Teachers rarely planned for effective group interaction among their pupils.

From a psychological perspective, interaction with pupil peers has a number of advantages. Interaction with peers has been associated with:

- the development of social awareness with regard to rules for games (Piaget 1932/65)
- knowledge about social conventions, e.g. gender relationships, authority relationships (Hartup 1978)
- development of friendships (Maxwell 1990).

The particular case of 'co-operative learning' (Slavin 1990) draws upon psychological theory and structured classroom practice, and shows that peers can learn while overcoming within-class racial and social prejudices. Peer interaction has also been shown to be an important element in cognitive development (explained in research developed from the ideas of Piaget and Vygotsky, which are discussed below).

In a more practical sense, there have been a number of studies (mainly undertaken in the United States) which identify successful strategies for the grouping of children in classrooms. These studies rely upon interaction between pupils, but do not focus on the quality of relationships between them. A good amount of information concerning the use of groups can be gleaned from these studies. For instance:

- there is a direct relationship between the size of group and the type of learning task that pupils may be asked to undertake (Kutnick 1994b)
- individuals may be best suited for drill and practice tasks, pairs for cognitive problem solving tasks, small groups (4–6 children) for application and extension tasks (found in a number of co-operative learning studies), and whole class for information transmission and control
- if tasks are inappropriate or ambiguous for the group, learning amongst the pupils will be ineffective (Bossert *et al.* 1985)
- discussions within groups have been found to be more effective if there is a mixture of ability among the pupils (Webb 1989); low ability groups may not have enough knowledge to initiate and sustain discussion and high ability pupils often have problems working amongst themselves
- if there is an imbalance between the number of boys and girls in a group, the quality of discussion will be inhibited (Webb 1989); although children have been found to express a preference for working with a same-sex partner or friend (Bennett and Dunne 1990).

The groupings described above all assume that effective learning in classroom-based groupings provide an 'intrinsic' reward for the pupils; the children do not need to be provided with any external 'tokens' or rewards for them to work effectively (Damon and Phelps 1989). Finally, the highly structured and external reward-based co-operative learning described by Slavin (1990) appears to have much in common with the research cited above, and shows that this long-term co-operative learning approach has educational and social benefits for the children who participate.

Positive developments that result from peer interaction do not 'just happen'. The paragraph above identified a number of classroom issues concerning group tasks and group composition. There appears to be an assumption that an 'appropriate' structuring of task and composition will lead to effective learning. On the other hand, children must have a positive and supportive relationship amongst themselves if they are to interact effectively. Teachers know that they cannot place two children who dislike each other together and expect them to work effectively; yet children will benefit from working with a range of their peers. Teachers must consider that it is their responsibility to 'train' children to get along with others (a nurturing side to interaction) rather than assuming that children have a natural ability to get along with others. If children are unable to relate to one another, their social and cognitive development will be inhibited.

Thus, from a psychological perspective, there is great potential in asking children to work together; they can work as collaborators, peer tutors, social supporters and friends. Classroom studies show that children are frequently placed in groupings, but pupils are rarely expected to work with one another. Many pupils feel that teachers do not support their working together, and many do not have the skills to work effectively with others. The contradiction between potential and reality may be exacerbated by lack of opportunities for teachers to learn about effective grouping for learning and the teacher-based perception that their role is to promote 'curriculum' knowledge rather than social knowledge. In a large-scale survey of teachers' use of pupil groups in classrooms (Blatchford, Kutnick and Baines 1998), a vast majority of teachers stated that they used a range of groupings but received little (or no) training concerning how to use and promote groupings. The lack of training may be due to the emphasis in current initial teacher training on curriculum-subject knowledge to the detriment of classroom management skills. The rest of this chapter will attempt to redress that imbalance by discussing the importance of peer interaction for development, exploring different methods used to enhance peer interaction in the classroom and suggesting some practical activities to undertake there.

Significance of peer interaction and social relationships for development

> There are no ... such things [as] isolated individuals. There are only relationships.
>
> (Piaget 1932/65)

All higher mental functions are internalised social relationships. ... Their composition, genetic structure and means of action – in a word, their whole nature is social.

(Vygotsky 1991).

As the quotations above clearly indicate, key theorists in the fields of psychology and education (Piaget and Vygotsky) were convinced of the role that social relationships play in cognitive development. However, it is also clear that they had different types of relationship in mind. In his early writings, concerning children's interactions, Piaget (1932/65) distinguished two types of relationship in which children are engaged, those with adults and those with peers. Relationships between adults and children were described by Piaget as being relationships of constraint, typified by unilateral authority and asymmetry of social power. Such relationships cannot develop mutuality due to the asymmetry of social power vested in the adult partner; they are, however, capable of taking on an 'instructional' dimension. Relationships between peers were described as relationships of co-operation, typified by reciprocity and mutuality and seen by Piaget as being conducive to the co-construction of new ideas and meanings usually in the form of open-ended 'problem-solving'. Piaget is quite specific that co-operation is needed in order to create new knowledge.

Conversely, for Vygotsky, it is precisely the asymmetrical nature of social relationships between child and adults, and children with more knowledgeable peers, that is the key to cognitive development. Research inspired by Vygotsky's ideas notes that the child is immersed in a pre-existing social order. It is the manner in which, through social activity, the child is immersed in the social and the manner in which this immersion transforms her/his capabilities that is his object of study. Cognitive development is seen as the child's active internalisation of existing problem-solving practices. The interaction between the 'expert' and the 'novice' leads to a transfer of knowledge. However, social authority is vested in the 'knower' by virtue of knowing that which the 'novice' desires to know. The means by which this transfer of knowledge occurs is 'instruction'. The task of the tutor is to 'scaffold' the learning situation for the tutee (Bruner 1978).

Thus, for Vygotsky, effective learning is based upon a sensitive relationship between the child and someone who can structure the learning process, whereas Piaget emphasised the role of peers in 'inventing' new knowledge and understanding. Underlying the Vygotsky/Piaget contrast is the premise that while each generation can pass on the benefit of its knowledge to the next, it cannot pass on its experience of it. Ownership of this knowledge can only be obtained via peer interaction and validation. While there are benefits accruing to instruction, the effect of instruction without the opportunity of interaction is limited.

Evidence from the study of collaborative learning lends support to these contentions and has indicated important characteristics for effective group work. David Wood and colleagues (Wood 1991) has demonstrated the importance of scaffolding in classrooms. Amongst children, the advantage of collaborative grouping lies in the relationships that such groups engender (Bennett 1994). In such groups the relationship of co-operation predominates. Especially when task structures do not demand a 'right' answer, a co-operative atmosphere is less threatening than in instruction-based groups and making mistakes need not be a cause of concern or embarrassment. Rogers and Kutnick (1994) argue that the primary motivators in such groups are interactive (learning) goals rather than getting the answer correct (performance) goals. The advantage of the collaborative group is that it fosters these learning goals by locating ownership of the task and control over it within the group, within a relationship of shared co-operation rather than one of constraint, which is controlled by someone more 'powerful'.

The discussion concerning Piaget and Vygotsky emphasised the differing nature of relationships in the development of knowledge and understanding. Both of these descriptions, however, lack an account of the socio-emotional background in which relationships operate. In referring to socio-emotional background, we mean the quality of a relationship which may either enhance or detract from the child working with others. In a simple sense, we are aware that the 'closer' a relationship between people, the more likely that trust and mutual support is developed (for example, attachment and also close friendship). It does not require a 'leap of faith' to further acknowledge that if a close relationship exists between the child and others, then learning is enhanced. If children do not like working or playing with one another then there is little likelihood of discussion, exchange of ideas or learning. Yet it has already been shown (Galton 1990) that simply seating children together is unlikely to promote co-operation. Another way of looking at this problem has been undertaken by Kutnick (1988) who noted that if we understand the socio-emotional nature of the development of close relationships between people, then principles to enhance the quality of relationships (and learning) can be derived. He argues that common 'deep structures' underlie the development of relationships, both between adults and children and amongst peers. Fundamental to the development of these 'deep structures' is a relationship of reciprocity based upon mutual trust and concomitant dependency. The manner in which the relationship develops and with whom the relationship develops, is a function of social context – exposure to and quality of experience with others. A model of the development of these quality or close relationships shows that early relationships develop:

- from schemes that promote an affective tie between the child and specific others,
- to a realisation of dependence and attachment, and
- to communicative understanding of the rules of interaction which incorporate respect for others (and gives rise to the ability to change and develop new rules and perspectives).

Similar to the description of the child's first quality relationship with the care-giver (i.e. attachment, see Ainsworth, Bell and Stayton 1974), the model suggests that effective and close social relationships are based upon trust and dependence. And these elements may be enhanced in the Primary school classroom setting in such a manner as to enable children, through co-operative interaction, to obtain ownership of the knowledge that such experience engenders. However, in order to obtain these benefits, children have to be able to enjoy good quality social relationships and for this they must be socially competent. This quality relationship is found more often between children and adults than between peers; this is due to upbringing practices (generally in western societies) which place greater emphasis on early, home-based child-adult experience than early, quality peer experience. As will be discussed later, there are methods of enhancing quality socio-emotional relationships amongst children based upon developmental principles; in order for these to be used to effect in the classroom, teachers must give time and effort to promoting social and learning development.

Social competence

For children to take advantage of the social interaction needed for cognitive development, we can agree that they must demonstrate 'social competence'; especially with regard to their relationships with others. This simple sentence leads to complicated problems of definition and perception of social interaction as well as two predominant avenues that teachers may pursue to develop the social skills that promote effective social interaction.

Rather than provide a definition of social competence, many researchers have resorted to the identification of certain outcomes of childhood interactions (e.g. good relationships, respect, empathy, communication skills). The use of outcome rather than definition leads to three problems:

- each of the outcomes assumes that it is 'normal' to achieve that outcome and any deviation from the norm indicates that the child is somewhat 'abnormal'
- any attempt to identify what is normal must account for the society or culture within which the child is living
- the defining of what is normal will only identify aspects of social competence (that is, we do not gain the complete picture of social competence, only some components).

Katz and McClellan (1996) support this outcomes-based approach and identify 'aspects' of social competence which include:

- peer status
- friendship
- ability to regulate emotions, social knowledge (ability to identify common interests and activity with others)

- social skills (especially of communication, joining in, maintaining conversation and conflict avoidance)
- social dispositions of care and concern for others.

This outcome approach involves both knowledge and feelings among children; the socially competent (or non-abnormal) child is balanced somewhere between autonomy and shyness.

In criticism, we note that it may be useful to identify these outcomes but too much emphasis on this approach may disguise the fact that children's social competencies are developed through and support their relationships with others. An alternate approach derived from the work of Piaget and Vygotsky identifies that children who relate well to adults and peers will naturally demonstrate a range of the above mentioned outcomes. The relational approach will be discussed in greater detail below.

Focusing on the school and school-aged children, we find that the expectation of social competence is present in a number of their activities and that some teachers may actually teach some forms of social competence. Research on the school playground finds this is a natural arena for the display of social competence. Opie and Opie (1969) have shown that children participate in social activities such as singing and game playing. These studies also find that children encourage and teach one another the songs and games. The playground also promotes social knowledge including authority, friendship and gender relationships, moral development and social sensitivity (see Figure 5.2). The current move to abolish 'afternoon' play, which has characterised a number of English Junior schools, is heavily criticised by Blatchford (1998) who notes that potential development of social competencies is being hindered.

There are few studies which demonstrate that social competence is being enhanced within normal classrooms, although experimental studies with school-aged children have shown that:

- children working in pairs on cognitive problems were more competent than children working as individuals (Perret-Clermont 1980)
- children working with partners are effective problem solvers, but the quality of the relationship between the partners will affect their performance (Light and Littleton 1994).

This research coincides with Hartup's (1996) speculation that friendship provides a close relationship which supports learning and should be used with greater frequency in the classroom.

Children's social competencies have been found at pre-school ages, with many children bringing these social competencies into the school in their reception year. Social competencies have been seen at home and with friends. Within families, Judy Dunn (1988) found complex social competencies used in joking, teasing, playing with, questioning and responding to questions, and understanding the needs of others in their family. The main

Figure 5.2 The playground is a natural arena for the development of social
competence. Activities and games children play here promote friendship,
moral development and social sensitivity

point of Dunn's research is that children from as young as eighteen months
demonstrated these competencies in the loving and supportive contexts of
their homes. The sophistication of children's interactions with friends
(Avigitidou 1994) is even more interesting. Noting that most close friendships among children develop in late childhood and adolescence, Avigitidou
observed and talked to children aged four years. Surprisingly, she found a
number of very complex friendship relationships – where children not only
identified a close, best friend and friendship was reciprocated, but where
children would also speak of friendship obligations. These close friends
helped and looked after one another. They were able to assume various roles
such as social and communicative (symmetrical) equals and teacher/learn-
ers (asymmetrical) partners. Within these secure friendships children could
separate from one another and return to work/play together. Less secure
friendships brought periodic 'clinging' between children; the clinging often
inhibited the children from productively working or playing together.

How can teachers nurture social competence and close relationships to promote learning in schools?

The above review strongly supports the view that social competencies and
relational skills must be nurtured through the teaching experience. If a
teacher sided with a 'natural' explanation (that children inherently have

these social competencies and skills in their make-up), then children with poor social competencies and relational skills might be seen as inadequate with little or no chance for remediation. If the competencies and skills can be 'nurtured', how can this be undertaken in the classroom?

While many teachers recognise that social relationships and competencies are important, they may not have the knowledge or practical skills to develop the skills in class. The nurturing of social and relational skills (or competencies) is not usually associated with the role of the teacher, especially in Primary schools where the teacher's role is more strongly related to curriculum instruction. Even in the early years of the Primary school, Katz and McClellan's (1996) review of studies in the USA concerning the development of social competence found 'no experimental studies of the general effects of teachers on young children's social development'. Katz and McClellan do point out an essential dilemma for teachers: whereas the whole class should be the basis for developing social competence, this is unlikely to be practised and many teachers focus solely on particular aspects of social competence that may be lacking in an individual child. Neglect of whole-class social competence for individual skills identifies two distinct approaches that the teacher may use to 'nurture' social competence and relational skills. The two approaches are derived from two distinct psychological traditions, the social behavioural and the social relational; they may be discussed in terms of a 'virtues' versus a 'development' approach.

The 'virtues' approach draws upon behavioural or learning theory wherein pupil actions (that a teacher would like repeated) will be rewarded (for further discussion see Kutnick and Manson 1998). For the virtues approach to be effective, the teacher must decide what competencies or relational skills should be demonstrated by the pupil; these may include empathy, altruism, communication, turn taking, negotiation and so on. When any of these skills is displayed by a child, the teacher should reward the child, possibly in front of the class as a whole. Underlying this approach is a belief that the 'virtues' can easily be identified, while children's behaviours that deviate from the virtues are judged 'abnormal'. This belief has been challenged by Ogilvy (1994), who identified that:

- concepts of normal and abnormal are only as adequate as the teacher's definition, which can be highly prejudiced by background and expectation
- any behavioural definition may see the virtue as an isolated behaviour; neglecting the context within which the virtue may have arisen
- the behavioural approach does not focus on the thinking and decisions that may underlie the display of a 'virtue' and often has little to do with the emotions that facilitate close relationships.

The socio-cognitive approach (Dodge and Crick 1990) has been developed to integrate 'thinking about' virtues before or as they are displayed. Yet both the behavioural and socio-cognitive approaches still rely on a teacher's perception of 'normal behaviour'; the virtue is taken out of the full social context (and social interactions) and development of that virtue is focused on the individual child. Still, it is important for the teacher clearly to identify classroom virtues that support social and relational competence for children and to communicate that these virtues are to be adhered to in class. Teachers can, in fact, attempt to follow a 'virtues' approach with the whole class rather than focusing on an individual child – thereby helping to create a social context which supports these competencies. If this can be undertaken in an atmosphere of discussion and agreement with the class, the children will be more likely to be aware of the classroom expectations and perform to the expectations (for example see 'circle time', Ballard 1982).

The social relational approach to the development of social competencies and relational skills is a new/alternative approach that is still in an 'experimental' phase. The social relational approach works with children in their classroom groups involving real life settings and developing skills which allow the children to identify and use 'virtues' themselves. The approach is based upon an analysis of the development of close relationships previously described. Teachers, working with whole classes, draw upon a series of exercises to promote phases of trust and dependence (as in attachment), communication (of knowledge and feelings), and collaborative problem-solving. The reasoning behind the choice and process of these exercises includes:

- the ordering follows an identified developmental sequence
- if a good attachment-like relationship can be developed between children in a classroom, the child should be 'equipped' to enter a larger social world and make new relationships with peers and other adults. Children with a poor attachment relationship are hindered from forming quality relationships with others (especially at the school level) and it is not unusual to find these children with learning problems in schools (Geddes 1999)
- when pupil groups are ineffective (as described by Galton 1990) researchers use the opposite of the terms that describe effective social relationships (e.g. lack of trust, sensitivity and communication).

The social relational approach puts children in a situation where they are challenged to develop this trust and sensitivity among themselves. The social relational approach calls upon the teacher to be actively involved in promoting social and relational competence, that is providing time within the school day to develop and practise these skills. Early results obtained by incorporating this approach into the classroom show that children are more likely to co-operate with one another, they are able to work with a broader range of classmates (than friends), and this co-working with classmates facilitates their solving of cognitive problems (Kutnick 1994a).

Towards a socio-relational programme

The basic framework for a socio-relational programme is derived from the theoretical perspective outlined above. The programme requires three types of exercise: trust and dependency, communication and problem solving. These types of exercise are used sequentially and their use is 'spiral' in nature, that is, the specific social skills that the exercises focus upon are repeated, extended and applied over time. Learning is not a one-off experience. Indeed, as these exercises are primarily experiential, repetition of them is essential. The programme of exercises described below should take place over a whole term or even longer, trying to fit at least two 'exercise' sessions into the timetable each week.

Some whole-class exercises are used, normally in the pre-programme relaxation stages (some very effective trust and dependency exercises also require a whole-class approach). Minimally, the class can begin with a 'circle-time' exercise where exercises can be explained, and ways of listening to a partner or variations on the exercises suggested by the children can be discussed. The majority of the exercises are undertaken in pairs or multiples thereof so that children will extend the breadth of classroom partners (rather than relying predominantly on their friends). Central to the programme is the notion of pairing the children undertaking the exercises in non-gendered, non-friendship based couples. Over the length of a term it is not possible to avoid some gendered or friendship-based pairing given the limited number of children in the class, but these should be the exception rather than the rule. In our experience most children respond favourably when the reason why they should be so paired is explained. Another basic ground rule is that participation in the exercises is not obligatory. Some children will find some of the exercises very different to their usual experience and may want the opportunity to observe prior to committing themselves. It is essential to start any session with a series of relaxation and warm-up exercises. These will include the whole class. Versions of 'Simon Says' ending up with star jumps and loud 'whoops' are especially effective in creating a necessary transition from normal classroom activity prior to embarkation upon the programme. Less energetic (and noisy) relaxation exercises may also be used. These warm-ups will encourage children to work together and to listen to the teacher for direction. Further, at the end of each of the exercise sessions, the class can be brought back into a circle to 'debrief' the children by explaining what they have accomplished and asking children what they have gained by working with their partners.

At the start of the programme are a series of exercises designed to promote relationships based upon trust and dependency; they include and are similar to sensitivity training procedures used with adults (Pfeiffer and Jones 1976). Among these are exercises such as blindfold walks and mirroring. The children are paired for these exercises. The basic format of the blindfold walk has one child steering another who has a blindfold (or scarf) over their eyes and then changing over. This exercise can be enlivened by making it into a game ('Night-time Escape from Prison during a Power Failure' was a much requested version of the exercise with older children). Mirroring asks partners to face one another and to mirror their partner's every move of head and arms. Turns are taken to take the lead. Partners are initially asked to touch palms together and, as they improve, partners must not come into physical contact with each other. All of these exercises require the active partner's attention to the passive partner's requirements. One popular whole-class trust and dependency exercise is 'Circle Sitting'. The whole class stands face-to-back of the child in front, in a tight circle and are asked to slowly sit upon the knees of the child behind (this should be used judiciously with younger children). There are many similar exercises to promote trust and sensitivity; Robin Dynes' *Creative Games in Groupwork* (1990) is a useful source book.

Such trust and dependency exercises predominate in the early stages of the programme. Each session, however, should contain at least some of communication and problem-solving exercises as well. Very simple paired communication exercises (especially useful with younger children) include 'Three Things' (Leech and Wooster 1986). Each child is asked to recount three things that they did between leaving school the previous evening and returning to school in the morning. Their partner has to remember them and recount them at the end of the exercise. Pairs can be doubled up and each pair will decide who will tell the three things to the other pair. For older children the number of things to be remembered can be increased. Communication can include 'emotional' content as well; partners can be asked to tell one another 'what makes me happy or sad' or 'my favourite television programme'. Partners must listen to one another and reciprocate. This emotional variation is exceptionally effective when undertaken first in pairs, then in pairs of pairs and finally in a plenary session with the whole group. A favourite whole-class communication exercise is the 'Whisper Game'. Everyone sits in a circle and whispers the message to their neighbour who in turn whispers it to their neighbour and so on round the circle. Beware of the peer pressure that can be exerted upon anyone who gets the message wrong!

Towards the end of the programme, the problem-solving exercises will be the main focus (Fountain 1990, is a very rich source of co-operative problem-solving exercises). Pairs can be given one sheet of paper and one pencil, and then asked to draw, for example, a house, car, tree. Individuals within pairs can also be allocated a number of blocks or parts of a puzzle, and the pair is asked to build a tower or complete the puzzle. Pairs and larger groups (of four and six) can undertake 'co-operative shapes and letters' where they are asked to use their bodies to make circles, diamonds, triangles and letter shapes.

So far, the exercises have been undertaken with a number of age groups. The basic format of the sessions has proved effective using essentially the same exercises throughout the age range. A formal evaluation of a socio-relational programme of the type described above is currently being undertaken. The initial findings from staff and pupils involved are positive. Children like and remember the exercises, often asking to repeat them many times. Other evidence (Kutnick 1994a) found that children were more able to co-operate with one another and were more effective in shared problem-solving when compared to classes that did not undertake the programme. Considerably more evaluative work is needed from Primary teachers by way of action research before firm conclusions regarding such interventions can be obtained. The authors are also painfully aware that the current emphases on individualised learning programmes and outcome results from SATs mitigate against a classroom climate wherein the benefits, so clearly available in the research literature, of social relational programmes and interventions can be explored.

In conclusion, this chapter has identified that research concerning the use of pupil groups in classrooms has found 'groupwork' to be largely ineffective and offered some suggestions to enhance the likelihood of children working together (to share support and learning). Creating the conditions within classrooms to promote effective interactional skills requires that children relate well to one another. Relationships do not simply 'happen' among the individual children that make up a class. Teachers cannot rely upon an 'individualised' national curriculum to promote learning relationships. The chapter has considered the classroom as an arena for potential interaction that can support or deny learning. The challenge for teachers is to decide how they wish to promote 'learning' and then create the relational conditions that will enhance interaction and learning. We trust that the analysis and suggestions offered above will be of use when teachers consider this challenge.

Activities

These exercises are to be undertaken with the class as a whole. Before starting the exercises, the class should be 'briefed' about the range of exercises to be undertaken during the session. The briefing should include consideration of safety factors (such that silliness in the blindfold walk may cause injury to a partner) and initial warm-up and relaxation. At the end of each session, the class should be brought together to consider the exercises undertaken, how they felt about the exercises, possible benefits of the exercises and any safety features that have to be considered in the future.

Blindfold walk: a sensitivity and trust exercise

Children are paired off. One child is designated as 'leader', the other as 'walker' (if appropriate, children may choose these roles themselves). It is important that each child in the pair has the opportunity to take both roles in the session. The leader stands behind the walker and places one hand on each of the walker's shoulders. Steering is effected by the leader giving directions by gently pushing the partner's shoulder. Thus, to go right is effected by pushing forward gently on the left shoulder. Stopping is effected by pulling (gently) simultaneously on both shoulders. Practice sessions may be held without the use of a blindfold. The blindfold should be made of light-proof material (such as a winter scarf). Initial attempts to do the blindfold walk should take place in a large room without obstructions. After the leader–walker pair has moved around the room for about five minutes, the partners are asked to stop and change roles. As the children gain confidence in the exercise, they can be asked to manoeuvre around obstacles.

Three things: a communication exercise (from Leech and Wooster 1986)

Start by pairing the children. One child is asked to tell their partner three things they did between the end of school the day before and arrival at school today. The first child must then 'check back' with the partner to see what was remembered and how accurately. Partners then reverse roles. As the children gain experience in listening and communicating, the same exercise can be undertaken in groups of four, with two pairs exchanging information and assessing recall and accuracy.

Co-operative shapes and letters: a problem-solving exercise

Begin with children working in pairs. As partners gain competence in the exercise, two and three pairs may work together. Initially, pairs are asked to physically form a simple shape or letter (e.g. a circle, letter Y or a square). Once the pairs understand that they must form the shape or letter with their bodies (they can talk to one another to aid progress), more complicated shapes can be attempted (e.g. a triangle, letter Z or W, parallelogram). If multiple pairs are brought together, simple words can be formed (e.g. hi, go, hat).

Further reading

Blatchford, P. (1998) *Social Life in Schools; Pupils' Experience of Breaktime*, London: Falmer.

Dynes, R. (1990) *Creative Games in Groupwork*, Bicester: Winslow Press Ltd.

Fountain, S. (1990) *Learning Together: Global Education*, Cheltenham: Stanley Thornes (Publishers) Ltd.

Kutnick, P. and Rogers, C. (eds) (1994) *Groups in Schools*, London: Cassell.

References

Ainsworth, M., Bell, S. and Stayton, D. (1974) 'Infant–mother attachment and social development: 'socialisation' as a product of reciprocal responsiveness to signals', in M. Richards (ed.) *Integration of a Child into a Social World*, Cambridge: Cambridge University Press.

Avigitidou, S. (1994) 'Children learning about friendship in the context of an English reception class', in H.C. Foot, C.J. Howe, A. Anderson, A.K. Tolmie and D.A. Warden (eds) *Group and Interactive Learning*, Southampton: Computational Mechanics Publications.

Ballard, J. (1982) *Circlebook*, New York: Irvington.

Bennett, N. (1994) 'Co-operative Learning', in P. Kutnick and C. Rogers (eds) *Groups in Schools*, London: Cassell.

Bennett, N., Desforges, C., Cockburn, A. and Wilkinson, B. (1984) *The Quality of Pupil Learning Experiences*, London: Lawrence Erlbaum Associates.

Bennett, N. and Dunne, E. (1990) 'Implementing co-operative groupwork in classrooms', in V. Lee (ed.) *Children's Learning in Schools*, London: Hodder & Stoughton.

Blatchford, P. (1998) *Social Life in Schools; Pupils' Experience of Breaktime*, London: Falmer.

Blatchford, P., Kutnick, P. and Baines, E. (1998) *Grouping practices in primary school classrooms, what do the teachers say?* Paper presented at the British Psychological Society Annual Conference, Brighton.

Bossert, S., Barnet, B. and Filby, N. (1985) 'Grouping and instructional organisation', in P. Petersen, L. Wilkinson, and M. Hallinen (eds) *The Social Context of Instruction*, Orlando, Fla.: Academic Press.

Bruner, J. (1978) 'The role of dialogue in language acquisition', in A. Sinclear, R. Jarvis and W. Levett (eds) *The Child's Conception of Language*, New York: Springer Verlag.

Damon, W. and Phelps, E. (1989) 'Critical distinctions between three approaches to peer education', *International Journal of Educational Research*, 13, 9–19.

Dodge, K.A. and Crick, N.R. (1990) 'Social information-processing bases of aggressive behaviour in children', *Personality and Social Psychology Bulletin*, 16, 8–32.

Dunn, J. (1988) *The beginnings of social understanding*, Oxford: Blackwell.

Dynes, R. (1990) *Creative Games in Groupwork*, Bicester: Winslow Press Ltd.

Fountain, S. (1990) *Learning Together: Global Education*, Cheltenham: Stanley Thornes (Publishers) Ltd.

Galton, M. (1990) 'Grouping and Groupwork', in C. Rogers and P. Kutnick (eds) *The Social Psychology of the Primary School*, London: Routledge.

Galton, M. and Williamson, J. (1992) *Groupwork in the Primary School*, London: Routledge.

Geddes, H. (1999) *Attachment and learning: an investigation into links between maternal attachment experience, reported life events, behaviour causing concern at referral and difficulties in the learning situation*, PhD dissertation, Roehampton Institute, London.

Hartup, W. (1978) 'Children and their Friends', in H. McGurk (ed.) *Issues in Childhood Social Development*, London: Methuen.

Hartup, W. (1996) 'The company they keep: friends and their developmental significance', *Child Development*, 76, 1–13.

Katz, L. and McClellan, D. (1996) *Fostering children's social competence: the teacher's role*, Vol 8, NAEYC Research into Practice Series.

Kutnick, P.J. (1988) *Relationships in the Primary School Classroom*, London: Paul Chapman Publishing.

Kutnick, P. (1994a) 'Developing pupils' social skills for learning, social interaction and co-operation', in H.C. Foot, C.J. Howe, A. Anderson, A.K. Tolmie and D.A. Warden (eds) *Group and Interactive Learning*, Southampton: Computational Mechanics Publications.

Kutnick, P. (1994b) 'The use and effectiveness of groups in classrooms', in P. Kutnick and C. Rogers (eds) *Groups in Schools*, London: Cassell.

Kutnick, P. and Manson, I. (1998) 'Social life in the primary school; towards a relational concept of social skills in the classroom', in A. Campbell and S. Muncer (eds) *The Social Child*, Hove: Psychology Press.

Leech, N. and Wooster, A.D. (1986) *Personal and Social Skills: a Practical Approach for the Classroom*, Exeter: Religious and Moral Education Press.

Light, P. and Littleton, K. (1994) 'Cognitive Approaches to Group Work', in P. Kutnick and C. Rogers (eds) *Groups in Schools*, London: Cassell.

Maxwell, W. (1990) 'The nature of friendship in the primary school', in C. Rogers and P. Kutnick. (eds) (1990) *The Social Psychology of the Primary School*, London: Routledge.

Ogilvy, C.M. (1994) 'Social Skills Training with Children and Adolescents: a review of the evidence on effectiveness', *Educational Psychology*, 14(1), 73–83.

Opie, P. and Opie, S. (1969) *Children's Games in the Street and on the Playground*, Oxford: Oxford University Press.

Peiffer, J.W. and Jones, J.E. (1976) *Handbook of Structured Exercises for Human Relations Training*, La Jolla, CA.: University Associates.

Perret-Clermont, A. (1980) *Social Interaction and Cognitive Development in Children*, London: Academic Press.

Piaget, J. (1932/65) *The Moral Judgement of the Child*, London: Routledge & Kegan Paul.

Rogers, C. and Kutnick, P. (1994) 'Evaluating group work', in P. Kutnick and C. Rogers (eds) *Groups in Schools*, London: Cassell.

Slavin, R. (1990) 'Co-operative learning', in C. Rogers and P. Kutnick (eds) *The Social Psychology of the Primary School*, London: Routledge.

Tizard, B. and Hughes, M. (1984) *Young Children Learning*, London: Fontana.

Vygotsky, L.S. (1978) *Mind and Society: The Development of Higher Mental Processes*, Cambridge, Mass.: Harvard University Press.

Vygotsky, L. (1991) 'Genesis of higher mental functions', in P. Light, S. Sheldon and M. Woodhead (eds) *Learning to Think*, London: Routledge.

Webb, N. (1989) 'Peer interaction and learning in small groups', *International Journal of Educational Research*, 13, 21–39.

Wood, D. (1991) 'Aspects of teaching and learning', in P. Light, S. Sheldon and M. Woodhead (eds) *Learning to Think*, London: Routledge.

6 Helping children to persevere and be well motivated

Roland Chaplain

EDITOR'S SUMMARY

This chapter explains how Attribution Theory helps us to understand why some children will persevere through difficulties and why others are poorly motivated and give up at the slightest opportunity. The origins and consequences of different motivational styles, such as 'mastery orientation' and 'learned helplessness', are explored. The chapter then sets out the crucial significance of teachers' attributions about children and their consequent expectations of them. The overriding importance of developing strategies to enhance children's feelings of self-worth are emphasised.

Introduction

All teachers at some time in their careers come across pupils who refuse to engage with their work, or those who start something only to give up when they encounter the slightest difficulty, whilst other pupils continue to make an effort even after failing at a task. These individual differences are not easily explained but recent research into achievement motivation has gone some way to providing insight and practical advice on how to help pupils engage more effectively with their learning – an asset to any member of the teaching profession.

In this chapter I will draw on contemporary social psychological evidence relating to differences in pupil motivation and how these are affected by the quality of relationships between teachers and their pupils. Contemporary theories argue that it is a combination of cognitive and affective responses to success and failure following a task which determines expectation of future success on similar tasks and thus influences the likelihood of engaging or

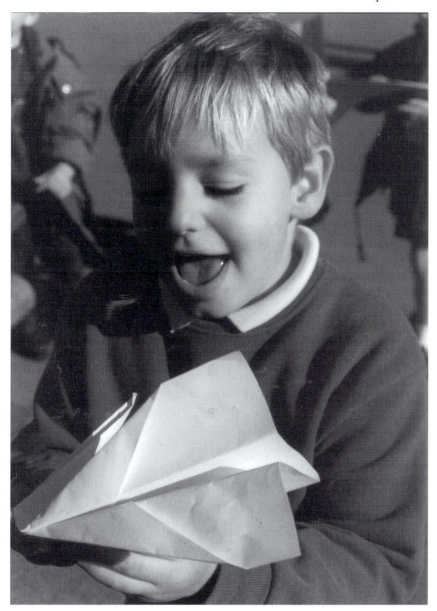

Figure 6.1 How can we ensure that all children think positively about themselves as learners?

sustaining effort. As well as the expectation of success, other mediating factors include the *value* to the individual of being successful on a particular task and the salience of feedback from significant others. Much of what I have to say in this chapter relates to what social psychologists call *social cognition*, that is, the cognitive processes involved in understanding and guiding social behaviour. At its core is the process of categorising people and things in order to make sense of our personal and social worlds as quickly and effectively as possible. Social cognition can be defined in a broad or narrow sense; in this chapter the broader definition will be used. Thus social cognition includes: attitudes, social perception, impression formation, attribution theory, attraction, cognitive dissonance and equity theory – some of which I will discuss in more detail later.

Teachers' models of the well-motivated child, in achievement terms, are inextricably linked to their social behavioural expectations of children. The academically well-motivated are typically perceived as being better behaved, or, more realistically, their behaviour is viewed in a different light. For instance, disruptive behaviour is linked to creativity and high spirits as opposed to delinquency and unpleasantness. The processes by which we come to extrapolate a whole range of inferences about people based on relatively limited knowledge is of particular interest to social psychologists concerned with social cognition. These processes are also of interest to those concerned with young people's education, since the consequences of these associations can result in knock-on effects in terms of opportunities and access which can influence a whole range of life chances.

This chapter focuses on:

- the role of cognition and emotion in understanding individual differences in motivation
- the development of adaptive and maladaptive motivational styles
- the role of teacher–pupil interaction in enhancing or reducing pupil motivation.

Psychological explanations of motivation

I have chosen to use the general term motivation here but the reader may feel it would be more appropriate to talk of *achievement motivation* in school settings. My reason for using the more inclusive term is to highlight differences between what teachers consider to be a well motivated pupil and what actually motivates the pupils themselves. Some pupils may be highly motivated to attend school and engage with their own agendas which may be very different from those of the teaching staff. Such pupils, for instance, may be motivated to challenge teachers verbally in a very competent, if not contextually acceptable way. Their engagement in what might be termed off task activities can be as a result of teachers not being successful in engaging them on legitimate tasks in the first place. After all, logic dictates that pupils who are engaged with a task are less likely to disrupt than those who are not. A key question for those engaged with the study of motivation is why some pupils are prepared to engage and continue with difficult tasks whilst others give up, despite seemingly similar circumstances.

There are at least as many theories of motivation as there are psychological perspectives to explain human behaviour – hardly surprising given the fact that many definitions of motivation see it as the basis for explaining 'why human ... organisms think and behave as they do.' (Weiner 1992:1) Early theories of motivation tended to view motivation in quantitative terms, that is, some people were more motivated than others with, in the case of some theories, 'obvious' connections to innate qualities. Motivational level was viewed as being a more or less fixed characteristic of an individual. These explanations are now seen as too simplistic and more recent theories focus on identifying qualitative differences between individuals.

Early explanations

Early theories of motivation offered mechanistic explanations (e.g. Hull 1943, Lewin 1952) which viewed motivation in terms of the relationship between a temporary state of the individual (tension or drive), the properties of their goal object (incentive value) plus a learning factor (habit). This thinking could also be found in certain more recent cognitive theories such as the expectancy–value theory of John Atkinson (1964) who added an emotional component: pride versus shame. Atkinson also saw motivation with reference to the degree of imbalance between the tendency to approach and avoid a goal object. Success on a task results in experiencing the emotion pride, whereas failure results in the experience of shame. Whether or not an individual attempts (approaches) a task or does not attempt it (avoidance) depends on the power of the anticipated emotion which is likely to follow. Atkinson used the phrases 'need for achievement' versus 'fear of failure' to describe these contrasting psychological experiences. Thus achievement motivation results from the conflict between the expectation of success (approach) and the fear of failure (avoidance). These in turn are fired by the relationship between need for success, perceived likelihood of success or failure and the perceived value of being successful.

Attribution theory

One of the leading contemporary researchers in achievement motivation, Bernard Weiner (1992), has produced a comprehensive model of motivation and emotion based on *Attributional theories*. A number of social psychologists have identified with this group of theories, which argue that human beings act as 'naïve scientists' trying to make sense of, and exercise some control over, the world in which they live. In other words people seek to find perceptions of causality or determine why an event occurred, by what amounts to hypothesis testing (a scientific process) in order to predict and understand human behaviour. When an event occurs we often start with some idea of why it occurred (hypothesis) and then seek to find evidence to support (or not reject) our evidence. If whilst walking through town I am hit on the head by a piece of masonry I might be inclined to think that part of the building above my head is collapsing. As a result I would probably look up in order to determine whether more masonry is falling, which will in turn influence my next action (e.g. dive for cover). If on looking up I observe two youngsters with more masonry in their hands pointing to me and laughing I may decide on a different course of action since I am likely to ascribe a different explanation to the event. The process I have outlined parallels the types of general questions attribution theorists might ask about the event, namely:

- What are the *perceived* causes of the event?
- What evidence exists to support these causal inferences?
- What are the consequences of making these causal inferences?

Whilst this may sound a logical analytic process, attribution theorists would argue that it is what we believe or infer about the causes, as opposed to the actual causes, that we tend to rely on. Put another way, the perceiver imposes causality; causes *per se* are not observable. I can only infer that the two youngsters had deliberately intended to cause me harm by dropping masonry on my head. I infer it from my observations of their behaviour and my beliefs and knowledge about the sort of behaviour individuals in their 'category' might engage in. Would I, for example, make the same inference if I looked up to see two nuns with masonry in their hands and looking shocked? Indeed, even in the presence of minimal information, people are able to use partial evidence to reach 'logical' causal inferences. Typically, it is usual not to have the full information nor the time required to make a complete analysis. Individuals therefore rely on 'causal schemata' or general rules related to cause and effects. Such rules are developed over time from prior experiences which become activated when triggered by appropriate circumstantial cues. Think about going into a classroom of pupils as a student teacher; you will no doubt very quickly categorise them on the basis of how they look at you, the way they dress, what they appear to be doing at the time and so on. The psychological advantage of this is that humans are able quickly to make sense of their surroundings in which limited information is available. The disadvantage is that we can make inaccurate judgements and that these become routinised and accepted, rather than reviewed on the basis of further evidence.

What has all this to do with achievement motivation? Well, attribution theories have been applied to a whole range of areas in psychology including health psychology: the causal ascriptions of people with mental health problems and how they differ from those made by people functioning normally; forensic psychology: how attributions can influence judgments about offenders; and educational psychology: how differential explanations for success and failure can influence achievement motivation and indeed social behaviour.

Attribution theory and achievement motivation

Complete Activity 1 before reading further.

Activity 1

(a) In this activity you are asked to imagine that you have just completed a test in which your performance is entirely dependent on your personal skill. You have completed the first six questions and your answers are as follows: incorrect, correct, incorrect, incorrect, incorrect, incorrect. How confident do you feel that your next answer will be correct? Use the scale below to rate your answer by putting a circle around the number which best indicates your level of confidence that your next answer will be correct.

Certain it will be correct				Unsure			Certain it will be incorrect	
1	2	3	4	5	6	7	8	9

(b) Now imagine you are dropping two-pence pieces into an arcade game in the hope that a large stack of coins will be pushed off the shelf and into the win tray. The likelihood of you succeeding is entirely dependent on luck. Your first six attempts result in the following: loss, win, loss, loss, loss, loss. Use the scale below to rate your answer by putting a circle around the number which best indicates your level of confidence in the likelihood you will win on your next attempt.

Certain I will win				Unsure			Certain I will lose	
1	2	3	4	5	6	7	8	9

These activities are examples of the questions used in experiments to identify the degree to which subjects attribute failure (or success) to internal or external sources. The two situations reflect two conditions of expectations following repeated failure. In (a), a test of your skill level, future success is dependent on your problem-solving skill, whereas in (b), an arcade game, future success is dependent on chance. Attribution theory suggests that expectations of success in situations where success depends on personal skill will be more affected by previous experiences than those which rely on chance. If this is true then in the above examples you would be more likely to have expected to fail in (a) than in (b) since the results are suggesting that your skills are not up to this test. Whereas in b), since winning is down to chance, you may feel that your luck is about to change ('gambler's folly'). Personal skill then is internally controlled (*internal locus of control*) whereas luck is externally controlled (*external locus of control*).

Internal versus external causes

The reputed father of attribution theory Fritz Heider (1958) argued that when people make causal ascriptions about events, they tend to do so by reference to either personal disposition or environmental factors. Applying this to a school learning context one might ascribe success on a task to personal competence (disposition) and failure to poor teaching (environment). Conversely one might attribute success to luck (environment) and failure to lack of personal competence (disposition). Clearly the former explanation is the more adaptive of the two since the power to control success is within the individual. One gauge of ability is the differential amount of effort required to complete a task. The successful person who makes the least effort is seen as having most ability in contrast to the person who makes the most effort to complete the same task – who is viewed as having less ability. We do not, however, come to these conclusions in a vacuum: our decisions are influenced by the presence of others. In the classroom the relative success or failure of other pupils on a task will influence the direction of our causal ascriptions. If one succeeded and all others failed we are likely to attribute success to personal disposition (personal competence). If we succeed when everyone else in the class succeeds, the outcome is ascribed to the easy nature of the task (environment).

Stable versus unstable causes

The story, as might be expected, is actually far more complex than that outlined thus far. Weiner and a number of other researchers (such as Covington 1992; Dweck 1991; Ames 1991) have developed, and continue to develop attribution theories of achievement motivation and their application to the classroom. Weiner's extension of the simple uni-dimensional explanation of Heider led to his recognition of two further dimensions: stability and controllability. Weiner argued that although the personal disposition–environment (or internal–external) dimension was important, it failed to address a number of other issues. For example, if we take two common constructs 'ability' and 'effort', they may share commonality in terms of both being considered internal constructs but may differ in terms of their stability over time. Ability is considered by most people to be fairly fixed whereas effort is changeable. Whilst you might assume your ability remains constant you are capable of making more or less effort when approaching a task. Thus ability can be seen as stable over time whereas effort tends to be unstable over time.

Complete Activity 2 before reading further.

Activity 2

Think about your own successes and failures. When did you last pass or fail an exam or do badly in an essay? If you passed did you put it down to your ability or to luck? If you failed did you think you did so because you lack ability or because you did not make enough effort? Do you tend to make similar explanations in all subjects or does it differ from subject to subject (for instance, when you fail at maths you lack ability, whereas a poor essay is down to lack of reading?)

When did you last ask somebody out and were successful or rejected? If you were successful did you put it down to your incredible good looks or was it because you had won two tickets for a weekend in Paris? If you were rejected was it perhaps because you think you are ugly or because you were in your decorating clothes and looked a mess?

Those explanations considered most likely to persist over time (e.g. lack of ability or being ugly) are referred to as stable causes since they are perceived as difficult to change. In contrast those explanations which can be more easily changed (e.g. you can make more effort or tidy yourself up) are considered unstable causes. From a motivational perspective you are more likely to expect a repeat of consequences which you perceive as being caused by stable factors than those you perceive as being caused by unstable ones.

Controllable versus uncontrollable causes

Complete Activity 3 before reading further.

Activity 3

You have just locked your new bicycle to a lamp post and are about to walk away when a car skids across the road and crashes into your bicycle, squashing it. You discover that the driver had swerved to avoid a blind person who had walked on to the road. When you get home you receive a telephone call from your friend who had experienced something remarkably similar. Like you she had fastened her bicycle to a post and a car had also crashed into it. However, the driver in her case had been drinking and had momentarily taken his eyes off the road. What do you think and feel about the two incidents – would you view them in the same way? If not, why?

It is likely that you would feel less sympathetic to the driver who ran into your friend's bike than the one who ran into yours, since the latter had chosen to drink alcohol (something within his control) whereas the driver in your case had tried to avoid an accident with someone who could not see where they were going (which is less within his control).

Table 6.1 An eight cell model to illustrate causal ascriptions across three dimensions

	Internal		External	
Controllability	Stable	Unstable	Stable	Unstable
Controllable	Usual level of effort	Temporary effort	Teacher bias	Unusual help from others
Uncontrollable	Ability	Mood	Level of task difficulty	Luck

Which of the drivers do you think is most likely to repeat their behaviour? Do you think your answer would be the same if a child had been run over instead of your bicycle? Why? What role, if any, do emotions have in your conclusions?

The third dimension examined by Weiner is the concept of controllability. Here the concern is the degree to which an individual can reasonably be expected to have control over events which influence outcomes. Teacher bias, for instance, is outside the pupil's control whereas temporary additional effort is within his or her control.

The three dimensions briefly outlined represent a framework for explaining the way in which individuals explain or attribute the causes of their success and failure, Weiner's three-dimensional framework is summarised in Table 6.1. It is important to focus on the co-variation of the three dimensions (or the way in which they interact) to make sense of the causal ascriptions made by pupils. In the diagram, ability is described as uncontrollable, internal and stable. In terms of academic achievement the pupil who attributes success to internal, stable and uncontrollable factors (ability) and failure to internal unstable and controllable factors (effort) will develop a more adaptive learning style. Conversely, the pupil who attributes success to external unstable factors (luck) and failure to internal stable factors (ability) is more likely to develop more maladaptive learning styles. The more an individual attributes their successes and failures in one or other direction the more reinforced a particular style becomes.

The repeated attribution of explanations for success and failure in a particular direction leads, over time, to the development of attributional styles. Three styles have been identified and are represented by differences in terms of pupil's expectations of success (and failure) on tasks and hence level of persistence.

These three motivational styles are now described.

Mastery orientation   This attributional style is represented by pupils who have a tendency to be more concerned with achieving success then avoiding failure; a realistic and reasonably high level of self esteem; a concern to gain mastery over their learning rather than proving they are better than others in the class; a healthy attitude to failure in that they will view it as a temporary setback, almost an opportunity to develop more effective learning skills. This style is considered the most adaptive motivational behaviour since the student is committed to the task for the purpose of learning and not for self-image enhancement – though this is likely to occur with repeated success on difficult tasks.

Learned helplessness   This is perhaps the best known of the maladaptive styles in both clinical and educational psychology and is represented by pupils who have a general belief that they lack ability, and that raising their ability is beyond their control; a global lack of control over their lives, with a tendency to externalise responsibility; expectation that they will fail on a task, so that if a task becomes difficult they will give up rather than work harder; and a belief that help from teachers reaffirms their lack of competence. In extreme examples of these pupils, failure is inevitable and trying to coax them to make more effort is akin to telling a depressed person to pull themselves together. Once established, this pattern of behaviour is hard to break. Furthermore, there is a correlation between pupils who exhibit these qualities and acute depression in adulthood. Attribution theorists argue that breaking the cycle comes through changing attributional patterns (attribution retraining) rather than adjusting the level of success or failure on a task or even a succession of tasks. In other words, they advocate getting the pupil to make more effective causal explanations, shifting the pupil's explanations for success and failure from stable and uncontrollable to those which are unstable and controllable, rather than making the tasks they have to complete more simple.

Self-worth motive   The second of the maladaptive styles is represented by pupils who believe that being viewed as having ability is more important than being seen as successful; ability sets limits on performance and attainment level, the latter only being exceeded through good luck. While learned helpless pupils have given up hope, self-worth individuals still believe they may have the required competence to be successful. However, ability level is negatively correlated with effort – high effort equals low ability; protecting their self image is all-important and they will utilise a whole range of defensive strategies to do so (e.g. procrastination, refusal to work). Whilst success is the best way to protect one's self image, in some cases the risks involved in trying to achieve it are too great so they avoid the likelihood at all costs believing it's best not to bother trying than to try and fail. Such strategies are relatively short-lived – others eventually see through the excuses and then uncertainty about one's self-worth becomes a certainty. This results in self-anger for feeling stupid, feelings of hopelessness and resentment of those believed to have caused such feelings (often teachers). A pupil who is settled into this attributional style is more anxious when confronted with an optimal task than one in which there is a high likelihood of failure – if most pupils are successful on a task and he is not, it lowers his-self-worth. If, however, he and everyone else fails on a task then his self-worth is largely unaffected.

Whilst self-worth protection and learned helplessness are both maladaptive, they are qualitatively different, which means they do not respond to the same types of intervention. Whilst learned helpless individuals can be taught to reattribute their failures, through attribution retraining, to internal unstable and controllable factors (usually effort) this is notably less successful with the self-worth group. Suggesting that more effort will result in success is unacceptable to the self-worth group since more effort implies less ability – an assault on the self worth. Working with this group requires attention to issues regarding their self image at both general and specific levels.

A piece of research carried out by Craske (1988) demonstrates these differences in the classroom. In her experiment Craske set a group of Primary school pupils four maths tests (A–D). Three of the tests (A, C, D) were of equal difficulty whilst the fourth (B) was very difficult and designed so that all the pupils would fail. Pupils received performance feedback on each before starting the next one. All pupils performed well on test A. However, as expected, all pupils failed on test B and were told of their results. Following this they completed test C which was exactly the same level of difficulty as A. Pupils who were mastery oriented either scored as they had on A or improved. Those whose performance deteriorated following failure were deemed to have maladaptive motivational styles. To further distinguish between members of this group they were given a fourth test (D) which they were led to believe would be very difficult and that they should therefore just attempt as many sums as they felt they could (a 'mitigating circumstance'). Those pupils whose performance improved were labelled self-worth motivated whereas those whose performance further deteriorated were labelled learned helpless. The explanation for this is that the self-worth motivated pupils had nothing to lose in attempting a test which was so difficult most pupils would not do well, thus failure after making an effort would not be attributed to lack of ability. Their scores improved when they did not have to protect their self-worth. In contrast the learned helpless group expected to fail and having been told to expect failure gave up prematurely.

Craske designed an activity to help pupils with maladaptive styles overcome their difficulties. This involved pupils playing a maths game which lasted between thirty and forty minutes. In the game a number of sums were written on the blackboard and each pupil in turn was invited to attempt as many sums as they could. They were given immediate feedback as to whether they had succeeded or not. They were then asked to make an attribution from a list to explain their success or failure, these choices were:

I got the sum right because:
    I had good luck
    It was easy
    I tried hard
    I am clever

I got the sum wrong because:
    I had bad luck
    It was too hard
    I didn't try hard enough
    I'm not clever enough

Where the pupil spontaneously selected an effort attribution it was reinforced: 'Yes, you got it right because you did try hard'. Where the pupil did not select an effort attribution they were prompted to do so by the experimenter: 'I think you got the sum wrong because you did not try hard enough'.

The results were promising, notably in the case of the learned helpless group who increased their attributions to effort and decreased their attributions to ability and produced better performances following failure. These successes were not measured in the case of the self-worth group.

Activity 4

You could try to replicate Craske's experiment; if you do so make sure to read the reference in detail first and follow the procedure carefully. There are other examples of similar experiments: see, for example, Rogers *et al.* (1994) and Galloway *et al.* (1996).

Alternatively you might start your study by spending some time talking with a group of pupils who appear to lack the will to learn or give up easily in some or all subjects. It may take a little time for them to open up. Make a note of the words they use to describe their failures and successes and those used to describe how they feel about themselves and others. Categorise these under the headings used in Table 6.1. Are their explanations adaptive or maladaptive? How do their explanations of success and failure compare with your explanations of their successes and failures? To what extent does the language they use to explain their situation contain expressions you tend to use? If you want to know more about how to obtain information from pupils see Rudduck, Chaplain and Wallace (1995).

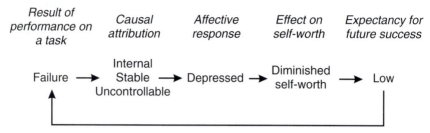

Figure 6.2 Cognitive and affective consequences of ascribing failure to an internal, stable and uncontrollable cause

A different approach is suggested for the self-worth group in which a greater emphasis is put on development of their self-worth which is not dependent on ability and competition. To achieve this such students need help to develop strategic thinking, how to think and not just what to think (Covington 1998), task orientation and problem-solving skills (Chaplain 1995). At a more structural level others have suggested the rethinking of competitive structures so prevalent in schools, advocating a more cooperative approach in which the price of failure is less threatening (Slavin 1983). This is not to suggest that such approaches should be reserved for self-worth protectors – they are relevant to all pupils.

Attributions and emotions

The resultant effects of making causal ascriptions in a particular direction have both cognitive and emotive components. The consequences of making a causal attribution for failure in the direction of internal stable factors tend to generate feelings of shame or depression which in turn lower self-worth and so expectation of future success is reduced. This downward spiral of self-defeating thoughts and affect is summarised in Figure 6.2.

The relationship between specific affective outcomes which result from making causal ascriptions for success and failure to particular attributional

Table 6.2 An example of the relationship between attributional dimensions and effect

	Attributional dimension × *Affective consequence*		
	Locus	*Stability*	*Controllability*
Failure due to internal stable attributions (lack of ability)	Worthlessness	Hopelessness	Shame
Failure due to internal unstable attributions (lack of effort)	Reduced self-worth	Hope	Guilt

dimensions have also been investigated by Weiner. The locus of control dimension (internal–external) is associated with pride and self worth. Attributions to stability result in the experience of hope or hopelessness. Attributions to controllability result in feelings of guilt or shame. An overall picture of these interactions under failure conditions is given in Table 6.2.

Complete Activity 5 before reading further.

Activity 5

Take a few minutes to list what you consider to be the characteristics of the ideal pupil. Include their physical attributes, dress, behaviour and ability level.

What did you conclude? That they were physically attractive, smart, clean, courteous, well-behaved and bright? The next question is how many pupils have you come across who meet your criteria? My guess would be hardly any or possibly none at all! Such pupils do not exist but are mental constructions against which we measure real pupils. Furthermore, would you really want to teach such pupils? Part of the excitement of teaching is working with individuals of differing ability, background and personality. This behaviour is not limited to school. When people are asked to describe their ideal partner their descriptions are often very similar to that of the ideal pupil. But again, how many partners fit the bill perfectly?

Attributions about other people

What relevance does the latter activity have in explaining differences in levels of pupil motivation? Research into social cognition shows that people's expectations and early impressions of others influence our verbal and non-verbal signals which we mediate to them. These in turn influence how such other people respond to us. If we represent significant others to them then such messages may influence the way they think about themselves. We will examine this cycle of events in detail later.

Up to this point I have concentrated on the attributions people make about themselves but people also draw causal inferences about other people's behaviour, a process known as interpersonal attribution. Attributional processes also operate at other levels including inter-group and societal level. Interpersonal attributions are of particular importance in the classroom, particularly those made by a teacher to explain pupil behaviour, those by the pupils to explain teacher behaviour, and dynamics resulting from the interaction of the two. The teacher who attributes a child's misbehaviour to the child's personality is likely to respond differently than if the teacher believes the child behaves that way because of home circumstances. Which social psychological factors lead us to attribute causes of other people's behaviour in one direction or another? To shed some light on this I will look at some of the variables which affect impression formation and interpersonal expectancy.

There has been considerable research carried out into the potential outcomes of holding particular expectations of other people's behaviour. Some of this work has been carried out in educational settings and has attempted to prove how teachers can unwittingly influence educational outcomes for pupils. Whilst it is essential that teachers are able to assess children's abilities and behaviour based on accurate measurement, when expectations act as causal factors in determining pupil outcomes they become a cause for concern. Most research in this area has concentrated on the positive effects (for ethical reasons) of holding high or higher than warranted expectations (the Halo effect). The hypothesis here is that holding higher expectations of pupils can result in their performance being enhanced. This effect is believed to occur because the teacher's expectation translates into a self-fulfilling prophecy. In other words the teacher forms an impression that a pupil is a high flyer (when in fact he/she is not) and as a result behaves towards the pupil in more positive ways; the pupil's self-efficacy (belief in their own ability) is then raised and performance is enhanced. Whilst this example is an over-simplification of a complex process, the evidence collected from a number of sources over the last forty years using a variety of methods indicates that teacher expectancy can, under the right conditions, have a powerful effect. Although there have been a great many studies of teacher expectancy using different methodologies, perhaps the two most famous historical examples are firstly the Pygmalion experiment by Rosenthal and Jacobson (1969) in which a group of teachers were led to believe, albeit incorrectly, that certain pupils in their class had latent talents and would 'bloom' in due course; all of the pupils were in fact 'average'. The results revealed some evidence to support the hypothesis that holding an inaccurate expectancy could have influenced the consequences. The methodology used was questioned and spurious conclusions drawn by the popular press – however, some significant findings were recorded.

A second well-documented study based on anecdotal description (where the pupils were tracked over a two-year period) was carried out by Rist (1970). Here teachers' expectations, based on socio-economic criteria, of Kindergarten pupils were found to have negative effects on the pupil's subsequent academic performance. Rist highlighted how linking high academic expectations with high social status and vice versa could result in unacceptable stigmatisation of those pupils from families with low social status. Rist's study therefore looked at the mediation of teacher expectations to their pupils; other studies have looked at the effects either side of the mediation process, that is, the formation of expectations about pupils on one hand and the outcomes for pupils on the other.

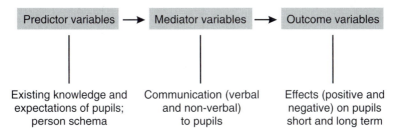

Figure 6.3 The expectancy process

The expectancy process

What conditions are required for this process to take place and what socio-cognitive activities are involved? Harris and Rosenthal (1986) identified a model for conceptualising interpersonal expectancy effects. This model categorises the process into three divisions: predictor, mediator and outcome variables (see Figure 6.3). Predictor variables moderate the way in which we form our expectations. You will no doubt be aware that in any interpersonal encounter you form impressions of people as potential partners, friends or perhaps business colleagues. The phenomena of 'person perception' and 'impression formation' are well documented in contemporary texts of social psychology. These processes include the identification of features we as individuals value or find attractive. These features might include dress sense, smell or beauty, for instance. From these pieces of information we infer a whole range of other characteristics, for example smart attractive people are generally expected to be intelligent; people who cannot look you in the eye are untrustworthy. Our database for holding these person schema are developed over time from a combination of innate dispositions, information from others and personal experience. These implicit models should be modified in the light of new information which contradicts existing knowledge but this is often not the case. Our impressions of people are often formed quite quickly and utilise a combination of information gathered over time and information about the current situation from which we form expectations. For such expectations to have any effect, however, they must be conveyed to, recognised by and responded to by the pupils concerned. These are referred to in Harris and Rosenthal's model as mediator and outcome variables respectively.

Expectations of pupils' social and academic performance can be conveyed in a number of ways including social organisation, for example, which group a pupil is placed in, along with the nature of the tasks they are expected to complete. Coupled with this are the interpersonal behaviours of the teacher towards the pupil, including the quantity and quality of verbal and non-verbal messages to pupils. However, interpersonal interaction is not one-sided. In order- for these expectations and resultant behaviours to have any effect on pupils requires them to be perceived and responded to by the target pupils. This does not mean that the pupil will necessarily be directly aware of what's going on – just as we don't have to be directly aware that someone does not appear to like us: we tend to talk of 'feeling' that they don't. This is not to suggest that the pupil's inferences will always be accurate – people often misread or misinterpret the motivational intent of others.

Harris and Rosenthal (1986) identified four mediating factors salient to the mediation of teachers' expectations to pupils and which result in differential effects on pupils. These four factors are summarised below:

Climate	teachers' positive or negative attitudes, teacher's 'warmth' towards students, non-verbal messages, especially eye contact
Feedback	levels of praise, positive and negative evaluation, criticism, acceptance of students' ideas, degree to which the teacher ignores students
Input	the amount and level of difficulty of material presented to students
Output	frequency of questioning and interactions initiated with students

Finally, the effect of a teacher's expectations also depends on how much the pupil values the teacher mediating them. If the pupil does not value the teacher, effects may be negligible. If on the other hand the pupil places a high value on the teacher the effects can be considerable.

Where there are resultant effects on a pupil these can be reflected in his or her academic performance, social behaviour, motivation (general and/or specific) and self-concept. All or some of these effects will manifest themselves in changes to social behaviour and academic performance. Both types of change will be fed back to the teacher by various classroom mechanisms which reinforce the original expectations formed by the teacher, thus maintaining the cycle. The effectiveness of the cycle depends upon all aspects of the sequence holding up. If a teacher's expectations are not translated into behaviours then they will not be conveyed to pupils. So having an expectation, even a distorted one, does not mean it will necessarily be conveyed to a second party. Furthermore, even if that expectation is mediated to a second party, this does not necessarily mean that it will have an effect if the second party does not value the mediator. From a social psychological perspective the expectancy process is thus a complex one, but it is also a phenomenon that in a simplified form has proved attractive to lay observers (notably the media and politicians). The expectancy cycle appears to operate only under certain conditions. For instance, the relative value of adults as significant others' changes over the socialisation process – younger pupils placing a higher value on adults than their older counterparts – which can reduce the potential influence a teacher's action might have. So to understand the effects of holding particular expectations requires attention to both sides of the interpersonal process; in reality, however, the main focus has tended to be on the teacher's frame of reference. In addition, there are a series of other issues operating at different levels of analysis. Understanding the process, with a view to intervening and enhancing pupils' life chances, requires attention not just to perceptions of others but also to perceptions of other people's perceptions, that is, metaperception.

Pupils' perceptions of their teachers' views of them influence their self-concept. If a pupil perceives his teacher as having low expectations of him then he is likely to develop low levels of self-efficacy and low levels of achievement motivation. The pupil can experience anxiety through uncertainty about his ability to succeed and about how to cope with failure. Sensing the teacher's low expectation activates an avoidance tendency: why ask someone for help who you believe doesn't value you? This may in turn lead to that pupil developing defences to compensate for these feelings, which can include work avoidance and disruptive behaviour to avoid on-task behaviour which offers potential damage to self-worth.

Making a difference

How might teachers take advantage of some of the findings outlined in this chapter? First, some understanding of the cognitive and affective processes inherent to interpersonal activity is of central importance. Taking time to consider and reflect upon our thinking about how we categorise pupils will provide insight into how we represent and respond to different pupils. It is also important to understand the attributional processes underlying our own causal explanations for interpersonal behaviour along with understanding the differential effects of pupils making causal ascriptions in one direction or another. We should also understand the qualitative differences of different attributional styles and how to distinguish between them and respond to each effectively. This should include activity at a number of levels including:

- encouraging pupils to focus on controllable and unstable explanations for failure
- enhancing pupils' self-worth in a manner which is not dependent on having a particular ability
- helping pupils to develop their problem-solving and strategic thinking skills
- developing cooperative classroom structures which develop individual and group problem solving skills
- developing whole school policies which encourage and value the above.

We should take time to explore with pupils how they believe we as teachers view them. There is a paucity of research evidence, beyond anecdotal description, examining pupils' perspectives on person perception, metaperception and expectations.

This summary is not intended overly to simplify the process nor offer 'fix it quick' solutions. Like so many other areas of human science there can be a wide gulf between recognising difficulties and overcoming them. Pupil motivation and interpersonal processes in school are no exception.

Further reading

Covington M. V. (1998) *The Will to Learn: A guide for motivating young people*, Cambridge: Cambridge University Press.

Galloway, D. and Rogers, C.G. (1998) *Motivating the difficult to teach*, London: Longman.

Weiner, B. (1992) *Human Motivation: Metaphors, Theories and Research*, California: Sage Publications Inc.

References

Ames, C. (1991) 'Achievement goals and the classroom motivational climate', in D.H. Schunk and J. Meece (eds) *Student Perceptions in the Classroom*, Hillsdale NJ: Lawrence Erlbaum Associates.

Atkinson, J.W. (1964) *An introduction to Motivation*, Princeton NJ: Van Nostrand.

Chaplain, R. (1995) 'Making a Strategic Withdrawal: Self-worth protection and disengagement among male pupils', in Rudduck, J., Chaplain, R. and Wallace G. *School Improvement: What Can Pupils Tell Us?* London: David Fulton Press.

Covington, M.V. (1992) *Making the Grade: A Self-worth Perspective on Motivation and School Reform,*. Cambridge: Cambridge University Press.

Covington, M.V. (1998) *The Will to Learn: A guide for motivating young people*, Cambridge: Cambridge University Press.

Craske, M-L. (1988) 'Learned helplessness, self-worth motivation and attribution retraining for primary school children', *British Journal of Educational Psychology*, 58, 152–164.

Dweck, C.S. (1991) 'Self-theories and goals: their role in motivation, personality and development', *Nebraska Symposium on Motivation*, 38, University of Nebraska.

Galloway, D., Leo, E.L., Rogers, C. and Armstrong, D. (1996) 'Maladaptive motivational style: the role of domain specific task demand in English and mathematics', *British Journal of Educational Psychology*, 66, 197–207.

Harris, M.J. and Rosenthal, R. (1986) 'Four factors in the mediation of teacher expectancy', in R.S. Feldman (ed.) *The Social Psychology of Education: Current research and theory*, New York: Cambridge University Press.

Heider, F. (1958) *The Psychology of Interpersonal Relations*, New York: Wiley.

Hull, C.L. (1943) *Principles of Behavior*, New York: Appleton-Century-Crofts.

Lewin, K. (1953) *Field Theory in Social Science*, New York: Harper.

Rist, R.C. (1970) 'Student social class and teacher expectations', *Harvard Educational Review*, 40, 411–451.

Rogers, C.G., Galloway, D., Armstrong, D., Jackson, C. and Leo, E.L. (1994) 'Changes in motivational style over the transfer from primary to secondary school: subject and dispositional effects', *Educational and Child Psychology*, 11, 26–38.

Rosenthal, R. and Jacobson, L. (1969) *Pygmalion in the Classroom*, New York: Holt, Rhinehart and Winston.

Rudduck, J., Chaplain, R. and Wallace, G. (1995) *School Improvement: What Can Pupils Tell Us?* London: David Fulton Press.

Slavin, R. (1983) *Cooperative Learning*, New York: Longman.

Weiner, B. (1992) *Human Motivation: Metaphors, Theories and Research.* California: Sage Publications Inc.

Part II

Teaching the curriculum

7 Organising activities to help children remember and understand

David Whitebread

EDITOR'S SUMMARY

Formal education poses particular problems for young children because it requires them deliberately to remember information with which they are presented as a planned curriculum. This chapter outlines what is known from research about the structure of the human memory system and its impact on learning and understanding. The memory system is divided into sensory stores, working memory and long-term memory. Each of these elements of our memory has its own structural characteristics and processes which affect the ways in which we can more easily remember and understand new information. Some very clear indications emerge as to what teachers of young children can do in order to help them understand and remember more effectively. These include adopting a multi-sensory approach to activities, encouraging children's self-monitoring of performance, using explicit discussion and modelling to encourage children to try a wide range of memory strategies and setting new information in the context of an event, story or dramatisation. The overriding significance of devising tasks which stimulate children's mental activity is also emphasised.

It is one of the fascinations and challenges of teaching young children that they not only have much to learn, but have also much to learn about learning itself. The Primary school teacher cannot simply place the material to be learnt in front of the children and expect them get on with it. If this were the case Primary school teaching would be very straightforward and probably extremely dull.

It is one of life's ironies that children learn very effectively before they arrive at school and before anyone starts trying to teach them anything.

Amongst many other accomplishments, they achieve the astonishing feat of learning to speak a language, and sometimes two, in the first few years of life and very rapidly indeed. It is only in school that significant numbers of children begin to find learning difficult. The learning they are required to do in school, however, is distinctive and challenging in two important ways:

- it requires them *deliberately* and *explicitly* to memorise information of various kinds, much of it arbitrary (letters of the alphabet, phoneme-grapheme correspondences, written numbers) or unrelated to their everyday world (Tudors and Stuarts, the properties of a triangle, energy and forces)
- it requires them to understand and develop ideas and concepts which are part of a *planned and delivered 'curriculum'* rather than arising naturally from their life experiences.

The challenge for the Primary school teacher, therefore, is to devise activities which will present information to children in ways which are memorable, which make it easy for them to understand, but at the same time help children to develop their memory and learning capabilities; or, in other words, help them to become increasingly independent learners.

An understanding of the ways in which children's memory and learning capabilities develop is clearly fundamental to devising such activities. The aim of this chapter, therefore, is to set out what psychologists currently understand about the structure and development of human memory and the ways in which children learn and make sense of their world. As we shall see, recent research by neuroscientists on the workings of the brain has combined with insights from cognitive developmental psychology to provide some very clear guidelines which, properly applied in the hands of a skilled teacher, can transform the effectiveness of attempts to teach young children.

The structure of the human memory system

Research on memory has shown it to be a complex and multi-faceted aspect of human cognitive processing. We do not have a memory so much as several memory systems, each with its own structural characteristics which fit it to performing a different function. This aspect of human memory can easily be demonstrated by considering the things which we find easy and difficult to remember. To illustrate this, before reading any further, write down which of the following you find easiest to remember, and which you find most difficult:

the melodies of songs
the letters of the alphabet
how to ride a bicycle
the names of people you meet
lecture notes

the 51 states of America
telephone numbers
how to draw a face
what happened at an important interview
where your keys are when you have lost them
the colours of the rainbow
new information about something in which you are interested
important information about something uninteresting

If you try this activity with a group of adults, typically there are areas of agreement and disagreement. That some people can remember melodies but not numbers, while others can remember telephone numbers but not people's names, suggests very strongly that there are separate systems for the different types of information. In the same way, some people have strong visual memories, while others can remember information expressed verbally much more efficiently.

In other areas there is usually almost unanimous agreement. Practical memories like how to ride a bike and draw a face are unproblematic. The letters of the alphabet and colours of the rainbow have been made secure through a combination of repetition, song and mnemonics. We would recognise the 51 states of America even if we couldn't actually recall them all. We know how to work out where our keys are by 'rewinding' our internal videotape of our recent experiences. What happened at an interview and new information related to an interest seem to stick, while lecture notes and information about things which don't interest us just disappear into the ether. I have looked at lecture notes I have written, sometimes fairly recently, and have no recollection of them at all – although the interesting new idea they included might by now be a central part of my thinking.

All this is a testament to the complex but very particular ways in which the human memory system works and its impact on our learning. It is a system perfectly adapted to perform certain kinds of memory and learning task highly efficiently; in order to do this, however, it has developed the ability to discard unimportant information as efficiently as it remembers the important.

The seminal work in analysing the structure of the human memory system was the *multi-store model* proposed by Atkinson and Shiffrin (1968). They proposed that there are essentially three different kinds of memory store, namely Sensory, Short-term and Long-term. This model was supported at the time by detailed research evidence and much of the subsequent work in this area has simply developed this basic model in more detail. Figure 7.1 sets out diagrammatically what is broadly the current consensus model of the various structures and processes in human memory. We will refer to this model throughout the chapter. In the remainder of the chapter, research related to each part of the human memory system and its development will be reviewed and major implications for teaching explored.

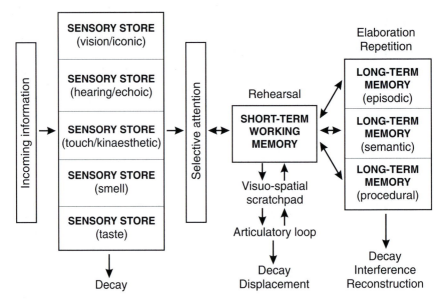

Figure 7.1 Multistore model of memory (based on Atkinson and Shiffrin 1968)

Sensory stores, recognition and selective attention

Incoming information from the environment is first received via the various sensory receptors into the Sensory Stores (one for each sense modality). These appear to operate as an initial screening device which hold information for just long enough (approximately half a second) for the important, significant or relevant information to be sorted out from the rest and transferred to the Short-term Store (or Working Memory). The overwhelming majority of the information which is not selected rapidly decays and is lost.

An example of how this works is the classic 'cocktail party' experiment where you are in a crowded room, listening intently to the conversation in your group and filtering out the rest, until someone on the other side of the room says your name. Immediately your attention switches to the other conversation. This demonstrates two important features of our memory system: the primacy of *recognition* and the power of *selective attention*.

Recognition

Although we are not aware of it, we are continuously monitoring all the information coming in to our sensory receptors. This process of monitoring involves the earliest and simplest form of memory, namely recognition. The human brain is astonishingly good at recognising information it has already attended to and received on a previous occasion. Recent work by neuroscientists has revealed that knowledge is stored in the brain as patterns of links between neurones, or brain cells. Learning is thus a process of establishing patterns, pattern matching and making links between patterns. When some information we have already encountered before is received again, it excites an already established pattern of neurones, and this exact match is perceived as recognition. As this is fundamental to the way our long-term memory system works, it is an ability with which we are born. Experiments with very young children have shown that their pure recognition memories are equal to those of adults.

This neurological work explains why we can always recognise information more easily than we can recall it. For example, we will reliably recognise someone's face, but recalling their name may be more difficult. Recognition simply requires that the incoming pattern of sensory information be matched. Recall, however, requires us to to do this and then to find a linked pattern. As we shall see later, the strength of the links between different neuronal patterns depends upon repetition. At this point, however, it is most important to note that our attention is largely guided by the recognition process.

Selective attention

This leads on to the second point, that the 'cocktail party' phenomenon also demonstrates the power of selective attention. A situation which all too often arises at parties is that where you are politely listening to someone droning on about something boring, while the people in the next group are talking excitedly about your favourite film, sharing some juicy gossip about someone you know, or having an uproarious time telling one another what are obviously some extremely funny jokes. Maintaining attention on the conversation about your companion's plumbing problems, or which route they took to the party, becomes quite impossible.

The Primary classroom, of course, shares certain characteristics with a crowded party: there are many opportunities for children to be distracted. Whereas adults might be capable of forcing themselves to attend to one element of their current sensory input rather than another, young children have not yet learned this control. Hagen and Hale (1973) demonstrated the development of selective attention by asking 5–6-year-olds and 14–15-year-olds to remember pictures on a series of cards. Each card actually contained two pictures, but one of the pictures was identified as the important one to be remembered. In these circumstances, the older children remembered many more of the important pictures than the younger ones; however, the younger children remembered many more of the pictures they were not asked to remember. So the total amount of information remembered was the same for both groups of children, but the older group has focused their attention much more effectively.

Recognition of the powerful and active nature of our selective attention makes it very clear why it is vital that activities intended to help young children learn must first and foremost interest them, intrigue them and be personally relevant for them. Only then can their attention be held, because they have not yet learnt to exercise deliberate control very effectively.

Importantly, grabbing young children's attention will involve a strong element of recognition together with the promise of new information related to what they already know. If it does not, attention will be easily diverted and all the important information the teacher has carefully planned and prepared will be discarded from their Sensory Stores within 0.5 seconds.

Sensory channels

A separate but equally important characteristic of the Sensory Stores mechanism is that each seems to be a unitary channel capable of passing on just one item of information at a time. As a consequence, different pieces of information coming in through the same sense modality tend to interfere with one another. It is, therefore, impossible to listen to two people talking at once, even if they are both trying to tell you the same thing. Related pieces of information coming in through different modalities (e.g. sound and vision), on the other hand, tend to support and reinforce one another.

When new information, ideas or concepts are being introduced to Primary children, enlisting the power of this multi-sensory message support is vital. Young children find it particularly difficult to acquire knowledge simply through listening to talk or reading text. The power of illustrations in young children's picture books and information books is a testament to this. Particularly when they are being introduced to something new, they need to see and hear, touch and physically experience in as great a variety of ways as possible. A multi-sensory approach to activities designed to help children's learning is always likely to be most successful. This is why the sensory richness of first-hand experiences will always help children's learning.

As we shall see, sense-specific processes and representations are also an important element in both short and long-term memory.

Short-term Store and Working Memory

The central structure of the human memory system identified by Atkinson and Shiffrin was the Short-term Store. Subsequent work by Baddeley and Hitch (1974), however, redescribed this as Working Memory, which is the usual term now used. The point here is that this aspect of the memory system can be more accurately characterised as a set of dynamic processes, rather than as a static store.

Importantly, the Working Memory is where we bring information into consciousness so that we can work on it. It has three distinctive features which have major significance for children's abilities to carry out a wide range of cognitive tasks and which determine the ways in which memory develops.

Rehearsal and the articulatory loop

The first distinctive feature of the Short-term Store or Working Memory system is that information held here, as with the Sensory Stores, is also subject to decay. However, the process of decay here is rather slower. Whereas information is lost after half a second from the Sensory tores, research indicates that information lasts about half a minute in the Working Memory. Furthermore, if information is needed longer than this, it can be restored afresh by the process of *rehearsal*. It is as though information in working memory is travelling along a conveyor belt; the journey from one end to the other lasts thirty seconds, after which items fall off the end and are lost. However, it is possible to pick up items just before they fall and place them back on the beginning of the conveyor again, giving them another thirty seconds. This re-inputting of items of information can be done repeatedly.

As well as allowing information to be held in memory for as long as we need to use it, rehearsal has also been shown to serve another purpose, which is the transfer of information from short-term to long-term memory. A range of evidence has demonstrated that the more information is rehearsed, the longer lasting it will be. For example, a well-established pattern in list learning experiments is that the first few items on a list are recalled better than items later on. This is known as the *primacy effect*. If more rehearsal is allowed by, for example, slowing down the speed at which the list is presented, then the primacy effect is increased. On the other hand, if the opportunity for rehearsal is removed by, for example, requiring subjects to engage in the 'distractor task' of counting backwards between the presentation of the words in the list, then the primacy effect disappears.

The central role of rehearsal in both holding information in Working Memory and transferring items to Long-term Memory has enormous educational implications. This is particularly the case because of evidence that the use of rehearsal itself develops through the Primary school age range. In a very influential series of experiments, Flavell, Beach and Chinsky (1966) revealed that, in a short-term memory task, the percentage of children spontaneously using rehearsal grew from 10 per cent for 5-year-olds to 60 per cent of 7-year-olds and 85 per cent of 10-year-olds. Not only the quantity, but also the quality of rehearsal develops, with older children and college students using more sophisticated, cumulative and flexible patterns of repetition in their rehearsal strategies.

In the Working Memory model, which Baddeley (1986) has continued to work on and develop, the process of rehearsal is reconfigured as the *articulatory loop*. This title recognises more recent evidence that conscious rehearsal is a process specific to verbal information, and that it involves articulation by an 'inner voice'. Detailed research has linked the development of an effective articulatory loop with reading fluency; amongst this is clear evidence that children with developmental dyslexia have greatly reduced memory spans.

Multi-sensory representations

A second feature of short-term memory that must also be acknowledged is its multi-sensory nature. We are all aware, for example, of our ability to hold visual images in our minds and this has been recognised in more recent versions of the Working Memory model (Baddeley 1986) with the inclusion of a second system referred to as the *visuo-spatial scratch pad*. This system allows the storage of a visual image which can be manipulated to carry out tasks. Just as the reception of information through more than one sensory modality appears powerfully to reinforce the message initially, its representation in more than one sense modality in Working Memory appears to dramatically increase its memorability. Teaching strategies and practices which encourage children to form and use visual images as representations of their understanding, particularly in areas such as mathematics and problem-solving, have been shown to be highly beneficial.

Limited capacity

A third point is that the Working Memory system has *limited capacity*. In a very early and seminal article, Miller (1956) reviewed evidence that the adult human can usually hold around seven pieces of information in short-term memory. As new pieces of information enter, either from current sensory inputs or retrieved from long-term memory, some existing pieces of information are displaced. This can easily be demonstrated. Try the following letter translation task. For each item there are some letters and a number. Having looked at each item, you must shut your eyes while you start with each letter in turn and count on the number of letters through the alphabet, so that you produce a new list of letters. When you have the new list formed in your mind, you open your eyes and write them down. Keep going until it becomes impossible.

> A + 6
> B K + 4
> M J C + 5
> K S D P + 3
> R L T E N + 4
> F O H Q G I + 2

It has long been established that young children appear to have a smaller Working Memory capacity than adults. Dempster (1981), for example, investigated how many randomly selected numbers or letters children of different ages and adults could remember and found a clear developmental sequence, the causes of which we will examine below. For the moment, however, it is important to recognise how fundamental the Working Memory is to a wide range of cognitive activity and that children may often have difficulty with tasks not through a failure of understanding, but because they cannot hold sufficient information in their minds. Thus, when young children are attempting to articulate their thoughts, or to read, or to carry out a numerical task, you will often experience them 'losing the thread' for this very reason.

In these circumstances, it is an important function of an adult to 'scaffold' the task for the child by providing support in the form of reminders of the vital pieces of information that have been displaced from the Working Memory. To understand the nature of the child's experience it is perhaps helpful to remember the experience of learning to drive a car. To begin with, there is simply just too much to think about all at once. It is possible to change gear just so long as one is not required to steer at the same time. For young children in Primary school this must be a very common state of affairs.

The mechanisms by which novice learners come to be able to cope with the large amounts of information involved in such complex tasks as articulating an argument, reading, solving a mathematical problem or driving a car turn out to have major pedagogical implications. To begin with, psychologists advanced the view that children simply had smaller working memory capacities which gradually grew (like their arms and legs). However, subsequent work has shown that adults' apparently larger capacity is really a consequence of two aspects of development which allow them to use their fixed capacity more efficiently. These relate to an improved knowledge base and the increasing self-awareness and control of our own cognitive processes.

Improved knowledge base

In a very elegant experiment, Chi (1978) demonstrated that it is knowledge rather than age which determines memory abilities in any particular area. She asked 10-year-olds and adults to recall lists of 10 digits, and to recall the positions of chess pieces on a chess board. As you would expect, the adults outperformed the children on digit recall, but, surprisingly, the tables were turned with the chess pieces. The result was explained, however, by the fact that the children were all regular chess players and the adults were not. It turns out that the improved knowledge base of the expert helps memory in a number of ways, and we will return to this when we look at long-term memory below. Chi's experiment, however, appears to illustrate the phenomenon of *chunking*. This is the process by which, as we become more expert and knowledgeable in a particular area, we do not simply acquire more information, but we also increasingly structure the information. Common structures, originally made up of lots of individual pieces of information, themselves become just one piece of information. This is illustrated by the following memory task. Try to remember each of the following sets of twelve numbers or letters. Look at each for three seconds, then cover them up and try to write them down.

```
9 5 8 2 3 5 4 1 6 7 0 3
1 0 6 6 1 9 4 5 2 0 0 1
1 2 3 4 5 6 7 8 9 1 0 1
q g u d x v n y r p l a
c a t d o g l e g a r m
a b c d e f g h i j k l
```

Clearly, the sequences which contained structures with which you were already familiar are far easier to remember than those which do not, because you can remember the information in meaningful 'chunks' and this reduces the load on working memory. In Chi's experiment, similarly, the child chess players were able to remember structures of chess pieces in 'chunks'.

It is important to recognise that young children's relative lack of experience in most knowledge domains means that the vast majority of even apparently simple tasks will place a heavier load on their working memory capacity. This is one reason why children can often manage a new task more easily when it is put in a familiar context.

Metacognitive monitoring and strategic control

The ability to use our limited Working Memory capacity more and more efficiently is also achieved by our increasing self-awareness of our own memory abilities and the development and use of strategies based on this knowledge. This 'metacognitive' aspect of children's developing abilities to learn and carry out more sophisticated tasks was first identified by Flavell, Beach and Chinsky (1966) in their explorations of rehearsal. They asked the question whether young children failed to rehearse because they were incapable of doing so, or because they were not aware this might be a useful strategy. So they used a simple memory task, involving sequences of pictures, and attempted to teach 5-year-olds to rehearse. As it turned out, these young children were perfectly capable of rehearsing, and performed as well as older children when they did so. However, when subsequently asked to carry out another such task, about half of them reverted to their original pattern of not rehearsing and failing to remember.

This early work has led to an emormous body of research concerned with the development of children's 'metamemory', or their increasing awareness of their own memory abilities, and its relation to the construction and use of increasingly sophisticated strategies. Children's lack of self-awareness has been well-documented. For example, Wellman (1977) investigated the 'tip-of-the-tongue' phenomenon and showed that children's awareness of when they know something, but cannot currently recall it, is far less accurate than that of an adult. Istomina (1975) revealed young children's gradually emerging self-awareness in a memory task which consisted of a game within which the children had to go to a 'store' to buy an agreed list of five items for a pretend tea party. Valerik displayed the typical behaviour of a 3-year-old. When asked to go to the store:

> 'Valerik, obviously pleased with the proposition, turns his head immediately toward the store and takes the basket. "O.K.", he says, and runs off without waiting to hear the experimenter's last words.
>
> In the store, Valerik inspects all the wares on display with great curiosity. When the store manager (experimenter's assistant) asks him "What have you been told to buy?" Valerik nods his head towards the toys and then says, "Candy."
>
> "And what else?" says the manager.
>
> Valerik begins to glance about nervously and frowns ... "Can I be the sales clerk?" he asks.'

By 4 years old, however, some kinds of primitive strategy are beginning to emerge:

> 'Igor ... listens to the instructions patiently, attentively looking at the experimenter with an air of importance; he then runs off, forgetting even to take the basket with him. "Give me noodles, a ball, butter, and that's all," he says quickly ... "And hurry, because the children are hungry."'

Igor's recognition of his need to listen with his full attention and then to rush to carry out the task demonstrates some awareness of his own memory abilities and limitations. It is not until 5 years old, however, that Istomina found children commonly beginning to rehearse and to be aware of any forgetting:

> 'Serezha listened attentively to the list and repeated each of the experimenter's words in a whisper. He recalls four items, but could not recall the fifth. He looked confusedly at the experimenter, and repeated the same words one more time. "There's something else I have to buy, but I've forgotten it," he said.'

It is not, of course, until we become aware that we are failing to remember or to understand that we recognise the need to carry out a task differently. Self-monitoring of performance is thus fundamental to developing our ability to be more effective learners. The common experience of suddenly realising that you have been 'reading' a text but haven't taken in any of the meaning is a testimony to this. Has this happened to you so far in this chapter? Let's hope not too often. But if it did, you would recognise it and do something about it.

As a consequence, encouraging children to self-monitor their performance on tasks can be enormously effective in developing their ability to learn. Children can also be asked to predict how they are likely to do on a task. They can also be usefully taught strategies such as:

- rehearsal and cumulative rehearsal

- using visual imagery
- making arbitrary information more meaningful so that it can be chunked, e.g. Richard Of York Gave Battle In Vain (colours of rainbow), Big Elephants Can't Always Understand Small Elephants (how to spell 'because') and so on
- turning recall into recognition by generating possibilities, e.g. the alphabetic method
- thinking back to the context in which the to-be-remembered item was first encountered.

This is by no means an exhaustive list; the ingenuity with which the human brain constructs a wide range and variety of such strategies is astonishing. Each of these strategies depends for its success upon a structural feature of our memory systems. As children become more self-aware about their own memories and ways of learning, so they become more adept at generating their own strategies and matching them ever more appropriately to particular tasks. Nisbet and Shucksmith (1986), amongst others, have also shown that Primary-aged children can be taught strategies and will adopt them if they are clearly associated with successful performance. Explicit discussion and modelling by an adult are effective means of encouraging children to try a wide range of memory strategies. There is also evidence that once children have used one strategy successfully, they are more likely to behave strategically on other occasions. It is by this means that the fundamentals of true independent learning would appear to be established.

Long-term memory

Atkinson and Shiffrin's original conception of a Long-term Store has also been refined and developed by subsequent research. The generally accepted current model is that originally proposed by Tulving (1985) who argued that long-term memory has, in fact, three distinct components: *procedural, episodic* and *semantic memory*. The evidence for this mainly arises from the study of amnesiac patients who, in different circumstances and conditions, lose certain kinds of memories but not others.

These three different kinds of long-term memory depend on different kinds of representations and store different kinds of knowledge. Intriguingly, the forms of representations used appear to relate closely to those identified by the eminent developmental psychologist, Jerome Bruner (1974), in his very influential model of the development of learning. Bruner's model emphasises the role within intellectual development of the use of different modes of representation:

- *enactive* memories of actions
- *iconic* memories of unreconstructed perceptions: visual images, sounds, smells, etc.

- *symbolic* memories of experience transformed into a symbolic code (language, mathematics, etc.): thoughts, ideas, concepts, etc.

Each of these modes is increasingly accessible to our conscious awareness and increasingly flexible. Thus, procedural memory relies on enactive representations, episodic memory on iconic (mainly visual) representations, and semantic memory on symbolic (mainly verbal) representations. The evidence from studies of the evolution of the human brain suggests that these modes of representation and their related memory systems emerged in this order. Perhaps as a consequence, while there are complex interactions between them, the more primitive enactive–procedural and iconic–episodic memories seem to be able to support symbolic–semantic memory more than is the case the other way around.

Procedural memory

The procedural memory is the repository of our developing knowledge about how to carry out actions: for example, feed ourselves with a spoon, fasten a button, hop, ride a bicycle, write with a pencil, hit a ball. The memories or knowledge of how to do these things is stored enactively and is not accessible to conscious verbalisations.

It is, of course, possible to describe our physical actions in language, but doing so does not seem to help improve their quality or efficiency very much if at all. I have, for example, read countless descriptions of the perfect golf swing, but the way I have improved my own performance is through practice; when I hit a great shot is when I remember how a good swing feels physically, not how to describe it verbally.

Conversely, there is some evidence to suggest that encoding verbal information enactively can be a very powerful mnemonic. Spelling, it has been claimed by some, is 'in the hand', and it is a commonly reported experience that when we have forgotten momentarily how to spell a word (i.e. cannot access our symbolic representation of it) that it helps to write it out by hand. Certainly, there is good evidence that linking new information to actions for children can be very helpful: for example, making the patterns of letters and numbers with whole arm movements in the air, or in sand, or linking new words or songs to be remembered to sequences of actions.

Episodic memory

Episodic memory appears to be a system whereby an initially quite detailed record is kept of our experiences. Although the most significant of these is probably the visual record, it includes information from all the sensory inputs. It is indicative of the way in which these memories are recorded that we have to run through them in the sequence in which they originally occurred in order to locate any particular memory. For example, if we have misplaced our keys, glasses or wallet, it is possible and often very effective, to 'rerun' our memories of the day so far, starting at the point where we have a definite memory of the lost item. It is as though we can rerun a kind of video-tape of our experiences in our head.

While the rather fixed and 'iconic' nature of the memories within episodic memory have their limitations, this is nevertheless a very powerful aspect of human long-term memory. Research has shown that everything we learn, even as adults, is initially most strongly linked to the particular context and sequence of events in which we first experienced it (see, for example, Conway 1997). It is also a common experience that revisiting somewhere we have not been for a long time, or coming across a particular smell or sound, will trigger memories of particular events which were originally associated with them (and which we often had previously not recalled).

Reminding ourselves of the context in which it was originally learned or encountered is consequently often one of the most effective ways of recalling information, and this is a technique we can teach to children. We can also make use of the power of episodic memory in other ways. It is no accident that important cultural information is mainly transmitted in pre-literate cultures by means of stories, myths and legends. As experienced teachers are well aware, setting new information in the context of an event, story or dramatisation can be enormously helpful for young children also. Acting out an historical event, transforming a phonic rule into a little story, visiting the fire station and so on, are not simply devices to improve motivation; they also embrace the power of episodic memory to help children learn and remember (see Figure 7.2). I recently came across a very effective way of remembering chemical equations which involved changing them into stories, devised in preparation for GCSE examinations. The process of photosynthesis, for example, became a moving love story between Mr Carbon and Miss Hydrogen, who met and were forever joined together. Such was their love that they constantly gave off little sounds of joy: 'O! O!' (Oxygen!) they would coo.

Semantic memory

Semantic memory is the latest evolving and uniquely human aspect of long-term memory because it depends upon our ability for *symbolic representation*, most significantly exemplified in our development and use of language. This is the part of our memories where we remember, rather than particular episodes or events, those thoughts, ideas, general rules, principles, concepts and so on which we infer from our particular experiences. Much more than either of the other long-term memory systems, semantic memory is subject to constant restructuring as we organise and reorganise our internal models of the world. As we gain more experience we re-categorise items, we make new connections, we invent, build and develop new hierarchies and webs of meaning.

In this system, it emerges that what determines how well remembered an item of information will be, and how easily it will be recalled, is dependent

Figure 7.2 Carrying out a field trip or acting in a play utilises episodic memory to make learning memorable and help understanding

upon how well embedded, connected and elaborated it is within our semantic structures. The neuroscientific evidence suggests that this has two elements: the strength of connections and the extent of connections.

Strength of connections

As long ago as 1949 the psychologist D. O. Hebb postulated that learning consisted of forming connections between neurones in the cerebral cortex. These connections form when a pattern of neurones 'fire' together; the more often they fire together, the stronger the connection becomes. This essential model has been subsequently confirmed by neuroscientific research. The strengthening of connections does indeed occur through repetitious firing via the now well-established electrochemical mechanism of long-term potentiation (LTP).

This goes a long way to explaining the golden rule of learning, which is 'little and often'. If you want to learn anything, ten minutes a day is much more effective than an hour a week because the former will oblige the learner to re-input the infomation on many more separate occasions, thus strengthening the neuronal connections. This probably also goes some way to explaining the evidence that once children have been introduced to some new information or ideas, in order to achieve long-term transfer, pedagogical practices which immediately require children to rehearse their new knowledge are highly effective. Children who are asked to learn some information and then immediately tested on their recall of it retain the information in the long term far more effectively than those who are not tested.

Extent of connections

As well as strengthening existing connections, learning also consists of constantly making new ones. When we are able to connect new information or ideas to ones we already have established, then we experience the new information as having meaning or making sense. The more connections we can make, the more sense we can make of the new information, and the more likely we are to remember it. In order to demonstrate how this works, try to remember each of these 14 letter words. Look at them for 5 seconds, then cover them up and try to write them down.

   Constantinople   Gwrzcwydactlmp   χονσταντινοπλε

Of course, you will have found the first one relatively easy, the second one difficult and the third one (unless you read Greek) extremely difficult. This is clearly related to the extent to which you can connect these new pieces of information to your existing knowledge. The first is bristling with connections to things you already know, at several levels (meaning, phonic sounds, letters), whereas it is increasingly difficult to make any connections to the other two.

A delightful example of this crucial relationship between knowledge, meaning and memory was provided by Chi and Koeske (1983), who carried out a study of a 5-year-old budding dinosaur expert. This particular boy owned nine books about dinosaurs and could name forty types. Figure 7.3 is a semantic network representation of his knowledge about dinosaurs that they constructed by asking him on six separate occasions to recall the names of dinosaurs he knew, and by seeing which clues he found most helpful in identifying dinosaurs. The dinosaurs were grouped by noting which ones he tended to remember together and which ones shared properties of which he was aware. As they hypothesised, on subsequent recall tests, the boy was most adept at remembering dinosaurs which had many links with other dinosaurs; the ones he tended to forget were the ones with fewest links.

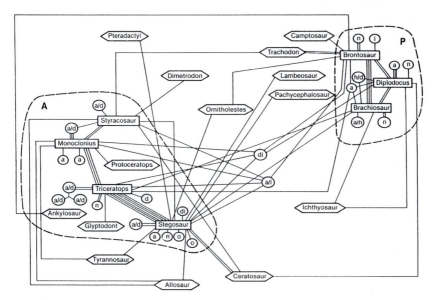

Figure 7.3 Semantic network representation of a 5 year old's knowledge about dinosaurs. Dinosaurs in the A group are armoured. Those in the P group are giant plant eaters. Multiple lines between dinosaurs indicate especially close connections. Small letters connected to dinosaur names indicate known traits: (a) appearance; (d) defence mechanism; (di) diet; (n) nickname; (h) habitat; (l) locomotion.

Craik and Lockhart (1972) developed a model of memory which emphasises its close relationships with knowledge, meaning and under-standing. This was known as the *'Levels of processing' model* within which they argued that the more 'deeply' new information is processed the more likely it is that it will be remembered. By 'deeply' they meant connected to exist-ing knowledge and semantic networks. For example, they demonstrated that if we are given a list of words and asked to say if they are printed in capi-tal letters or rhyme with 'lemon' (which requires only superficial process-ing of the appearance or sound of the words), we are less likely to remember them than if we have to say, for example, whether they are ani-mals or objects you would find in the kitchen (requiring deeper processing of the words' meanings).

A number of very important implications for effective teaching flow from these insights into the processes within semantic memory. To begin with, it becomes very clear why it is so vital to help children *connect new infor-mation or ideas to what they already know.* We know that children are not nearly as efficient as adults in searching their existing knowledge for connections to help them; we need to construct strategies to help and encourage children to do this. When introducing something new, it is always helpful to remind children, or, even better, through careful questioning, oblige them to remind themselves, of what they already know that is related.

Second, when new information or ideas are being presented to children, it makes a very remarkable difference if they are required to do something with it, rather than just passively receive it. In this regard Howe (1983), for example, has written very persuasively about the importance of *mental activity*. If children are asked to re-express the idea in a variety of media (talking, writing, drawing, modelling, etc.), or asked to use the new information creatively, or use it to solve a problem, these processes will oblige them to make extensive connections, to reorganise their semantic networks and so on. In the process, the new learning will become securely embedded. Just one small example comes to mind: I recently saw a class teacher giving out the week's spellings, but she gave them out in the form of anagrams. The children had to solve the anagrams and then learn the spellings – the extra mental activity seemed to do the trick.

Summary

In this chapter we have reviewed evidence accumulated by psychologists and neuroscientists which has helped us understand a good deal about the structure and development of human memory and the ways in which children learn and make sense of their world. Some very clear indications emerge as to what teachers of young children can do in order to help them remember and understand more effectively, as follows:

- gain their attention by making activities purposeful and personally relevant
- adopt a multi-sensory approach to activities
- place new tasks in familiar contexts
- encourage and foster children's self-monitoring of performance
- use explicit discussion and modelling to encourage children to try a wide range of memory strategies
- link new information to actions
- set new information in the context of an event, story or dramatisation
- require children to rehearse their new knowledge
- help children connect new information or ideas to what they already know
- remember the importance of mental activity

These notions sound, in many ways, obvious and straightforward. They have very profound implications, however, for the planning and structuring of Primary school teaching. Applied imaginatively by skilled teachers, what evidence we have suggests that they are capable of transforming children's learning.

Activities

Strategies

Children can sometimes use strategies when they are suggested by a real situation, but cannot deliberately use them in isolation. For this procedure you need to set up a situation in which there is a genuine need to remember, e.g. a dinner party in the home corner and a shop on the opposite side of the room; or taking a message to another teacher; or asking the children to remind you about something later which is important to them. For comparison, you need to give the children something to remember which is equivalent but which they have just 'to remember' for no particular purpose, except you are going to ask them what they can remember later.

You need to make careful observations of the children's responses to these situations, particularly noting any signs of a strategy being used to help themselves remember the information, e.g. rushing before they forget, rehearsing, making connections or elaborations on what they have to remember. You should note down what they say at each stage, and record how much they could remember, and their apparent awareness of whether they had forgotten anything.

Metamemory

Children's knowledge about their own memory abilities, about memory strategies, and about the ease or difficulty of different memory tasks, do appear to develop. In order to investigate this you need a tray of twenty objects, some familiar and some unfamiliar to the children, and which can be sorted into 3–5 categories. You then interview individual children and carefully record their responses, under these three headings:

1 **own abilities:** show the child the tray of twenty objects, arranged randomly on the tray and covered over by a cloth, and ask them to estimate how many objects they will be able to remember if you let them look for thirty seconds. While they are looking you could note down any strategies they use. Record how many they are actually able to remember

2 **strategies:** ask the children what they could do to help themselves remember such a collection of objects

3 **memory tasks:** ask them how you could have made the twenty objects task easier; record any ideas the child has; if they do not offer much, make some suggestions (e.g. arranging them differently,

having fewer objects, giving them a longer time, choosing more familiar objects) and see how they respond.

Helping children to remember and understand

Mental activity

The key idea here is mental activity. The more mental activity we engage in when we are inputting information the more likely we are to remember it. This can be achieved by asking children to generate some of what is to be remembered themselves, or do something with it, like re-arranging it, and by asking them to relate it to what they already know (including the use of mnemonic strategies). Choose something you want the children to remember and try to devise active ways of helping them to remember, for example, ask them to make up a mnemonic (Richard of York Gave Battle in Vain), or a sentence or story or a picture, or ask them to reorganise the material to be remembered (e.g. spellings), or spot patterns in it (e.g. multiplication tables) or groupings in it, or talk about what it reminds them of. Test the children to see what they remember the next day.

Compare this with what they remember of some equivalent information which they have been given and simply asked to copy down and remember.

Repetition

Ask the children to learn something first thing in the morning (and give them 15 minutes) and then get them to tell you what they can remember at the end of the day. Next day, do an equivalent task on three five-minute occasions during the day, and then test at the end of the day. Is there a difference?

Further reading

Baddeley, A.D. (1993) *Your Memory: a User's Guide,* London: Penguin.

Baddeley, A.D. (1997) *Human Memory: Theory and Practice,* Hove, E. Sussex: Psychology Press.

Cassells, A. (1991) *Remembering and Forgetting,* (Open Learning Unit) Leicester: BPS Books.

Coulson, M. (1995) 'Models of Memory Development', in Lee, V. and Gupta, P.D. (eds) *Children's Cognitive and Language Development,* Oxford: Blackwell.

Kail, R. (1990) *The Development of Memory in Children,* 3rd Ed., New York: Freeman.

Parkin, A.J. (1993) *Memory: Phenomena, Experiment and Theory,* Oxford: Blackwell.

Siegler, R.S. (1991) 'Memory Development', in *Children's Thinking*, 2nd Ed., Englewood Cliffs, N. Jersey: Prentice Hall.

References

Atkinson, R.C. and Shiffrin, R.M. (1968) 'Human memory: a proposed system and its control processes', in Spence, K.W. and Spence, J.T. (eds) *The Psychology of Learning and Motivation, Vol. 2*, London: Academic Press.

Baddeley, A.D. (1986) *Working Memory*, Oxford: Oxford University Press.

Baddeley, A.D. and Hitch, G. (1974) 'Working memory', in Bower, G.H. (ed.) *The Psychology of Learning and Motivation, Vol. 8*, London: Academic Press.

Bruner, J.S. (1974) 'The Growth of Representational Processes in Childhood', in *Beyond the Information Given*, London: George Allen & Unwin.

Chi, M.T.H. (1978) 'Knowledge structures and memory development', in Siegler, R.S. (ed.) *Children's thinking: What develops?* Hillsdale, N.J.: Erlbaum.

Chi, M.T.H. and Koeske, R.D. (1983) 'Network representation of a child's dinosaur knowledge', *Developmental Psychology*, 19, 29–39.

Craik, F.I.M. and Lockhart, R.S. (1972) 'Levels of processing: a framework for memory research', *Journal of Verbal Learning and Verbal Behaviour*, 11, 671–84.

Conway, M.A. *et al.* (1997) 'Changes in memory awareness during learning: the acquisition of knowledge by psychology undergraduates', *Journal of Experimental Psychology*, 126 General, 393–413.

Dempster, F.N. (1981) 'Memory span: Sources of individual and developmental differences', *Psychological Bulletin*, 89, 63–100.

Flavell, J.H., Beach, D.R. and Chinsky, J.M. (1966) 'Spontaneous verbal rehearsal in a memory task as a function of age', *Child Development*, 37, 283–99.

Hagen, J.W. and Hale, G.A. (1973) 'The development of attention in children', in Pick, A.D. (ed.) *Minnesota symposium on child psychology, Vol. 7*, Minneapolis: University of Minnesota Press.

Hebb, D.O. (1949) *The Organisation of Behaviour*, New York: Wiley.

Howe, M.J.A. (1983) *A Teacher's Guide to the Psychology of Learning*, Oxford: Basil Blackwell.

Istomina, Z.M. (1975) 'The development of voluntary memory in pre-school-age children', *Soviet Psychology*, 13, 5–64.

Miller, G.A. (1956) 'The magical number seven, plus or minus two: some limits on our capacity for processing information', *Psychological Review*, 63, 81–97.

Nisbet, J. and Shucksmith, J. (1986) *Learning Strategies*, London: Routledge & Kegan Paul.

Tulving, E. (1985) 'How many memory systems are there?' *American Psychologist*, 40, 385–398

Wellman, H.M. (1977) 'Tip of the tongue and feeling of knowing experiences: a developmental study of memory-monitoring' *Child Development*, 48, 13–21.

8 Teaching children to think, reason, solve problems and be creative

David Whitebread

EDITOR'S SUMMARY

Within education there is increasing recognition that, in a changing world, children need to learn more than just a body of knowledge. They need to learn to be creative in their thinking and become expert problem solvers. This chapter reviews the evidence about the development of children's thinking. It emerges that, contrary to the earlier views of such as Piaget, even very young children are able to reason to a high level in context. What needs to be recognised by educators, however, is that they learn by induction and by analogy, and that they learn to be flexible in their thinking through play. A problem-solving approach to learning which encourages children to be playful and creative, and to take risks, is, therefore, always going to be the most powerful. The final part of the chapter looks at approaches to teaching children to think, solve problems and develop their creativity which encourage the key developments of becoming more exhaustive in their information processing, more able to comprehend relations of successively higher orders, more flexible in their use of strategies and information and more sophisticated in their reflections upon and control of their own thinking.

The title of this chapter may appear to many readers to be nonsensical. Children, they will say, are perfectly capable of thinking and reasoning (as I have discovered on countless occasions when I have tried to persuade my own children to do anything at all that they don't wish to do, and have finished up having to agree with them that my request was clearly unreasonable and probably immoral, hypocritical and just plain dangerous, and further evidence of my inadequacies as a parent!). Children, many readers will also agree, are very often quite ingenious in their problem-solving abilities and highly original and creative – you only have to watch them at play on a computer game, effortlessly outscoring their elders and betters, or at play making up mythical adventures, inventing extraordinary games or building their own weird inventions and contraptions to realise that.

Yet it is also clear that there are, in fact, huge individual differences in these kinds of highly valued abilities. It is also clear that teachers can have a very powerful role in either encouraging and stimulating this kind of mental activity or, sadly, in discouraging and extinguishing it. This chapter attempts to review what psychologists have discovered about the essential nature of these aspects of human intellectual functioning, and the implications of what they have found for Primary school teachers. Evidence will be reviewed which indicates that children can be helped to think and reason more effectively, to become better problem-solvers and to be much more creative. Notwithstanding the examples above, it is, of course, the case that children do become more able generally in these areas as they develop through childhood and into adulthood. What psychologists have attempted to unravel is the precise nature of this development and why it blossoms so much more powerfully in some individuals than in others.

The other key element in the argument of this chapter is the fundamental contribution in these areas of learning through play. Evidence will be reviewed which has indicated that human beings' capacity for playfulness of all kinds – humour, games, imaginative pretending and so on – are all very much a piece with our more general intellectual abilities.

Piaget and his influence

Any discussion in this kind of area has to begin with the work of Piaget. His contribution to our understanding about the nature of the development of children's intellectual abilities is, of course, enormous. He was active professionally for around sixty years, carried out thousands of studies of young children's thinking and published hundreds of books and learned articles. There is not space here to review his research and theory in any detail (see Ch. 11 in Smith, Cowie and Blades 1998 for a good introduction and Chs 1 and 2 in Meadows 1983, for a review of his theory and analysis of his impact on Primary education). However, the point which we need to address here is his general view of the nature of children's learning and thinking and how it develops. Essentially, he made two major claims:

- that children are active thinkers and learners who construct their own understandings
- that development consists of acquiring a range of logical structures or understandings about the world

As we shall see, subsequent research has very much borne out and supported the first claim, but largely dismissed the second.

Constructivism

Piaget's view of the child as actively attempting to construct their own under-standings of the world was very enthusiastically welcomed by psychologists and educationalists in the early 1960s when very large cracks were beginning to appear in the behaviourist view of human learning which was predomi-nant in the first half of the twentieth century. The behaviourist view was that learning consisted of forming simple associations between events and was dependent upon external reward or reinforcement. Increasingly, psycholo-gists began to recognise that such a model could not explain the richness, diversity and sheer creativity of human learning. The behaviourist model viewed the learner as a passive recipient of learning. What became clear, however, through the work of Piaget and others, was that much of human learning takes place for its own sake and as a consequence of an intrinsic desire actively to make sense of the world.

The kind of model of human learning which developed from this view is illustrated in Figure 8.1. Here every aspect of the interaction between the learner and the environment is seen as active and dynamic. Rather than pas-sively receiving information, the learner actively perceives and selects the information they are seeking. The information is not simply stored, it is sifted, categorised and re-organised, patterns are detected and rules, 'schema' or concepts constructed. Similarly, the consequent actions or behaviour of the learner are not simply a 'response' to a 'stimulus', as the behaviourists would have it, but are consequent upon hypotheses and pre-dictions generated about the way the world works and strategies and plans developed to act effectively upon it.

The example is often quoted of the way in which children learn language. According to a behaviourist view, this is a laborious process whereby every word and utterance the child learns is initially imitated from an adult and learnt as a consequence of reinforcement by external reward (adult smil-ing). However, it is clear that the rate at which children learn to understand and use language is far too rapid for this kind of explanation and, in any case, they typically produce a constant stream of completely novel utterances (in my family we even have words and whole phrases which we now all use, but which were originally invented by the children). In English, many of these novel words and phrases that children produce, furthermore, are clearly the consequence of misapplying patterns and rules which they have constructed for themselves. For example, you will hear young children say that yesterday they 'goed to the shops and buyed something'. They will not have heard an adult say this; nor has any adult taught them that you create the past tense by adding on 'ed'. This is a pattern or regularity that they have detected from the huge variety of their experience of spoken English.

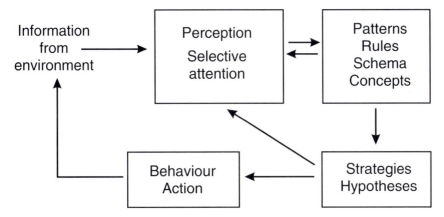

Figure 8.1 How children learn: a constructivist model

Young children's reasoning

While Piaget's notion that children actively construct their own understandings of the world has been largely confirmed by later research, his view of the nature of children's intellectual development has not. Essentially, his view was that there are certain 'logical structures' or 'schema' which young children do not understand, and which are fundamental to logical thinking. Young children's thinking was seen as being dominated by their immediate sensory perceptions and thus illogical.

He claimed, for example, that young children could only see the world from their own point of view and were thus 'egocentric' in their reasoning and understanding. This was demonstrated by his famous 'three mountains' experiment (see Figure 8.2). Here, the child was required to demonstrate that they could understand the point of view of a doll sitting opposite them on the other side of the three mountains by selecting a picture of the correct 'view' from a selection offered. Many young children under the age of 6 or 7 years failed this task and selected a picture of their own 'view'. However, subsequent work has demonstrated fairly conclusively that it was the demands of this particular task which confused young children and not any deficiency in their reasoning. For example, when Hughes (cited in Donaldson 1978) used a task which involved taking another's point of view, but which made far more 'human sense' to young children, many more young children were successful. This was the 'hiding game' task which involved hiding a naughty doll from a policeman (or policemen) behind some walls (see Figure 8.2). In some versions of this game the child was required to 'hide the doll from the policemen' in a position in which the doll was clearly in view from the child's point of view (quadrant C).

Other researchers have shown that young children do understand the 'object concept' (that an object continues to exist even when we can't see it),

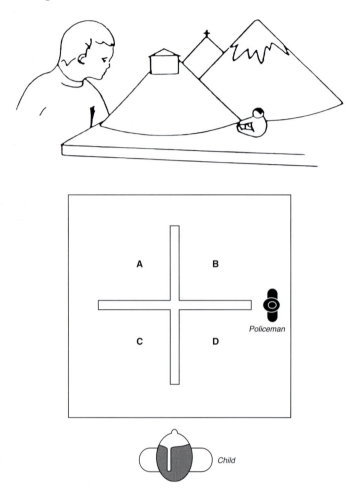

Figure 8.2 Piaget's 'three mountains' experiment and Hughes' 'hiding game'

and can make 'transitive inferences' (if A>B and B>C, then A>C) but fail Piaget's tasks through short-term memory problems (see Brainerd 1983). They can also understand the conservation of number, weight, volume, etc., but fail Piaget's tasks because they are abstract, misleading and rely upon over-sophisticated linguistic skills (Donaldson 1978). Even fairly sophisticated aspects of human cognition such as reasoning by analogy turn out to be well within the compass of very young children, provided that the context is meaningful to them and within their experience (Goswami 1992).

Indeed, all the evidence suggests that young children's abilities to think and reason are considerable and are in many respects comparable to those of adults. Thus, Klahr (1978) provided the following scenario (from his own experience) as an example of the power of young children's reasoning:

Child and father in yard. Child's playmate appears on bike.

CHILD: Daddy, would you unlock the basement door?
DADDY: Why?
CHILD: 'Cause I want to ride my bike.
DADDY: Your bike is in the garage.
CHILD: But my socks are in the dryer.

The stages of reasoning accomplished in an instant by Klahr's young child are explicated as follows:

Top goal: ride bike
Constraint: shoes or sneakers on
Fact: feet are bare

Subgoal 1: get shod
Fact: sneakers in yard
Fact: sneakers hurt on bare feet

Subgoal 2: protect feet (get socks)
Fact: sock drawer was empty this morning
Inference: socks still in dryer

Subgoal 3: get to dryer
Fact: dryer in basement

Subgoal 4: enter basement
Fact: long route through house, short route through yard entrance
Fact: yard entrance always locked

Subgoal 5: unlock yard entrance
Fact: Daddies have all the keys to everything

Subgoal 6: ask Daddy

(Klahr 1978:181–2)

Reasoning by induction and analogy

There are, however, certain kinds of logical reasoning which children find very difficult. Contrary to Piaget's belief, adult humans do not appear to reason logically either and have the same kinds of logical problems as children. The kinds of reasoning problems experienced by both adults and children are very useful, and have been extensively researched, because they give us clear indications of the nature of human reasoning. I will just mention three kinds of problems.

First, with certain kinds of syllogistic and deductive reasoning adults commonly make exactly the same kinds of errors as children (see Garnham and Oakhill 1994, for a useful review). Thus, consider the following problem:

There are two kinds of aliens, Blobs and Blips.
Blobs are blue.
I meet an alien. It is blue.
What kind of an alien is it?

Many children and adults will confidently tell you that it is a Blob. However, this is not necessarily the case. Because we have been told Blobs are blue, the human tendency is to infer that Blips are not blue, but we have not been told this. They could be blue also, and the alien could be a Blip.

Second, we know that adults as well as children find abstract reasoning problems more difficult than ones placed in a real, practical context. Wason and Johnson-Laird (1972), for example, posed the following 'four card' problems (see Figure 8.3). In the numbers and letters version (a), we are told that each card has a number on one side and a letter on the other. Our task is to name those cards, and only those cards, which need to be turned over in order to determine whether the rule (set out below the cards) is true or false. In the open and sealed envelopes version (b), we are asked to pretend that we are working for the Post Office and our job is to make sure that no one is under-paying, that is, we have to say which envelopes, and only which envelopes, we would need to turn over to make sure that customers were obeying the rule set out below the envelopes.

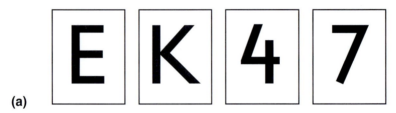

(a)

If a card has a vowel on one side,
then it has an even number on
the other side.

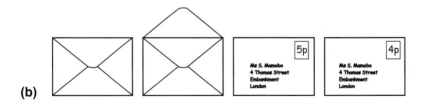

(b)

If a letter is sealed, then it has
a 5p stamp on it.

Figure 8.3 Wason and Johnson-Laird's 'Four card' problem

The correct answer to (a) is the vowel (E) and the odd number (7), not the even number (4). The correct answer to (b) is the sealed envelope and the one with the 4p stamp on. Most adults (even University undergraduates!) find the more abstract version (a) difficult and often make mistakes. The more practically contextualised version (b) is nearly always found to be much easier although logically it is an identical problem.

Third, it turns out that human beings are good at generating hypotheses about the world, but they are not good at testing them out logically or 'scientifically'. Consider, for example, the '2, 4, 6' problem invented by Wason (1960), which you might like to try out on a friend. In this, the subject is told that they have to discover the rule for the production of series of three numbers. To start them off the experimenter writes down a series which conforms to the rule: 2, 4, 6. The subject then has to write down other series of three numbers and each time the experimenter tells them whether the series conforms to the rule. When they think they know the rule, the subject states what they think it is, and the experimenter tells them whether they are correct or not. If they are not correct, they continue writing down series. The rule is: any three numbers in ascending order.

Typically, it turns out to be remarkably difficult to discover this rule. Most subjects generate a hypothesis from the initial series of three numbers – numbers going up in twos, perhaps – and adopt a 'confirmation strategy', producing other series which conform to this rule: 24, 26, 28, for example. After a few trials like this, they will then announce the rule and are surprised when they are told it is incorrect. This is because generally humans are predisposed to learn by the inductive process of pattern matching and not by the hypothesis falsification strategy of formal science, which you need to adopt in order to solve this problem (i.e. by testing out series which do *not* conform to your rule).

From all this various evidence a picture of human reasoning emerges as consisting of two enormously powerful and fundamental processes, namely *induction* and *analogy*. Induction consists of constructing general rules or patterns from a variety of particular instances as illustrated earlier in the case of children learning language. This combined with the use of analogy presents human beings as predominantly learning by pattern detection and matching, or understanding and interpreting new phenomena by trying to find existing knowledge upon which it may be mapped. When confronted with a new problem we do not analyse it logically; rather we try to find an analogous problem with which we are already familiar and apply the same rules or strategies. As we shall see, these fundamental processes have enormous implications for teaching children to think, solve problems and be creative.

What develops?

If it is the case, then, as we have seen, that it is not the ability to reason *per se* which develops through childhood, what is it that develops and enables the adult to think, reason, solve problems and be more creative than the young child? If we can discern this, then we have a guide as to what the Primary school teacher might do to facilitate useful developments.

There is, of course, a huge body of psychological research and theory devoted to this question and there is not space here to give anything like an adequate review. Siegler (1991) and Meadows (1993) both do this job admirably. Certain key elements do emerge, however, from this literature, which have important implications for teaching young children. Sternberg and Powell (1983), after an extensive review of psychological approaches to learning, including Behaviourism, Piagetian constructivism and more recent Information-processing approaches, provide a useful synthesis of four key areas in which there is clear development, which follow.

More exhaustive information processing

As regards the first point, there is extensive research showing that, as children grow older, they become less impulsive and more reflective, that is, less likely to respond too quickly to a situation or problem before they have had chance to assimilate all the relevant information. We will all have experienced the tendency of young children to do this. Sometimes when being given instructions about a new task they rush off (out of pure excitement!) and then have to come back to find out what it was exactly that they had to do. There are also, however, considerable individual differences in this area of 'cognitive tempo' and these can have important consequences for children's learning. Borkowski *et al.* (1983), for example, demonstrated significant relationships between impulsivity-reflectivity, metamemory, strategy use and performance on a range of memory tasks. It is also a well-researched finding that gifted children and adults spend longer 'encoding' a problem before responding than do average children (see, for example, Sternberg and Rifkin's 1979 study of analogical reasoning).

In the light of this evidence, it is perhaps worth reflecting on the balance which is struck in many Primary school classrooms between encouraging children to get on quickly and complete tasks and to take time to reflect carefully and systematically upon the task before attempting it. The evidence in this area would suggest that a curriculum which requires too much breadth at the expense of any depth may be dangerously counter-productive.

The ability to comprehend relations of successively higher orders

There is a clear and well-documented progression in children's thinking from being only able to consider the particular task, problem, object or incident at hand to being able to consider issues at a more abstract level, where a range of different instances might be taken on board simultaneously. As the work of Donaldson (1978) and others have shown, children's ability to reason is particularly context dependent. Primary school teachers are very familiar with this phenomenon, whereby children appear to understand an idea on one day, but can be completely baffled by a slight change to the way it is presented on the next.

The development of the ability to see relationships between different tasks would appear to be dependent upon the accumulation and continual restructuring of knowledge, driven by the processes of induction and analogy discussed above. This issue of 'transfer' is a crucial one in learning. Research reviewed by Meadows (1993) indicates that children are more likely to be able to transfer understandings or processes from one task to another where:

- the skill or procedure has been thoroughly learned
- the learner encounters a range of examples with a common structure but different irrelevant characteristics
- the abstract rule is made explicit
- the new task 'appears' similar to the old task.

Often the problem is simply that young children do not search their own existing knowledge as thoroughly as they might in order to find previous experiences which would be helpful. Several studies have indicated that showing a group of children the materials for a new task and, before setting the actual task, asking them to brainstorm ideas of what the task might involve dramatically increases their chances of successfully tackling the task when it is set. Resnick and Glaser (1976), for example, taught 7 and 8 year old children to change a parallelogram into a rectangle and to find the area of a rectangle. Their subsequent success at finding the area of a parallelogram was enormously increased by questioning beforehand aimed at reminding the children of what they already knew.

The ability to deal with higher order and more abstract relationships is also dependent upon the use of language and other forms of symbolic representation. These enable information to be 'chunked' into larger units which can then be processed and manipulated more easily. The work of Vygotsky (1986) on tools, signs and symbols in the development of human thinking, and Bruner (1973) on the development of enactive, iconic and symbolic modes of representation, has been most significant in this area. In the 'Nine glasses' experiment Bruner (Bruner and Kenney 1966) demonstrated the power of one form of symbolic representation, namely language, as a 'tool of thought'. In this experiment young children were presented with nine glasses arranged in a pattern on a 3 × 3 matrix (see Figure 8.4).

The children were asked to describe the pattern. The nine glasses were then removed from the matrix and jumbled. The children were asked to replace them onto the matrix in the original pattern. The glasses were removed and jumbled again, but this time the bottom left glass in the original pattern was placed in the bottom right corner of the matrix, and the children were then asked to replace the glasses in a similar pattern to the original. Bruner discovered, very significantly, that, while most of the

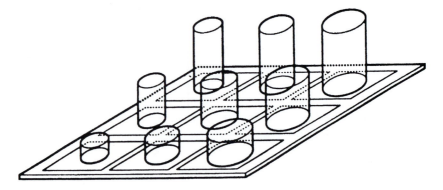

Figure 8.4 The 'Nine glasses' problem (from Bruner and Kenney 1966)

children could reproduce the original pattern, there was a very close association between the ability to describe the original pattern by using words such as 'tall', 'wide', 'short', 'thin', etc. and the ability to produce the second, transformed pattern. He thus argued that the ability to process and transform information is dependent upon the ability to represent it symbolically.

This kind of evidence suggests very powerfully that requiring children to express and represent their understandings in a variety of symbolic ways – talk, writing, drawing and so on – is enormously beneficial. As anyone who has ever taught knows, being required to explain something to someone else is often the best way to come to understand it oneself.

It is worth noting at this point that some important approaches to teaching children to think and be creative, which are reviewed below, are significant mostly for their contribution in this area. Philosophy for Children, for example, focuses quite explicitly on encouraging children to articulate and represent their thinking and consequently reconstruct their understandings.

Flexibility in the use of strategy or information and the development more sophisticated control strategies (metacomponents)

The last two key areas of development identified by Sternberg and Powell are very much inter-linked and so we can deal with them together. We now know, through the work of neuroscientists, that, unlike a computer, the human brain carries out several processes simultaneously. As a consequence, we are capable of carrying out intellectual or physical tasks and simultaneously monitoring what we are doing. That this is fundamental to human learning has been established by a huge amount of research in the last twenty years or so concerned with the development of what have become known as metacognitive processes and abilities. What emerges from this literature is a three stage process whereby we become increasingly able to construct, select and customise cognitive strategies to enable us to carry out ever more different and demanding tasks with maximum mental efficiency. This process consists of:

- monitoring and evaluating our cognitive processes
- building up metacognitive knowledge about tasks and our own intellectual processes and abilities
- constructing and selecting ever more appropriate strategies.

I have written more fully about these processes in Ch. 7 of this book and there are many other excellent reviews (e.g. Robinson 1983; Roberts and Erdos 1993). What it is important to note here, however, is that developing these kinds of abilities is crucial to children's development as thinkers and learners, precisely because they enable children to take what they have learnt in one area and use it in another. A wide range of evidence has shown that it is in these abilities that many children with learning difficulties are particularly weak (e.g. see Sugden 1989). As we shall see, the development of metacognitive abilities is a central element in most programmes designed to improve children's thinking.

The other point to note here is that the development of human thinking is characterised by increasing flexibility. Uniquely, as human beings, we are capable of dealing with new situations, of solving new problems and of being genuinely creative. Within neuroscience this flexibility of thought is commonly referred to as the 'plasticity' of the human brain (e.g. Greenfield 1997). We are unlike any other species in the extent that our brain grows after birth (it roughly quadruples in size in the first four years and continues growing well into our teenage years). This enables us to adapt to the circumstances in which we find ourselves, and to continue to adapt to changing circumstances, to a degree far beyond the capacity of any other species.

This growth in size is not accommodating the growth of new cells; rather it is accommodating the growth of new connections. We are born with all the brain cells we are ever going to have, but throughout life these cells continually form literally hundreds of thousands of connections with other cells. The connections made in the first few years are overwhelmingly important, however, because they construct the basic neural architecture upon which further learning will be imposed. This finding has led to the increased recognition of the importance of Nursery and Primary education over recent years. It has also lead to the increasing recognition of the importance of children's play for their intellectual development and it is to this issue which I now wish to turn.

Play and the development of flexible thinking

Psychologists have been researching and developing theories about the nature and purposes of children's play since the middle of the nineteenth century. It has been suggested as a mechanism for letting off steam, for providing relaxation, for relieving boredom, for practising for adult life, for living out our fantasies and many more. That it is important in children's development, however, has never been in doubt. As Moyles (1989) demonstrated, for every aspect of human development and functioning, there is a form of play.

It is only in the last twenty to thirty years, however, that its significance for thinking, problem-solving and creativity has been fully recognised. Bruner (1972), in a famous article entitled 'The nature and uses of immaturity', is generally credited with first pointing out to psychologists and educationalists the relationship across different animal species between the capacity for learning and the length of immaturity, or dependence upon adults. He also pointed out that as the period of immaturity lengthens, so does the extent to which the young are playful. He argued that play is one of the key experiences through which young animals learn, and also the means by which their intellectual abilities themselves are developed. The human being, of course, has a much greater length of immaturity than any other animal, plays more and for longer, and is supreme, of course, in flexibility of thought. The more recent neuroscientific evidence has very much supported Bruner's position.

Play, in Bruner's view, is all about developing flexibility of thought. It provides opportunities to try out possibilities, to put different elements of a situation together in various ways, to look at problems from different viewpoints. He demonstrated this in a series of experiments (e.g. see Sylva, Bruner and Genova 1976) where children were asked to solve practical problems. Typically in these experiments, one group of children was given the opportunity to play with the objects involved, while the other group was 'taught' how to use the objects in ways which would help solve the problem. Consistently, the 'play' group subsequently outperformed the 'taught' group when they were then left alone to tackle the problem. The children who had the experience of playing with the materials were more inventive in devising strategies to solve the problem, they persevered longer when their initial attempts did not work, and so were not surprisingly more successful in their attempts to solve the problem.

Observation of children at play gives some indication of why it might be such a powerful learning medium. During play children are usually totally engrossed in what they are doing (see Figure 8.5). It is quite often repetitive and contains a strong element of practice. During play children set their own level of challenge, and so what they are doing is always developmentally appropriate (to a degree which tasks set by adults will never be). Play is spontaneous and initiated by the children themselves; in other words, during play children are in control of their own learning.

Guha (1987) has argued that this last element is particularly significant. There are many examples in psychological research of tasks where being in control has turned out to be crucial for effective learning. Guha cites, for example, experiments concerned with visual learning in which subjects are required to wear 'goggles' which make everything look upside down. They are then required to sit in a wheelchair and learn to move safely through an

Figure 8.5 During play children are usually totally engrossed in what they are doing

environment. The results of such experiments show that subjects moving themselves around the environment (and having a lot of initial 'crashes') learn to do this much more quickly than those who are wheeled safely about by an adult helper.

The parallels here with Bruner's 'play' and 'taught' groups are striking. There are also clear implications for how we can most effectively help young children to learn. Whenever a new material, task or process is introduced, it is clear that children's learning will be enhanced if they are first allowed to play with them in a relatively unstructured manner. When new information is being introduced, children need to be offered opportunities to incorporate this into their play also. The other important finding for teachers, however, is that there is an important role for the teacher in participating and intervening in children's play. Smith (1990), in an extensive review, examines the evidence relating to the issue of structured and unstructured play. He concludes that there is a role in learning for both kinds of play; sensitive adult intervention can usefully enhance the intellectual challenge, mainly by opening up new possibilities and opportunities. Manning and Sharp (1977) have provided a very thorough and practical analysis of ways in which teachers can usefully structure and extend children's play in the classroom. I want to conclude this chapter by looking at approaches to developing children's thinking, reasoning, problem-solving and creativity, the most successful of which, I would want to argue, are those which are playful.

Teaching children to think and reason

In the last ten years or so there has been an enormous blossoming of interest, within the psychology of education community, in teaching children to think. As McGuinness (1999) has concluded, however, while a whole wealth of different programmes have been developed and trialled, they have had an almost negligible impact within Primary schools. This is perhaps not surprising, given all the other developments and innovations with which Primary schools have had to cope over the last decade. However, the latest version of the National Curriculum for England (DfEE/QCA 1999) quite explicitly sets out a range of thinking skills which it is intended will be enhanced by teaching throughout the curriculum, so it seems likely that this concern will now be given more attention.

A major area of debate has been whether it is more effective to teach thinking skills as a separate activity from the rest of the curriculum, or whether this teaching should be embedded in the teaching of curriculum subjects. What we know about children's reliance on meaningful contexts to enhance their learning (e.g. Donaldson 1978) would suggest that an embedded approach is more likely to be successful, and this is the certainly the conclusion reached by a number of general reviews of the evidence, including that of McGuinness (1999). Burden and Williams (1998) have produced a comprehensive review of work analysing the thinking skills embedded in a wide range of National Curriculum subjects, and methodologies for teaching them.

Essentially, there are two general approaches embodied within the programmes which appear to be most successful, namely what has become known as 'cognitive apprenticeship', which includes 'scaffolding' techniques and metacognitive and strategy training.

Scaffolding and cognitive apprenticeship

Several successful approaches rely upon particular styles of interaction to support and stimulate children's thinking; Collins, Brown and Newman (1989) and Tharp and Gallimore (1988) have both analysed ways in which scaffolding, coaching, modelling, questioning, cognitive structuring and so on by skilful teachers can make their thinking explicit to children and provide clear feedback; this combination appears to enable children to learn to think much in the same way that the special way we talk to very young children (sometimes referred to as 'motherese') enables them to learn to speak a language.

These approaches also require children to articulate their own thinking in ways which, as we have seen, the work of Bruner and Vygotsky has indicated are likely to help children think more flexibly and at more sophisticated levels. A notable example here is the Philosophy for Children programme.

Philosophy for Children was originally devised by Matthew Lipman (1988) in America and has been extensively developed there and in the UK (Costello, 2000, provides an excellent up-to-date review of work in this area). Essentially the approach consists of starting with a children's story which raises moral or personal or philosophical issues. By various carefully structured procedures the teacher then draws out from the children which issues particularly interest or intrigue them: it might be related to the motivation and feelings of one of the characters in the story, or how one character has interacted with another. This then develops into a kind of Socratic philosophical discussion where the teacher raises questions of clarification and so requires the children to articulate their views and arguments ever more clearly. Carried out with skill and sensitivity, it can be an extremely involving experience for young children who, as we know, care desperately about fairness, people's feelings, and so on, and are deeply intrigued by some of the big human issues such as love and death.

Children can learn a great deal from this kind of approach. They develop their abilities to articulate their ideas, their ideas themselves become better structured and, particularly if there is an element of playfulness in the approach adopted, they learn to enjoy 'playing around with ideas', which is fundamental to so much high level problem-solving and creativity.

Metacognition and cognitive strategies

As McGuiness (1999), Ashman and Conway (1997), Schunk and Zimmerman (1994) and many others have reviewed, metacognitive training is a fundamental element in nearly all approaches to teaching children to think. Essentially, this involves requiring children to think and reflect upon their own thinking or the strategies they use to carry out particular cognitive tasks. Perhaps the most obvious example, frequently observed in Primary classrooms, involves children in carrying out some mental arithmetic and then, rather than just seeing who arrived at the correct answer, discussing all the different strategies that different people used. A variety of methods have been developed within different programmes to enhance reflection and promote self-regulation (i.e. deliberate selection and control of strategies). These include thinking aloud, pair problem-solving, co-operative learning, reciprocal teaching and group discussion. These can be occasional, one-off events or, as in the case of the Thinking Books approach (involving children keeping journals of their reflections on their own learning) developed by Swan and White (1994), they can be a long-term and fundamental aspect of the children's lives in the classroom. Fisher (1990) has provided a highly readable and practical account of a number of these approaches. What is excitingly clear is that once children begin to reflect upon their own thinking, the quality of their achievements dramatically improves and their new-found self-regulatory abilities snowball, as they become increasingly strategic in a range of areas (e.g. see the model of the 'good strategy user' in Pressley *et al.* 1987).

Teaching children to solve problems

Problem-solving approaches to teaching children in the Primary school have long been advocated and, in places, have been well developed. The relatively new area of the curriculum devoted to Design Technology embodies the essentially problem-solving approach of the Design Process (see Figure 8.6). Other areas of the curriculum, such as mathematics and science, have also contained a strong element of problem-solving. Fisher (1987) and de Boo (1999) have both provided inspiring reviews of work being carried out in Primary schools using problem-solving and investigational approaches across the curriculum. Such approaches, I would wish to argue, are highly effective in motivating and helping children to learn because they rely upon the strengths of the human brain as a learning organism. The processes of induction and analogy, to which I referred earlier, lend themselves naturally to solving new problems and discovering general rules and principles from them (rather than having to learn the same rules and principles in the abstract).

I have written elsewhere (Whitebread 1997) about the particular opportunities which adventure games and other story-based 'problems' or database software, available on Primary school computers, offer in relation to developing children's problem-solving. In that article I attempted to demonstrate that, through the use of these resources, children could gain practice at each of the processes involved in solving any problem, which are as follows:

- understanding and representing the problem (including identifying what kinds of information are relevant to its solution)
- gathering and organising relevant information
- constructing and managing a plan of action, or a strategy
- reasoning, hypothesis testing and decision-making

Figure 8.6 Problem-solving through design technology

- using various problem-solving tools (drawings, maps and other representations).

Analysis within the psychological literature of expertise (e.g. see Mayer 1992) has shown that the skill of an expert in solving problems in any particular area fundamentally amounts to having a bigger repertoire of previous problems to draw upon and being able to identify more reliably which of these known problems is appropriately analogous to the new one. Once again, we come back to the issue of playfulness and flexibility of thinking. My enthusiasm for adventure games is precisely because they require and encourage a playful and flexible approach and are set in motivating, narrative scenarios which give purpose and meaning to the children's endeavours.

Teaching children to be creative

The issue of flexible representations is also central to the notion of creativity. As Edward de Bono, the inventor of the term 'lateral thinking', has been arguing for many years, in many different books (e.g. de Bono 1970, 1976) being creative is not an activity confined solely to the Arts, but is fundamental to thinking in any area of human activity and is about being able to see problems in new and different ways. This can involve looking at things from different points of view, putting together two apparently unrelated ideas, seeing one problem as analogous to another rather different one, and so on. This has been true of great inventions and brilliant insights throughout history. It

Figure 8.7 A bicycle for postmen

is also, of course, at the root of much of what passes for humour. Children's delight in all kinds of verbal, physical and visual humour is not unrelated to their essential creativity. In a distinguished review of the psychological study of creativity, Finke *et al.* (1992) address a range of processes, fundamental to creativity, which are about flexible representations and being playful with ideas: creative visualisation, creative invention, conceptual synthesis, structured imagination, insight, brainstorming and divergent thinking all feature in their review.

One of the most delightful of de Bono's books (de Bono 1972) involved a technique for stimulating children's creative problem-solving which can be used directly by Primary school teachers. In this, he asked young children to draw solutions to a variety of imaginative problems, cleverly designed to intrigue them and inspire their imaginations. Such problems included 'stop a cat and dog fighting', 'weigh an elephant', 'improve the human body' and 'a bicycle for postmen' (see Figure 8.7). In the introduction to the book, de Bono bemoans the fact that children produce much more imaginative and innovative solutions to such problems than do adults (well, business executives, at any rate!) Perhaps justifiably, he sees this as a problem of education, and he may be right in saying that creativity has been under-valued in our

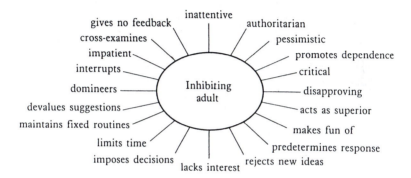

Figure 8.8 Creating a climate in which creativity and problem-solving can flourish (from Fisher 1990)

education system hitherto. What is clear, however, is that creativity and problem-solving are increasingly valued abilities in the modern world, and within Primary education we have the opportunity to make a real contribution in this area. Anna Craft (2000) has recently produced an excellent guide to the development of creativity across the Primary curriculum.

The classroom environment

I have tried to argue that in fostering and encouraging playful approaches to thinking, reasoning, problem-solving and creativity we are likely to have considerable and real impact on children's learning at a very fundamental level. Rather than being a set of techniques, however, this has to be a whole approach to our classroom teaching, including the basic ways in which the class operates, works, makes decisions and so on. The kinds of thinking and learning we have been discussing are about trying things out, being ridiculous or outrageous, taking risks, 'seeing what happens if', having a go and so on. These approaches will not flourish unless the teacher sets the right kind of tone and ethos. This is particularly important since it is precisely the children who are not such confident learners, and who are not so sure of their own abilities, who may well benefit the most from these more creative and open-ended approaches, but whose first little forays into uncertainty will be the most easily crushed. Fisher (1990) discusses this issue helpfully in terms of the 'encouraging' adult and the 'inhibiting' adult (see Figure 8.8). I would ask you to conclude your reading of this chapter by spending a few moments looking at this diagram and thinking about the implications for your practice in your classroom. There are clear and powerful reasons why many teachers will often inhibit children's creativity. We have a National Curriculum to teach, we have to keep order, we have to provide for the needs of over thirty little persons simultaneously and we have to remain sane! It is more difficult to always be an encouraging adult, but it is worth thinking about, because the rewards are enormous, and are why many of us wanted to teach young children in the first place.

Activities

Learning to think: philosophy for children

The complete Philosophy for Children approach is quite extensive and you would be advised to go on a training day, or at least to read up about this a little more first. As a starter, though, you might like to try reading a story which raises issues about fairness, friendship, freedom or some other big issue and then leading a discussion amongst your class. Here are some golden rules to follow and some ways of stimulating and supporting the discussion:

- Let the children choose the topic or issue for discussion.
- Practice active listening – repeat back what children say, summarise, point out links.
- Be accepting of opinions, but point out contradictions, where one child's view disagrees with another.
- Point out implications of children's views.
- Record main points on the board where everyone can see and refer back.
- Give examples which are 'tricky'.
- Play the devil's advocate.
- Make it clear that these are difficult areas, that you don't know all the answers.
- Allow completely off-the-wall ideas and have fun, but don't seriously accept 'magic' solutions.

If it goes well you will have to do this again and again because the children will demand it. If it doesn't go well, think about how you could do it better next time. It's probably a good idea to start working in this way collaboratively with one or two colleagues, then you can compare notes and learn from one another. Good luck!

Problem solving

There are, of course, endless practical problems that can be set in a Design Technology framework. Building towers and bridges with newspaper is always a favourite. Given a standard amount of newspaper and sticky tape, who can build the tallest, strongest, (etc.) bridge? There are lots of books available with these kinds of challenges in, of the 'Great Egg Race' variety. I would also recommend trying a computer adventure game: Grannies Garden, Lemmings, Crystal Rain Forest, Dinosaur Discovery are all excellent, and there are many more. I also like intellectual puzzles of all kinds. For example, there are all kinds of crossing the river problems.

The canoe problem

> Two men and two boys want to cross a river.
> Their canoe will only take one man or two boys.
> How do they all get across?

Hobbits and Orcs

> Three Hobbits and three Orcs need to cross a river.
> There is only one boat which they must share.
> The boat can only hold two creatures at a time.
> The Orcs must never be allowed to outnumber the Hobbits on
>   either bank of the river, or they will overpower and eat them.
> How do they all get across safely?

Remember that perhaps the most important part of all these problem-solving activities is the talk and discussion that they generate, so always have children working collaboratively in small groups (a pair is a group!)

Being creative

A good starting point is to ask the children in your class to do drawings of the kind suggested by de Bono (1972). Some ideas are listed in this chapter. Here are some more: devise a dog-exercising machine, devise a way of building a house quickly, devise a machine to get you up in the morning. A good starting point to stimulate ideas might be, for example, the Wallace and Gromit videos or any good book about a mad inventor. The key thing here is to be very accepting, not to worry about whether the ideas would actually work, and have fun!

Further reading

Burden, R. and Williams, M. (1998) *Thinking through the curriculum*, London: Routledge.
Costello, P.J.M. (2000) *Thinking Skills and Early Childhood Education*, London: Fulton.
Craft, A. (2000) *Creativity across the Primary Curriculum*, London: Routledge.
de Boo, M. (1999) *Enquiring Children, Challenging Teaching*, Buckingham: Open University Press.
Fisher, R. (1987) *Problem-solving in Primary Schools*, Oxford: Blackwell.
Fisher, R. (1990) *Teaching Children to Think*, Oxford: Blackwell.
Moyles, J.R. (1989) *Just Playing? The role and status of play in early childhood education*, Milton Keynes: Open University Press.
Whitebread, D. (1997) 'Developing children's problem-solving: the educational uses of adventure games', in A. McFarlane (ed.) *Information Technology and Authentic Learning*, London: Routledge.

References

Ashman, A.F. and Conway, R.N.F. (1997) *An introduction to cognitive education*, London: Routledge.
Borkowski, J.G., Peck, V.A., Reid, M.K. and Kurtz, B.E. (1983) 'Impulsivity and strategy transfer: metamemory as mediator', *Child Development*, 54, 459–73
Brainerd, C.J.(1983) 'Working-memory systems and cognitive development', in Brainerd, C.J. (ed.) *Recent advances in cognitive-developmental theory*, New York: Springer-Verlag.
Bruner, J.S. (1972) 'The nature and uses of immaturity', *American Psychologist*, 27, 1–28.
Bruner, J.S. (1973) *Beyond the Information Given*, London: George Allen & Unwin.
Bruner, J.S. and Kenney, H. (1966) 'The development of the concepts of order and proportion in children', in J.S. Bruner, R.R. Olver and P.M. Greenfield (eds) *Studies in Cognitive Growth*, New York: Wiley
Burden, R. and Williams, M. (1998) *Thinking through the curriculum*, London: Routledge.

Collins, A., Brown, J.S. and Newman, S.E (1989) 'Cognitive Apprenticeship: Teaching the Crafts of Reading, Writing and Mathematics', in Resnick, L.B. (ed.) *Knowing, Learning and Instruction: essays in honour of Robert Glaser*, Hillsdale: Erlbaum.

Costello, P.J.M. (2000) *Thinking Skills and Early Childhood Education*, London: Fulton.

Craft, A. (2000) *Creativity across the Primary Curriculum*, London: Routledge.

de Bono, E. (1970) *Lateral Thinking*, London: Ward Lock.

de Bono, E. (1972) *Children Solve Problems*, Harmondsworth: Penguin.

de Bono, E. (1976) *Teaching Thinking*, London: Temple Smith.

de Boo, M. (1999) *Enquiring Children, Challenging Teaching*, Buckingham: Open University Press.

DfEE/QCA (1999) *The National Curriculum; handbook for primary teachers in England*, London: HMSO.

Donaldson, M. (1978) *Children's Minds*, London: Fontana.

Finke, R.A., Ward, T.B. and Smith, S.M. (1992) *Creative Cognition: theory, research and applications*, Cambridge, MA: MIT Press.

Fisher, R. (1987) *Problem-solving in Primary Schools*, Oxford: Blackwell.

Fisher, R. (1990) *Teaching Children to Think*, Oxford: Blackwell.

Garnham, A. and Oakhill, J. (1994) *Thinking and Reasoning*, Oxford: Blackwell.

Goswami, U. (1992) *Analogical reasoning in children*, London: Erlbaum.

Greenfield, S. (1997) *The Human Brain: a guided tour*, London: Weidenfeld and Nicolson.

Guha, M. (1987) 'Play in School', in G.M. Blenkin and A.V. Kelly (eds) *Early Childhood Education: a developmental curriculum*, London: Chapman.

Klahr, D. (1978) 'Goal Formation, Planning, and Learning by Pre-school Problem-solvers or: "My Socks are in the Dryer"', in Siegler, R.S. (edi) *Children's Thinking: What Develops?*, Hillsdale: Erlbaum.

Lipman, M. (1988) *Philosophy Goes to School*, Philadelphia: Temple University Press.

Manning, K. and Sharp, A. (1977) *Structuring Play in the early years at school*, Cardiff: Ward Lock Educational.

Mayer, R. (1992) *Thinking, Problem Solving, Cognition*, 2nd edition, New York: W. H. Freeman & Co.

McGuinness, C. (1999) *From Thinking Skills to Thinking Classrooms: a review and evaluation of approaches for developing pupils' thinking*, Research Report RR115, London: DfEE/HMSO.

Meadows, S. (ed.) (1983) *Developing Thinking*, London: Methuen.

Meadows, S. (1993) *The Child as Thinker*, London: Routledge.

Moyles, J.R. (1989) *Just Playing? The role and status of play in early childhood education*, Milton Keynes: Open University Press.

Pressley, M., Borkowski, J.G. and Schneider, W. (1987) 'Cognitive Strategies: Good Strategy Users Co-ordinate Metacognition and Knowledge', in R. Vasta (ed.) *Annals of Child Development*, 4, 89–129.

Resnick, L.B. and Glaser, R. (1976) 'Problem-solving and intelligence', in L.B. Resnick (ed.) *The Nature of Intelligence*, Hillsdale: Erlbaum.

Roberts, M.J. and Erdos, G. (1993) 'Strategy selection and metacognition', *Educational Psychology*, 13, 259–66.

Robinson, E. (1983) 'Metacognitive development', in S. Meadows (ed.) *Developing Thinking*, London: Methuen.

Schunk, D.H. and Zimmerman, B.J. (1994) *Self-regulation of learning and performance*, Hillsdale: Erlbaum.

Siegler, R. S. (1991) *Children's Thinking*, 2nd Ed., Englewood Cliffs: Prentice Hall.

Smith, P.K. (1990) 'The role of play in the nursery and primary school curriculum', in C. Rogers and P. Kutnick (eds) *The Social Psychology of the Primary School*, London: Routledge.

Smith, P.K. , Cowie, H. and Blades, M. (1998) *Understanding Children's Development*, 3rd Ed., Oxford: Blackwell.

Sternberg, R.J. and Powell, J.S. (1983) 'The development of intelligence', in P.H. Mussen, J.H. Flavell and E.M. Markman (eds) *Handbook of Child Psychology, vol. 3*, New York: Wiley.

Sternberg, R.J. and Rifkin, B. (1979) 'The development of analogical reasoning processes', *Journal of Experimental Child Psychology*, 27, 195–232.

Sugden, D. (1989) 'Skill generalisation and children with learning difficulties', in D. Sugden (ed.) *Cognitive Approaches in Special Education*, London: Falmer.

Swan, S. and White, R. (1994) *The Thinking Books*, London: Falmer.

Sylva, K., Bruner, J.S. and Genova, P. (1976) 'The role of play in the problem-solving of children 3–5 years old', in J.S. Bruner, A. Jolly and K. Sylva (eds) *Play: its role in development and evolution*, Harmondsworth: Penguin.

Tharp, R.G. and Gallimore, R. (1988) *Rousing Minds to Life*, Cambridge: Cambridge University Press.

Vygotsky, L. S. (1986) *Thought and Language*, Cambridge, MA: MIT Press.

Wason, P.C. (1960) 'On the failure to eliminate hypotheses in a conceptual task', *Quarterly Journal of Experimental Psychology*, 12, 129–40.

Wason, P.C. and Johnson-Laird, P.N. (1972) *Psychology of Reasoning: Structure and Content*, London: Batsford.

Whitebread, D. (1997) 'Developing children's problem-solving: the educational uses of adventure games', in A. McFarlane (ed.) *Information Technology and Authentic Learning*, London: Routledge.

9   Teaching reading

Isobel Urquhart

EDITOR'S SUMMARY

This chapter reviews recent research on the development of children's literacy and how teachers can best help children learn this complex activity. Different approaches to the teaching of reading are analysed, together with research about the developmental stages in children's learning. The significance of phonological awareness is emphasised. The chapter provides a thorough analysis of teaching and assessment techniques related to onset and rime, the alphabetic principle, miscue analysis and so on. Finally, features of successful teaching interactions with children with reading difficulties are outlined, which include developing a warm and supportive relationship between the teacher and the learner, frequent scaffolded reading and writing experiences and considerable explicit cognitive modelling of reading and writing processes by the teacher. In these ways children develop the key metacognitive skills and understandings about literacy, such as self-monitoring, which are fundamental to becoming a fluent reader.

Reading is an extraordinarily complex activity, involving all sorts of mental processes that enable us to recognise written words and to make sense of the texts and print we read (Clay 1979), including media texts and new technologies. Reading should also be taken to include a social understanding of reading as a range of recognisable, meaningful and different activities (see Figure 9.1).

Whatever our personal purposes for reading, our competence leads to a deep sense of satisfaction. Conversely, to be unable to read and write in a print-saturated environment places an individual at a sharp disadvantage, jeopardising his or her chances of personal and social fulfilment and

Figure 9.1 Reading is an extraordinarily complex activity

happiness in life, and placing him or her at the mercy of those more powerful and able to negotiate the authority of text. Illiteracy reduces our personal autonomy because it limits all our other educational achievement, and impairs our ability to be other than passive recipients of others' interpretation of texts to us. Early reading failure can also be shown to result in a diminution of cognitive skills:

> Slow reading acquisition has cognitive, behavioural, and motivational consequences that slow the development of other cognitive skills ... The longer this is allowed to continue, the more generalised the deficits will become.

> (Stanovich 1986)

The development of writing and reading are mutually enhancing and reciprocal (Frith 1985) and reading difficulties impair written development. This has serious consequences in that, in writing, we can justify, argue, explain or movingly and originally express our perceptions and opinions. We live in a society that writes to itself (Meek 1992), and it is specifically our ability to participate in this written discourse, highly valued and highly influential both at school and in the wider world, that empowers us (Christie 1998).

The complexity of reading is reflected in the variety of ways in which it is studied. Psychological research into reading development, for example, has traditionally investigated reading as word-recognition, testing children's ability to read lists of single words or detecting sounds in words. Other approaches offer new ways of understanding the development of children as readers and writers, for example examining how different cultural communities 'do' reading in different ways, with some children entering school with ways of 'doing reading' that map readily onto school reading practices, while other children may not find their reading culture acknowledged or taken seriously as part of what is meant by reading in school (Heath 1983). Children may therefore become reading failures because they are initially unable to participate fully in school reading activities, and may then be positioned as reading failures by a set of literacy practices which privilege an advantaged elite, thus perpetuating existing social differences between social groups.

Because of its complexity, reading poses interesting challenges to those of us who are interested in understanding how children learn to read and why some children do not progress despite the very best efforts of teachers and families. In this chapter, I am focusing particularly on psychological contributions to theories of reading and reading development, and how teachers may help children develop into competent and discriminating readers and writers.

Word recognition

By far the most extensive psychological research into reading has been into how children learn to pronounce individual words when they are written down in the form of groups of letters. Adams (1990) opens her comprehensive, unashamedly 'scientific', and readable account of the process of learning to read with the sentence: 'The ability to read words, quickly, accurately and effortlessly is critical to skilful reading comprehension'. Her sentence is carefully worded. Notice that she emphasises the fact that word recognition serves a wider purpose. The goal of reading, in her estimation, is comprehension, and the ability to recognise words quickly and, without too much brain power, working out what they say, is critical to this purpose. Word recognition studies have proved to be a very productive line of enquiry, helping us to understand how children's reading develops, some of the factors which predict ease of learning to read, and where children's difficulties might lie in the reading process.

The alphabetic principle

The ability to read written words involves children coming to understand that English is an alphabetic writing system. It is central to our writing system, because it is a particularly efficient way of generating any number of words from a small and re-usable set of letters. The alphabetic principle is very economic: we combine and recombine our limited set of letters to represent sounds in a less than straightforward one-to-one mapping of sounds (phonemes) onto letters (26 letters, 44 sounds), e.g. the letter 'a' represents different sounds in 'sat', 'star' and 'shake'. This adds a further complexity because it means our writing system is not purely phonic, unlike Urdu, another alphabetic system, nor even like Italian in our own alphabetic system. Nevertheless, understanding how this alphabetic principle works as a system of correspondences between letters and the individual, separable sounds in a spoken word is the key to cracking the 'code' of words written down (Ehri 1999). If we think of this system as a code, then in order to read words accurately, a reader has to be able to decode the letters by associating them correctly with individual phonemes and then pronouncing them fluently as words. The test of whether children can be assumed to have grasped the alphabetic principle is if they can read sequences of letters they have never seen before. This explains why so many research studies ask children to read nonsense words as well as unfamiliar words, or ask children to remove or add phonemes in words; researchers want to be sure that they are observing the application of decoding skills and not some other skill, such as sight recognition or use of contextual cues.

However, despite the importance of the alphabetic principle, it appears that young children who have not yet learned to read find it very hard to identify the separate phonemes in words. It appears that it is not as obvious as it seems to hear those separate sounds. Young, non-reading children who listen to other people speak are not necessarily aware of how to break up an utterance into the abstract segmentations we take for granted: words, sounds. And yet, in order to develop into successful readers, it is critical that they can eventually do so (Adams 1990).

Sensitivity to sounds in spoken words is described as phonological awareness and, although pre-reading children are not very good at detecting phonemes, other kinds of sensitivity to the sounds in words do occur. The significance of phonological awareness prior to reading instruction is discussed below. The important point is that children seem to become aware of the relationship between phonemes and letters once we begin to *teach* children to segment words in these ways. Full phonemic awareness, the ability to detect the individual sounds that make up a word, comes only after children have begun to be instructed in reading, rather than being a factor that precedes and causes reading achievement (Goswami and Bryant 1990). Indeed, it is likely that the relationship between reading achievement and phonemic awareness is reciprocal: the ability to detect phonemes is first promoted by literacy acquisition and then enables further gains in literacy as word recognition becomes more automatic with increased practice in reading, and a more comprehensive grasp of the letter–sound correspondences (Perfetti 1999; Underwood and Batt 1996). Commonly, children also begin to understand the relationships between letters and sounds as they experiment with writing words, where the need to write letters in sequence is immediately apparent and where children begin to develop their own mental models of the relationships using whatever learned associations between letters and sounds they have already acquired in their invented spellings (Clay 1975).

Phonological awareness

An important area of research, therefore, has sought to identify what factors seem to assist children's discovery of the alphabetic principle (Oakhill and Beard 1999; Goswami and Bryant 1990; Byrne 1998). Investigations have explored whether some kinds of sensitivity to sounds are better than others at predicting subsequent success in reading achievement. This would address the problem posed by the fact that ability to segment words at the level of phonemes is highly correlated with success in reading acquisition while the ability to segment words into phonemes appears to be difficult for young pre-reading children (Ehri 1999; Adams 1990; Goswami and Bryant 1990).

Onsets and rimes

The interesting conclusion seems to be that pre-reading young children can detect *some* sounds within words. For example, they can segment words into syllables, although this does not seem to be particularly helpful to them in learning to read. However, they can also subdivide the syllables in words into an *onset* (made up of the initial phoneme of the syllable) and the *rime* (made up of the vowels and any subsequent phonemes) (Treiman 1985; Goswami and Bryant 1990). Thus, children might be able to identify that the word 'catkin' contains the sounds 'c-at' and 'k-in'. An ability to do this is a good predictor of how readily children will learn from instruction in phonics. That is, children who can detect onsets and rimes will usually rapidly develop the ability to detect phonemes in words when reading instruction begins. This seems to be, as Goswami argues, because they can use a fundamental cognitive ability, analogy, to generate the pronunciation of new words on the basis of known words, using a segmentation process that is relatively easy for them. Rimes in particular are highly regular in terms of sound and spellings, so that knowing how to read 'b-eak', a child may well be able to read 'w-eak'. Note that some phonemic ability is present, in that the child also needs to be able to pronounce the onset, 'w' (Ehri 1995).

Not all children are equally able to distinguish onsets and rimes. This ability is more well developed in those children who are also able to detect rhyming and alliterative sounds in spoken words, and thus it is unsurprising, perhaps, to find that children who have had lots of experiences of rhymes and word play are more able to segment words in this way. When this information is put together with the research that shows rhyme-detection is itself a good predictor of later reading achievement, we can begin to see that onset-rime ability may be a very useful precursor for reading (Goswami and Bryant 1990).

The role of instruction

Few children learn to read without some instruction (Seymour and Elder 1986). In particular, instruction is necessary for children to understand the alphabetic nature of the links between letters and sounds. As has been stated above, children who can already identify some separation of sounds in spoken words seem to be better able to break words down into separate phonemes, when they are instructed in how to do this. Commonly, systematic instruction only occurs once children enter school, but the effect of instruction in identifying phonemes and associating them with letters, commonly known as phonics, has been shown to enable slow-learning Primary-aged children and even pre-schoolers to identify new words (Adams 1990).

While phonics instruction is necessary for most children to develop an independence and automaticity in decoding skills, a persistent dilemma has been how to give a proper balance between emphasising reading as a meaningful and enjoyable engagement with texts by children actively hypothesising about how to make the text make sense, while teaching the 'nuts and bolts' of the alphabetic code. Indeed, analyses of phonic programmes by Bond and Dykstra (1967) showed that those which combined both systematic phonics and a great deal of emphasis on meaningful reading of connected text were the most effective of all. All the most powerful programmes, such as Clay's Reading Recovery, make certain that phonic instruction is embedded in engagement with well written texts at a level that is meaningful and engaging for the children concerned.

Reading experts talk about the 'deep play' of children's engagement with texts and literature, and the danger with phonics instruction has always been its losing sight of what motivates children to want to read and write (Britton 1972; Meek,1988).

> No matter how well authenticated the method, children do not want to read unless they discover what's in it for them and what could be pleasing to teachers. One thing only is certain; if they never find out what reading is good for, they won't want to read enough of it to learn the real reading lessons: how to read new texts with the confidence of being able to make them mean.
>
> (Meek 1994:227)

Anyone who has watched the way children read and re-read their favourite books, or talk excitedly to each other about their discoveries in the pictures and the words on the page, or who use books to find out more about their current interests, or who 'get lost' in a story or poetry book, can vouch for the importance of 'what's in it for them' as part of what it means to be a reader. We must not lose sight of this serious engagement with text. Integrating word and sentence level within an authentic engagement with text is critical, therefore, for children to understand that school literacy promotes not just the correct pronunciation of words, but engagement, purpose, pleasure and meaning at text level.

Table 9.1 Frith's model

Step	Reading	Writing
1(a)	Logographic	(Symbolic)
1(b)	Logographic	Logographic
2(a)	Logographic	Alphabetic
2(b)	Alphabetic	Alphabetic
3(a)	Orthographic	Alphabetic
3(b)	Orthographic	Orthographic

How reading develops

Various models describe the developmental landmarks of children's grow-ing abilities in reading and writing (e.g. Frith 1985; Ehri 1992), although stage models should not necessarily be taken to demonstrate discrete steps in a determined progression. Some cognitive theorists would propose that the development is driven as children partially relinquish less efficient means of processing print in favour of faster and more efficient methods, hence their emphasis on the development of automaticity in descriptions of skilful read-ers reading behaviours. Theorists differ in whether children exchange one strategy for another, or whether they accumulate a complex and reciprocal network of strategies. I favour the latter, partly because it links with other studies (e.g. Siegler 1996) that show children's learning proceeding more like overlapping waves, where both more and less efficient strategies may operate alongside each other, with more efficient strategies eventually pre-vailing under the influence of feedback on the success of the strategy. In reading, it may be even more complex, with alternative strategies continuing to be potentially useful and reciprocating, giving children a rich repertoire to draw on when trying to read new words.

Uta Frith's stage-theory of reading development is based on the accumula-tive model of reading acquisition. At the end of the developmental sequence, children have at their disposal a repertoire of all the strategies, and use all of them. Frith's model also demonstrates the reciprocation between learning to write and spell and learning to read, with causal links in both directions (see Table 9.1).

In Frith's model, children begin to read using a spontaneous strategy of attempting to memorise as visual entities all the significant words that they encounter. The stimulus to move away from that strategy begins when, par-ticularly under the influence of learning to write, children start to think about separate letter–phoneme relationships. The introduction of reading instruction in phonics gives children a more effective strategy based on the alphabetic principle, and most children learn to apply this with increasing efficiency until, with greater reading and writing experience, they find that words can be stored and memorised using larger 'orthographic' chunks of information, which increases the speed and accuracy of their reading and writing.

Children take to the memorisation of sight words more quickly when they read than when they write, and so the child's experience of reading words has a causal relation to the development of the same strategy in writing. However, the causal links proceed the other way, from writing to reading, in the alphabetic stage: children use alphabetic knowledge first in their writing, as they attempt to spell words, and this is eventually how children read new and unfamiliar words. Finally, reading leads to memorisation of larger, orthographic chunks of letters, and these are eventually exploited in spelling new words.

Logographic stage

Most models identify that children's first attempts to read involve, not a phonological strategy, but a visual one. Children begin to recognise some words by memorising the look of words as holistic entities, word-shapes, called logographs. In schools, these are often known as sight-words, words children recognise and can read on sight. Pre-school children's ability to read some words in their story books, or in the print they notice in their environment – words on television, advertisements, packaging, parents' writing, etc. – is best explained by this kind of visual memorisation and associative process. But this ability is not generative; it is not, in itself, a technique that enables children to recognise further examples of unfamiliar words (Gough 1999). It does not give children insight into the alphabetic principle they need to understand in order to decode print into sounds that can be spoken.

Alphabetic stage

The new stage involves the reader in making some degree of analysis of both spoken words and visual displays of words, i.e. grasping the alphabetic principle. This stage rarely occurs spontaneously, unlike the first stage, and almost always requires some kind of intervention from more experienced learners – parents, teachers, siblings – who give cues that support the child's analytic processing, or who present words to the child in ways that encourage him or her to analyse spoken and written words into their component sounds and letters.

Subsequently, under the influence of instruction, and also the influence of practice in writing and invented spelling, children make the important transition to an alphabetic analysis of written words.

Orthographic stage

This final stage involves detecting larger non-phonic sequences of letters, also known as 'spelling patterns', that recur across words, and connecting these to sounds within the child's store of known words. Orthographic reading and writing recognises patterns that are not phonetically regular, but contain spelling conventions that are visually recognised. Examples include spelling patterns such as '-tion', or words such as 'said'. Fluent readers thus go beyond a purely phonic analysis in favour of a faster, and therefore more efficient visual analysis of the way letters combine in spellings rather than as representations of individual sounds (Frith,1985; Ehri 1999; Adams 1990). In this stage, children can make use of larger letter patterns memorised as single units to analogise to new or unfamiliar words.

Making sense of text

Forrester remarks about most word-recognition studies:

> Few ... have moved beyond the level of the letter and the word [and] while this methodologically rigorous approach has certain advantages, it tells us very little about everyday reading processes.
>
> (Forrester 1996:160)

As we have seen, word-recognition approaches can become divorced from meaningful reading, and the ability to understand text. Even Marilyn Adams, a champion of word recognition and good phonic instruction, admits that phonics teaching has often been characterised by uninteresting texts and a chronic overemphasis on decontextualised phonic exercises. One outcome has been that some children can apparently read, in word recognition terms, very well, but have so lost sight of its purpose (to make meaning), that they cannot tell you very much at all about what their reading was about (Whitehead 1997). It is only when these children are questioned about the text or asked to explain or retell what they have read that their difficulties are revealed.

A wider criticism of word-recognition studies is the conviction that children can only learn to read through formal instruction, which tends to dismiss the child's active participation in learning to read, and their innate drive to make sense of what reading is *for* as well as what reading consists *of*. Other psychological approaches have therefore investigated reading from the child's point of view: they look for evidence of how children construct their own ideas of reading and writing, drawing on their observations of how print is used around them, as well as their participation in reading and writing activities.

Nigel Hall described a number of charming experiments (Hall 1987) in which he asked very young children if animals could read and write. The children told him that animals could not read because they said bow wow or miaow, and they did not have hands. In a similar study (Scollon and Scollon 1981), the little girl thought her baby brother would one day be able to read when his hands grew. Reading is thus interpreted as an oral and physical activity by small children – you have to be able to speak words and you have to be able to hold up a book.

In answering these questions about reading, it is clear that 'children are attempting to make sense of the activity of being a reader in ways that are clearly sensible' (Hall 1987). The children's answers show them actively making reasoned sense of the human activities they see around them, making astute inferences based on the kinds of experience they have had so far of reading and books. The point Hall makes is that children do not wait until we give them reading instruction to begin to develop their own mental models of what reading is all about.

Elsewhere in this book you will read how children learn from more experienced adults. Another important contribution to reading theory has been made from this theoretical standpoint, examining how adults assist children in developing the practices of reading and writing, through sharing books, notes, lists and environmental print, as well as sharing talk about books and reading (Bruner 1983; Clay and Cazden 1992; Graham 1994). Through their social participation in authentic reading experiences, e.g. going shopping and making lists, reading stories together, children learn important lessons about reading (Hall 1987; Meek 1988). First and foremost, they learn in what ways reading is constructed as enjoyable and useful by the significant adults around them. They also learn, in their conversations with adults, what to call some of the features of print they notice in their shared reading: e.g. 'word', 'letter' and 'sound' as well as finding out that the story is *in* the words, and that print goes left to right, top to bottom. They notice some features of text, especially if these are surprising or arresting, such as big letters, or a letter from their name, or they may notice punctuation features such as a full stop, capital letter and commas. Marie Clay called these the early concepts about print which contribute to children's first attempts to make sense of how texts work (Clay 1985).

Gordon Wells (1986) identified further lessons that children learn about reading in collaboration with their parents. He found that children who had had plenty of experience of stories prior to attending school were better prepared to make sense of literacy activities in school. They had internalised the structures, the 'tunes' and cadences of written language, the structures of narrative and other genres of texts that would support their text-level reading in the early years of schooling.

Here is Judith Graham, reading *Where the Wild Things Are* by Maurice Sendak, with Jessica.

> She already knows how the print is different from the illustrations and that it '*tells*' me what to say ... I can reinforce this in many ways. When I open the book at the first sentence and wait, Jessica says 'One day Max weared his wolf suit'. (Text: The night Max wore his wolf-suit and made mischief of one kind ... or another). I ask her where it says that, and she runs her finger backwards and forwards over the line of writing. I say 'That's right,' and we turn over. Sometimes Jessica turns over before I have finished reading and I say, 'Wait for me to finish reading' and I point to where I am. We come to words made distinctive by Sendak,

either because they are alone on the page or printed in upper-case letters. We both stab our fingers on the 'BE STILL!'

(Graham 1994:213)

In this episode, the child takes the role of an apprentice reader, participating as far as she is able, with the adult ensuring that her assistance leaves the child with as much independence as possible. Although Graham argues persuasively that Jessica is learning to read from the text itself, it should also be noted that this learning occurs within a collaborative and mediated relationship with a very skilled reader whose questions, comments and responses (including galumphing round the sofa being Wild Things) confirm and reinforce her young reader's surmises both about what reading is (print) and what it is for (the glorious experience of being a Wild Thing for a while). This scaffolding of children's skills through assistance that is contingently matched to children's learning helps children to develop problem-solving strategies by actively making sense of reading.

Teaching children strategies for making sense of text

In shared reading and writing with classes and in guided and one-to-one reading sessions, teachers try to build on the collaborative experiences of reading in the home, and to work within an apprenticeship model that allows children to participate more and more in the reading act. Frank Smith (Smith 1984), who championed psycholinguistic approaches to reading development which have now been partially disproved, nevertheless made some persuasive statements about children as readers. One phrase he used extensively was the importance of children 'joining the literacy club', i.e. letting them learn to read by participating in the reading of whole texts rather than through drills and worksheets. What was perhaps not emphasised enough in Smith's approach was the skill of the teacher's instruction and expert assistance, as she draws the child further and further into that club. Through what Juel calls a facilitative dialogue, teachers assist children to internalise strategies that will help them develop their own hypotheses and mental schema about how to make sense of text (Oakhill and Beard 1999).

Let us look at an example. Before reading a book together, the teacher may briefly talk to the pupil, Paul, about what he expects it to be about, perhaps commenting on the picture on the front cover or discussing what he likes about this kind of book: 'What sort of things do you like in animal stories?' While sharing the book together, she might help Paul work out a not instantly recognised word by asking him to look at the pictures, or direct his attention to consider the first letter-sound in order to pronounce a word, and to invite him to self-monitor whether the reading then makes sense. Paul may be encouraged to read from the beginning of a sentence up to the difficult word to help him use his implicit knowledge of the cadences of written narrative, or his knowledge of syntax and spoken language. The teacher might ask him what word would 'make sense', encouraging him also to look carefully at the graphophonemic information to make sure it also 'fits'. She may cover up part of a word in order to get him to look closely at the middles of words, or may encourage him to notice grammatical elements (morphemes) or prefixes and suffixes, e.g. '-ed', '-ing', '-less'. She may make a note of words that are particularly difficult and give some direct phonic instruction after the reading is over. She will reinforce his ability to monitor his own reading, e.g. positively encouraging Paul when he says things like 'horse ... no ... hang on ... house' or when he notices that something did not make sense and goes back over the sentence without prompting: 'That was good, Paul, the way you checked the meaning there.' She will encourage him to talk about the text, getting genuinely involved in the story or the topic, sharing his pleasure, and encouraging him to make inferences, or to draw on information from different parts of the text, to speculate and draw conclusions, perhaps about a character, or to predict what might happen next.

Miscue analysis

One major contribution made by theories of reading that focus on the development of these metacognitive strategies in learning to read has been the development of a diagnostic assessment procedure. Miscue analysis examines the errors children make in response to 'cues' in a piece of continuous text, in a situation as close as possible to normal reading behaviour. The teacher can infer from the child's reading behaviour the strategies they are bringing to the problem of reading unfamiliar words and making sense of the text, and build a picture of the strengths and weaknesses of individual readers. She can use this to plan reading sessions which reinforce strengths or teach and encourage the missing or weak strategies.

Here are the main problem-solving strategies for making sense of unfamiliar words:

- using the letter–sound information to sound out words
- using semantic knowledge (word meanings) to predict an appropriate word
- using knowledge of how language works at a syntactic level (grammar, morphemic transformations, etc.) to predict a word that 'fits' grammatically
- using the context – life experience, pictures on the page – to predict a word.

What has been established beyond much doubt is that the use of *context* as the predominant strategy is favoured by weaker or less experienced readers. As children become more confident about their word-recognition skills, they tend to use context less frequently.

Here is an example of miscue analysis in action. Rahina enjoys stories; she listens avidly to stories the teacher reads, and she also has stories read to her at night. She likes stories 'with an adventure in them' and hates stories where nothing happens. In her miscue analysis, it was clear that when she came to difficult words, she substituted words that made sense to the story, but she did not pay much attention to the graphophonemic (letter-sound) information, so that her substitutions, although usually reasonably sensible, were not accurate. She read with panache, with the clear implication that her construction of 'reading' was that an impression of fluency and speed had to be sustained, even if this was at the cost of accuracy. Eventually the accumulation of slight inaccuracies meant that the sense did break down, and Rahina then tended to skip words, keeping the text going with a vague gist of the meaning. Following a detailed analysis, her teacher planned to focus on drawing her attention to the initial letter of the words for which she was giving semantic substitutions, and to say to her, 'What sound does this first letter make?' or 'How does this word end?' In teacher-directed sessions, and in independent work, questions to Rahina focused on noticing patterns of letters, making phonic connections, playing phonic games, and on reading non-fiction texts in other subject areas, where the tasks required Rahina to provide very accurate information. Rahina liked using the word processor for writing because she had lots of ideas which she could get down quickly, using the spellchecker as she went along rather than afterwards. The teacher encouraged her to proofread and identify her own remaining spelling errors, and to learn spellings using 'Look Say Cover Write Check' as a visualisation strategy. She regularly encouraged Rahina to find words that made the same pattern as her target word, so that she learned groups of words together.

Christa likes comics and looking at the pictures in books. Her big brother listens to her read, and expects her to learn the words she had to sound out. In the miscue analysis, she spent ages hesitating before words she found difficult. She would take several runs at it, repeating a phrase preceding the word several times before she tried, under her breath, to sound out the letters. Eventually she would pronounce the word, often accurately, but having particular difficulty with vowel digraphs. She also used a short phrase preceding the difficult word to help her predict a word that would make sense, but her lack of experience of written texts and her concern to be accurate meant that this was not very effective. Reading seemed a big effort and her construal of reading was obvious: it was to read words correctly. Afterwards, she was not very sure what she had been reading about. Her teacher set up group reading of familiar stories, and encouraged the group to retell the story afterwards. As it was a group activity, it felt more like fun and Christa did not feel exposed. The group then retold another story, changing the ending for one of their own. The teacher also encouraged Christa to predict events and reactions in the shared reading sessions, and helped her to identify how the text and pictures gave the reader clues. The teacher also decided to work with the whole class on some selected vowel digraphs, beginning with words found in the texts the class were reading at the time, and inferring rules and building families of words from these. Christa was also given times for writing her own stories and reading these and other favourite books with her friends.

Reading as a social activity

In the introduction to this chapter, I mentioned that some studies of reading concentrate on the cultural differences in reading that impact on reading success in schools. The kinds of literacy events and practices children experience and how these are talked about and construed in their families and cultural communities form part of what children come to understand as reading. When they enter different cultural locations, children quickly learn that reading may be done in different ways, with different meanings and values attached to those practices. This could include the way a holy book is read in churches, temples or synagogues, and the reading together of an enlarged text while sitting on a carpet that is a current feature of primary classrooms (Minns 1990).

What comes to count as literacy in schools reflects the values of those who have sufficient authority to present their views about literacy as the ones that matter. Schools therefore have their own set of reading activities that tell children what 'reading' means in school. These activities confirm and build on some children's existing experience of texts and reading while failing to recognise as legitimate other children's reading and writing experiences. This is powerfully demonstrated in Heath's anthropological study into the literacy practices of three different communities in America (Heath 1983) where she was able to demonstrate how particular kinds of preschool literacy experiences were evaluated differently in school.

Gregory (1992) argues that schools should build on early home learning in teaching reading but goes on to ask: 'But whose home learning is it to be?' Can 'all children be acculturated into reading in school through practice that is only real for some?' When the teacher says to her class, 'We're going to read a story together' in a literacy hour session, she is likely to assume that it calls up a framing concept of stories and books which children from school-oriented backgrounds have already experienced and can work within. However, children who do not share this background may not be able to frame the task this way and consequently may not understand what is expected of them in early reading lessons. Such school reading activities may mean very little to some children and they may then be unlikely to do well as readers and to be seen to be failing at reading. We have seen that the consequences of reading failure are very great and yet, just as Heath had discovered, it is not that these children come from families who 'don't read' but that they may not read in the ways sanctioned by school models of literacy.

Reading difficulties

Currently, there is growing evidence that many children with persistent reading difficulties suffer impairments in phonological processing. Typically, phonological processing skills are delayed or, in very severe cases, deficient (Adams 1990; Snowling 1987; Stanovich 1999). Snowling (1980) argues that the difficulties children with specific reading difficulties display are characteristic of younger children with a similar reading age. Children with reading difficulties seem to be operating at an earlier stage of the reading process, making the same kinds of errors that younger children of average reading ability make in learning the alphabetic code, or in persisting with trying to memorise whole word-shapes, a strategy typical of the earliest stage of reading. Higher order reading skills such as inference and the ability to draw together information from different parts of the text remain unimpaired, however, in some children with dyslexia.

For example, a 12-year-old dyslexic boy was able to discuss with me, with unusual articulacy and insight, the Phillip Pullman novels *His Dark Materials* and *The Subtle Knife*. He liked the way Pullman created complex plots, as these made him want to read further in order to find out how Pullman resolved them, and he enjoyed the complexity of the characters and was interested in how they would deal with new twists in the tale. He was very upset when he read about the death of one of the characters in *The Subtle Knife*. However, he was unable to read the novels for himself; his mother read them with him. Sadly he had not been able to share his enjoyment or understanding in school. We can see how this boy could certainly see how to make texts meaningful, but was seriously hindered by his difficulties in decoding.

Recently, psychologists have begun to work closely with neuroscientists, examining data such as information from MRI brain scans, and linking the data with cognitive theories about neural connectivity, to produce evidence that may demonstrate the neurophysiology of reading difficulties. For example, neurological irregularities in motion sensitivity have been discovered in some dyslexics who report that they see text jumping around, and it has been suggested that both auditory processing – a frequent difficulty for dyslexics – and motion sensitivity are controlled by a particular network of cells located just below the hypocampus where information from the eyes crosses over into the opposite hemisphere (Stein 1999).

Interesting questions then arise about how and whether experience (nurture) in the form of teaching and frequent practice can modify neural pathways (nature), perhaps by strengthening existing, or by finding alternative, pathways which may lead to more effective processing of phonological and visual information.

Children who find phonological processing difficult will show problems with the phonological analysis of words, for example finding it hard to segment words into sound units, both in spoken language and in written representations; finding it difficult to spell words phonetically; to blend sounds into words; or to use analogy based on phonological elements (Bryant *et al.* 1990; Goswami and Bryant 1990; Tunmer and Hoover 1992).

Without systematic and intensive phonics instruction, children with these difficulties will have continuing problems in building up their knowledge of the spelling-to-sound correspondences and reading will not reach the effortless, automatic and fluent levels expected of skilled readers (Stanovich

1999). Because children's sensitivity to sounds in words is relatively easy to identify early on, children who are not able to process sounds can be noticed quickly and teaching interventions can be quickly implemented. Furthermore, children can receive training in phonological sensitivity prior to schooling which could lead to accelerated progress in word-recognition and spelling skills.

Snowling's argument (Snowling 1987) that children with specific reading difficulties display the kinds of errors and problems of average younger-aged readers suggests that we can help children by working at their developmental stage. This might include work on developing phonological sensitivity to rhyming words, and using their visual similarities to learn spellings and make analogies between 'families' of words with similar spellings. Regularities in sound at syllabic level are more regular in their spelling than at phoneme level, and so early reading can be assisted by helping children to see how regularities in spoken words, such as rhymes, are also regular in their spellings. Children can thus learn 'word families' that contain the same spelling pattern, e.g. 'cold', 'old', 'told'. Children can be encouraged to use a powerful cognitive tool, analogy, to hypothesise about how to read unfamiliar words, e.g. 'sold', on the basis of known words. Most programmes designed for children with specific literacy difficulties systematically teach all the phonic relations between letters and sounds, using multi-channel learning, that is, using all sensory inputs – sight, sound, and movements in hand muscles – to help build up memory. They also attempt to develop automaticity, by rehearsing and overlearning the targeted element. This involves frequent exposure to the target, frequent practice to the point of automaticity. The problem with this, of course, is that it can be tedious, and this is why such programmes often use phonic games and more recently computer-based tasks to try to maintain motivation (e.g. Additional Learning Support Materials, DfEE 1999).

However, as we have seen, programmes designed to treat difficulties that are only analysed at word level – identifying difficulties in processing phonic information – can often fail to move children on to applying their newly learned phonic skills to real and varied reading practices in schools and elsewhere. This view of word-attack skills as only a partial analysis of the reading process, and only a partial description of the difficulties children can experience with reading, is supported by Kershner (Chapter 14 in this book) in which she refers to Reason's diagram of the reading process which describes the full reading process as occurring at three levels of analysis. Children who experience reading difficulties therefore benefit from teaching which has carefully and thoroughly analysed each individual child's needs at all three levels.

Thus, children with reading difficulties also benefit from learning reading strategies which, by working on children actually engaged in making meaningful sense of texts, help them to self-monitor how they are reading and to use all the available information and cues in the text to sustain meaning.

Children also need teachers to be sensitive to and respectful of their existing literacy practices, and to use these as the platform on which further reading and writing can become relevant and important to children.

Features of successful teaching interactions with children with reading difficulties may be summarised as follows (Juel 1999):

- A warm and supportive relationship between tutor and learner. There is evidence from the analysis of successful dyadic reading instruction (where a more experienced reader teaches one less experienced) that 'obvious affection, bonding and verbal and non-verbal encouragement of children's progress' makes a significant contribution to children's progress (Juel 1999; Lawrence 1981).

- Frequent scaffolded reading and writing experiences in which the tutor provides just enough information for the child to do the task with the tutor's 'hands-off' assistance; for example, as the child starts to write the 'f' of the word 'full', the tutor may remind the writer of another word she knows such as 'pull'; as the reader makes a substitution that breaks down the meaning of the text, the tutor may cue her by asking her 'Does that make sense?' In both cases, the learner is given as much autonomy as possible.

- Considerable explicit cognitive modelling of reading and writing processes by the tutor. Effective tutors frequently explain to children how reading and writing work, and, as Juel puts it, '"walk" the children through the processes so that the tasks [are] clearer, more accessible and less mysterious.' Interestingly, Juel found that one very effective method of doing this was to reverse roles with the learner, where the child pretended to tutor the tutor. In this process, not only did the learner verbalise her metacognitive understanding of the knowledge, skills and strategies needed to read, the tutor could model and explicitly refer to the thought-processes used in approaching a difficult word or self-monitoring her reading.

Finally, in all our work with children with literacy difficulties, we need to reflect on our own deep engagement with books, because it is the power of our own conviction that all children can enter the world of books and writing and find something of value for themselves there that will fuel our creativity and conviction in offering interventions and literacy experiences that will introduce children to the same excitements and discoveries. Drawing deeply on our own discovery of the pleasures and uses of reading and writing, empathising with the very particular way an individual endeavours to make meaning that we know is at the heart of reading and writing, will guide our judgements about what works and does not work for children with reading difficulties.

Activities

Reading difficulties

Observe a child with reading difficulties in Year 4 in class or talk to the class teacher or SENCO or examine an intervention programme (e.g. Additional Learning Support materials for children in Years 3 and 4).

- What kinds of specific teaching interventions are made with the child you observe, or are suggested by the class teacher or SENCO or characterise the programme?
- How successfully is the tension between direct instruction at word-recognition level and the serious engagement with meaning and texts reconciled?

Listen to a child reading

- What strategies does he or she use to make sense of the reading?
- What does he or she do when 'stuck' on a word?
- What do you find yourself saying to help the child?
- What does this reveal about your own views about how children read?

Books in your home

Think about the role books have in your family home and what it tells you about the social practices of reading in your family.

- Are books plentiful or few in number?
- How are the books housed? Are they visible to people coming to visit? Are they on display, e.g. in a book-lined room, in a glass cabinet in the living room? Are children's books thrown in with the toys in the toy box, given away when you were too old for them, etc.?
- Who reads what? Where and when?
- Are there different kinds of books: series, DIY, novels? Are they used differently? (My recipe books have food stains and bits of pastry on them.)
- What other kinds of texts are read? (TV, video, computer texts, letters, adverts, notices)
- How are books handled? Left out in the rain, tidied up and put away? (I read books in the bath so that the pages of many of my books are buckled, but my colleague keeps her books carefully. For her, bathtime is not a time for reading!)
- How have *you* learned to treat books, and what does it tell you about how you construe reading?

Further reading

Adams, M. J. (1990) *Beginning to Read. Thinking and Learning about Print*, Cambridge, MA: MIT Press.

Goswami, U. and Bryant, P. (1990) *Phonological Skills and Learning to Read*, Hillsdale: Erlbaum.

Hall, N. (1987) *The Emergence of Literacy*, London: Hodder & Stoughton.

Oakhill, J. and Beard, R. (1999) *Reading Development and the Teaching of Reading*, Oxford: Blackwell.

Whitehead, M. (1997) *Language and Literacy in the Early Years*, 2nd Edition, London: Paul Chapman.

References

Adams, M. J. (1990) *Beginning to Read. Thinking and Learning about Print*, Cambridge, MA: MIT Press.

Bond, G.L. and Dykstra, R. (1967) 'The cooperative research programme in first-grade reading instruction', in *Reading Research Quarterly* Vol 2, 5–142.

Britton, J. (1972) *Language and Learning*, Harmondsworth: Pelican.

Bruner, J. (1983) *Child Talk*, Oxford: Oxford University Press.

Bruner, J. (1986) *Actual Minds, Possible Worlds*, Boston: Harvard University Press.

Bryant, P.E., Maclean, M. and Bradley, L. (1990) 'Rhyme, language and children's reading in *Applied Psycholinguistics* 11, 237–52.

Byrne, B. (1998) *The Foundation of Literacy. The Child's Acquisition of the Alphabetic Principle,*. Hove: Psychology Press.

Christie, F. (1998) *Literacy and Schooling*, London: Routledge.

Clay, M (1975) *What did I write?* London: Heinemann.

Clay, M. (1979) *Reading: The Patterning of Complex Behaviour*, 2nd edition, London: Heinemann

Clay, M. (1985) *The Early Detection of Reading Difficulties*, London: Heinemann.

Clay, M. and Cazden, C. (1992) ' Vygotskian interpretation of the whole-language approach to literacy development', in *Educational Psychologist* 29, 173–222.

DfEE (1999) *Additional Learning Support Materials*, London: DfEE

Ehri, L.A. (1992) 'Reconceptualising the development of sight word reading and its relationship to recording', in Gough, P.B., Ehri, L.A. and Treiman, R. (eds) *Reading Acquisition*, Hillsdale: Erlbaum.

Ehri, L.A. (1995) 'Phases of development in learning to read words by sight', *Journal of Research in Reading* 18, 118–25

Ehri, L.A. (1995) 'Phases of development in learning to read words', In Oakhill, J. and Beard, R. (eds) *Reading Development and the Teaching of Reading*, Oxford: Blackwell

Forrester, M.A. (1996) *Psychology of Language*, Oxford: Blackwell

Frith, U. (1985) 'Beneath the surface of developmental dyslexia', in K.E. Patterson, J.C. Marshall, and M. Coltheart (eds), *Surface Dyslexia: Neuropsychological and Cognitive Studies of Phonological Reading*, London: Erlbaum.

Goswami, U. and Bryant, P (1990) *Phonological Skills and Learning to Read*, Hillsdale: Erlbaum.

Goswami, U. (1992) *Analogical Reasoning in Children*, Hillsdale: Erlbaum.

Gough, P.B. (1999) 'The New Literacy: caveat emptor', in Oakhill, J. and Beard, R., *Reading Develooment and the Teaching of Reading*, Oxford: Blackwell.

Graham, J. (1992) 'Teachers learning about literacy', in K. Kimberley, M. Meek and J. Miller (eds) *New Readings. Contributions to an understanding of literacy*, London: A. & C. Black.

Gregory, E. (1992) 'Learning Codes and Contexts: a psychosemiotic approach to beginning reading in school', in K. Kimberley, M. Meek and J. Miller (eds) *New Readings. Contributions to an understanding of literacy*, London: A & C Black.

Hall, N. (1987) *The Emergence of Literacy*, London: Hodder & Stoughton.

Heath, S.B. (1983) *Ways with Words*, Boston: Harvard University Press.

Juel, C. (1992) 'The Messenger may be Wrong but the Message may be right', in K. Kimberley, M. Meek and J. Miller (eds) *New Readings. Contributions to an understanding of literacy*, London: A. & C. Black.

Lawrence, D. (1988) *Enhancing Self-Esteem in the Classroom*, London: Paul Chapman.

Meek, M. (1988) *How Texts Teach what Readers Learn*. Thimble Press.

Meek, M. (1992) 'Literacy: rediscovering reading', in K. Kimberley, M. Meek and J. Miller (eds) *New Readings. Contributions to an understanding of literacy*, London: A. & C. Black.

Minns, H. (1990) *Read it to me now!* London: Virago.

Oakhill, J. and Beard, R. (1999) *Reading Development and the Teaching of Reading*, Oxford: Blackwell.

Perfetti, C. A. (1999) 'Cognitive Research and the Misconceptions of Reading Education', in Oakhill, J. and Beard, R. *Reading Development and the Teaching of Reading*, Oxford: Blackwell.

Scollon, R. and Scollon, B. (1981) *Narrative, Literacy and Face in Interethnic Communication*, Ablex Publishing.

Seymour, P.H.K. and Elder, L. (1986) 'Beginning Reading without Phonology', *Cognitive Neuropsychology* 3, 1–36.

Siegler, R. S. (1996) *Emerging Minds. The Process of Change in Children's Thinking*, Oxford: Oxford University Press.

Smith, F. (1984) *Joining the Literacy Club*. London: Centre for the Teaching of Reading.

Snowling, M (1987) *Dyslexia. A Cognitive Developmental Perspective*, Oxford, Blackwell

Stanovich, K.E. (1986) 'Matthew effects in reading: Some consequences of individual differences in the acquisition of reading', in *Reading Research Quarterly* 21, 360–406.

Stanovich, K.E. (1999) 'Speculation on the causes and consequences of individual differences in early reading acquisition', in Oakhill, J. and Beard, R. *Reading Development and the Teaching of Reading*, Oxford: Blackwell.

Stein, J. (1999) 'Language and Literacy', paper given at Learning and the Brain. A Public Enquiry. The Lifelong Learning Foundation and the Royal Institution.

Treiman, R. (1985) 'Onsets and rimes as units of spoken syllables: evidence from children', *Journal of Experimental Child Psychology* 39, 161–81.

Tunmer, W.E. and Hoover, W (1992) 'Cognitive and linguistic factors in learning to read', in Gough, P.B., Ehri, L.A. and Treiman, R. (eds) *Reading Acquisition*, Hillsdale: Erlbaum.

Underwood, G. and Batt, V. (1996) *Reading and Understanding*, Blackwell.

Wells, G. (1986) *The Meaning Makers*, Routledge.

Whitehead, M. (1997) *Language and Literacy in the Early Years*, 2nd Edition, Paul Chapman Publishing.

10 Teaching numeracy: helping children become confident mathematicians

David Whitebread

EDITOR'S SUMMARY

This chapter reviews evidence that common difficulties in learning and becoming confident with mathematics are a consequence of a dominant style of teaching in schools which has exposed the weaknesses of human beings as learners, rather than exploited our strengths. School maths has typically been bereft of any real, meaningful or supporting context, has been reliant upon abstract symbolism, involved the learning of new 'pencil and paper' strategies unrelated to naturally developed mental strategies, and has been taught as a set of unexplained and prescribed procedures. The chapter sets out an analysis of how we learn by processes of induction, by developing more efficient ways of using our limited 'working memory' capacity, and through increasing metacognitive awareness and control of our own learning. This analysis supports the development of a new 'emergent' approach to teaching mathematics which involves placing tasks in meaningful contexts, requiring children to make their own representations, encouraging and developing children's strategies, and employing a style of teaching which focuses on processes rather than products.

The difficulties and frustrations of mathematics teaching in schools are widely recognised. Far too many of our young children find learning mathematics in school difficult, lose their confidence in mathematics, and go on to join that large swathe of the adult population that panics at the first sight of

This chapter is a slightly modified version of one originally published as 'Emergent Mathematics *or* How to Help Young Children become Confident Mathematicians', in Anghileri, J. (ed.) (1995) *Children's Mathematical Thinking in the Primary Years*, London: Cassell. It is reprinted here with the permission of the original publisher.

numbers. This chapter reviews a dramatically different and new approach to teaching mathematics to young children which promises to eradicate many of these problems. This new approach grows out of exciting recent work by psychologists and others exploring the ways in which young children learn. In recent years teachers' thinking about the teaching of literacy has been revolutionised by these ideas and developed into a new approach encapsulated in the term 'emergent writing'. This chapter attempts to describe how these same ideas relate to the teaching of early numeracy and together suggest an approach which might be termed 'emergent mathematics'.

In relation to literacy, the 'emergent writing' approach encourages children to begin writing by playing with written symbols, inventing their own 'writing' and using it for their own purposes (notes, lists, thank you letters, diaries, etc). The teacher models the writing process by engaging in writing for her own real purposes explicitly in the presence of the children. The children's writing is valued by the teacher; stories written, for example, might be 'published' in the form of books and placed alongside other books in the class reading corner. This approach to the written word represents an attempt to build on what children already know, and it appears to be very successful (e.g. Hall 1989). Children in classes where this approach is adopted have been found to write much more, much earlier and with more meaning, confidence and enjoyment than children taught to write by more traditional methods.

After the written word, mathematics, of course, is the second major symbol system which young children need to understand. The 'emergent mathematics' approach recognises, therefore, that as with writing, children need to develop an understanding of numbers by playing with them and using them for their own purposes. They need to talk about their mathematical ideas with other children and with teachers, begin by representing mathematical processes in ways which make sense to them, and become more aware of their teacher's, and thus their own, mathematical thinking.

This chapter is divided into three sections. The first section presents an analysis of the nature of children's difficulties with school mathematics. The second section reviews recent findings from developmental psychology which have demonstrated some of the causes of these difficulties, and begun to indicate new ways of assisting children's learning. The final section examines practical implications of these new ideas for teaching mathematics to young children, and itemises the essential elements of an 'emergent mathematics' approach.

Why do young children find school mathematics difficult?

When we are considering the difficulties young children have with mathematics it is important to draw a distinction between what we might call 'home' mathematics and 'school' mathematics. Home mathematics is learnt (rather than taught!) in real world contexts for real purposes. It invariably involves particular objects and is rarely if ever recorded. It involves such things as counting the number of stairs, playing snakes and ladders, handling pocket money and sharing out sweets. School mathematics, by contrast, is often carried out for its own sake, unrelated to any real or particular context, and almost always involves recording using written symbols. All the evidence we have suggests that children become very confident in relation to the kind of mathematical problems they come across in the home, but that the story is very different with the type of mathematics they often face in school. Some important pointers towards making formal mathematics more accessible to young children can therefore be gained by examining the differences between these two contexts, and young children's responses to them.

Many Primary school teachers over the last twenty or thirty years have been influenced in their approach to young children's mathematics by the work of Piaget (1952). This suggested that before they arrived at school young children understood very little about numbers. Researchers such as Gelman and Gallistel (1978), however, have demonstrated that preschool children from as early as the age of two know a lot more about numbers than had previously been thought. Given more appropriate tasks than those designed by Piaget, preschool children could demonstrate some understandings about counting and an ability to conserve number (in one of their experiments, for example, they noted the surprise registered by young children when items 'magically' disappeared).

Studies of children and adults in developing countries, where they either have not been to school or have dropped out early, have found that individuals who cannot cope with 'school mathematics' at all can devise and perform sophisticated mathematical operations to solve real, everyday problems. Studies of unschooled Liberian adults, Kpelle traders and Brazilian street children have all revealed the ability to develop very effective mental calculation routines in relation to real and meaningful everyday practical situations. Brazilian street children trade at street markets from as young as eight or nine years of age. These children have been found to be capable of carrying out mental arithmetic calculations involved in street trading quickly and accurately. Learning 'pencil and paper' routines to solve exactly the same problems proves to be much more difficult. Indeed, researchers found that attempts to follow school-prescribed routines often interfered with Brazilian street children's abilities to solve problems (Nunes *et al.* (1993) usefully review work in this area).

If mathematical understandings seem to develop so easily and naturally out of school, why is it that young children often find learning mathematics in school so difficult? John Holt (1964), in his classic book *How Children Fail*, was among the first to describe the bewilderment of young children when faced with school mathematics. The book is full of examples of children attempting to apply formal procedures they have been taught in school and getting into the most appalling muddles because they don't really understand what they are doing.

Subsequent work has repeatedly confirmed this position. By the end of their Primary schooling, the vast majority of children are capable of carrying out arithmetical calculations using pencil and paper methods they have been taught in school. Many of them, however, have a very poor understanding of what they are actually doing. The Assessment of Performance Unit, reporting in 1980, found a great deal of evidence that children lack understanding of the formal mathematical symbols which are the everyday currency of school mathematics. Children aged 11–13 years, for example, were presented with problems such as this:

> The Green family has to drive 261 miles to get from London to Leeds. After driving 87 miles, they stop for lunch. How do you work out how far they still have to drive?

87×3	$261 + 87$	$87 \div 261$	$261 - 87$
261×87	$261 \div 87$	$87 - 261$	$87 + 174$

As many as 40 per cent of 12-year-olds were unable to select the correct answer ($261 - 87$).

The problem of school mathematics as it has traditionally been taught is illustrated beautifully by an incident recounted to me by a former mathematician colleague, Alison Wood. This began with a conversation between Alison and her younger daughter Susannah, who was seven at the time:

SUSANNAH: Mummy, set me some taking aways with carrying.

ALISON: How do you set them out?

SUSANNAH: You put TU at the top and then two numbers under one another, like this:

Susannah writes

$$\begin{array}{cc} T & U \\ 4 & 2 \\ -2 & 7 \\ \hline \\ \hline \end{array}$$

ALISON: Forty-two minus twenty-seven; how do you do it?

SUSANNAH: No, four two take away two seven.

ALISON: What do you mean?

SUSANNAH: That's the sum.

ALISON: But if you went along the street and saw a door with 42 on it, you wouldn't say that's number four two!

SUSANNAH: No, of course you wouldn't, but that's nothing to do with it.

ALISON: So what does it mean?

SUSANNAH: Nothing, silly, it's a sum.

By this stage, Susannah was beginning to get cross, and so Alison allowed her to finish demonstrating how she did the sum. She used decomposition and found the correct answer, which she read as 'one five', with no difficulty.

ALISON: Good, Susie, can you do forty-two minus twenty-seven?
SUSANNAH: Fifteen.
ALISON: Did you use the sum you have written down?
SUSANNAH: No, I said, 27 + 3 = 30, 30 + 10 = 40, 40 + 2 = 42, so I added 15 altogether in my head.
ALISON: Look at the answer to the sum.
SUSANNAH: The numbers are the same *but the sum is different!*

Alison was then able to help Susannah discover, with the help of Unifix cubes, why the two different sums produced the same answer. The mysterious and meaningless process of 'taking aways with carrying' thus began to be related by Susannah to real mathematics that she already understood, and thus dawned the possibility that school mathematics might mean something.

Not every child, however, is blessed with a mother who is a mathematician. One of Alison's colleagues at the time, David, also had a daughter in the same class, and she asked him to enquire about Anna's mathematics. A few days later he described a conversation he had with his daughter:

DAVID: What sort of sums are you doing?
ANNA: Taking aways.
DAVID: Show me one.
ANNA: T, U, four, two.

Anna writes   T   U
                4   2

She then crossed out the 4, replaced it by a 3 and changed the 2 to 12.

DAVID: So where's the sum?
ANNA: That's it.
DAVID: But why is it a taking away?
ANNA: I took 1 from 4, silly!
DAVID: I thought you put another number underneath like this:

David writes   T   U

                4   2
              −2   1
               ─────

               ─────

ANNA: Oh yes, we do.
DAVID: Can you do it?

Anna tries but fails because she doesn't need to borrow:

She writes: T   U

$$
\begin{array}{cc}
{}^3\!4 & {}^1\!2 \\
-2 & 1 \\
\hline
1 & 11
\end{array}
$$

DAVID: I don't think that's right, is it? How do you do them at school?
ANNA: I ask Susannah.

The nature and source of Anna and Susannah's failures of understanding are very typical. Their teacher has taught them a very clear and precise procedure for carrying out this particular kind of calculation, and both children would no doubt eventually master it. Their level of understanding of what it all means, however, is zero. The nature of the calculation required, or the instructions surrounding it, have only to be changed in the slightest degree and they are left completely stranded.

Four key features of school mathematics clearly emerge from this anecdote, and from the other more systematic kinds of evidence to which we have alluded, each of which contribute to making school mathematics difficult for young children.

- First, it is commonly *bereft of any real, meaningful or supporting context.* In the words of one, often quoted, aspiring young mathematician, the trouble with mathematics is that 'it isn't about anything'.
- Second, school mathematics commonly involves the use of *abstract symbolism.* We will review below evidence which Martin Hughes, a British psychologist, has collected to suggest reasons why this should cause young children such difficulty.
- Third, school mathematics often requires children to use new *'pencil and paper' strategies* which are not simply written versions of the mental strategies which they have already developed for themselves (compare, for example, Susannah's mental strategy for calculating $42 - 27$ with the written method she has been taught).
- Fourth, school mathematics is often taught as a set of *prescribed procedures,* without any attempt to help children really understand numbers and the ways they behave. There is often more emphasis placed on 'getting the right answer' than on understanding the processes involved.

It is important to recognise, however, that the answer to these difficulties cannot be to scrap the kind of mathematics that children learn in school. Formal mathematics may present certain difficulties to the learner, but these largely stem from features which make this kind of mathematics such a powerful analytic tool. Formal mathematics is a very significant human achievement which enables all kinds of complex and important problems and phenomena to be more accurately described and explored. Even in our everyday lives, particularly in technologically advanced societies, the ability to use formal mathematical procedures is of enormous benefit, without which individuals are disadvantaged.

The argument of this chapter is that formal 'school' mathematics can, indeed, be learnt much more easily by young children than at present. If we are to achieve this, however, teaching methods need to be adapted towards an 'emergent mathematics' approach. This approach can be defined in relation to the four key features of school mathematics identified above. An 'emergent mathematics' approach involves placing tasks in meaningful contexts, helping children to understand the nature and purpose of mathematical symbols, encouraging children to develop and explore a variety of mental and written strategies, and requiring children to reflect upon mathematical processes.

These key elements of the 'emergent mathematics' approach will be further developed in the third and final section of this chapter. To get a thorough understanding of this approach, and the ways in which its key elements hang together, however, it is important to understand some recent work carried out by developmental psychologists. This work has revealed a number of important aspects of the ways in which young children think and learn which are of enormous significance to us as teachers. These recent findings underpin the 'emergent writing' and 'emergent mathematics' approach to teaching young children in these two most important areas. The next section reviews this work.

Psychological research: how do children think and learn?

There have been a number of models of human learning developed by psychologists. The dominant model in contemporary psychological research on human learning is of the child as an information processor attempting to make sense of, and derive meaning from, experience (i.e. to classify, categorise and order new information and to relate it to what is already known). This model characterises the young child as actively processing information and generating predictions and hypotheses about their world which they are constantly testing against experience.

There are three main features of the human information processing system which are worth briefly reviewing. Each has very direct implications for introducing young children to the world of formal mathematics.

Learning by induction

The first major feature of human learning which has strong implications for approaches to teaching young children is that it appears to be very predominantly a process of identifying patterns and regularities from the variety of our experience. As human beings we appear to be very able to engage in the process of *induction* (inferring general rules or patterns from a range of particular cases), but relatively less well equipped for *deductive* reasoning (the opposite process of inferring particular cases from a general rule).

Inductive reasoning is the basic process whereby we make sense of our world, by classifying and categorising experience into increasingly structured conceptual structures and models. The overwhelming significance of inductive processes for human learning has long been recognised, and has always been a strong element, for example, within intelligence tests. 'What is the next number in the sequence 1, 2, 4, 8, ?' is a test of inductive reasoning.

By contrast, research involving syllogisms, for example, has consistently shown that humans have very real difficulties with deductive logic . The relative facility with which we all learnt the grammar of our first language, by working out the rules for ourselves (aided by a little 'motherese') as contrasted against the horrendous difficulty many experience attempting to learn the grammar of a second language by being taught the rules, and being asked to apply them, is a good example of the superiority of inductive processes.

This search for patterns and regularities within the variety of experience has important implications for the ways in which young children make sense of new experiences. They expect to find pattern and regularity, and they expect new experiences to fit together in some way with what they already know. This is the means by which any of us makes sense of anything new with which we are faced, by relating it to what we already know. This natural and powerful human way of learning is, of course, vastly inhibited when we are presented with new information or experience which does not relate at all to what we already know. This has clear and major implications for the ways we go about introducing young children to the formal rules and procedures of school mathematics. It is clear that tasks and procedures within school mathematics are often not placed in contexts which make them meaningful to young children. This is a point to which we will return.

Limited 'working memory' capacity

The second major feature of human learning which has strong implications for approaches to teaching young children is that the human being is a limited capacity processor of information. Miller (1956), in his paper 'The Magic Number 7 Plus or Minus 2', demonstrated from a whole range of evidence that we can hold only about seven separate pieces of information in our short-term or 'working' memory. This is why as adults we can easily process in our heads a sum such as 17×9, but have much greater difficulty with 184×596. We know the procedures we must go through to get the answer to the second sum, and we can carry out each of the separate computations involved. What we cannot do, however, is hold all of the information in our heads at once. While we are working out one part, the result of the previous computation is very likely to be forgotten. This happens all the time for children, of course, with much smaller numbers and less complicated procedures.

In order to cope with this structural limitation, a number of features of our information processing system develop. That each of these features are relatively under-developed in children is significant for their learning, and has implications for ways in which we can go about helping them to learn most effectively. Three features which are particularly significant are those relating to the development of *selective attention, structured knowledge* and *processing strategies.*

Selective attention

To begin with our processing is characterised by the development of the ability to selectively attend to those features which are relevant to the task in hand. This is largely achieved by the processes of inductive reasoning discussed above, and is vital if we are not to be overwhelmed by the huge array of information which is bombarding us through our five senses every moment of our waking life. The commonly observed ability of children to notice and observe features of a situation or event which adults have missed or overlooked is just the positive side of their inability, through lack of experience, to selectively attend to relevant information. I well remember my own elder daughter's account of a machine she had been impressed by during a school visit to the Science Museum in London. From her description it could be deduced that what she had seen was a 'working model' of an internal combustion engine. When asked what she thought the machine did, however, she expressed the opinion that it had something to do with gravel, as it had been 'surrounded by the stuff'!

Young children's inability to sort out the relevant from the irrelevant is a very significant feature of their early difficulties with school mathematics. Relevant features of situations or tasks are learnt by the processes of inductive reasoning. These processes depend upon the new task being presented within a variety of meaningful contexts (just as a new word or aspect of grammar might be 'presented' to a young child in their everyday experience of language). Often, within school mathematics, quite the opposite has been the case, with new tasks being presented in one particular way only, and divorced from any meaningful context. It is not surprising that Susannah, in our earlier example, had seen no connection between the 'home' and 'school' mathematics versions of subtraction, because the task had not been presented to her in a way which enabled her to relate it to anything she already knew. Often children taught to do sums vertically cannot do the same calculations when they are presented horizontally, and will say that sums cannot be done like that. They have not sorted out the relevant from the irrelevant because they have not been presented with the opportunity to do so.

Interestingly, much of the criticism of Piaget's work in relation to young children's mathematical understandings is concerned with the abstract and meaningless nature of his tasks. Margaret Donaldson (1978) and her collaborators reported, in her classic book *Children's Minds,* a whole series of experiments which demonstrated that children often failed Piaget's tests of, for example, number conservation, because they had been unable to sort out the relevant features of the task. This book is an excellent introduction to the importance of meaningful contexts in young children's learning.

Structured knowledge

A second feature of human processing which equips us to deal with the structural limitations of our memories concerns the way we store what we know. As we learn more about any particular topic, not only does our knowledge become more extensive, but it also becomes more structured. There are two aspects to this of which we need to be aware, namely 'chunking' and 'elaboration'.

Chunking is the process whereby several separate pieces of information become commonly associated together, and so come to be remembered as one piece of information. Consider the following two sequences of 9 numbers:

    4 6 2 9 7 1 8 3 5
    1 2 3 4 5 6 7 8 9

It is clear that as an adult the second sequence would be infinitely easier to remember, because it can be stored as one piece of information i.e. the numbers from 1 to 9. For a child who could not count in sequence, however, both sets of numbers would be equally difficult to remember.

Elaboration refers to the process whereby, as we become more experienced in an area, we make more connections between different parts of our knowledge. This has the consequence that we have much more chance to make connections with new information, to classify and categorise it, to make sense of it and understand its significance, and thus, once again, to select out the relevant features.

Both these features of the ways in which our memories develop are dependent upon processes of representation. This has been an enormously important area of investigation for developmental psychologists in recent years, and much research has been carried out to try to explore the ways in which our knowledge is represented and stored in our brains, and how these representations develop in children. There is still a great deal to be discovered about these processes. What is clear, however, is that the ability of humans to use various kinds of symbolic representation, such as pictures, words and numbers, is crucially important in the development of our cognitive abilities. This would appear to be because the use of such representation allows more extensive processing and manipulation of larger units of information. Bruner and Kenney (1966) demonstrated this very clearly with their famous 'Nine glasses' experiment (which I review in more detail in Chapter 8).

The implications for teaching young children school mathematics are fundamental, and twofold. First, it is clearly important that they become confident users of mathematical symbols. If they are going to be of any use to young children, however, these symbols must be meaningful and integrated into their mathematical knowledge. As we shall see below, Martin Hughes, in his important research on children's understandings about numbers (Hughes 1986), has shown that mathematical symbols often carry very limited meaning for young children. Second, it is clear that young children need to learn to represent their mathematical understandings in language. The implications of both these aspects of the development of mathematical representation are discussed below. The encouragement of young children to actively represent their mathematical understandings to themselves and others is clearly fundamental to the 'emergent mathematics' approach.

Processing strategies

The third major feature of human cognitive development, related to the need to work with our limited processing capacity, is the development of increasingly sophisticated intellectual strategies. These can be broadly categorised as general processing strategies, related to improving the efficiency with which the various parts of the human information processing system are used themselves, and domain-specific strategies, which relate to particular areas of knowledge.

Research has demonstrated that children appear to have very much the same processing capacities as adults, but they are very largely unstrategic in their use. For example, at the general processing level young children, relative to adults, search visual arrays for information less systematically, search their existing knowledge less thoroughly in order to make sense of new information or problems, are less likely to rehearse or categorise new information to help them remember it, and so on (see Siegler 1991, or Meadows 1993).

At the domain-specific level, in relation to mathematics, a lot of research has explored the way in which children gradually develop more sophisticated strategies, particularly in relation to counting and mental calculation. A number of researchers have looked at the emergence of the so-called MIN strategy for addition. At an early stage children faced with a problem like 3 + 9 will either count 3, or start at 3, and then count on 9. At some point, however, they realise that it is more efficient to always start from the larger number (i.e. start at 9 and count on 3). This is the MIN strategy.

The emergence of such strategies appears to be a very gradual process. Rather than just appearing out of the blue, new strategies are often extensions, modifications or combinations of existing strategies. After a new strategy has been used for the first time, an older simpler strategy is often reverted to for quite a while, and the new strategy only takes over very slowly. When faced with a more difficult problem, a simpler, more well-used strategy often reappears. Children often appear to lack confidence in new strategies, and will double-check the results by using a simpler strategy. My own daughter, for example, frustrated me for years by insisting on counting out in 'ones' sums such as 23 + 10, even though she 'knew' (in some sense) that the answer must be 33.

This issue of confidence appears to be crucial in this area. How we might go about helping children confidently to develop and explore a sophisticated range of strategies for dealing with numbers we will explore below. What is clear is that the present approach within school mathematics of ignoring strategies that children have already developed, and teaching them 'pencil and paper' strategies which bear no obvious relation to their existing strategies, is not helpful.

Developing 'metacognitive' awareness and control

After the dominance of learning by induction and the limited capacity of 'working memory', the third general feature of the human information processing system which we must consider is that it is a system which not only learns, but learns how to learn. The American psychologist, John Flavell (1981), was a prominent early investigator in this area. He pointed out that not only do individuals develop strategies, but also they develop the ability to use them appropriately. This is a consequence of what he termed 'metacognitive' processes, whereby we all become more aware of our own intellectual processes, and more in control of them. These metacognitive processes have been an area of enormous research effort within developmental psychology over the last fifteen to twenty years.

Flavell and his collaborators carried out a series of experiments in the 1960s and 1970s which demonstrated the development of 'metamemory' in young children. Children of different ages were shown sets of objects, and some of the objects were pointed to in sequence by the experimenter. After an interval of fifteen seconds, the children were asked to repeat the sequence. While 7-year-olds were perfectly capable of using a rehearsal strategy and remembering the sequence, 5-year-olds did not rehearse and failed in the memory task. When instructed to rehearse, however, the 5-year-olds turned out to be perfectly capable of doing so, and with consequent success in the task. But when the task was repeated, without the specific instruction to rehearse, many of the 5-year-olds reverted to not rehearsing, and failing to remember the sequence of objects. Flavell termed this failure to use an appropriate strategy, of which the 5-year-olds were clearly perfectly capable, a 'production deficit'.

Subsequent research in many areas of intellectual functioning has revealed exactly the same pattern. As adults we have learnt to monitor our own functioning very closely; we are usually aware when we do not understand something, when we have forgotten something, or when our current way of trying to tackle a problem is not working. Young children often show none of this self-awareness. Experiments carried out with the 'tip-of-the-tongue' phenomenon, for example, show that adults are very much more accurate than children in deciding whether they will recognise the name of something they have forgotten if they are told it.

As a consequence of this kind of metacognitive monitoring, adults build up a store of knowledge about their own abilities and limitations, the characteristics of various tasks, and the potential uses of a wide range of strategies. Young children also show severe limitations in these areas. They are regularly, for example, wildly optimistic about the number of objects they will be able to remember when playing Kim's Game (where objects are shown briefly and then hidden under a cloth). Adults are generally very accurate with this kind of metacognitive knowledge.

The implications for children's learning of mathematics are clearly highly significant. As we have indicated within the earlier part of this chapter, and has often been noted by commentators, children's problems with school mathematics are not so much related to an inability to carry out taught routines or strategies, but more to their inability to be aware of when they are appropriate. How often have we all set children some 'problems', of the type:

> Johnny has 3 apples. Timmy has 4 apples.
> How many apples do they have altogether?

only to be faced with the inevitable question,

> 'Is it an add, Miss?'

And this from children who could work out the answer to this kind of problem in their own way when they were several years younger. The teaching of 'pencil and paper' strategies for tackling certain kinds of mathematics problems is all too often done in a way that does not encourage children to reflect upon the processes involved, so that they can become in control of the new strategy. Sadly, all that often seems to be achieved, as has been found with such as the Brazilian street children, is to interfere with young children's natural problem-solving abilities developed in more meaningful surroundings. It is clearly important within the 'emergent mathematics' approach that children are encouraged to be reflective about their own processing, and to adopt and develop strategies in ways that put them in control.

Implications for early mathematics teaching

The new understandings which derive from all this recent and current research into the processes by which children think and learn have clear and major implications for teaching mathematics to young children. To date, as we have reviewed, these new understandings have been taken on board most notably in the area of introducing young children to writing. What it is intended to argue here is that the introduction of young children to formal, written mathematics would benefit enormously from the same kind of approach. The final section of this chapter attempts to develop and illustrate four key ideas or themes which together define what is beginning to be called 'emergent mathematics'. This approach has been very much inspired by the work of Martin Hughes (1986).

Sue Atkinson (1992), in her book *Mathematics with Reason* has provided an edited collection of classroom applications and examples of practice. In the introduction to her book she defines 'mathematics with reason' by reference to fourteen points, from which the following nine are selected to serve as a definition of the 'emergent mathematics' approach.

- It is mathematics which starts from the secure 'home learning' established in the child before she comes to school.
- It is mathematics based on understanding.
- It puts great emphasis on the child's own methods of calculating and solving problems and rejects the previous practice of heavy emphasis on standard written algorithms.
- Mathematics is regarded as a powerful tool for interpreting the world and therefore should be rooted in real experience across the whole curriculum … Mathematics is brought out of the child's everyday situations.
- Mathematics with reason is rooted in action: learning through doing.
- Mathematics with reason puts less emphasis on representing numbers on paper as 'sums' and more emphasis on developing mental images in the child.
- The main tool for child and teacher to employ in the mastery of mathematics concepts is language, not pencil and paper exercises from textbooks. The child is encouraged to talk about what she is doing.
- Errors are accepted as an essential part of the learning process. The child, freed from the fear of criticism, will more readily experiment.
- Mathematics with reason emphasises the thinking processes of mathematics, and these are made explicit in the conversations between adult and child.

(Atkinson 1992:12–13)

These ideas can be encapsulated in four essential ideas or themes which derive directly from what we now know about the development of children's thinking and learning, as outlined in the previous section. They also have clear and radical implications for our approach to introducing young children to the world of formal mathematics. These four themes involve placing tasks in *meaningful contexts*, requiring children to make their *own representations*, encouraging and developing *children's strategies*, and employing a style of teaching which focuses on *processes rather than products*.

Placing tasks in meaningful contexts

Most fundamentally, this new approach recognises the lessons of research into 'home mathematics' and 'school mathematics'. As we have reviewed, children learn to understand and use numbers with confidence and enthusiasm before they enter school. In real situations, where the mathematics serves real purposes, young children quickly and easily develop their own informal and largely effective methods. The difficulties start when they enter school and are expected to operate in the abstract, to use formal 'pencil and paper' routines and procedures and to do mathematics for no clear purpose. The example of Susannah and Anna's attempts with subtraction illustrate this point well.

Evidence about the way children learn would seem to suggest that what we need to do is to start with real problems, and work from them to abstract representations, not the other way around (see Figure 10.1). As Margaret Donaldson's work has amply illustrated, placing tasks in meaningful contexts enables children to understand what it is that they are required to do. The point is illustrated well by Hughes' (1986) box game, which he reports in *Children and Number.* Here bricks are placed in a box, and, as bricks are added or taken away, the child has to say how many bricks are now in the box. Hughes found that many young, even pre-school children were able to do this with small numbers, but they were completely flummoxed by being presented with the same sum in the abstract. Here is a typical piece of dialogue between Hughes and a 4 -year-old, Amanda.

HUGHES: How many is two and one? (*Long pause. No response.*) Well how many bricks is two bricks and one brick?
AMANDA: Three.
HUGHES: Okay. So how many is two and one?
AMANDA (*Pause*): Four? (*hesitantly*)
HUGHES: How many is one brick and one more brick?
AMANDA: Two bricks.
HUGHES: So, how many is one and one?
AMANDA: One, maybe.

(Hughes 1986:46)

It is clear that when Amanda is faced with the real, concrete problems of numbers of bricks, she understands what is required and is able to carry out the calculation. She is able to produce some kind of internal representation of these real problems, and carry it out in her head, perhaps by producing images of the real bricks in the box. The same problems posed in the abstract clearly fail to trigger the same kind of process.

There are, of course, abundant opportunities in the everyday activities of young children to get them involved in real mathematics. Playing games, sharing biscuits, deciding what is fair, finding out how many days it is to someone's birthday, cooking and shopping are all examples quoted by Atkinson (1992). In her book, teachers recount inspiring examples of exciting mathematics projects with titles such as 'Young children plan a picnic', 'Tracey and Jason make a map' and 'Children build a natural area and pond'. In one chapter, entitled 'Real "real problem-solving"' Owen Tregaskis argues that for problems to be real they must have direct relevance to the lives of the children. He describes a project in which his class planned, organised and ran a mini-sports day. This was done on their own initiative as

Figure 10.1 Children need to start from real problems and work out the mathematics from there

their way of improving the school. They were involved in buying and selling refreshments, designing and making shields for prizes, and designing and running the various events (including marking out the running track).

With young children in particular (although this is certainly true throughout the Primary range and probably beyond) problems can be real yet essentially born of the imagination. Problems arising through imaginative play or stories, indeed, can often be even more vivid for young children than genu-inely real life problems. A superb example of the possibilities of mathematics from imaginative play is to be found in the ideas and activities developed by Zoe Evans (see references). This British early years educator has developed a whole series of activities based upon all kinds of cuddly toys, including fami-lies of ladybirds, snakes and dogs (see Figure 10.2). These sets of animals are, of course, enormously appealing to young children, and each set has its own story to stimulate all kinds of sorting, matching, counting and other mathe-matical activities.

While young children may be helped to develop their mathematical abili-ties and understandings by tackling real problems placed within contexts which are meaningful to them, it is important, however, as we have stated earlier, that they learn to depend less upon the support of such contexts. Mathematics gains its power from its abstractness, and children need to be helped to become confident with abstract mathematical processes.

There are two elements to this. First, the same process or concept needs to be presented to them in a variety of meaningful contexts. In this way, by the natural processes of induction which we have discussed, children are able to sort out the relevant from the irrelevant. Indeed, they are ultimately able to abstract for themselves the essential elements of the process or concept (see James 1985).

Requiring children to make their own representations

The second element which is required to help children move towards abstract thinking in mathematics involves helping them to develop their rep-resentational abilities. This is also my second key idea or theme within the 'emergent mathematics' approach. Perhaps the newest element within this approach is the suggestion that children should be given opportunities to make their own representations of mathematics problems, processes and procedures before they are introduced to the conventional symbols. In this respect 'emergent mathematics' parallels very closely the ideas of 'emergent writing', where young pre-literate children are encouraged to make their own writing for their own purposes.

The significance of representational processes within the development of human knowledge and thinking has been indicated above in the earlier review of the work of Bruner and others. Within mathematics it is clear that if children are to become able and confident mathematicians, they must be able to represent mathematics to themselves and to others, in language and in mathematical symbols. In this section I want to review a range of work which has indicated, at least in broad terms, the kinds of ways that teachers can help children to develop these abilities.

That there is a problem in relation to children's understanding and confi-dence with the conventional mathematical symbolism is the central thesis of Hughes' (1986) enormously valuable book. He began by asking children

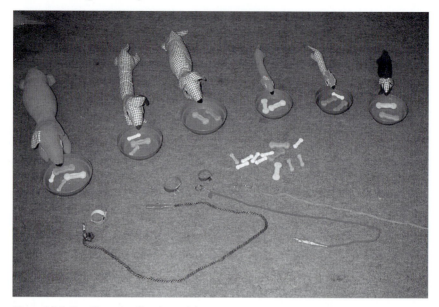

Figure 10.2 Zoe Evans' collection of dogs

aged 3–7 years to represent particular mathematical phenomena. For example, they were presented with paper and pencil, and a quantity of bricks was placed on the table in front of them. They were then asked, 'Can you put something on the paper to show how many bricks are on the table?' (Hughes 1986:55). The children produced all kinds of responses, which Hughes goes on to analyse. What he found to be highly significant, however, was that, despite the fact that the children from Class 1 onwards (5-year-olds) had mathematics workbooks full of the conventional symbols, it was not until Class 3 (7 year olds) that these symbols became the predominant response. The children's lack of confidence with the symbols they had been taught in school was even more marked in relation to representing zero and the processes of addition and subtraction.

Intrigued by these findings, Hughes went on to invent the 'tins game' to explore children's ability to develop their own mathematical symbols. This game consisted of presenting young children (aged 4–5 years) with a number of tins, each of which held a different number of bricks, and asking the children to 'put something on the paper' on the top of each tin so that they would know how many bricks were inside.

Hughes found that not only could these young children make their own representations on the tins, but they were very able to read these invented symbols back. Sue Atkinson has conducted similar experiments and has also found that children's own invented symbols hold enormous meaning for them. The conclusion that they both draw, paralleling the work which has been done with emergent writing, is that children gain an understanding and confidence in written symbols by first inventing and using their own.

Atkinson (1992) also provides a number of useful pointers to helping children make the transition from their own to the conventional symbol system. To begin with she notes that many teachers have found that children's development of the use of recording in mathematics is best sustained when they are allowed to record when they feel the need to do so. Processes of successive shorthanding and, interestingly, the use of calculators, both naturally lead children to introduce the conventional symbols into their recordings, in the same way that standard letters rapidly appear in children's emergent writing.

If children are to become confident and competent mathematicians, however, the development of written symbolism must be accompanied by the development of mathematical language. Indeed, many mathematics educators now believe that it is important that children express their mathematical thinking in language, through talk, before they begin to represent it on paper. James (1985) reviews the evidence of Bruner and others of the inter-relationships between language and thought, and propounds a mathematics teaching procedure which he terms 'do, talk and record'. This involves children in doing mathematics practically, and then following a five-step sequence of activities towards recording, thus:

- the learners explain their thinking to others
- they demonstrate their mental images either with objects or by sketches
- they record in writing the 'story' of what their sketches show
- they make successive abbreviations of the process they used
- finally, they can see the relevance of and adopt standard notations.

(James 1985:43)

An enormous amount has been written about the need for young children to talk about mathematics with their teachers, and in groups with their peers. What follows is a review of some work carried out by a student of mine which demonstrates a way in which teachers can use a certain kind of talk to help children develop representations of mathematical processes. This is an example of the way in which children's representational processes can be encouraged to help them to make the transition from context-bound to abstract understandings.

The student, Douglas Mayther, worked with 3- and 4-year-old children in a local Nursery school and adapted a procedure originally devised by Hughes (1986), once again involving tins and bricks. In the control group children were asked to do computations related to the number of bricks put in and taken out of the tin, and exactly the same computations presented as abstract verbal 'sums'. As Hughes reported, Douglas found that the children could tell you that there were two bricks in the tin, and now you had added one more there were three. But they were unable to respond at all to the question, 'How many is 2 and 1 more?'

With a second group of children, however, Douglas carried out some versions of the task which appear to have helped the children to represent the problem to themselves in ways which facilitated the move from the concrete, real life situation to the abstract mathematics. First of all, he used a tin without bricks and asked the hypothetical question:

If I put 2 bricks in the tin, how many would be in the tin?

Then:

If I put 1 more brick in the tin, how many would there be?

The next development was to use a hypothetical tin. With neither tin nor bricks in the child's vision, the same kinds of questions were asked again. These children were then finally also asked questions of the type 'How many is 2 and 1 more?' Strikingly, they were much more able to answer this kind of formal mathematical question.

The procedure carried out by Douglas, he argued, required and enabled the children to internally represent the problem to themselves. This began with a specific image, in this case of a tin and some bricks, but the children were clearly able to use this to help themselves solve the more abstract (or, in Donaldson's words (Donaldson 1978), 'disembedded') problems. This is related to the processes by which placing tasks in meaningful contexts help children to see what is relevant and irrelevant in a task, and which processes are required. Essentially, Douglas's technique appears to have helped children to provide their own meaningful representation of a disembedded piece of mathematics.

Given this kind of experience in a variety of contexts, the ability to make sense of abstract mathematics by reference to particular, concrete representations may well be encouraged to develop. For this reason, the development of children's representational processes is a hugely important area in relation to building confidence and understanding in mathematics. As well as encouraging talk and graphical representations, Hughes also argues that children should be encouraged to use their fingers. These are, after all, almost universally the first symbols that we all use to represent mathematical quantities.

Encouraging and developing strategies

As well as being faced with abstract symbolism and new mathematical language, the child in making the transition from 'home' to 'school' mathematics is also faced with a range of new paper and pencil strategies. The difficulties this causes can also be alleviated by new approaches to encouraging and developing children's strategies, and this is my third key theme within 'emergent mathematics'.

The new approach, as Atkinson (1992) reviewed, puts:

... great emphasis on the child's own methods of calculating and solving problems and rejects the previous practice of heavy emphasis on standard written algorithms.

(Atkinson 1992:13)

As we have seen from the example with Susannah, and as researchers have found with unschooled children and adults, natural and informal methods of mental calculation are developed, and these often bear little obvious relation to written 'paper and pencil' methods. To take the example of the problem facing Susannah, many children and adults solve subtraction problems by counting on.

This lack of a relationship between informal and formal methods is a major cause of young children's loss of confidence with school mathematics. In line with other features of the approach, 'emergent mathematics' attempts to tackle this difficulty by recognising the ways in which children learn new strategies, and devising a way forward which builds on these processes. As we have reviewed, children need to be confident with new strategies, and this involves understanding how a new strategy relates to their existing strategies, and what are its appropriate uses. This can only be achieved by teachers first recognising the significance of children's existing strategies, allowing children to use them, devising ways of representing them (either verbally in discussion, or graphically on paper, or both) and making it explicit that a range of strategies are acceptable, and all have their uses.

What is clear is that children cannot be encouraged to use new strategies very effectively by simply being taught them as an abstract procedure. It has long been accepted that children have great difficulty in using or applying the mathematical strategies and procedures they are taught in school. It is well-documented, for example, that children aged around three to six years are often capable of counting, and yet they fail to use this as a strategy for solving particular problems where it might be applied. A second student, Angela Root, recently carried out a study related to this particular 'production deficit'. This study very successfully illustrated one quite powerful way of encouraging young children to use a strategy by giving them confidence in it.

Angela identified children in this age range who could count a row of 9 bears, but used matching one-to-one rather than counting when shown a row of 7 blue bears and asked to put out the same number of yellow bears. She then split these children into two groups. With the first group she instructed the children directly to use counting to solve the bears problem. The children were told to count how many blue bears were on the table and then to count out the same number of yellow bears. With the second group, Angela asked the children to set up the bears problem for her to solve. She then modelled how to use counting as a strategy for solving it, explicitly describing to the child what she was doing at each stage, and why.

All the children were then set a further bears problem of the same type, and were also posed a second, rather different problem. In this second problem, two rows of bears were set out on the table, a row of 6 red bears, and a row of 7 green bears. The bears were placed in such a way so that the line of red bears was longer than the row of green bears, and the children were asked to say which row contained the biggest number of bears.

The results of this study were very interesting. On the original matching problem there was no significant difference between the direct instruction and modelling teaching styles. Both groups of children increased their use of counting as a strategy. However, the difference between the two teaching styles for the second problem comparing the rows of bears was quite dramatic. On this problem none of the children in the direct instruction group used counting (and nearly all of them failed to answer correctly), while around a half of the modelling group successfully solved the comparison problem by using counting.

This research has indicated that one way in which children can learn most effectively is when they are engaged in particular kinds of 'dialogue' with adults. As such, it is in line with the findings of quite a body of research, as reviewed in the first part of this chapter, which has been inspired by the approach of the Russian psychologist, Lev Vygotsky (see Moll 1990). Vygotsky argued that all learning is essentially social in origin. It is not difficult to see why the 'modelling' approach adopted by Angela might help young children develop a confidence and understanding with regard to a new strategy or way of proceeding. The children have seen that this is how an adult tackles the problem, and they have also been provided with an insight into the adult's thinking.

Employing a style of teaching which focuses on processes rather than products

This kind of research has also gone on to suggest that it is by such processes of social interaction and dialogue with more experienced learners (i.e. adults, or more experienced peers) that children learn to be reflective about their own processing and so begin to learn how to learn. This relates to the kinds of 'metacognitive' developments first identified by Flavell (1981) reviewed above, and is my fouth key element within an 'emergent mathematics' approach.

All too often school mathematics is about getting the right answer, by whatever means. Many teachers have a fund of stories of the ingenious ways young children have devised for getting the right answer without having to trouble themselves with understanding the mathematics. I once, for example, came across a child called Mark who was faced with this on a page of his mathematics book:

Making 7

7 + __ = 7	0 + __ = 7
6 + __ = 7	1 + __ = 7
5 + __ = 7	2 + __ = 7
4 + __ = 7	3 + __ = 7
3 + __ = 7	4 + __ = 7
2 + __ = 7	5 + __ = 7
1 + __ = 7	6 + __ = 7
0 + __ = 7	7 + __ = 7

'What's all this about?' I said.

'Oh, it's easy. I know how to do these,' Mark replied, and proceeded to write in the numbers from 0 to 7 down the first column, and then again up the second column. The whole procedure took a few seconds. He proudly demonstrated how the same technique had worked for 6, 5, 4 and 3 on previous pages in his book, which were festooned with masses of lovely red ticks. It was not immediately obvious that he had appreciated the commutative law of addition (i.e. that 3 + 4 must be the same as 4 + 3), or that he was engaged in 'algebra', or that he had even noticed which numbers he was writing next to which, or even that there were addition sums on the page.

But he was getting them all right, and that was all that mattered. It appeared that his teacher never saw how Mark completed these pages, and never discussed it with him. Since he was getting them all right, there was obviously no need!

It is the final key element in an 'emergent mathematics' approach that processes must be more important than products. Mathematics with reason, as we noted Atkinson lists earlier,

> emphasises the thinking processes of mathematics, and these are made explicit in the conversations between adult and child.
>
> (Atkinson 1992:13).

Such explicit discussions about mathematical processes serve a number of important purposes. They clearly make it much more likely that children are going to develop understanding of the mathematics they are doing, and be enabled to make sense of it, and become more confident with it. They are the only clear way in which a teacher can reliably assess children's understanding, and become aware of the true nature of any misunderstandings, which must inform and vastly improve the effectiveness of subsequent teaching.

And finally, we have strong evidence that such conversations help children considerably to become more aware of and reflective about their own processing. The benefits in terms of helping children to become effective learners of this kind of approach have been well demonstrated by such as Nisbet and Shucksmith (1986), who trialled a programme of metacognitive training for young children with Primary school teachers.

The development of metacognitive abilities may be fostered by 'dialogues' of a number of different kinds. As we mentioned above, one approach which a number of researchers have found useful involves an adult explicitly modelling and explaining a strategy in relation to a particular problem. Another approach is to encourage children routinely to question themselves about their understandings, and to reflect upon and record their achievements. Teachers can ask children to explain their approaches to problems, and discuss with groups different approaches to the same problem. James (1985), some of whose work was reviewed above, provides a range of examples of teachers talking to children about mathematics, and children talking to one another, in ways which are helpful in fostering these kinds of developments. He particularly singles out the value of children working collaboratively to solve mathematical problems. This obliges children to make their thinking explicit to others, and to reflect upon their own reasoning and choice of strategies and approach. In his examples, the children were required to work out problems together, and then show the class teacher the answer they have arrived at and, most importantly, to justify their method.

Summary

This chapter has attempted to describe what is potentially a very exciting and powerful set of ideas to guide the introduction of young children to formal 'school' mathematics. It would be arrogant and foolhardy to suggest that we yet know all the answers. What is hopefully clear from this review is that, from the practical experience of mathematics educators, from research in children's mathematical understanding, and from the explorations of developmental psychologists related to children's learning, we do have some strong indications of the kinds of direction in which we ought to move. If we want to help many more young children make a confident start into the world of school mathematics, we need to:

- start with real problems, in order to present children with mathematical processes embedded in a variety of meaningful contexts
- encourage children to represent their mathematical understandings both verbally and graphically, beginning with symbols of their own devising
- allow and encourage children to develop their own mathematical strategies
- involve children in a variety of kinds of dialogue which encourage awareness of and reflection upon mathematical processes.

As we have reviewed, the human information processing system has great strengths, but also inherent weaknesses. The current dominant methods of introducing young children to the world of abstract symbolic mathematics exposes the weaknesses of human learning. What we need to do is to harness its strengths. If we can begin to do this, the benefits for children's confidence and performance in mathematics could be very remarkable.

Activities

Real problems

Set children a 'real' problem with some mathematical content. Some suggestions might be: planning a picnic; working out how many pieces of apple or orange they can each have from a bowlful presented to them; or how many coloured pencils are needed if each table is to have one of each colour; finding out how many days it is to their birthday; organising a class shop; sorting out the dolls' clothes and making sure they all have enough to wear; comparing the number of boys and girls in the class; working out a rota for time on the computer or in the home corner.

Observe the children attempting to tackle the problem and note the strategies they use; try to identify mathematical content and processes; try to identify ways in which the real context helps the children with the mathematics. What do they show you that they understand that they might not otherwise have revealed?

Hidden number games and written representations

If you have a young class (up to 7-year-olds), play a game like Hughes' 'tins game' and see how the children in your class respond. You could use any kind of counter (stone, button, pound coin) and any kind of container (tin, envelope, handbag, etc.) Here are some possibilities for what you might try:

* show the child counters in each container and ask him or her to make a mark on container 'to help us remember how many there are inside'
* add or subtract some counters and ask the child to record what has happened
* ask the child to read back the numbers he or she has recorded
* have three containers with different numbers in each; show the child and ask him or her to find the one with most in ('the winner') after you have switched them around a lot; ask the child if there is anything he or she could do to help – allow marks to be made on all three containers and see if it helps; discuss with the child how they could tell which was which.

With older children you could ask them to carry out an arithmetical procedure with practical apparatus and then record what they have done on paper.

In each case, do the children use conventional symbols, or do they invent their own even if they have maths books full of conventional symbols? (Hughes suggests children will do this up to the age of 7.) Can they interpret their own symbolic representations immediately, the next day, or a week later? Do you think this kind of exercise helps in any way?

Strategy games

Play games which require children to use their maths and work out strategies in a competitive situation. This is often a very good stimulus of heated mathematical and strategic discussion! Here are two examples.

- Provide a set of cards with the numbers 1 to 9 on them and set them out face up on the table. Two children must take a card alternately; the winner is the first to have three cards adding up to 15.
- Space Invaders! Provide three dice and two calculators. The children throw the dice and must use the three digits to make a number on their calculators. They then take turns to 'shoot' down the number of their opponent using 'ammunition' marked –100, –10 or –1. The first child to make their opponents number zero is the winner.

Listen to the talk generated by these games. Are the children learning anything? Can you learn anything about what they do and do not understand?

Further reading

Atkinson, S. (ed.) (1992) *Mathematics with Reason*, London: Hodder & Stoughton.
Hughes, M. (1986) *Children and Number*, Oxford: Basil Blackwell.
Nunes, T. and Bryant, P. (1996) *Children Doing Mathematics*, Oxford: Basil Blackwell.
Thompson, I. (ed.) *Teaching and Learning Early Number*, Buckingham: Open University Press.

References

APU (Assessment of Performance Unit) (1980) *Mathematical Development*, Primary Survey Report No. 1, London: HMSO.
Atkinson, S. (ed.) (1992) *Mathematics with Reason*, London: Hodder & Stoughton.
Bruner, J.S. and Kenney, H. (1966) 'The development of the concepts of order and proportion in children', in Bruner, J.S. *et al.* (eds) *Studies in Cognitive Growth*, New York: Wiley.
Donaldson, M. (1978) *Children's Minds*, London: Fontana.
Evans, Z. booklets available from Hendre Craft, 'Old Barns', Newton St. Cyres, Exeter, EX5 5BY, UK.

Flavell, J.H. (1981) 'Cognitive monitoring', in Dickson, W.P. (ed.) *Children's Oral Communication Skills*, New York: Academic Press.

Gelman, R. and Gallistel, C.R. (1978) *The Child's Understanding of Number*, Cambridge, Mass: Harvard University Press.

Hall, N. (1989) *Writing with Reason*, London: Hodder & Stoughton.

Holt, J. (1964) *How Children Fail*, New York: Dell Publishing.

Hughes, M. (1986) *Children and Number*, Oxford: Basil Blackwell.

James, N. (1985) *Learning Mathematics, Unit 14, E206, Personality, Development and Learning*, Milton Keynes: Open University Press.

Meadows, S. (1993) *The Child as Thinker*, London: Routledge.

Miller, G.A. (1956) 'The magic number seven plus or minus two: some limits on our capacity for processing information' *Psychological Review* 63, 81–97.

Moll, L.C. (ed) (1990) *Vygotsky and Education*, Cambridge: Cambridge University Press.

Nisbet, J. and Shucksmith, J. (1986) *Learning Strategies*, London: Routledge and Kegan Paul.

Nunes, T., Schliemann, A.D. and Carraher, D.W. (1993) *Street Mathematics and School Mathematics*, Cambridge: Cambridge University Press.

Piaget, J. (1952) *The Child's Conception of Number*, NJ: Humanities Press and Routledge and Kegan Paul.

Siegler, R.S. (1991) *Children's Thinking*, 2nd Ed., Englewood Cliffs, N.J: Prentice-Hall.

11 Assessing children's learning

Colin Conner

EDITOR'S SUMMARY

This chapter begins by discussing the different views which have been held about assessment and its purposes and illustrates the ways in which these views have arisen from different psychological theories of intelligence and ability. Earlier psychometric views, where IQ was seen as fixed and directly measurable, regarded learning and assessment as entirely separate activities. More current social constructivist views, however, recognise that any particular performance will be influenced by a range of contextual factors, and support a much more dynamic view of learning and its assessment. In this view, assessment is itself seen as part of the teaching and learning process. The chapter then reviews recent research which has demonstrated ways in which formative assessment and particular kinds of feedback from teachers can dramatically enhance children's learning. The chapter concludes by briefly discussing the related issues of reliability, validity, manageability and moderation.

Introduction

Assessment is an extremely important and topical issue in education at the present time and it is one that is the subject of international debate. In the United Kingdom, changes in assessment practice have affected all stages of education. James (1996) lists the following examples to illustrate the range of the assessment debate as it currently affects all levels of the education service:

- the baseline assessment of young children entering school
- National Curriculum assessment and testing for school pupils from 5 to 14 in England and Wales and comparable arrangements in Scotland and Northern Ireland

- the diagnostic assessment of children with special educational needs for the purposes of 'statementing' and the allocation of special resource provision
- the nature and value of examinations at 16+, especially coursework elements in the GCSE
- the construction and use of league tables of test and examination results and the relative advantages and disadvantages of 'raw' or 'value-added' versions
- the development of vocational assessment post 16 (NVQs and GNVQs) and the relationship with the academic 'gold standard' of 'A' levels
- the assessment of modular courses in further and higher education and the accreditation of prior learning (APL) and prior experiential learning (APEL)
- work-based assessment and performance appraisal.

Many of these issues are not of immediate relevance to Primary teachers, but since the introduction of the 1988 Education Act it is probably true to say that one of the most significant effects on Primary education has been the overwhelming demands of the assessment process. It has resulted in considerable additional expectations being placed upon Primary teachers and has been the subject of continual change.

But have we learned anything from our experience of the last ten years? This chapter draws upon some of the research evidence related to the implementation of National Curriculum assessment and considers what it tells us about effective ways of assessing children's learning. The next section opens the debate by a reflection on some of the different ways in which assessment has been interpreted.

Contrasting views about assessment and its associated purposes

> Assessment of school children is an inexact science. We are hampered in our endeavours by both the misconceptions of history and the misrepresentations of politics. Our children are owed more than this.
>
> (Lyseight-Jones 1994:32)

The word 'assessment' can conjure up a wide variety of images: rows of desks in quiet examination halls, working to a set deadline, trying to remember the answers to obscure and seemingly irrelevant questions. Sometimes it dredges up long-forgotten memories of the 11+, a musical examination, a driving test, an interview, or being observed in a classroom. Often these memories are tinged with uncertainty, unhappiness and even a feeling of failure. It is important to remember, therefore, that assessment for many of us has been an emotional experience and it is not surprising that we should be concerned about placing learners in such situations too early in their lives. Assessment is defined in a wide variety of ways in the literature. A classic example comes from Macintosh and Hale (1976), who identified six main elements of assessment:

- *diagnosis* finding out what precisely a child or group of children have learned with a view to planning the curriculum and teaching to meet their needs
- *evaluation* using assessment information as evidence in judging the value of educational provision
- *guidance* helping children to make appropriate career or course choices
- *grading* identifying the level at which a child is performing and assigning a number or letter to signify the standard attained
- *selection* identifying those children most suitable for a particular set, class, school or form of employment
- *prediction* identifying the potential or aptitude of individuals for a particular kind of training or employment in order to avoid the waste of talent.

This overview of potential interpretations and purposes of assessment can be extended further. For example, Berwick (1994) identified two main categories, those concerned with the educational development of pupils and those concerned with the outcomes of the educational process.

Assessment and the educational development of pupils

- assessment to motivate pupils and improve future performance
- assessment to provide feedback (to the pupil, parents and other teachers)
- assessment to diagnose strengths and weaknesses so that future performance can be improved
- assessment to differentiate learning opportunities appropriately
- assessment to guide the pupil in making appropriate choices
- assessment to select a pupil for a course, a teaching group or a career

Assessments concerned with the outcomes of education

- the grading of pupil performance
- the ranking of pupils against external norms and against each other
- assessments to identify and maintain a school's standards
- assessments to evaluate a school's effectiveness
- assessments to evaluate a teacher's effectiveness

(Berwick 1994)

A final alternative definition and associated purpose of assessment is obtained by tracing the roots of the word assessment. Satterly (1989) traces this to the Latin *assidere*, to sit beside. If you combine this with 'education', which can be traced back to the Latin *educare*, 'to bring out', educational assessment should be seen as the process of sitting beside the learner and bringing out the potential that exists within them, creating an opportunity for them to demonstrate what they know, what they can do and what they understand. Given such an interpretation, assessment in education has to be seen as a dynamic process, which should be a positive experience for both the teacher and the learner, a fundamental feature of teaching and success-ful learning. Considering assessment as a regular feature of planning for learning is likely to contribute significantly to children's progress, and also to improve the quality of the learning provided in school as a whole. This was recognised as being of particular significance in the Gulbenkian Report on *The Arts in Schools* (1982), where it was suggested that:

> Assessments of pupils are not, nor can they be, statements of absolute ability. They are statements about achievements within the framework of educational opportunities that have actually been provided. In some degree every assessment of a pupil is also an assessment of the teachers and of the school.
>
> (Calouste Gulbenkian Foundation 1982: para. 130)

This report went on to argue that it is essential that schools continually moni-tor and review the quality of their educational provision and their methods of working, that is, to engage in a process of educational evaluation, which is seen as

> ... a more general process than assessment in that it looks beyond the pupil to the style, the materials and the circumstances of teaching and learning. If teachers need to assess pupils they also need to evaluate their own practice. Although they have different purposes, assessment and evaluation are obviously linked. Teachers and pupils alike need in-formation on each other's activities and perceptions if their work to-gether is to advance. Assessment and evaluation should provide this as a basis for informed description and intelligent judgement.
>
> (ibid.: para. 131)

The Gulbenkian report concluded that if we are to regard teaching as a pro-fession, it is insufficient to rely on 'gut reaction' or what we feel to be the case. It is important that any judgements, whether they are about the prog-ress of an individual or about the effectiveness of a school's practice, must be supported by evidence. Before any serious consideration can be given to the organisation and structuring of assessment in a school or classroom, it is essential that beliefs, understandings and expectations are made explicit. This is because such beliefs considerably influence practice often without our realising it. As Sotto (1994) suggests, we tend to see things in terms of our past experience, that is, in terms of a theory we already have. In the case of assessment our theory will be made up of all our past experiences of being assessed. We will then tend to view assessment from that frame of reference, and mostly without being clearly aware of it.

In short, our theories tend to come before our practice. And not only
do they help to determine our practice, they also shape how we see our
practice.

(Sotto 1994:13)

A number of writers on assessment argue, therefore, that a fundamental fea-
ture of effective assessment is to have a set of clearly articulated principles.
For example, the OMEP (Organisation Mondiale pour l'Éducation
Préscolaire) suggest the following:

- that there should be respect for the individual child
- that parents should be recognised as the primary educators of their
  own children, and as partners in the education process
- that assessment is in the interest of the child and is effected through
  the child's interests
- that assessment forms part of the on-going teaching and learning
  process.

(OMEP 1993:5–6)

Conner (1995) has argued that views about assessment are influenced and
informed by particular psychological theories. This is an issue that has been
emphasised by Paul Black, the former chairman of the Task Group on Assessment and Testing (DES 1988). In a pamphlet written with his colleague
Dylan Wiliam (1998), they make a distinction between a 'fixed IQ' view and
an 'untapped potential' perspective.

… there is on the one hand the 'fixed IQ' view: a belief that each pupil has
a fixed, inherited, intelligence, so that little can be done apart from accepting that some can learn quickly and others hardly at all. On the other
hand, there is the 'untapped potential' view, prevalent in other cultures,
which starts from the assumption that so-called 'ability' is a complex of
skills that can be learnt. Here, the underlying belief is that all pupils can
learn more effectively if one can clear away, by sensitive handling, the obstacles set up by previous difficulties, be they cognitive failures never diag-
nosed, or damage to personal confidence, or a combination of the two.
Clearly the truth lies somewhere between these two extremes.

(Black and Wiliam 1998:14)

The next section distinguishes between the 'fixed IQ ' and the 'untapped
potential' perspectives of assessment.

The 'fixed IQ' and the 'untapped potential' perspectives
on assessment

By and large, we are still working with models of ability and assessment
developed in the first decade of the twentieth century.

(Raven 1992:112)

At an in-service session on assessment several years ago, I invited a group of local authority inspectors to reflect upon an occasion where they had been assessed, to consider what came to mind and what they remembered feeling like at the time. The purpose of the activity was to remind them that assessment was as much an emotional activity as it was a cognitive one. One member of the group went back nearly thirty years to the time when she had failed the 11+, which she believed had classed her as a failure at that very early age. She explained that most of her effort in life since then had been an attempt to prove that her examiners were wrong in their assessment of her. At that time there was a view that intelligence was fixed and that it was easy to distinguish between children and decide which form of education was most suitable to their capacities. It was grounded in the views of theorists of intelligence whose ideas had been generated at the turn of the century. Alfred Binet, for example, had developed the first successful intelligence test in 1905 to select those children who should be institutionalised, who were regarded as 'educationally sub-normal', 'mentally defective' or 'feeble-minded'! Such views still exist and dominate the educational debate today. Berlak and Newman (1992) and Gipps (1994) refer to this view of assessment, with its basis in conventional views about intelligence as the psychometric model of assessment. The underlying idea of this model is that intelligence is fixed and innate, that we inherit our abilities from our parents. Since it is fixed it can be measured and on that basis, each of us can easily be assigned to groups, classes, schools and employment. As Gipps suggests:

> ... with its formulae and quantification comes an aura of objectivity; such testing is scientific and therefore the figures it produces must be accurate and meaningful. The measurements which individuals amass via such testing: IQ scores, reading ages, rankings, etc. thus come to have a powerful labelling potential.
>
> (Gipps 1994:5)

Berlak and Newman (1992) add that assessment procedures are inherently political because whoever controls the assessment process shapes the curriculum, approaches to teaching and ultimately each student's life chances.

> Mass administration of standardised tests ... is largely suited to exercising control from the centre. ... Such tests provide virtually no information about what students are capable of doing or where they may need help. These tests produce relative rankings but little substantive information about what students know and can do which is useful to teachers, parents, prospective employers or to students themselves for making programme or individual decisions. ... The psychometric tradition only enables us to classify and rank students (or teachers) and to constitute individuals as a 'case' – that is, as belonging to a class or category which possesses a particular set of objective characteristics (e.g. high, average or low achiever.)
>
> (Berlak and Newman 1992:18–19)

Gipps (1994) comments that one of the major differences between the psychometric approach to assessment and more recent approaches is a different view of the learner and a different relationship between the pupil and assessor. At the heart of this lies an understanding that performance in any assessment is affected by the context in which the assessment takes place. The assessment context includes:

- the relationship between pupil and assessor
- the pupil's motivational state
- the characteristics of the assessment task.

She argues that research on cognition and learning throughout the 1980s has shown that the following factors are particularly significant in affecting performance in assessment:

- motivation to do the task and an interest in it
- the relationship between the assessor and the individual being assessed and the conditions under which the assessment is made
- the way in which the task is presented, the language used to describe it and the degree to which it is within the personal experience of the individual being assessed.

> The conclusion is inescapable ... assessment (like learning) is highly context specific and one generalises at one's peril.
>
> (Gipps 1994:5)

Gipps also suggests that in the development of assessment we should 'elicit the individual's best performance' by offering tasks and activities that are:

- concrete and within the experience of the individual
- presented clearly and unambiguously
- perceived to be relevant to the current concerns of the pupil and related to recent curriculum experience
- under conditions that are not unduly threatening, something that is helped by a good relationship between the assessor and the student.

As a result of reflection on the issues discussed above, Berlak and Newman advocate the use of 'contextual' assessment which is based upon assessments in the context of activities related to what has been taught, to the skill or idea that has supposedly been achieved. Gipps prefers the term 'educational assessment' which is concerned with 'How well' an individual does rather than 'How many' he or she has got right in comparison to some external norm. Gipps draws upon the discussion by Wood (1986) which argues that educational assessment:

- deals with an individual's achievement relative to himself rather than to others
- seeks to test for competence rather than for 'intelligence'

- takes place in relatively uncontrolled conditions and so does not produce 'well-behaved' data
- looks for 'best' rather than 'typical' performances
- is most effective when rules and regulations characteristic of standardised testing are relaxed
- embodies a constructive outlook on assessment, where the aim is to help rather than 'sentence' the individual.

Rather than base his views on dated theories of intelligence, Wood draws upon more recent suggestions which adopt a 'social constructivist' view of learning (Pollard 1990). The central arguments of this perspective are that:

- learning requires opportunities for the 'active' construction of meaning
- new learning should be related to and should build upon previous learning
- learning is significantly influenced by the context in which it takes place.

But what do these claims mean in practice and what are their implications for assessment?

Learning as an active construction of meaning

The term 'active learning' is one that is often misunderstood, with the assumption that it implies undirected free choice with little consideration of the experience in relation to previous or future learning and an emphasis on practical, physical activity. Accepting a place for activity does not just mean physical activity, it also includes the importance of opportunities for mental activity.

Jacqueline and Martin Brooks (1993) have attempted to describe the classroom implications of developing a 'constructivist' approach to learning and assessment. In constructivist classrooms, they suggest, the pursuit of children's questions is highly valued. Students are viewed as thinkers with emerging theories about the world. Curriculum activities rely heavily on primary sources of data and provide plenty of opportunities for physical and mental manipulation. Teachers seek the students' points of view in order to understand their current perceptions and conceptions and to see where to take them next. Assessment is interwoven with teaching and occurs through observations of students engaged in the process of learning as well as creating opportunities to display the products of their learning in a wide variety of formats.

Learning should be related to and should build upon previous learning

Ausubel *et al.* (1978) are strong advocates of the importance of building learning on what is already known, and suggest that:

> The most important single factor influencing learning is what the learner already knows. Ascertain this and teach him accordingly.
>
> (Ausubel *et al.* 1978:i)

At the heart of these suggestions is the need for teachers to become enquirers into childrens' understanding of their classroom experiences. The National Curriculum advice on planning in the Primary school (NCC 1989) described the curriculum in three ways: the curriculum as planned, the curriculum as taught and the curriculum as received. Reflection on of each of these reminds us that if we are not clear about childrens' current understandings and the sense that they have made of their learning, any new learning experience can fall on deaf ears or be totally misunderstood. In this context, it is important not to assume that what a child currently knows is based upon what we most recently taught them. A great deal of learning goes on outside school and children bring well established understandings to their learning in school. There is also a lot of evidence that some of these understandings are wrong. (See for example the findings of the SPACE project directed by Paul Black and Wynne Harlen (1990) and the study of children's informal ideas of science by Black and Lucas (1993) which illustrated that many children's ideas about science are wrong, but that because they have been established by the children themselves, they are not easily changed by teaching. The only way to move children beyond these erroneous conceptions is to bring them out into the open and subject them to scrutiny.) If we do not attempt to find out what children currently know, our attempts to extend their understanding will be severely hampered. This is why assessment is fundamentally important. Developing ways of getting access to children's current understanding is a crucial element of effective assessment. Since the teacher is closest to this understanding, he or she is in a good position to gather the necessary information to plan the next stages in learning so that more effective learning takes place, learning that builds on and extends the learner's current understanding and competence.

Learning is significantly influenced by the context in which it takes place

Elsewhere, I have argued that context has three important elements (Conner 1992), each of which need to be considered when planning learning experiences and which influence assessment. Firstly, there is the *physical* context; is the learning environment welcoming and comfortable? As adults, a cold, untidy working environment is a disincentive to our learning. This principle applies just as much to children. The second feature of context is concerned with the *affective* side of learning; can I expect to feel confident as I approach new learning? Am I likely to be supported in my learning and can I take risks and learn from mistakes? Or am I likely to be placed in a potentially negative learning situation where I have a fear of failure? As is explained in Ch. 6, the work of Dweck (1986) illustrates the differences between learners in this context. She distinguishes between positive and negative approaches to learning. Positive attitudes are evidenced by a belief that effort leads to success, an acceptance of one's ability to improve and learn, a preference for challenging tasks, and satisfaction from completing difficult tasks. Those who adopt a negative orientation believe that success is related to ability, satisfaction is gained from doing better than others, and there is a tendency to evaluate oneself negatively when the task is too difficult. An assumption of 'learned helplessness' can become established where any success is attributed to luck rather than effort or competence. Careful assessment enables the teacher to identify children adopting either of these reactions and to modify teaching accordingly. A number of writers have argued that one way of overcoming learned helplessness is to ensure that children understand what is expected of them. Clarke (1995), for example, argues that:

> Firstly, knowing the purpose focuses the child towards a particular outcome. Very often, children have no idea why they have been asked to do something, and they can only look for a clue or 'guess what's in teacher's mind' as a means of knowing what is expected of them. Secondly, they are being invited to take more control over evaluating their achievements. If the purpose is known, this is more likely to encourage the child to be weighing up the relative strengths and weaknesses of their work as they are doing it.
>
> (Clarke 1995:14)

The importance of this is also recognised by Black and Wiliam (1998), who argue that pupils can only assess themselves when they have a clear picture of the targets that their learning is meant to attain.

> Surprisingly, and sadly, many pupils do not have such a picture, and appear to have become accustomed to receiving teaching as an arbitrary sequence of exercises with no overarching rationale. It requires hard and sustained work to overcome this pattern of passive reception. When pupils do acquire such an overview, they become more effective as learners: their own assessments become an object of discussion with teachers and with one another, and this promotes even further that reflection on one's own ideas that is essential to good learning.
>
> (Black and Wiliam 1998:10)

The final feature of context relates to the *social* context of learning. For many of us, our experience of learning was as a solitary process with each of us responsible for making our own sense of situations and experiences. Now there is strong support for the inclusion of opportunities to work with and alongside others, peers and friends as well as teachers. Vygotsky emphasised the co-operative nature of learning when he said:

> … what the [learner] can do today in co-operation he [she] will be able to do tomorrow on his [her] own.
>
> (Vygotsky 1962)

In support of this thesis, Vygotsky described the 'Zone of proximal development', which refers to:

> … the gap between what a given child can achieve alone, their potential development as determined by independent problem solving, and what they can achieve through problem solving under adult guidance or in collaboration with more capable peers.
>
> (Wood and Wood 1996:5)

Or, as Galton and Williamson (1992) describe it:

> … the difference between what children can do independently and what they can accomplish with the support of another individual who is more knowledgeable and skilled.
>
> (Galton and Williamson 1992)

Again, it is through the processes of assessment that the teacher is able to identify each learner's needs, the support and 'scaffolding' that may be required, and the extent to which they should be given the opportunity to 'go it alone'. Assessment, therefore, has to be seen as a dynamic process with the teacher reflecting on the implications of children's responses for future planning and learning. Appropriate assessment is an essential feature of effective scaffolding by:

> … recruitment of the child's interest in a task, establishing and maintaining an orientation towards task relevant goals, highlighting critical features of the task that the child might overlook, demonstrating how to achieve goals and helping to control frustration.
>
> (Wood and Wood 1996:5)

Government advice, however, is concerned primarily with securing standards for end of key stage statutory teacher assessment rather than the implications for individual learners, and pays no attention to the on-going assessments that teachers are making every day in their interactions with children. Yet these assessments are at the heart of a school's assessment practice. It is these assessments which significantly influence the teaching and learning process and it is fundamentally important that sufficient attention is paid to developing expertise in this area. James (1996) has argued that government interest is now clearly focused on assessment for accountability, and that it is up to schools and teachers to rescue the potential of assessment for learning. At the heart of assessment for learning is the way teachers respond to children, and the feedback they provide. This is an issue that has been the subject of recent critical scrutiny.

Formative assessment and feedback

In a study of the feedback process by Black and Wiliam (1998) three main questions were framed.

- Is there evidence that improving feedback improves learning?
- Is there evidence that there is room for improvement?
- Is there evidence about how to improve our skills?

The answer to all three questions was overwhelmingly affirmative. Black and Wiliam conclude their review of over 680 world-wide studies of the issues involved with the recognition that:

> ... standards are raised only by changes which are put into direct effect by teachers and pupils in classrooms. ... Our education system has been subjected to many far reaching initiatives which, whilst taken in relation to concerns about existing practices, have been based on little evidence about their potential to meet these concerns. In our study ... there can be seen, for once, firm evidence that indicates a clear direction for change which could improve standards of learning.
>
> (Black and Wiliam 1998:19)

An attempt to summarise the important factors associated with feedback identified in the Black and William study was undertaken by the Eastern Region branch of the Association of Assessment Inspectors and Advisers (Swaffield 1998). The summary concludes that the quality of feedback is a key feature of formative assessment, and that giving specific comments on errors and suggestions for strategies for improvement have as great an effect on performance as prior attainment (see Figure 11.1). Successful feedback, it is suggested, needs to include the following features.

- Feedback is more successful in situations requiring higher-order thinking skills.
- Feedback should be related to the task itself.
- As much or as little help as is needed should be given, rather than providing the complete solution as soon as the pupil is stuck.
- Concentration should focus on specific errors and weak strategies.
- Pupils should be offered suggestions about how they might improve, rather than being offered one way of doing something.
- Feedback should be designed so that it stimulates a thoughtful response, building upon previous learning.
- Details of correct answers should be given, rather than just saying whether the pupil's answer is correct or not.
- Comments should focus on progress rather than absolute levels of performance.
- The focus should aim for deep rather than superficial learning.
- Following tests, feedback about strengths and weakness of responses should be given before providing the answers.

Figure 11.1 The quality of teacher feedback can enhance the quality of children's
        learning

- Feedback should help the pupil realise that success is due to 'internal,
  unstable, specific' factors (e.g. effort), rather than stable 'general' factors (e.g. ability, which is internal, or being regarded positively by the
  teacher, which is external).

It is also emphasised that some feedback activities can have negative consequences, and that feedback has been found to have negative effects in about
two out of five instances.

- Once a gap between actual and desired performance has been identified, feedback should help the pupil find ways of closing the gap and
  reaching the desired goal. However, other student responses may be
  that the goal is abandoned or changed, or the fact that a gap exists is
  denied. All of these can lead to the development of a negative self-concept and resultant lack of commitment to learning.
- Feedback which focuses on the self, rather than the task, is likely to have
  a negative affect on performance.
- The potential positive effects of detailing weaknesses and providing a
  plan of action for improvement can be negated by an initial congratula-
  tory message.
- The most effective teachers praise less than the average.
- Praise can lead to the perception of success, even if this is unfounded.

- Praise can increase pupils' interest in and attitude towards a task, whilst not improving the performance itself.

The above recommendations suggest that there needs to be much more careful reflection on the way in which we respond to children and support them in the learning process. In the Primary context, this has been the focus of an investigation undertaken by Gipps *et al.* (1997) which considered the nature and quality of feedback provided by Primary teachers to children. Drawing on the work of Sadler (1989) this study emphasises the importance of the feedback process, in particular how a reaction to a child's work can help that child to improve future performance. However:

> ... when teachers give students valid and reliable judgements about their work improvement does not necessarily follow. In order for the student to improve she must have a notion of the desired standard or goal, be able to compare the actual performance with the desired performance and to engage in appropriate action to 'close the gap' between the two. Feedback from the teacher, which helps the student ... needs to be of the kind and detail which tells the student what to do to improve; simply using grades or 'smiley' faces cannot do this.
>
> (Gipps *et al.* 1997:11)

Over a two-year period Gipps and her colleagues observed the process of feedback to children by Primary teachers. The major research questions of the project were, 'What sort of feedback do teachers give to children?' and 'How do the children interpret and act on this?' The research involved teachers and children directly in discussion of these issues through interview. Observations and recording in classrooms were also undertaken. The findings have shown that feedback is central in learning and has three main functions:

- as part of the classroom socialisation process
- to encourage children and maintain motivation and effort
- to identify specific aspects of attainment or good performance in relation to a specific task.

It is this last category that is vital for improving the teaching–learning process. The research generated a typology of teacher feedback, details of which are provided in Figure 11.2.

The feedback described as Type A and B focuses on helping children to understand what is correct or particularly good about their work and what needs to be done to improve it. These Gipps *et al.* describe as 'descriptive'; the teacher describes strengths and weaknesses to the child. For example, one of the children's responses in this category explained, 'All he does for my writing is write the words on the top so I know how to spell them properly.'

The feedback identified as Type C focuses on attainment, the specific aspects of successful steps in the learning process, or the identification of mistakes made by a child and how these might be improved. For example

	Type A	Type B	Type C	Type D	
	A1 **Rewarding**	**B1** **Approving**	**C1** **Specifying attainment**	**D1** **Constructing achievement**	
1 **Positive** **Feedback**	rewards	positive personal expression; warm expression of feeling; general praises; positive non-verbal feedback	specific acknowledgement of attainment/use of criteria in relation to work/ behaviour; teacher models; more specific praise	mutual articulation of achievement; additional use of emerging criteria; child role in presentation; praise integral to description	**1** **Achievement** **Feedback**
	A2 **Punishing**	**B2** **Disapproving**	**C2** **Specifying improvement**	**D2** **Constructing the way forward**	
2 **Negative** **Feedback**	punishing	negative personal expression; reprimands; negative generalizations; negative non-verbal feedback	correction of errors; more practice given; training in self-checking	mutual critical appraisal	**2** **Improvement** **Feedback**

Figure 11.2 Teacher feedback typology (from Gipps 1997:12)

one of the children explained, 'She thinks of things of how to improve it. She thinks of good ideas of how to improve it. She thinks of exciting things to put in my stories.'

In both of these cases the teacher *tells* the child. Feedback described as Type D represents a *collaboration* between the teacher and the child. Teachers using this kind of feedback shift the emphasis on to the child's role in learning, 'using approaches which seemed to pass some control to the child'. It was less of 'teacher to the child' and more of 'teacher with the child'. In particular, teachers in the category described as 'constructing the way forward' provided children with strategies that they could adopt to develop their work and it encouraged children to assess their own work. They were asked what they thought about their work, how it was or was not an improvement on previous work and how they might improve it further. It was also used to reinforce important skills so that the learner was more in control. For example, in interview, one child described a process for improving her spelling that she had discussed with her teacher and had now taken control of.

CHILD: After I've finished my writing she gives me words at the back I've done wrong. I have to write them. On one page I write it. The second time I cover my hand up and then I write it.

INTERVIEWER: Can you always do it? What if you can't?

CHILD: I do it again then.

INTERVIEWER: Do you always learn your words that way?

CHILD: Yes. I even do it at home.

Gipps *et al.* offer the important observation that:

Assessment has a role in valid accountability and reporting; but the main role of assessment in the classroom must be to support learning. By developing teachers' skills in assessment and feedback we can continue to build good practice in primary assessment.

(Gipps *et al.* 1997:14)

Other assessment issues

The concepts of validity and reliability are two of the most important concepts in assessment and each of them place conflicting demands on any assessment that is undertaken. 'Reliability' refers to the extent to which a similar result would be obtained if an assessment were to be repeated, whereas 'validity' is concerned with the extent to which the assessment really creates a means by which a particular skill, concept, area of knowledge or attitude is effectively assessed. Most teachers are much more concerned with validity; is this assessment a fair reflection of what the children have been taught? Whereas politicians and policy makers tend to be more concerned with reliability; can I have confidence in these results so that I can compare one result with another? Harlen (1994) reminds us that;

> ... validity and reliability can never both be 100% ... that we must recognise assessment is never 'accurate' in the way that the word is used in the context of measurement in the physical world. Assessment in education is inherently inexact and it should be treated as such. We should not expect to be able to measure pupils' abilities with the same confidence as we can measure their heights. This in no way makes educational assessment useless. It means that the interpretation of assessment results should be in terms of being an indication of what pupils can do but not an exact specification.
>
> (Harlen 1994:12–13)

It is probably impossible to create an assessment situation that achieves complete reliability and validity. Harlen suggests, therefore, that the best one can achieve in terms of quality assessment is the provision of information of the highest validity and optimum reliability suited to a particular purpose and context. Sutton (1990) offers some sensible advice with regard to these issues. To achieve reliable and valid assessments she suggests we need to reduce the main variables that can affect judgements.

> There are three major variables in most assessment by teachers: context (the circumstances of assessment): time (how many times and over what period of time you have to see an assessment criterion achieved); and 'rater' (that is, the person doing the assessment). To put it briefly, do what you can to agree with your colleagues how you can reduce these variables. ... Assessment is an art, not a science, and much of the time you will be relying on your professional judgement and common sense, employing more stringent techniques only when you're in doubt.
>
> (Sutton 1990:24)

There are two further important concerns that need to be added to reliability and validity, both of which have emerged as a direct result of attempting to implement the National Curriculum. These are:

- manageability; is the procedure we propose to adopt one that is manageable within our existing resources?
- consistency; what procedures are there in place to ensure that our assessments are as fair as they might be?

The most effective strategy for improving consistency has been moderation. Although it can be time consuming, it is the main way in which each teacher can confirm his or her assessment against the views of colleagues. Gipps, McCallum and Brown (1997) reinforce the importance of moderation:

> There is a clear picture of enhanced understanding and practice in assessment. ... All of this has been achieved, however, at a cost to teachers' lives and ways of working. Most importantly, we believe our evidence shows that the improvements in practice, both in teaching and assessing, would not have resulted from the introduction of traditional, standardised tests alone, but depended on a wider approach with moderated teacher assessment at its core.
>
> (Gipps, McCallum and Brown 1997:6)

Conner (1999) has described the benefits of moderation as follows.

- Participation in the moderation process contributes to the development of teachers' assessment skills.
- Teachers become clearer about assessment criteria and how to interpret them.
- Teachers become clearer about what they are teaching and how to teach it more effectively.
- It helps to establish recognised and agreed standards of achievement.
- It ensures that there are common standards and expectations between teachers in the same school.
- It contributes to the development of consistent procedures for marking, and recording and reporting.
- It contributes towards establishing common standards between schools.
- It helps teachers to convey consistent messages to pupils.
- It helps teachers convey consistent messages to parents.
- It contributes to improving the transfer of information from one school to the next.
- It is reassuring and develops confidence in assessment.

In addition to improving the quality of assessment, engaging in the process of review associated with the moderation process contributes to improving the quality of education provided by a school. Participation in discussions about assessments and the ways in which we respond to children about the products and processes of learning ultimately engages teachers in discussion about the curriculum and the most effective ways of organising children's learning and sustaining and motivating their interest. It is only in this way that standards are likely to be improved. Ultimately we have to focus on assessment *for* learning rather than the current pre-occupation with assessment *of* learning.

Activities

The experience of being assessed

Think back on your own experience of being assessed and focus on one specific example.

- How did you feel? Compare and contrast reactions with colleagues.
- What do you think the purposes of this assessment were? How do they relate to those identified at the beginning of this chapter?
- Was the assessment process used 'fit for its purpose'? What alternatives do you think could have been used to allow you to show what you knew, understood and could do?

Establishing a basis for our practice

A fundamental issue in the development of an effective system for assessment is that it should be based upon a clearly developed set of principles. The following questions might help to start that process. It is usually best to complete the questions individually and then compare and contrast them with a colleague. In agreeing or disagreeing with any of these categories it is essential that the decision is supported by an explanation. A comparison amongst the group will then identify the areas of agreement (and disagreement) and create the starting point for future discussion and the development of some agreed principles to inform practice and a set of ideas against which practice might be evaluated.

How far do you agree?	*Strongly agree*	*Agree*	*Disagree*	*Strongly disagree*
1 The emphasis in assessment should be on success and children's achievements.				
2 Learners should be involved in the assessment of their own progress and should understand the ways I/we assess them.				
3 Assessment should focus on a broad range of achievement.				
4 To assess effectively, we need to be clear about the kinds of learning we value and what our expectations are for that learning.				

How far do you agree?	*Strongly agree*	*Agree*	*Disagree*	*Strongly disagree*
5 Assessment should be used to inform our teaching and to help us to improve the curriculum.				
6 Assessment should be based on detailed observations of what learners do and say.				
7 Assessment should be based upon evidence, not hearsay or intuition.				
8 Assessment must take account of the possible effects of the context on the learner's performance, (e.g. the language used to explain a task, the learner's previous experience, the learner's emotional state).				
9 Assessment should draw upon a wide range of assessment opportunities.				
10 Assessments of individuals should be used in planning future learning activities for those children.				
11 Assessments made over a period of time should be used to review the learning opportunities provided during that time.				
12 Written records should include factual evidence, sensitive interpretation and tentative judgements.				
13 Written records should demonstrate progress and development for an individual.				
14 When appropriate, assessments of bi-lingual children should be made in the child's home language by a person who knows about the child's cultural heritage.				
15 Parents should be recognised as important providers as well as receivers of assessment information and should be involved in the assessment process.				

Source: Adapted from Drummond *et al.* 1992

Further reading

Assessment Reform Group (1999) *Assessment for Learning: beyond the Black Box*, Cambridge: University of Cambridge School of Education.

Conner, C. (1999) *Assessment in Action in the Primary School*, London: Falmer Press.

Drummond, M.J. (1993) *Assessing Children's Learning*, London: Fulton.

James, M. (1998) *Using Assessment for School Improvement*, Oxford: Heinemann.

References

Ausubel, D.P., Novak, J. and Hanesian, H. (1978) *Educational Psychology: A cognitive view*, 2nd edition, New York: Holt Rinehart and Winston.

Berlak, H. and Newmann, F. (1992) *Toward a New Science of Educational Testing and Assessment*, New York: State University of New York Press.

Berwick, G. (1994) *Factors which Effect Pupil Achievement. The develoment of a whole school assessment programme and accounting for personal constructs of achievement*, Unpublished PhD thesis, Norwich: University of East Anglia.

Black, P. and Harlen,W. (1990) *Nuffield Primary SPACE Project, (Science Processes and Concept Exploration Project)*, Liverpool University Press.

Black, P.J. and Lucas, D.M. (1993) *Children's Informal Ideas of Science*, London: Routledge.

Black, P. and Wiliam, D. (1998) *Inside the Black Box: Raising Standards through classroom assessment*, London: Kings College School of Education.

Brooks, J. and M.G. (1993) *In search of understanding: The case for constructivist classrooms*, VA: ASCD

Calouste Gulbenkian Foundation (1982) *The Arts in Schools*, London: Oyez Press.

Clarke, S. (1995) 'Assessing significant achievement in the primary classroom', *British Journal of Curriculum and Assessment*, 5, 3, 12–16.

Conner, C. (1992) 'Is there still a place for learning in School?', *University of Cambridge Institute of Education Newsletter*, Spring.

Conner, C. (1999) *Assessment in Action in the Primary School*, London: Falmer Press.

DES (1988) *Task Group on Assessment and Testing: A Report*, London: HMSO.

Drummond, M.J., Rouse, D. and Pugh, G. (1992) *Making Assessment Work: values and principles in assessing young children's learning*, NES Arnold in association with the National Childrens' Bureau

Dweck, C. (1986) 'Motivational processes affecting learning', *American Psychologist*, 41, 1041–1048.

Galton, M. and Williamson, J. (1992) *Group Work in the Primary Classroom*, London: Routledge.

Gipps, C. (1994) *Beyond Testing. Towards a theory of educational assessment*, Lewes: Falmer.

Gipps, C., McCallum, B. and Brown, M. (1997) 'Models of teacher assessment among primary school teachers in England', *The Curriculum Journal*, 7, 2, 167–83.

Gipps, C. (1997) *Assessment in Primary Schools: Past, Present and Future*, London, The British Curriculum Foundation.

Harlen, W. (ed.) (1994) *Enhancing Quality in Assessment*, London:Paul Chapman.

James, M. (1996) *The Assessment of Learning, Unit 5, Open University Course E208, Exploring Educational Issues*, Open University Press.

Lyseight-Jones, P. (1994) 'An inexact science – issues of assessment', in Keel, P. (ed.), *Assessment in the Multi-ethnic Classroom*, Stoke on Trent: Trentham Books.

Macintosh, H.G. and Hale, D.E. (1976) *Assessment and the Secondary School Teacher*, London: RKP.

National Curriculum Council (1989) *A Framework for the Primary Curriculum*, York: NCC.

OMEP (1993) *Executive Spring Review*, OMEP (UK)

Pollard, A. (1990) 'Toward a sociology of Learning in the Primary school', *British Journal of Sociology of Education*, 11, 3.

Raven, J. (1992) 'A model of competence, motivation, behaviour and a paradigm for assessment', in Berlak, H. (ed.) *Toward a New Science of Educational Testing and Assessment*, New York: State University of New York Press.

Sadler, R. (1989) 'Formative assessment and the design of instructional systems', *Instructional Science*, 18, 118–144.

Satterly, D. (1989) *Assessment in Schools*, 2nd edition, Oxford: Blackwell.

Sotto, E. (1994) *When Teaching becomes Learning*, London: Cassell.

Sutton, R. (1990) 'Issues for Teachers in Implementing National Curriculum Geography', in Lambert, D. (ed.) *Teacher Assessment and National Curriculum Geography*, Sheffield: Geographical Association.

Swaffield, S. (1998) *Assessment and Classroom Learning, Feedback*. Internal Paper for the Eastern Region Association of Assessment Inspectors and Advisers, unpublished.

Vygotsky, L.S. (1962) *Thought and Language*, Boston: M.I.T. Press.

Wood, D. and Wood, H. (1996) 'Vygotsky, Tutoring and Learning', *Oxford Review of Education*, 22, 1, 5–61.

Wood, R. (1986) 'The agenda for educational measurement', in Nuttall, D. (ed.) *Assessing Educational Achievement*, Lewes: Falmer.

Part III

Educating all the children

12 Recognising and responding to children as individuals

Ruth Kershner

EDITOR'S SUMMARY

One of the many challenges in the work of the Primary school teacher is to respond to the individual characteristics of each of the thirty or so children in their class, some of whom are very different from themselves. This chapter reviews the psychological processes whereby teachers form views of the children in their class and looks at children's own, perhaps surprisingly sophisticated, perceptions of how they vary. It goes on to examine the ways psychologists have described individual differences, through notions such as self-concept, temperament and personality, multiple intelligences and cognitive styles. In the final section the implications of going 'beyond the comfort zone' and developing inclusive approaches which help all children learn in school are explored. This includes consideration of processes whereby teachers can make their classrooms truly 'hospitable to diversity'.

Children in British Primary schools spend much of their time in class groups of 25–30 or more, generally organised by age or, increasingly, by attainment for subjects like mathematics and English. Many teachers enjoy the variety, stimulation and drama of interacting with a whole class of children, and a class can take on a character and a reputation of its own in a school. Yet the children in any class group have their individual characteristics, beliefs and feelings, and their interests and friendships often cut across age boundaries.

This chapter is about the implications for class teachers of children's individuality. After a brief discussion of teachers' responsibilities for balancing the needs of individual children with those of the whole class, I will go on to look at a range of ideas about how children differ in ways that are relevant to education and then put forward some principles for responding to children as individuals in school.

Recognising children's individuality in school

In school, the routines and opportunities can work either to highlight children's individuality or to emphasise their sameness as pupils. The systems and requirements of school life may lead children to identify with each other and group together in order to cope with the demands and challenges imposed on them, and there may even seem to be a 'self-fulfilling prophecy' effect in which teachers' expectations for individuals or groups of children are realised. It is a professional challenge and responsibility for teachers to take account of individual differences in children's learning without holding to fixed preconceptions about individual children's potential to learn or about 'normality'. Children are also challenged to manage the demands on them as individual pupils in an educational system which is, on the whole, geared towards conformity in behaviour and learning.

In making decisions about planning, teaching and classroom organisation, Primary class teachers have to rely to some extent on their understanding of how children of the same age tend to behave and learn in similar circumstances. Teachers cannot know all that is to be known about the individual children in their classes, and it is difficult to predict or assess children's achievements in school without making comparisons with others of the same age. The recognition of similarities between children helps us all to make some sense of our observations of them from day to day, and much psychological and educational research focuses on general trends in children's development and learning. However, focusing only on similarities between children can be misleading if it means ignoring individual differences that are educationally relevant.

Even highly experienced and committed teachers can have some difficulties in consistently 'matching' work to children's differing abilities and attainments. Simpson (1997) found in her research that Primary and Secondary teachers felt a need for more knowledge about individual pupils and the different curricular experiences which might help them to learn. They wanted more time to spend with individuals to talk to them, listen, observe and help. Simpson also interviewed 60 children early in their Secondary school career, asking them about how they learned best in school. The children said that what was important for them as learners were not individualised schemes, setting by ability or other types of grouping and organisation. Instead they placed most value on:

- a good relationship with the teacher
- constructive feedback, on weaknesses as well as strengths
- challenging and appropriate work.

Each of these factors relates in some way to the teacher's recognition of children as individuals.

How do children differ?

Attempts to describe and understand individual differences between children might focus on the following:

- physical characteristics and abilities: e.g. age, health, appearance, sensory abilities
- personal qualities: e.g. adaptability, determination, competitiveness, honesty
- emotions and motivation: e.g. responses to success and failure, self-esteem, curiosity, empathy, loyalties, anxieties
- social behaviour: e.g. aggression, communication skills, friendships
- learning skills and strategies: e.g. memory, problem-solving, imagination, literacy and numeracy, responses to teaching, awareness and control of learning strategies
- knowledge, attitudes and opinions: e.g. breadth and detail of knowledge in different subject areas, strength of opinion, interests, preferred sources of information
- environment and experiences: e.g. school attendance, family relationships, home language, hobbies and clubs, possessions, social class, membership of a religious community

This is a very mixed list of individual qualities and types of experience, and it raises questions about the perspective that is taken in understanding individual differences between children. Is 'race', for example, more appropriately placed as a physical characteristic or as social experience and activity? What about health, when we know that physical pain may be accompanied by the social experience of confinement to hospital? Should priority be given to understanding individual children's thoughts and feelings? Children, as active learners, form their own impressions of their environment and other people, so it is difficult to predict the impact of a particular experience on children's thinking and behaviour. Think, for example, of what different children remember from the same school trip.

The terms we use to describe children as individuals vary in the degree of detail and specificity of our observations: compare the phrase 'she's very sporty', with 'she's the only one in the class who plays hockey every week for the school team'. Some personal characteristics, such as height, are observable and even measurable. Others depend on impression and inference, as when we judge a person's attitudes or opinions from what they say or do. The ways in which children are described in school depend to a large extent on the context and the purpose of recognising children as individuals. A response to how a child is dressed, for example, depends on the existence of a uniform policy in school; and if the school curriculum does not include opportunities to compose music, make films or play chess, then children with particular strengths in these areas are not easily distinguished and given credit for their talents. The characteristics of the school context, including the curriculum, will affect the perceptions and judgements that are made about children as individuals, and the way they are treated as pupils.

The beliefs and expectations which influence the ways in which individual children are recognised operate at different levels, from social and cultural values to the thinking of teachers and individual children. There is also a long tradition in psychological research of studying individual differences, including the areas of self-concept, intelligence and personality. What follows are some examples of how individual differences are understood at these different levels.

Social and cultural values

Educational decisions have to be made in a context where views about individuality may be strongly held, and, as Bruner discusses, there can be apparent contradictions between educational aims for individual children and society.

> ... it is unquestionably the function of education to enable people, individual human beings, to operate at their fullest potential, to equip them with the tools and the sense of opportunity to use their wits, skills, and passions to the fullest. ... [Yet] the function of education is to reproduce the culture that supports it – not only reproduce it, but further its economic, political and cultural ends.
>
> (Bruner 1996:67)

Depending on which of these aims takes precedence, children's individual interests and skills will be valued differently in school and the educational system could be organised alternatively for vocational training, comprehensive education, or selection to schools specialising in subjects like music, sport and technology for pupils who show talent in these areas.

International studies have drawn attention to differences in the way cultural beliefs about the individual child's role in society may be reflected in school, and this can be particularly evident in the way young children are introduced to education in the early years. For example, the research of Tobin *et al.* (1989) on preschools in China, Japan and the United States suggests that different attitudes to children as individuals in these three countries has an effect on factors like the teacher's role, the children's relationships, and even basic routines like going to the toilet separately or together, on demand or all together. This is not simple and unthinking cultural determinism, however. The people involved in this study evaluated their own and each other's approaches, and they recognised differences within as well as between each country. Yet broad cultural beliefs about individuality can persist. The argument of sociologists like James and Prout (1997) and their co-authors is that in spite of the increasing 'globalization' of childhood and teenage culture, there remain specific cultural understandings, values, experience and expectations which inform our interpretations of children's behaviour, our beliefs about their developmental and educational needs and our responses to children as individuals.

Teachers' views of children as individuals

In school it is hard to ignore the fact of children's individuality from day to day. Teachers (and politicians) may hold the balance of power about what children should learn and how they should behave, but it is children's individual questions, conversations, interests, activities and moods that fill the school day. In a review of the historical and ideological traditions of British Primary and Infant schooling, Anning (1997:13) remarks on the 'the intense concern for the individual child in the English tradition of early education', leading to a strong belief amongst Primary teachers that children's personal and social development should be fundamental educational aims. Yet in the 1970s, it was recognised that the progressive rhetoric of Infant teachers did not match their practice in classrooms:

> ... children were not treated as individuals, not given free choice of activities, nor allowed to develop at their own pace. There was evidence also that teachers' typifications of pupils affected the way they responded to different groups of children within their classes, and that teacher responses to children and their expectations of them had tangible effects on pupil progress in schooling.
>
> (Anning 1997:17)

As suggested above, teachers form impressions of their pupils, and make judgements about the children's individual strengths, interests and needs. This is essential for teaching, which calls for insight into the perspectives of individual children and their parents. However, children can be complex, inconsistent and puzzling in their behaviour and learning, and teachers' perceptions of pupils are not always comprehensive, coherent or secure.

Some patterns of children's individual characteristics and their interactions with others are particularly salient and relevant to Primary teachers. Interviews with teachers highlight the ways in which they take account of a wide range of factors in deciding how to differentiate the curriculum for individual children. The factors include the children's behaviour, personality, daily moods, ability to work with other people, language, educational attainments, age group, and home situations (Kershner and Miles 1996). The teachers have to balance their knowledge of the children with the demands of the curriculum in order to make decisions about grouping, activities, teaching strategies and classroom organisation. Much of this happens minute-by-minute, almost intuitively, and it is only when teachers reflect on their practice that the underlying principles emerge. Anning (1997:55) gives an example of an Infant teacher who recognised when interviewed that she had treated two children differently according to her understanding of their likely emotional response to pressure and risk. This affected not only what she said to the children (e.g. 'keep going') but the phrasing of her instructions and questions and her tone of voice.

A systematic way of discovering the salience to teachers of children's individual differences makes use of Kelly's Personal Construct Theory, which is a model of how people organise and make sense of experience by perceiving or 'construing' the main dimensions of a situation (Kelly 1955; Salmon 1995). When I asked a small group of teachers attending a course on early years education to select five or six of their pupils and identify the various ways in which two of the children were like each other and different from a third, they came up with a list which included the following 'constructs':

active	passive
good attention span	poor attention span
leaves mother easily	screams when leaving mother
aggressive	non-aggressive (gentle, caring)
able to listen to each other	not able to listen to each other
shy	confident
flits from one activity to another	able to amuse themselves for long periods
right-handed	left-handed
able to initiate conversations with adults	not able to initiate conversations with adults
competitive in games	non-competitive in games

A rather different set of constructs was identified by one teacher in the group who worked in a school for children with severe learning difficulties. These referred to muscle tone and eye-contact, for example, both of which highlight aspects of children's development which would go unnoticed in most ordinary Primary schools. So we can see how the school context, the pupils' special needs, and the specific role of the teacher can frame a teacher's perceptions of pupils.

In the main group of constructs it is interesting to see how many of the teachers' perceptions relate to personality and behaviour, and how few to learning and educational attainment, or to more superficial features such as physical appearance. It seems that children's behaviour and their social and personal development are very important to these early years teachers who have a key role in socialising young children as school pupils.

The use of Personal Construct Theory focuses on teachers' individual perceptions of children. However, it has been suggested that teachers as a group may develop a common view of children's nature and development.

Carugati (1990), drawing on Moscovici's theory of Social Representations, argues that people come to use and understand terms like 'intelligence' as a way of explaining the inequalities and hierarchies that are seen in most social groups, including schools. Teachers, like parents, are particularly sensitive to children's individual differences, but they have to manage the daily routine and make practical decisions affecting all the children in their classes. Carugati suggests that the construction of a common social representation of intelligence helps teachers collectively to maintain a professional identity as practitioners. For example, teachers who are faced daily with the fact of children's individual differences in attainment and progress may be helped by a representation of children as naturally 'bright', 'average' or 'not very intelligent', rather than a more personally threatening representation of the effects of 'good' and 'poor' teaching. This can apply particularly when there is a mismatch between the school curriculum and the various ways in which children can excel, or when time runs out for trying different teaching strategies within the ordinary school day. For children at the extremes of apparent high or low ability, this process can have implications for the future choice of teaching strategies, activities, class groupings and even for school placement.

Beliefs about how children differ can affect teachers' interactions with children, setting up expectations and self-fulfilling prophecies. Yet it should be remembered that the subtleties and demands of teaching from day to day work against the consistent application of simplistic labels to particular children. Even if teachers have a general idea about underlying differences in intellectual potential, they can also be aware of, and eager to seek out, ways in which children's achievements and learning can be affected by particular experiences – as shown by this experienced Primary teacher interviewed in a study of teachers' approaches to differentiation:

> Some children have had experiences out of school that can make them able to contribute at a much higher level than you might normally expect. …
> A family interest can bring something extra to their work.
>
> (Kershner and Miles 1996)

Children's views about individuality in school

From a child's point of view as a pupil in school, we may wonder how she or he feels about sometimes being treated like other children, and sometimes differently from them. Do children need to feel similar to others in a working group in order to feel secure, motivated and able to learn? Do children evaluate themselves in comparison with others? Schunk (1990) refers to a long history of psychological research into the self concept to argue that children observe each other carefully in school, they judge how they stand in relation to their peers and they may model themselves on others who are seen to have similar attributes such as ability, age, gender and race.

Children also develop general views about learning and individuality. In a questionnaire which my colleague Pam Pointon and I gave to forty-eight 10–11 year olds, 59 per cent of the children disagreed with the statement that 'girls work better if they are sitting with boys'; 33 per cent took the opposite view, and 8 per cent were neutral. So, when asked about working with other boys and girls in a rather general and abstract way, the children showed a strong tendency to take gender as a significant factor, one way or the other, when they were prompted by the questionnaire to focus only on that broad characteristic. However, in interviews which encouraged them to talk in more detail about their own experiences in school, some of the children were very articulate in explaining that relying on characteristics like gender to choose working partners may not be the best way to learn. The co-operative or individual nature of the activity and the implicit aims for 'good work' and 'concentration' clearly makes a difference to the thinking of this child:

> Most girls like to have a group of girls, and boys like to have a group of boys. But sometimes, in music maybe, some boys are good at music and some girls are too. It you mix them together you make a good piece of music.

Children are likely to have their own ideas about how teachers ought to help individual pupils to learn in different ways – as shown, for example, by 10-year-old Lorraine's reponse to questions about whether children should be told to 'work hard' in school:

> Well if it was, say, PE, and they said they weren't very good at it, then I'd say 'well you can do a bit more'. ... Some people think 'oh, I've got to work hard', and then they get upset because they can't do it. ... Some people are really good at something and other people aren't so good. ... I'd help the person who wasn't as good, but keep helping the other person so that he or she remembered what it was they were doing.

Children can also be very sensitive and responsive to the school context, as is shown by this extract from an interview with 10-year-old Antony, in which he describes his own response to apparent inconsistencies between teachers:

INTERVIEWER: What do you get out of coming to school?

ANTONY: Well, I learn sort of writing, things. But then every class I go into, each teacher wants you to do different styles of writing. Like Mrs L. told me to join up my Ys and Gs to the next letter, but Mrs S. doesn't.

INTERVIEWER: So, what sense do you make of that when you're told to do different styles of writing?

ANTONY: Well, I sort of ... I get in between. I do some one way, and some the other.

Antony has developed his own coping strategy (perhaps at some cost to his writing), and his comments highlight the high expectations for children to adapt to school life. Even if based on misunderstanding of what his teachers actually said to him from year to year, it is clear that Antony's handwriting skills are closely linked to his perceptions of the demands and expectations in the school context. His teachers may well be unaware of his dilemma.

Many children may have an inclination to conform to school life, however inconsistent and puzzling it is to them. Yet there is a danger in conformity, as has been shown by interviews and case studies of children who become 'invisible' to teachers. Pye (1988) interviewed young adults whose education had been limited when they quietly conformed to school life or dropped out as soon as they could. From his own experience as a Secondary school teacher he knew that he had a gained only a vague understanding and memory of many of his pupils. Many of his interviewees felt that their rich and complex feelings about learning had not been recognised by their teachers. For example, 'Jane', seen as a 'sensible and pleasant' pupil, had been allowed to leave school on the understanding that she had come to what was seen as an appropriate decision about working as a clerk. Her fears about failure if she were to take her academic studies further had not been recognised or tackled. She had been 'over-simplified' and it was only as an adult that she retrieved and revived her confidence and pleasure in learning (Pye 1988:85).

Collins (1996) was similarly concerned about her 'quiet' pupils in Primary school and this prompted her to set up a research project. After interviewing the children over a period of three years as they transferred to Secondary education, interviewing other teachers and parents and carrying out classroom observations, she came to understand the different reasons why children might become passive, unenthusiastic and socially withdrawn in school. In her case studies she identified factors relating to anxiety, culture clashes and inappropriate expectations of school as significant in explaining different children's superficially similar quiet behaviour in class.

Psychological views of children as individuals

Psychologists ask many questions about children's development and learning, including:

- How do children resemble each other and how do they differ?
- What is the importance of children's individual actions, perceptions, beliefs and feelings for their development and learning?
- How do specific circumstances affect children's actions, thoughts and feelings?

One of main areas of psychological research relating to children as individuals focuses on the self-concept. Interviews with children of different ages show that there is both development and variation in children's self-understanding, including their perceptions of the reasons for their own physical attributes, behaviours, social relationships, thoughts, feelings and attitudes (Damon and Hart 1988).

There have also been long-running and often controversial attempts by psychologists to describe and understand individual differences in the areas of personality and intelligence (see Crozier 1997; Hampson and Colman 1995; Richardson 1991 for reviews of the literature). Yet attempts to understand individual differences in personality, for example, have often foundered in the face of evidence about the inconsistency of people's behaviour in different situations – as when a quiet child in class becomes lively and noisy with her friends in the playground. Hampson (1997), who has written extensively about the development of personality in terms of the meanings attached to people's behaviour in different social circumstances, proposes that the best way to understand the coherence of individual personalities is by looking for patterns of consistent and inconsistent behaviour, not by searching for underlying fixed personal qualities. She suggests that this approach provides a properly multidimensional picture of human behaviour and personality.

> Real people and good fictional characters are a complex blend of attractive and less attractive qualities and, at times, they behave in conflicting and even contradictory ways. The challenge for the observer (and the self-observer), is to make sense of their inconsistencies.
>
> (Hampson 1997:83–84)

Hampson gives an example from her research with adults in which she found that when people select adjectives to describe themselves, it is not unusual for them to include inconsistent qualities (e.g. daring and cautious). However, they will tend to be consistent in terms of overall positive or negative tone, even if the actual behaviours are inconsistent. With children as with adults we need to be aware of the tendency to produce an overall evaluation of the self or others and then fit new perceptions into this positive or negative view. The educational implications for future motivation and learning can be significant if children fall into a pattern of positive or negative thinking about their potential to be successful learners.

Why do children differ in their thinking and behaviour?

Certain children seem more resilient than others in what seem to be difficult life circumstances, and other children find learning difficult even in apparently the best of conditions. There are many conceptual and methodological problems in trying to identify causes and explanations for children's individual differences, however. Meadows (1993:252), in her discussion of change and variation in children's cognitive development highlights the difficulties in discovering causes which are 'sufficient', 'necessary' or 'contributory', bearing in mind the likelihood that complex behaviours and thinking are likely to be the result of several factors 'which may vary from person to person and time to time'. Much of the data gained from psychological research on personality and intelligence is correlational, meaning that the pattern of two sets of observations or scores is similar. However, this connection does not necessarily indicate a causal relationship, one way or the other.

The apparent correlation between IQ test score and school achievement, for example, could be explained by the resemblance to schoolwork of the intelligence test which was used (IQ tests often require high levels of reading skill or mathematical ability, for example); or there may be other factors which separately influence IQ test scores and measures of school achievement – such as children's skills and motivation in taking tests and examinations. In effect, the same thing has been measured twice and given a different name. Causal models arising from any statistical calculations need to be tested and replicated with further research.

There are both ethical and practical problems in gathering evidence about children's lives, as has been shown by the extensive research on twins which has aimed to gather evidence about the genetic and environmental causes of intelligence (Meadows 1993). Research can only produce a sample of information about children's lives, and it is limited by the nature of the research questions and the interpretation of findings about development in different social and cultural contexts. It is important not to be too simplistic; one only has to think about the different meanings life events carry for people who live closely together, e.g. the varying impact of the birth of a new baby on different brothers and sisters in the same family.

To understand children's differences, we need to bring together ideas about the physical nature of the human body, the psychological processes of consciousness and learning, social behaviour, and the aspects of the physical and social environment in which a child grows up. In her study of the workings of the brain, Greenfield (1997) uses the example of memory to show how experience leads to individual differences at a psychological and physical level, even for genetically identical twins. It is not the workings of the brain nor the distinctive genetic profiles of individual people which cause individual differences in their sets of personal memories. A person's unique set of memories depends on their individual perceptions and interpretations of a vast number of experiences from infancy as well as the nature and efficiency of the developing neuronal network in the brain, which can itself be directly influenced by other factors such as nutrition, drugs and physical damage. It is an interactive process throughout life, which relates to the activities of life.

There are subtle but significant social and psychological interactions from the time of birth. Chess and Thomas (1992), discuss the impact of children's different temperaments with reference to the evidence of their New York Longitudinal Study which followed 133 children from early infancy to adulthood. They observed early temperamental differences in factors like the children's activity level, adaptability, responsiveness, distractibility and mood, yet they argue that it is not the child's temperament in itself which determines later development and social adjustment. What is seen to be crucial is the 'goodness of fit' between the child and the parents. They argue that excessive, inappropriate or incompatible demands and expectations will jeopardise a child's healthy development. The growing child needs to adapt to the environment, but the people caring for the child also need to adapt to him or her.

The potentially magnifying effects of interaction between the child and the environment can be seen in school. For example, children who show aggression may be isolated from the opportunity to play with other children, and, over the long term, the effects can then spiral into classroom behaviour, curriculum choices and even to placement at a different school. Each new response provides a 'turning point' in life experience which has its own implications for the children's future development (Rutter 1994).

The debates about the interaction between a child and the environment relate strongly to different views on intelligence and learning. In his chapter in this book, Colin Connor explains the difference between the 'fixed IQ' and the 'untapped potential' perspectives on children's intellectual abilities and the implications for assessing children's learning. The 'untapped potential' view suggests that children's intelligence varies according to the context and the teaching received, and it works against the notion of natural inequalities in intellectual power or capacity. However, there is a field of psychological research which draws us back to look at the individual intellectual qualities which children bring to their experiences and learning in different settings. For example, Gardner (1993) has developed a model of 'multiple intelligences', which has become popular as a way of understanding and responding to children's individual strengths in school (MacGilchrist *et al.* 1998; Chamberlain *et al.* 1996). Drawing on a range of evidence from the lives of exceptional individuals, the effects of brain damage on different abilities, developmental processes, evolution and psychological task performance, he identifies the following independent areas of intelligence:

> Linguistic, Musical, Logical-Mathematical, Spatial, BodilyKinaesthetic, Interpersonal, Intrapersonal

These reflect the differing abilities of children and adults in the areas of language; musical composition and performance; hypothesis testing and problem-solving; navigation, imagery and drawing; physical co-ordination and skill; understanding of other people; and understanding of oneself. Gardner has more recently added a further 'intelligence' of the naturalist, and he has raised the possibility of an 'existential intelligence' which involves the ability to consider fundamental questions about human existence (Gardner 1998).

Other approaches to understanding individual differences in learning include ideas about individual differences in styles of cognition and learning. A review of research in this area by Riding and Rayner (1998) refers to the many attempts over the years to place individuals on the dimensions of, for example, risk taking or cautious; converging or diverging thinkers; adaptors or innovators; field-dependent or field independent; and impulsive or reflective. Riding and Rayner propose that cognitive style can in fact be reduced to two principle dimensions which cover the organisation of information and the way it is mentally represented, i.e. a 'wholist–analytic' dimension, which identifies a tendency to organise information into wholes or parts; and a 'verbal–imagery' dimension, which identifies an inclination to represent information verbally or in pictures. We can see that the verbal–imagery dimension shows some overlap with Gardner's linguistic and spatial intelligences, while the wholist–analytic dimension is more general and 'content-free'. Riding and Rayner's research suggests that cognitive style may affect children's learning by influencing their responses to the structure, presentation and content of what is to be learned. The implication is that some children will respond better than others to step-by-step verbal explanations, subject headings, diagrams, hypertext, etc., and that in activities like speaking, writing and drawing, individual children will find certain ways of expressing their knowledge easier than others. Riding and Rayner also note the extensive research on differences of learning style which include children's characteristic orientation to study and individual preferences for certain types of learning environment.

The work on multiple intelligences and on styles of cognition and learning brings together the traditional fields of psychological research into intelligence, personality, temperament and motivation. Sternberg (1997), for example, argues that a person's preferred thinking style can be the key to explaining why some situations, including formal tests, do not best display that person's abilities and achievements. By broadening our understanding of the relevance and interconnectedness of different aspects of children's thinking and behaviour, we can begin to recognise exactly what test scores and profiles can and cannot tell us about children's individuality. More research is still needed to confirm the validity of these models of individual difference, but even in their current form they are useful in suggesting ways of understanding differences between children which potentially link directly into learning and teaching. They open up possibilities, tentatively at least, to respond to children as individuals by developing the school curriculum. Similarly, a dynamic view of intelligence as 'learning potential' opens up the role of the teacher as a guide, prompter and model for all children's learning, whatever their individual starting points.

Responding to children as individuals in school

An awareness of children's individuality, together with an understanding of the differing perspectives and influences discussed in this chapter, suggests that it is important for teachers to:

- accept and acknowledge children as individuals
- identify individual differences between children which are clearly relevant to learning and teaching, bearing in mind the opportunities available in school for children to demonstrate and develop different interests and skills
- seek to understand the children's perspectives about learning in school

- understand how children and teachers may influence each other in the social world of the classroom, taking into account the relevant characteristics of the school context
- establish a body of principles, rights and professional expertise which ensures that all children are noticed and included in the educational system.

Each one of these points has implications for responding to children as individuals in school, at the individual and whole-school levels. Many of the ideas offered below are covered more extensively in other chapters of this book.

Accepting and acknowledging children as individuals
(attention, relationships, talk, participation and emotional processes)

One of the most important tasks for class teachers is to attend in some way to individual pupils and establish a relationship with them. Pye (1988), in his study of 'invisible' children stresses the importance of ensuring that children feel valued and 'acknowledged', by which he means that:

> ..a teacher treats a pupil as an interesting and unpredictable individual, not as an inhabitant of convenient generality. Pupils will gain from teachers with whom they make close relationships, time, patience and regard. But most important of all, they will gain from being acknowledged as not wholly known, as able to surprise.
>
> (Pye 1988:16)

Pye (1988) and Collins (1996), who writes about 'quiet' children, both emphasise the importance of somehow helping all children to talk and participate in classroom activities. This applies equally to children who are disruptive and disengaged in school. Simple encouragement and opportunity may not be enough, however: children need to develop the skills and motivation to participate more in class. For some children, structured groupwork and role play can help to bridge this transition, as can the use of activities designed to capture and respond to the individual knowledge and interests which children bring to school.

The emotional aspects of teaching and learning must also be acknowledged. It is important to respect children's needs for privacy, space and reflection, but a significant proportion of children may be quiet and withdrawn in class for reasons of confusion, fear and anxiety. They are unable to choose to participate and their learning is affected. Salzberger-Wittenberg (1983) writes about the role of the teacher in helping children to order their thoughts and cope with the pressures and fears of learning in school. Part of this process involves teachers in attending to individual children, being open and receptive to their feelings, and being prepared to empathize and think about the feelings which are aroused in themselves by individual pupils.

Identifying educationally relevant individual differences between children *(task analysis, differentiation, curriculum innovation and 'going beyond the comfort zone')*

The teacher's acknowledgement of children's individuality has to incorporate an understanding of children's responses to what the school curriculum is asking of them. This operates at different levels.

Task analysis and differentiation

'Matching' tasks to individual pupils is practically difficult, as was found by Bennett *et al.* (1984) and by the teachers interviewed by Simpson (1997). But many of the problems arise when attempts to make adaptations for individuals do not include an analysis of the actual priorities and demands embodied in the curriculum. For individual classroom activities, such as writing a story or carrying out a science investigation, the relevance of children's individual differences depends on what the task demands in terms of communication, social skills, literacy, reasoning, knowledge, physical co-ordination, and so on. A task analysis is needed to highlight not only the cognitive demands of the area of the learning in question, but also the often hidden expectations in any classroom activity for children to read, understand instructions, write, draw, work with others, handle objects, make a plan of action, and 'tune out' the noise from the corridor, for example. This analysis can be structured to take account of the ways in which children may differ in their thinking and learning. For example, Bayliss (1995) offers an approach to identify how a task calls on children's 'multiple intelligences'.

Curriculum innovation and going beyond the comfort zone

Task analysis and differentiation are important tools for teachers, but ultimately the recognition and inclusion of children as individuals in school has to lead to extension and innovation within the curriculum. Hart (1996) writes about 'innovative thinking' as a way of generating new insights into what might be done to support a child's learning in school. This approach includes the re-description of individual children in terms of hypotheses about how to help them learn in school, rather than in terms of their personal characteristics and limitations. The implication is that the whole-school curriculum ought to be open to change in response to the diverse population of pupils. The children's individual differences act as a spur to developments and innovations which can be for the benefit of all the children in school.

This process can be risky and uncomfortable for teachers and pupils, yet it is essential to 'go beyond the comfort zone' in education. Joyce and Weil (1996) argue that

> ... real growth often requires us to make our learners uncomfortable,
> and we have to help them deal with the unfamiliar situations that we
> must create for them.
>
> (Joyce and Weil 1996:386)

As they point out, this is particularly important when pupils may tend to
'pull' the teacher towards their preferred styles of learning. In an extended
and flexible curriculum, many children will need both teaching and encouragement to work in a collaborative group, for example, or to use visual rather
than verbal strategies for expressing their ideas.

Seeking to understand the children's perspectives about learning in school *(multiple goals and channels of communication)*

In acknowledging and responding to children as individuals, it is important
to recognise how they have to co-ordinate their own multiple goals in school.
Children are pulled by their own interests and friendships as well as the
demands of teachers and parents. Higher attaining pupils by definition can
manage these multiple goals successfully, whereas pupils who are not doing
so well in school may modify or abandon certain goals in favour of others:
they may stop working to be 'cool' with friends, or alternatively avoid their
friends in order to concentrate on their work. A teacher's response to apparently 'lazy' or 'lonely' children might be to help them to list their various priorities and map out their lives, in this way aiming to enhance children's self-
understanding and sense of autonomy, which in turn enhances their
learning.

The active process of seeking to recognise children as individuals with
their own relevant perceptions and views is not only important for practical
teaching purposes, it also has both legal backing and moral force in relation
to principles about children's rights (Gersch *et al.* 1996). The implication is
that as a matter of school policy, individual children's views should be represented, and, as with the curriculum, this will require some innovative thinking about the channels of communication in school and the ways in which
children can be helped to express their ideas using discussions, interviews,
writing and drawing. School Councils and similar bodies can offer a formal
structure for this.

Understanding the social world of the classroom *(perceptions, co-regulation and the management of multiple goals)*

We have seen earlier in this chapter that the social context of classroom
learning can hinder and skew teachers' understanding of individual children and children's understanding of themselves, locking children into

fixed categories and traits of personality and behaviour. From the teacher's point of view, strategies to counter this tendency include:

- making a point of monitoring one's own perceptions of pupils by, for example, regularly trying to recall which children have been memorable in the school day and why;
- trying on regular occasions to identify and understand how the teaching role can influence beliefs about children by identifying salient 'personal constructs' and 'social representations' about pupils, as described earlier in this chapter;
- setting aside time to look in more depth at how individual children are learning in different contexts, taking into account other people's observations and opinions. With the growing number of different adults in Primary schools this consultation about children is often done informally, but the process could be more systematic and extensive. For example, Shulman and Mesa-Bains (1993) show how teachers' written observations of individual children in inner-city, multicultural school settings, together with commentaries from other people, can offer a rich source of information and a powerful basis for understanding and responding to children's diversity.

The intrinsic 'socialness' of classroom life can also be used to acknowledge and enhance children's individuality. The basis of learning in school is a flexible co-regulation between pupils and between teachers and pupils:

> Co-regulated learning conveys a sense of 'we-ness'. Learning is not merely an individual struggle, nor is motivation.
>
> (McCaslin and Good 1996:660)

When children are engaged in a varied menu of classroom activities, lessons can be planned with a view of the different contributions individual children can make to the learning of the class as whole, including themselves. In collaborative groupwork, for example, children have to recognise each other's needs and take on the complementary roles which can prompt individual children to extend, practise or demonstrate their learning in a way that complements the needs of other children for a collaborator, helper or model. A teaching or helping role from time to time is especially important for children who are normally identified as having learning or behavioural difficulties, or who may be otherwise marginalised in class.

The management of a class of individual children depends on the co-ordination and review of multiple goals, from the teacher's perspective as well as the children's. As McCaslin and Good (1996:656) point out, some strategies for managing multiple goals are more positive than others. There is a danger for certain children that learning goals may be substituted or even abandoned in the face of other priorities – as when children with literacy difficulties may be withdrawn from certain class lessons in music or art, for example, in order to receive extra teaching in reading and spelling. It is important to examine what happens to the multiple goals for children's learning in practice, and to ensure from day to day that there is not a systematic exclusion of certain pupils from areas of classroom life.

Establishing a body of principles for inclusion
(being 'hospitable to diversity')

One of the main issues in responding to children as individuals is to establish whether the school curriculum, organisation, teaching strategies and resourcing can and should be developed to accommodate the full range of pupils in an inclusive educational system. In responding to children as individuals it is important to clarify the guiding principles about what the educational system and individual schools ought to be doing for all children. If the aim is to educate all the pupils in school, then, as writers like Levine (1996) and Bearne (1996) have put it, a school needs to be hospitable to diversity. Bearne (1996) discusses in general terms how the goal of being hospitable to diversity can be represented in the whole-school environment as well as within the curriculum. She alerts us to the significance of factors such as displays, physical access, and the nature of learning resources as demonstrations of the way children are perceived in school and the value placed on them as individuals.

Arguments about being hospitable to diversity pull together many of the points already discussed in this chapter about children as individuals in the social world of the school. We are coming to know a great deal about children as individual learners from a psychological perspective, but the attitudes and practices found in school can exclude certain children from learning. The processes of recognising and responding to children as individuals in school have to be active, creative and preferably collaborative between all involved, and they must be guided by principles and policies for all children's inclusion within an educational system which is tuned to children's individuality and diversity.

Activities

How should children be grouped in school?

A Primary teacher remarked in an interview that 'When you get a class you take a time getting to know the children. You've got to group them for management straight away, but ... as soon as you start to know them you actually want to regroup them. Ability is one of the factors, but it's not the only one.'

Which factors would you take into account in grouping children in the Primary classroom?

Multiple intelligences in the classroom

It has been suggested that Gardner's model of 'multiple intelligences' can be used to develop a varied range of teaching strategies to respond to children's individual strengths and weaknesses, as well as helping teachers to understand which aspect of a task may set up obstacles to children's learning.

Consider the following familiar activities in school: reading and writing; singing; constructing models; painting pictures; scientific investigation; working in a group; responding to the teacher's written feedback; tidying up.

How do these activities relate to children's 'multiple intelligences'? Are any aspects of intelligence not represented?

What teaching strategies and resources could be used to enhance children's skills and talents in the different areas of intelligence identified by Gardner?

How could an understanding of different aspects of intelligence be used with children of different ages to introduce a new concept or topic, like 'the local environment', 'magnetism' or 'multiplication'?

What is 'normal' in school?

Expectations about children's 'normal' behaviour and learning are shown when teachers discuss 'a particularly lively Year 3 child' or 'a hard working Year 5 class'. The issues of 'normality', and the implications for including children in the educational system are constantly debated. Some children are removed from the ordinary school setting because their learning abilities and behaviour seem so extraordinary and difficult to manage compared to other pupils. In a school in which 100 per cent of the children are bilingual it is 'normal' to place issues of language and communication near the top of any thinking that is done about curriculum planning, teaching strategies and parental involvement. However, what would be 'normal' and what action should be taken with a proportion of bilingual pupils of 60, 25 or 1 per cent?

Now answer the same question with reference to children with hearing impairments.

Further reading

Bearne, E. (ed.) (1996) *Differentiation and Diversity in the Primary School,* London: Routledge.

Collins, J. (1996) *The Quiet Child,* London: Cassell.

Cooper, C. (1998) *Individual Differences,* London: Arnold.

Crozier W.R. (1997) *Individual Learners: Personality differences in education,* London: Routledge.

Davie, R. and Galloway, D. (eds) (1996) *Listening to Children in Education,* London: Fulton.

Gardner H., Kornhaber M.I. and Wake W.K. (1996) *Intelligence: multiple perspectives,* Fort Worth: Harcourt Brace.

Hampson, S.E. and Colman, A.M. (eds) (1995) *Individual Differences and Personality,* London: Longman.

Richardson, K. (1991) *Understanding Intelligence,* Buckingham: Open University Press.

References

Anning, A. (1997) *The First Years at School: Education 4 to 8,* 2nd edition, Buckingham: Open University Press.

Bayliss, P. (1995) 'Teaching for diversity', in C. Desforges (ed.) *An Introduction to Teaching: psychological perspectives,* Oxford: Blackwell.

Bearne, E. (1996) 'Constructing a policy for differentiation', in E. Bearne (ed.) *Differentiation and Diversity in the Primary School,* London: Routledge.

Bennett, N., Desforges, C., Cockburn, A. and Wilkinson, B. (1984) *The Quality of Pupils' Learning Experiences,* London: Lawrence Erlbaum Associates.

Bruner, J. (1996) *The Culture of Education,* Cambridge, MA: Harvard University Press.

Carugati, F.F. (1990) 'From social cognition to social representations in the study of intelligence', in G. Duveen and Lloyd B. (eds) *Social Representations and the Development of Knowledge,* Cambridge: Cambridge University Press.

Chamberlain, V., Hopper, B. and Jack, B. (1996) *Starting Out MI Way: a guide to multiple intelligences in the primary school,* Bolton: D2/The Centre for the Promotion of Holistic Education, Edge Hill University College.

Chess, S. and Thomas, A. (1992) 'Interactions between offspring and parents in development', in B. Tizard and V. Varma (eds) *Vulnerability and Resilience in Human Development: a Festschrift for Ann and Alan Clarke,* London: Jessica Kingsley.

Collins, J. (1996) *The Quiet Child,* London: Cassell.

Crozier, W.R. (1997) *Individual Learners: personality differences in education,* London: Routledge.

Damon, W. and Hart, D. (1988) *Self-Understanding in Childhood and Adolescence,* Cambridge: Cambridge University Press.

Gardner, H. (1993) *Frames of Mind: the theory of multiple intelligences,* London: Fontana Press.

Gardner, H. (1998) 'A multiplicity of intelligences', *Scientific American Presents: Exploring Intelligence,* 9 (4), 18–23.

Gersch, I. (with Moyse, S., Nolan, A. and Pratt, G.) (1996) 'Listening to children in educational contexts', in R. Davie, G. Upton and V. Varma (eds) *The Voice of the Child: a handbook for professionals,* London: Falmer.

Greenfield, S. (1997) *The Human Brain: a guided tour*, London: Weidenfeld and Nicolson.

Hampson, S.E. and Colman, A.M. (eds) (1995) *Individual Differences and Personality*, London: Longman.

Hampson, S.E. (1997) 'The social psychology of personality', in C. Cooper and V. Varma (eds) *Processes in Individual Differences*, London: Routledge.

Hart, S. (1996) *Beyond Special Needs: Enhancing children's learning through innovative thinking*, London: Paul Chapman.

James, A. and Prout, A. (eds) (1997) *Constructing and Reconstructing Childhood: contemporary issues in the sociological study of childhood*, 2nd edition, London: Falmer.

Joyce, B. and Weil, M. (1996) *Models of Teaching*, Boston: Allyn and Bacon.

Kelly, G. A. (1955) *The Psychology of Personal Constructs*, New York: Norton.

Kershner, R. and Miles, S. (1996) 'Thinking and talking about differentiation: "It's like a bar of soap … "'. In E. Bearne (ed.) *Differentiation and Diversity in the Primary School*, London: Routledge.

Levine, J. (1996) 'Developing pedagogies for multilingual classes', in M. Meek (ed.) *Developing Pedagogies in the Multilingual Classroom: the writings of Josie Levine*, Stoke-on-Trent, Staffs: Trentham Books.

MacGilchrist, B., Myers, K. and Reed, J. (1998) *The Intelligent School*, London: Paul Chapman Publishing.

McCaslin, M. and Good, T.L. (1996) 'The informal curriculum', in D.C. Berliner an R.C. Calfee (eds.) *Handbook of Educational Psychology*, New York: Simon and Schuster Macmillan.

Meadows, S. (1993) *The Child as Thinker*, London: Routledge.

Pye, J. (1988) *Invisible Children: Who are the real losers at school?* Oxford: Oxford University Press.

Richardson, K. (1991) *Understanding Intelligence*, Buckingham: Open University Press.

Riding, R. and Rayner, S. (1998) *Cognitive Styles and Learning Strategies*, London: Fulton.

Rutter, M. (1994) 'Continuities, transitions and turning points in development', in M. Rutter and D.F. Hay (eds) *Development Through Life: a handbook for clinicians*, Oxford: Blackwell.

Salmon, P. (1995) *Psychology in the Classroom*, London: Cassell.

Salzberger-Wittenberg, I. (1983) 'Emotional aspects of learning', in I. Salzberger-Wittenberg, G. Henry and E. Osborne (eds) *The Emotional Experience of Learning and Teaching*, London: Routledge and Kegan Paul.

Shulman, J.H. and Mesa-Bains, A. (1993) *Diversity in the Classroom: a casebook for teachers and teacher educators*, Hillsdale: Research for Better Schools/Erlbaum.

Schunk, D.H. (1990) 'Self-concept and school achievement', in C. Rogers and P. Kutnick (eds) *The Social Psychology of the Primary School*, London: Routledge.

Simpson, M. (1997) 'Developing differentiation practices: meeting the needs of pupils and teachers', *The Curriculum Journal*, 8, 1, 85–104.

Sternberg, R.J. (1997) *Thinking Styles*, Cambridge: Cambridge University Press.

Tobin, J.J., Wu, D.Y.H. and Davidson, D.H. (1989) *Preschool in Three Cultures: Japan, China and the United States*, New Haven: Yale University Press.

13 Providing equal opportunities for boys and girls

Joan M. Whitehead

EDITOR'S SUMMARY

There is clear evidence that some children do not fulfil their academic potential because they conform to gender stereotypes. This can be damaging for both boys and girls. This chapter explores the mechanisms by which these stereotypes limit children's aspirations, and the ways in which schools can unwittingly contribute to this. The contribution that the processes of canalisation, reinforcement and role modelling make to the formation of gender schema and a gender identity are explored, together with factors that influence children's conformity to sex-stereotypes. It is argued that teachers need to be aware of these socialisation processes so that they can present positive role models, have high expectations of all pupils, reduce the significance of gender as a social category and challenge pupil attitudes. By these means, and by working to help all children be confident about themselves, it is possible to negate the worst consequences of gender stereotypes for children's education.

Gender is one of the most important and fundamental aspects of our identity; it is also a category that permeates the way society views individuals and how we come to view ourselves. In order to understand the role that education plays in its development, some knowledge of the psychological issues involved is essential. In the first part of this chapter I am going to look at some of these issues; at what constitutes the cultural norms regarding gender within our own society; at how these norms are taught through the socialisation process and the effect conformity to these norms can have on individuals of both sexes. The second part of the chapter will look at the role of education in the development of a gender identity, with particular reference to the role of teachers, and the relationship between conformity to sex-stereotypes and educational achievement.

A gender identity can be described, in simple terms, as our internal aware-ness of ourselves as a woman or a man, a girl or a boy. How we come to this internal awareness is, however, a complex process and although research has increased our knowledge of the process, it is as yet not fully understood. It is also an area of controversy, primarily about whether women and men 'natu-rally' behave in different ways or whether differences in behaviour are largely the result of the internalisation of culturally defined norms which prescribe appropriate feminine and masculine behaviour.

While some biologists and geneticists would argue that men and women are 'programmed' to behave in different ways, most social scientists would argue that while sex (being male or female) is undoubtedly a biological distinction, gender is a social construction. There are a number of reasons for this. What is considered appropriate feminine or masculine behaviour varies across cul-tures and within cultures depending on, for example, social class or ethnicity; what constitutes appropriate behaviour within a particular culture changes over time and there are differences in the extent to which individuals conform to culturally prescribed norms. So although individuals are born either male or female it is society that makes them masculine or feminine.

Once formed, however, a gender identity serves as an internal monitoring system for governing choices and directing behaviour. Thus individuals choose to behave in ways they believe are appropriate for them. It is also important to remember that a gender identity is both fixed and flexible; the internal awareness individuals have of themselves as a woman or man is gen-erally fixed, but what is regarded as appropriate behaviour can, and often does, change over time.

Three main factors, it can be argued, influence the formation of a gender identity:

- *biological factors* which assign individuals to the category male and female
- *social and cultural factors* which provide information about appropriate cultural norms relating to gender, taught through the socialisation process
- *individual choice*: individuals are not passive recipients of the socialisation process they are actively involved in it and make personal choices.

Sex-stereotypes

Sex-stereotypes are widely held cultural beliefs about the characteristics of men and women, which are based on characteristics that are largely assumed to be unique to one particular sex. Stereotypical thinking leads to individuals being seen primarily in terms of their group membership and to the assump-tion that they have the characteristics of the stereotype. An individual's sex, therefore, becomes important in defining who they are and what behaviour is expected of them. Stereotypes highlight and exaggerate group differences while largely ignoring individual differences within groups. Thus all men are seen as the same and different from all women.

What then are the sex-stereotypes within our culture? Those can be divided into two kinds, sex-role and sex-trait stereotypes.

Sex-role stereotypes relate to the roles men and women are expected to occupy within a particular culture, traditionally defined in Western cultures as the 'breadwinner' role for men and the 'homemaker' role for women. Sex-trait stereotypes relate to the personality characteristics and abilities that women and men are expected to have which will enable them to carry out their respective sex roles (see Table 13.1).

Table 13.1 Stereotypical sex-trait items

Warmth–Expressiveness cluster of traits, stereotypically associated with women	*Competency cluster of traits, stereotypically associated with men*
Interested in appearance	Leader
Neat and tidy	Ambitious
Sympathetic to others	Decisive
Emotional	Self-confident
Aware of others' feelings	Hides feelings
Talkative	Dominant
Finds expressing feelings easy	Assertive
Strong need for security	Outspoken
Gentle	Not easily influenced by others
Tactful	Competitive
	Not easily upset by others
	Independent
	Good at coping in a crisis
	Adventurous
	Aggressive
	Outgoing
	Logical
	Competent
	Ruthless

Source: Perceptions of sex-stereotypes in western cultures by a national sample of 16–18 year old pupils in Schools in the UK (Whitehead 1994).

Note: Similar results have been obtained in Western cultures by the following:
Bem, S.L. (1974) 'The measurement of psychological androgyny', *Journal of Consulting and Clinical Psychology* 42(2), 155–162.
Broverman, I.K., Broverman, D.M., Clarkson, F.E., Rosencranz, P.S. and Vogel, S.R. (1972) 'Sex-role stereotypes, a current appraisal', *Journal of Social Issues*, 28(2), 59–87.
Loo, R. and Thorpe, K. (1998) 'Attitudes towards women's role in society: a replication after 20 years', *Sex Roles* 39, 11/12, 903–913.
Williams, J.E. and Best, D.L (1990) *Measuring Sex-Stereotypes*, Newbury Park, California: Sage.

The two stereotypes form a complementary whole. Men who have to manipulate the environment in the public sphere of work are seen as assertive, rational, logical, competent, good at problem-solving and interested in the world of objects and phenomena. Women, on the other hand, who have to ensure good social relationships within the private sphere of the home, are seen as sympathetic, gentle, tactful, aware of the feelings of others and above all interested in people and their concerns.

Thus to be 'truly' feminine or masculine the individual has to develop the traits stereotypically associated with their sex and to avoid those associated with the opposite sex. This is particularly important for males. Doyle (1989) has argued that the avoidance of the feminine is one of, if not the, most important aspect of masculinity. Males must avoid at all cost being regarded as a 'sissy', that is, behaving in ways or participating in activities regarded as appropriate for women.

These stereotypes, like all stereotypes, do not accurately reflect the behaviour of individual women and men, although some individuals may 'fit' the stereotypes quite closely. Many women have careers and many men are involved in child rearing. Despite the blurring of roles, however, there is evidence that stereotypical views still linger. It is still assumed that working women are responsible for running the home and organising child care, even if their job is as demanding as that of their partner. As one adolescent boy put it, 'I know a women's place isn't in the home any more but at least she ought to keep it clean' (Whitehead 1995).

Given that stereotypes do not necessarily provide accurate information about individuals, what functions do they serve? Primarily they serve as categories to help us deal with the vast amount of information received from the environment. If an object or person can be assigned to a category then we can draw on knowledge about that category to help us cope with the situation. Therefore when we meet someone for the first time we notice (among other things) that they are female or male. Once assigned to this category we then draw on sex-stereotypes to tell us what to expect from this person and to predict how they might behave and respond to us.

Stereotypes also provide a 'cultural standard' to help individuals judge the behaviour of others and themselves as appropriate or inappropriate in a particular context. Stereotypes, therefore, come into play when we are faced with a degree of uncertainty. Once we get to know others well we are much less likely to use knowledge derived from stereotypes in responding to them.

Finally stereotypes can be important because they provide 'guidelines' for the socialisation process, allowing parents and others to know what to teach their children so that they behave appropriately for their sex.

Socialisation

The first thing to stress about socialisation is that children are not passive recipients of the process but are themselves actively involved. Children are motivated to achieve mastery over their environment and will actively seek out information that will both increase their understanding of the environment and their competence in dealing with it. Learning about gender and developing a gender identity, therefore, is an integral part of the normal learning process.

Sandra Bem (1981) in her gender scheme theory has suggested the following processes as being involved in the development of a gender identity. Children become aware from a very early age that gender is a very important social category in our culture. Parents go to great lengths to make children aware of their own gender and that of others. People are continually identified and differentiated by gender through the use of names, and pronouns. Thus children not only become aware of gender as a category but also learn that it is a useful tool in helping them to interpret and understand social information. Children also apply gender categories to themselves. Once they realise that they belong to one sex rather than the other and that this is a stable characteristic (usually between the ages of three and five) they seek to behave in ways that are appropriate for their sex. They do this first of all by building up schema of what it means to be a girl or boy, women or man in our society. They become aware, for example, that certain kinds of clothes are worn by men but not by women, that certain activities are appropriate for women and others for men. They may also realise that some clothes and activities are appropriate for both sexes. In order to build up these schema children will use all the information available to them.

However, children are not left to learn about gender through their own incidental learning, there is also a systematic input from significant others in the child's world, notably parents, who provide information and shape behaviour in a number of ways.

- *Canalisation:*   parents restrict the experiences of their children to those deemed appropriate for their sex through, for example, the toys, games and books they buy them and the activities they allow them to participate in.
- *Reinforcement:*   parents reward what they believe to be appropriate behaviour by giving approval and encouragement; at the same time they discourage inappropriate behaviour by disapproval and in some cases punishment. As most children want to please their parents they are likely, as a result of this process, to repeat behaviour that has brought approval and to desist from behaviour that brought disapproval.
- *Role models:*   children learn large 'chunks' of behaviour by observation and imitation of others whom they select as role models (Bandura 1977). If imitation of behaviour is reinforced by parents then children will be motivated to repeat it and encouraged to further observation and imitation of the same role model in order to gain further reward and encouragement. Bandura believes that children play a very active role in controlling this process. They set themselves the goal of reproducing

behaviour that will gain approval, thus they learn to select appropriate role models, in this case members of their own sex, and to regulate their own behaviour to act in ways that maximise the likelihood of reward.

This socialisation process is applied to a wide range of behaviours, and in many cases the same behaviour will be encouraged in both sexes, for example being helpful, and others discouraged equally, for example highly aggressive behaviour. However, it is also used to shape sex-appropriate behaviour; in particular it is used to discourage 'feminine' behaviour in boys. Fathers, generally speaking, are very concerned that their sons should not be seen as a 'sissy'. Girls who behave in masculine ways, however, are generally much more tolerated, as being a 'tomboy' is much more acceptable.

Through the mechanisms outlined above children develop their gender schema which, according to Bem, will reflect cultural and social norms about gender. Children then apply these schema to monitoring and evaluating their own behaviour. The end result is that they choose to exhibit behaviour which conforms to society's norms. Thus are sex-stereotypes, and sex-differences, maintained (Bem 1993).

Conformity and non-conformity to sex-stereotypes

The majority of researchers on gender identity have been concerned with explaining how individuals conform to sex-stereotypes, and consequently very little has been written about why some individuals don't conform. There are numbers of ways, however, in which non-conformity to sex-stereotypes can come about.

Different schema

Different experiences can lead to individuals developing different schema, some of which are more likely to be composed of strongly stereotyped images than others.

Importance of gender

Although developing a gender identity is important for everybody the extent to which individuals regard it as the most salient aspect of their identity will vary. Some individuals may regard other aspects of themselves as a more important to their identity – e.g. ethnicity, being a devout Christian, an active socialist or a good teacher – than being a 'good' woman or man. Thus for some individuals their gender identity would take priority over all other aspects of their identity, and would be for them the most salient dimension. For others a gender identity is only one dimension among other important aspects of their identity.

Intra-psychic conflict

Conflict between conformity to sex-stereotypes and personal development may lead to rejection of sex-stereotypes. For example, if having a high-powered career or being good at sport conflicts as it does with stereotypical femininity, then the individual may choose a career or being a good sports-woman in preference to being a stereotypically feminine woman. Men may choose to be a caring parent even though this conflicts with stereotypical notions of masculinity and involves developing traits associated with femininity.

Secure gender identity

Those who have a strong internal awareness of themselves as a woman or a man are more likely to have the confidence to pursue their own personal development irrespective of social norms concerning sex-stereotypes. Individuals, however, who are less confident about their gender identity, are more likely to conform to sex-stereotypes to convince themselves, and others, that they are a 'real man' or a 'truly feminine woman', even if they do not particularly like behaving in stereotypical ways.

The important point about conformity or non-conformity is not what individuals choose to do but why they choose to do it. Individuals may choose activities and roles that are regarded as appropriate for their sex, not because they wish to conform to sex-stereotypes, but because these are the activities and roles they see as important for their personal development. The problem arises if individuals are choosing activities or behaving in particular ways solely because they believe they have to do so because of their sex.

There are periods, however, in the development of a gender identity when most individuals experience insecurity. The first of these is when children are first establishing their gender identity, usually between the ages of three and seven; the second is during adolescence when individuals are moving from a 'childhood' to an 'adulthood' gender identity. During these two periods, therefore, individuals, may show greater levels of conformity to stereotypes, a point I shall return to later.

Finally before we leave this section it is important to remember, as mentioned in the introduction, that a gender schema is not a fixed entirety, new experiences can change the content of the schema and consequently change the criteria which individuals use to shape and monitor their own behaviour. Intra-psychic conflict can also produce changes and lead to a re-appraisal of what constitutes appropriate behaviour.

Sex-stereotypes and personal development

For some time there has been a debate about the desirability of individuals conforming to the sex-stereotypes. Many researchers and writers, including myself, regard both the stereotypes themselves and rigid conformity to them as undesirable because of the effects they can have on personal development.

Firstly, conformity to sex-stereotypes encourages individuals to develop only certain characteristics, those considered appropriate for their sex, while suppressing others, those considered inappropriate. Both competence and warmth-expressiveness, it can be argued, are necessary to function as a mature adult.

Secondly, demanding that individuals conform to patterns of behaviour deemed appropriate to their gender can both militate against personal choice and lead to an under-utilisation of individual talents. Both of these factors, particularly in the past, have strongly affected women. The debate about the effects on men of being forced to conform to rigid notions of masculinity is much more recent, but also raises similar issues, particularly about social relationships and feelings of failure about not living up to the 'masculine mystic' (Pleck 1981, 1995 and O'Neill *et al.* 1995). Indeed many writers would argue that non-conformity is now much more difficult for men than women.

Thirdly, extreme forms of masculine behaviour, e.g. aggressive and violent behaviour, are highly anti-social.

Conformity to sex-stereotypes also has an impact on the attitudes individuals have towards education.

Sex-stereotypes and education achievement: girls and women

Concern about the underachievement of girls in the education system became an important issue in the 1970s and conformity to sex-stereotypes was identified as one of the main factors in this underachievement (see, for example, Sharpe 1976). There was a fairly widespread belief that an 'academic' education was not necessary for girls as they were 'only' going to be wives and mothers, an attitude summarised well in the Newsom Report of 1963 in its discussion of an appropriate curriculum for girls:

> For all girls too, there is a group of interests relating to what many, perhaps most of them, would regard as their most important vocational concern – marriage. It is true that at the age of fourteen or fifteen, this may appear chiefly as preoccupation with personal appearance and boy friends, but many girls are ready to respond to work relating to the wider aspects of homemaking and family life and the care and upbringing of children.
>
> (Newson Committee 1963:37)

Many girls accepted this ideology and saw social success and finding a husband as their main aim in life; school achievement was not only regarded as irrelevant but as a distinct disadvantage. Girls were not supposed to be clever or competent, it was unfeminine. For other girls, however, it was not so straightforward. The formation of an adult gender identity was for many adolescent girls problematic. This was because they were faced with a conflict between the pressure and demands of femininity, embodied in the sex-stereotype, and the encouragement towards, and in many cases, the desire for high achievement on the other. This conflict was generated because only low achievement, combined with social success, was compatible with the feminine stereotype. High academic achievement and a successful career required the characteristics of the competency dimension, stereotypical masculine traits incompatible with traditional notions of femininity in our society.

How girls resolved this conflict was, and still is, a crucial factor in determining their success or failure within the education system. Those who choose to conform to stereotypical notions of femininity, both in terms of roles and traits, are likely to be unsuccessful in school. Successful girls are those who are high in intrinsic motivation and who reject stereotypical femininity in favour of combining a career with marriage and seeing themselves as high on the stereotypically masculine trait scale of competence (Whitehead 1994). Although ability (measured by a verbal reasoning test) obviously played a part in determining success, the attitudes of the female pupils themselves were more important in that girls of average ability who rejected the stereotypes were more successful, in terms of examination results, than high ability girls who conformed. Sharpe (1994) reported similar findings among predominantly working class girls.

Attitudes have changed, therefore, particularly those of girls themselves, and this is reflected in the results of national examinations. Statistics produced yearly by the DfEE show that over the past decade the educational achievement of all pupils has risen considerably. The improvement in the performance of girls, however, has been much greater than that of boys, such that they now outperform boys at all levels of education. Results from national testing at Key Stage 1 show that the 'gender gap' in achievement is already established at age seven. Sammons *et al.* (1997) looked at variation in pupil achievement at Key Stage 1 in inner London Primary schools and identified gender, along with fluency in English and low income, as one of the best predictors of performance. The highest achieving group are girls who are fluent in English and not from low income families; the lowest achieving group are boys from low income families who are not fluent in English.

There is evidence, therefore, that conformity to sex-stereotypes is likely to lower the educational achievement of girls, and that rejection of certain aspects of stereotypical femininity are associated with success.

Sex-stereotypes and educational achievement: boys and men

Does conformity to stereotypical notions of masculinity also lead to lower achievement? The answer to this question was originally thought to vary depending on social class. Because educational qualifications are necessary for middle-class occupations, academic success was assumed to be compatible with the middle-class view of masculinity, conformity to which would lead to success (Tolson 1977). For working-class boys, however, academic success was not only considered to be irrelevant to their concept of masculinity but was in many cases despised as 'unmanly' (Willis 1977). Thus conformity to working-class notions of masculinity usually lead to rejection of school. Later writers, for example Connell (1995), have pointed out that this dichotomy is simplistic and that many working-class boys succeed in the education system while some middle-class boys fail. It is argued however, that working-class boys succeed because they adopt a middle-class view of masculinity. While it is true that boys who embrace a working-class notion of masculinity are generally unsuccessful (see, for example, Connell 1995), it is not the case that all those who aspire to a middle-class view of masculinity are successful. Whitehead (1998) found that scores on a questionnaire to measure extrinsic motivation (desire for a high status job, recognition of achievement by others, etc. which represent a middle-class view of masculinity) did not correlate with achievement and did not discriminate between successful and unsuccessful boys; furthermore the boys who gave the strongest support to the maintenance of traditional sex-roles in society and who intended both themselves and their wives to follow this role were the least successful boys in the system. High achievement was associated with intrinsic motivation and with liberal views about sex-roles, both for society and for themselves.

Why boys who are the most stereotypically masculine should be less successful than boys who are less stereotyped is not an easy question to answer. There are, however, indications in the research literature that it is not only working-class boys who regard school work as 'unmasculine'. Eccles (1993) in the United States looked at the home experience of young children both before they entered school and in the early years of schooling. She found that parents were more likely to encourage their daughters to read in their leisure time and were more likely to buy books for them. Their sons, on the other hand, were more likely to be encouraged to play sport and engage in other physical activities. Eccles concludes, therefore, that from an early age girls are developing skills that will help them in school, particularly the ability to concentrate on intellectual tasks; boys on the other hand are encouraged to concentrate more on physical activities which are less adapted to school work. Furthermore, boys are not motivated to work on school tasks because they perceive them as 'girls activities' – what boys do are physical activities.

These findings are supported by work in this country by Lloyd and Duveen (1992) who found that boys, at nursery school, were much more likely to engage in noisy physical activities than girls. Research in Primary classrooms has shown that boys are much more likely to be 'off task' than girls, consequently much of the interaction teachers have with boys relates to discipline, while interaction with girls is generally about work (for a good review see

Brophy 1985). There is also evidence that these attitudes and patterns of behaviour persist into the Secondary school (see for example Arnot *et al.* 1997).

It can be argued, therefore, that boys can also face a conflict between masculinity and academic achievement, and that the failure to resolve this conflict could explain the why the educational achievement of boys has not improved as much as that of girls.

The role of education in the formation of a gender identity

It would appear from the discussion so far that a high level of conformity to sex-stereotypes is not only undesirable in terms of personal development, but also militates against academic achievement. It is important, therefore, that the process of schooling both challenges the sex-stereotypes themselves and helps individuals to be less conforming. To look at how this may be achieved we need to return to the socialisation process. The factors, discussed earlier, that will influence the extent to which individuals conform to sex-stereotypes can be summarised as follows.

Conformity to sex-stereotypes

- A gender schema that reflects stereotypical cultural and social norms about gender brought about by:

  (a) reinforcement of stereotypical behaviour by significant others who accept these norms
  (b) exposure to role models whose behaviour is stereotyped
  (c) only being given the opportunity to engage in sex-appropriate activities (canalisation).

- The individual is motivated to conform because they regard gender as the single most important aspect of their identity, therefore they:

  (a) want to behave in ways that are appropriate for their sex
  (b) match their behaviour to the gender schema in preference to other standards.

Thus the view that they have of themselves (self-image) is strongly linked to their gender identity, and self-esteem results from behaving appropriately.

Low levels of conformity to sex-stereotypes

- A gender schema that is more flexible and complex, recognising that many behaviours and activities can be exhibited by both men and women, and that the stereotypes themselves are culturally constructed, brought about because:

(a) stereotypical norms are not reinforced by others

(b) they have participated in a wide range of activities, particularly cross-gender activities

(c) they have been exposed to role models who do not behave in stereotypical ways.

- Less motivated to conform because they regard gender as only one aspect of their identity, and therefore:

  (a) regard other aspects of self as equally, if not more, important

  (b) are less concerned about conforming to stereotypes.

Thus the view they have of themselves (self-image) may be less focused on gender as the most salient aspect of self. Self-esteem is not linked to conformity to stereotypes.

Drawing on the above summary we can see that here are a number of ways in which schools and teachers can help pupils to be less conforming by providing a social and learning environment that is egalitarian, where stereotyped patterns of behaviour are not reinforced and which encourages the development of all aspects of the child. The key to providing such an environment rests primarily with teachers, as they are the main agents of socialisation within the education system, not just because they direct children's behaviour and determine the activities they will pursue, but also because they provide information about gender which children use to form their gender schema. It is important, therefore, for teachers to examine very carefully their own attitudes about gender and consider how these may influence their behaviour towards pupils. The next section will look at teacher behaviour within each of the areas of socialisation identified earlier.

Canalisation

As we saw earlier, some children may have had their experiences restricted to ones that parents deem appropriate for their sex. When they encounter the new and strange environment of the school they may tend to engage with what is most familiar to them and to shy away from the unfamiliar, particularly if given a choice. This may mean that some girls are reluctant to engage with construction kits, or tools, to build objects, because they have never used them before and don't know where to begin. Some boys may be reluctant to engage seriously with reading because this activity has not been encouraged at home and they may regard it as unmasculine. It is important, therefore, that all pupils are encouraged to participate in activities they find unfamiliar, and given positive support in learning new skills. Allowing too much free choice may mean that pupils build on existing strengths and continue to neglect areas in which they have few skills. Because pupils are choosing 'normal' gender appropriate activities teachers may fail to notice that

Table 13.2

Qualities or behaviour	Description if a girl	Description if a boy
Noisy, rushing around from one activity to the next	Disturbed, disruptive, over excited	Boisterous, lively, active
Showing emotions freely, crying if upset	Sensitive	Wet, cry-baby, big softie
Organising others, initiating activities	Bossy	Born leader

other areas are being avoided and may thus unwittingly perpetuate the process of canalisation (see Activity on pupil choices).

Reinforcement

Teachers reinforce certain patterns of behaviour in pupils by approval and praise and discourage others by disapproval and punishment. Although in many cases the same standards of behaviour are expected from all pupils, irrespective of their gender, research has shown that gender can influence our perception of behaviour and how we respond to it. Browne and Franc (1985), for example, looked at the way they, and other nursery school teachers, described children's behaviour. Some examples are given in Table 13.2.

We can see from these descriptions that behaviour can be regarded as positive or negative depending on the sex of the child. The term 'bossy' has never been a complement. Describing girls who are good at organising others in this way conveys to them that this behaviour is not approved of, and may discourage them from developing their potential for leadership. Boys, on the other hand, are given approval and encouragement for the same behaviour. Encouraging children to cry all the time is clearly undesirable; however, it is important that children learn to understand their feelings and to express them appropriately. Individuals who find this difficult, usually males, often have difficulties with personal relationships. Noisy and active children are clearly more problematic. Accepting that this behaviour is 'typical' of boys and doing little to discourage it can clearly work to their disadvantage, as they are not being encouraged to sit down and concentrate on more 'academic' tasks. Discouraging girls from this form of behaviour may help them academically but may discourage their participation in more active pursuits such as sport. Clearly a balance needs to be found for all pupils. What the above example illustrates is that 'taken-for-granted assumptions' based on sex-stereotypes about appropriate behaviour for boys and girls can influence the way we respond, often quite unconsciously, to their behaviour resulting in the reinforcement of sex-stereotyped patterns of behaviour.

Role models and teacher expectations

For many pupils the teacher will be regarded as a role model. How teachers behave, therefore, and how they present topics and learning materials to pupils are likely to have a significant impact on pupils' perceptions. It is particularly important that teachers do not convey the expectation that certain topics are for boys and others for girls and that differential rates of success are therefore expected. Research has shown that some pupils do take on board teachers' expectations for them and perform accordingly. The impact of expectations about gender are clearly demonstrated in the famous study by Palady (1969). This study looked at teachers' beliefs about sex differences in the ability to learn to read. One group of teachers (Group A) believed that boys and girls learn to read equally easily; another group believed that girls learned to read more quickly than boys (Group B). Reading readiness scores at the beginning of the first year of schooling were obtained for all pupils which showed no significant differences between the pupils of the two different groups of teachers. Reading achievement scores at the end of the first year, however, did show a significant difference. There was no significant difference between the reading scores of boys and girls in Group A, whereas in Group B girls had significantly higher reading scores than boys. How exactly these teachers conveyed their expectation to pupils was not investigated by Palady, but other researchers have drawn attention to the ways teachers do this, primarily by the level, amount and type of work they set and the feedback they give pupils (for a good review see Jussim and Eccles 1995)

Role models are also found in the books and materials that pupils encounter in the classroom. The content of teaching materials in the Primary school has in the past been heavily criticised for the stereotyped ways in which it represented the sexes. Males were shown as active individuals who engaged in a wide range of activities. Females, on the other hand, were either shown as passive watchers of male activity, or active only in the domestic sphere, producing the 'cult of the apron' whereby all adult female characters – humans, rabbits, cats, donkeys and alligators – were shown wearing aprons. As a result many of the materials were changed. However, producing non-stereotyped images that appeal to both boys and girls has not proved as easy as first thought. Looking at how individuals of different sexes are represented in teaching materials can, therefore, provide a useful activity around which discussions of gender issues, particularly roles, can be structured (see Activities).

The importance of gender as a social category

The point was made earlier that individuals who regard gender as only one aspect of their identity are likely to be less conforming to sex-stereotypes than those who regard it as the single most important aspect of their identity. How much gender is emphasised, and used, as a social category is likely to affect the individual's perception of its importance. Many researchers, for example Lloyd and Duveen (1992) and Thorne (1993), have shown that teachers, particularly in the Primary school, use gender as a social category with great regularity. The most common way of doing this is to evoke the terms 'girls' and 'boys', either singularly or together, in order to organise classroom activity. It is such a convenient way to organise the pupils into two groups in order to assign them different tasks or organise a competition. Continuous use of gender as a social category is likely to strengthen the pupils' perception that their gender is the most important thing about them, and encourage them to 'see' the world as fundamentally divided into two gender groups who are very different, thus encouraging stereotypical thinking. This is likely to militate against them realising that males and females have many characteristics in common and that individual differences are often far more salient in understanding others than sex group membership.

From the experience of trainee teachers on professional placement it is clear that Primary school teachers differ in the extent to which they use gender as a social category to mark behaviour and to group pupils. In some schools, girls and boys remain segregated within the classroom – boys sit with boys and girls with girls – and they play different sports and have little or no contact with one another in the playground. A student commented to me that in one school in which she was working a punishment for boys was to make them sit next to a girl; in another school girl pupils were made to stop doing physical exercise before boys because girls 'should not get hot and sweaty'. In other schools, however, there is little evidence of gender segregation; boys and girls sit and work together in the classroom and both sexes participate in all activities without comment or protest. These differences must in subtle, and not-so-subtle ways, be encouraged by teachers.

Challenging pupils' attitudes

Some pupils will clearly bring into school stereotyped attitudes relating to gender and may want to 'opt out' of activities on the grounds that they are only for boys or girls. If such stereotyped attitudes are encountered then the opportunity should be taken to discuss the issue and to challenge such attitudes. Pupils should be helped to recognise that activities within the classroom are for all pupils and that the designation of many as masculine and feminine are simply social and cultural conventions that are arbitrary and do not have to be followed. On a broader front they should learn to recognise that the majority of activities and roles are carried out by both women and men (see Activities).

Challenging attitudes can be a very successful way of changing them. Work that changed the attitudes of girls towards science and mathematics, which were regarded as masculine subjects, has not only increased the number of girls choosing these subjects (see, for example, Kelly 1988, Burton 1986 and Whitehead 1996) but increased their level of achievement such that they now outperform boys. It is likely, therefore, that a similar drive to encourage boys to change their perceptions of communication-based skills such as reading and writing and the subjects that draw heavily on these skills – English, other languages and art subjects – which tend to be perceived as feminine, would also be successful.

It has to be recognised, however, that it may not always be easy to persuade children at the lower end of the Primary school that all activities are equally appropriate for girls and boys. As discussed earlier, there are periods in the development of a gender identity when individuals feel less secure and confident about their gender. One such period is between the ages of three and seven when children are first establishing their gender identity. This insecurity tends to lead to high levels of conformity to sex-stereotypes because pupils of this age tend to believe (it is thought) that it is activities and behaviour that define you as a boy or a girl and if you engage in cross-sex activities then you may change from one sex to the other. As Paley (1984) pointed out:

> Kindergarten is a triumph of sexual self-stereotyping. No amount of adult subterfuge or propaganda deflects the five-year-olds passion for segregation by sex. They think they have invented the differences between boys and girls and with any new invention, must prove that it works.
>
> (Paley 1984:ix)

The situation, however, is not as desperate as it sounds. Thorne (1993) points out that segregation is most likely to occur when pupils choose groups and activities themselves. Teacher-organised groups and activities are much less likely to be gender marked. Segregation can be prevented by organising children into mixed sex groups for all activities. Commitment to conformity also tends to decline after the age of seven. This is due to the realisation that one's sex, and therefore one's gender identity, is constant and is separate from activities; participating in certain activities does not change your sex. The later years of the Primary school are, therefore, likely to provide an ideal opportunity to encourage non-conformity.

Adolescence is another period when insecurity may produce high levels of conformity. During this period individuals need to develop an 'adult' gender identity; the gender schema, therefore, needs to be expanded to incorporate specific ideas about adult behaviour. The adolescent's developing sexuality may also make it more likely that the need for peer group approval, particularly that of the opposite sex, may encourage sex-stereotyped behaviour in order to reaffirm femininity or masculinity. Adolescence, therefore, can be a key period for determining whether or not individuals conform to sex-stereotypes (for a good discussion of these issues see Eccles 1987). From the research quoted earlier in the chapter we know that many adolescents reject the traditional sex-stereotypes. For others higher levels of conformity may be a passing phase which will diminish once they feel confident in their more 'adult' gender identity. Clearly individuals who have, through earlier phases of development, been encouraged not to conform and to have gender schema that do not reflect sex-stereotypes will be less likely to become highly sex-stereotyped adolescents or adults.

Psychological conflict and intrinsic motivation

Conflict between personal development and conformity to sex-stereotypes can often lead to rejection of stereotypes. Intrinsic motivation, characterised by intellectual curiosity and the enjoyment of the challenge inherent in academic activities, has provided such a conflict for many female pupils. Thus girls in Secondary schools who enjoyed academic work and were good at it rejected attitudes that defined this as unfeminine. This rejection combined with equal opportunities initiatives changed the attitudes of society as a whole towards girls and education. It would appear that a similar process may also operate for boys; those who are intrinsically motivated are more likely to reject the idea that academic work is considered unmasculine. Fostering intrinsic motivation, therefore, can both improve the level of academic achievement and reduce the likelihood of pupils rejecting school work as inappropriate for their sex.

From this discussion it can be seen that teachers play a significant role in the development of a gender identity in their pupils. They could participate in the perpetuation of these stereotypes with all their disadvantages for individuals of both sexes. However, teachers have the potential to help pupils develop a gender identity that does not enclose them within the rigid confines of sex-stereotypes.

Activities

Understanding pupils' attitudes

Before we can challenge pupils' attitudes we need to know what they think about classroom activities. Do they think boys or girls are better at certain things? If so, this may mean that some pupils believe they are 'no good' at certain things. As a result of this attitude they may either avoid certain activities if they can, or if they have to do them, make little effort to complete the work. A useful activity, therefore, is to design a questionnaire to find out what children think. List all the common activities that go on in the classroom for the age range you are teaching, e.g reading, building with blocks, topics for projects, number work, etc., then ask the pupils to say, for each one, whether boys and girls are equally good at this activity or whether boys or girls are better at it. An example of the format you might use, with hypothetical results for a class of thirty, is given below.

Instructions to pupils

For each of the activities and/or subjects listed below I would like you to say whether you think:

(a) girls in general are better at these activities/subjects

(b) boys in general are better at these activities/subjects

(c) boys and girls are equally good at these activities/subjects

	Girls better at these activities	Boys and girls equally good at these activities	Boys better at these activities
Reading aloud	10 (33%)	20 (66%)	0 (0%)
Building things	5 (17%)	10 (33%)	15 (50%)

Depending upon the age of the pupils this could be done either as an individual written exercise, or each pupil could be interviewed by the teacher.

Quantifying the results

WHOLE CLASS RESPONSE

The number of pupils who endorse each response should be calculated as a percentage of the number of the pupils in each class, as shown above. This will allow you to see if there any activities that are generally regarded by the majority of pupils as being sex-stereotyped.

INDIVIDUAL RESPONSES

Individual pupils, however, may differ greatly in the extent to which they regarded activities/subjects as stereotyped by sex. Just as informative for the teacher, therefore, would be to look at each response. The object here would be to identify those pupils who show strongly stereotyped responses, believing that boys are better at some activities and girls at others. Pupils with such attitudes may show a lack of motivation, and low achievement, if they believe that the opposite sex is better at a particular activity. Understanding pupils' attitudes, therefore, may help teachers to tackle under-achievement.

Results from work I have done on school subjects with Secondary school pupils showed that the majority of pupils (over 66 per cent) thought that boys and girls were equally good at most subjects. There were, however, notable exceptions. The craft subjects – needlework, metalwork – were still seen as strongly stereotyped, as was physics, but not to quite the same extent. Similar results on classroom activities would indicate to teachers which activities they need to target to break down stereotypes in order to get boys (or girls) to participate fully in them. There were large individual differences, however, some pupils having a very stereotyped view of subjects while others showed little stereotyping of subjects. These attitudes strongly influenced subject choice, particularly for boys (see Whitehead 1996). Work may be needed, therefore, with individual children to change their attitudes.

Classroom materials and role models

Looking at how males and females are represented in classroom materials can be instructive. Not only can it provide teachers with information about the role models pupils are being exposed to, but it also provides a good activity on which to build a discussion of sex-stereotypes. The following questions can be looked at by both pupils and teachers.

1   What activities are women/men/boys/girls shown doing? Are they shown doing the same activities or different ones?
2   What clothes are they shown wearing, e.g. is the 'cult of the apron' still with us?
3   What kind of people are men/women/girls/boys shown to be? Are they shown, for example, as kind, aggressive, helpful, active?
4   Do males or females appear more often in illustrations? Does this depend on what the materials are about?

The answers to these questions can then be used for discussion purposes. Comparisons can be made between what is shown and the pupils' own experiences and ideas. If some of the materials are very stereotyped then the opportunity can be taken to challenge these images. Another activity could be to ask pupils to provide their own alternative illustrations for materials. This activity can also be used to look at how different ethnic groups are represented. For older pupils the exercise can be extended to look at television programmes, newspapers, computer games, comics or magazines.

Pupil choices

Observation of pupils' behaviour, particularly their choices of toys and activities, is useful to see whether or not the effect of 'canalisation' is apparent in the school. Pupils can be observed in 'free play' situations within the classroom or in the playground during breaks. The following areas can be explored.

1   How many of the pupils are involved in
    (a) single-sex groups or dyads
    (b) mixed-sex groups or dyads?
2   In what games or activities are:
    (a) girl-only groups involved
    (b) boy-only groups involved
    (c) mixed groups involved?

Which of the activities you have identified would you say are gender-appropriate activities?

3   What happens if a member of the opposite sex tries to join a single-
sex group? Are they accepted or rejected?

Maccoby (1998) and Thorne (1993) among others have shown that
peer group interaction can reinforce sex-stereotyped behaviour. For
example, children who play with sex-appropriate toys or engage in sex-
appropriate activities are rewarded by being joined in their play by
same-sex peers. Children, on the other hand, who play with cross-
gender toys are ignored by their peers and left to solitary play. Do you
see any evidence of this?

 If you find that segregation and canalisation are common then
action is going to be needed! *Dolls and Dungarees. Gender Issues in the Primary School Curriculum* edited by Eva Tutchell (see Further Reading)
provides some very good ideas on how to go about tackling these issues.

Further reading

Bem, S.L. (1993) *Lenses of Gender*, Yale: Yale University Press.
Connell, R.W. (1995) *Masculinities*, Cambridge: Polity Press.
Doyle, J.A. (1989). *The Male Experience*, Dubuque, Iowa: William. C. Brown.
Doyle, J.A. and Paludi, M.A. (1998) *Sex and Gender*, New York: McGraw Hill.
Lloyd, B. and Duveen, G. (1992). *Gender Identities and Education*, London:
    Harvester/Wheatsheaf.
Sharpe S. (1976 and 1994) *Just Like a Girl*, London: Penguin.
Whitehead J.M. (1994) 'Academically successful schoolgirls: a case of sex role
    transcendence', *Research Papers in Education*, 9, 53–80.
Thorne, B. (1993) *Gender Play. Girls and Boys in School*, Buckingham: The Open
    University Press.
Tuchell, E. (ed.) (1990). *Dolls and Dungarees. Gender Issues in the Primary School
    Curriculum*, Milton Keynes: The Open University Press.

References

Arnot, M., David, M. and Weiner, G. (1997) *Educational Reforms and Gender Equity in
    Schools*, Manchester: E.O.C.
Bandura, A. (1977). *Social Learning Theory*, Englewood Cliffs, N.J.: Prentice-Hall.
Bem, S.L. (1974) 'The measurement of psychological androgeny', *Journal of
    Consulting and Clinical Psychology* 42, 155–162.
Bem, S.L. (1981) 'Gender schema theory: a cognitive account of sex typing',
    Psychological Review 86 354–364.
Bem, S.L. (1993) *Lenses of Gender*, Yale: Yale University Press.
Brophy, J.J.E. (1985) 'Interaction of male and female students with male and female
    teachers', in Wilkinson, L.C. and Marrett, C.B. (eds) *Gender Influences in Classroom
    Interaction*, London: Academic Press.
Browne, N. and Franc, P. (1985) 'A look at sexist talk in the nursery', in Weiner, G.
    (ed.) *Just a Bunch of Girls*, Milton Keynes: Open University Press.
Burton, L. (1986) *Girls in to Maths Can Go*, London: Holt Education.

Connell, R.W. (1995) *Masculinities*, Cambridge: Polity Press.

Department for Education and Employment (Yearly) *GCSE/GNVQ and GCE A/AS Examination Results – England*, Statistical Bulletin, London: HMSO.

Department for Education and Employment (Yearly) *National Curriculum Assessment of 7, 11 and 14 Year Olds in England*, Statistical Bulletin, London: HMSO.

Doyle, J.A. (1989). *The Male Experience*, Dubuque, Iowa: William. C. Brown.

Eccles, J.E. (1987) 'Adolescence: gateway to gender-role transcendence', in B.D.Carter (ed.) *Current Conceptions of Sex-roles and Sex-traits*, New York: Praeger.

Eccles, J. (1993) 'Age and gender differences in children's self and task perceptions during elementary school', *Child Development* 64, 830–847.

Jussim, L. and Eccles, J. (1995) 'Naturally occurring interpersonal expectancies', in Eisenberg, N. (eds) *Social Development*, London: Sage Publications.

Kelly, A. (1986) 'The development of girls' and boys' attitudes to science: a longitudinal study', *European Journal of Science Education* 8, 319–412.

Kelly, A. (1988) 'Sex-stereotypes and school science: a three year follow-up', *Educational Studies* 14, 151–63.

Lloyd, B. and Duveen, G. (1992). *Gender Identities and Education*, London: Harvester/Wheatsheaf.

Maccoby, E.E. (1998) *The Two Sexes. Growing Apart, Coming Together*, Cambridge Massachusetts: The Belnap Press of Harvard University Press.

O'Neil, J.M., Good, G.E. and Holmes, S. (1995) 'Fifteen years of theory and research on men's gender role conflict: new paradigms for research', in Levant, R.F. and Pollack, W.S. (eds) *A New Psychology of Men*, New York: Basic Books.

Newsom Committee (1963) *Half our Future*, Report of the Advisory Council for Education Committee, London: HMSO.

Palady, J.M. (1969) 'What teachers believe – what children achieve', *Elementary School Journal* 69, 370–374.

Paley, V.G. (1984) *Boys and Girls Superheroes in the Doll Corner*, Chicago: University of Chicago Press.

Pleck, J.H. (1981) *The Myth of Masculinity*, Massachusetts: MIT Press.

Pleck, J.H. (1995) 'The gender role strain paradigm: an update', in Levant, R.F. and Pollack, W.S. (eds) *A New Psychology of Men*, New York: Basic Books.

Sammons, P., West, A. and Hind, A. (1997) 'Accounting for variation in pupil attainment at the end of Key Stage 1', *British Education Research Journal* 23, 4, 489–511.

Sharpe, S. (1976 and 1994) *Just Like a Girl*, London: Penguin.

Thorne, B. (1993) *Gender Play. Girls and Boys in School*, Buckingham: The Open University Press.

Tolson, A. (1977) *The Limits of Masculinity*, London: Tavistock Publications.

Whitehead J.M. (1994) 'Academically successful schoolgirls: a case of sex role transcendence', *Research Papers in Education*, 9, 53–80.

Whitehead, J.M. (1995) 'Is there really a new man?', paper to the First International Multi-Disciplinary Congress on Men, Ottawa.

Whitehead, J.M. (1996) 'Sex stereotypes, gender identity and subject choice at 'A' level', *Educational Research* 38 147–160.

Whitehead, J.M. (1998) 'Masculinity, motivation and academic success: a paradox', paper to the International Conference 'Gendering the Millenium', University of Dundee.

Willis, P. (1977) *Learning to Labour*, England: Gower.

14 Teaching children whose progress in learning is causing concern

Ruth Kershner

EDITOR'S SUMMARY

This chapter reviews ways of understanding and responding to children with learning difficulties. It begins by arguing that, rather than viewing the child alone, or the context alone, we will achieve a better understanding of learning difficulties if we observe the child in the context in which the difficulties are arising. Strategies for teaching children to enhance achievement, participation and active learning, and the links between them, are then explored; these include target-setting, scaffolding and teaching thinking skills. Finally, it is argued that the teaching of children with learning difficulties, in the current absence of a solid, generalisable and educationally applicable theory of learning problems, works most effectively when professional knowledge of learning difficulties is shared amongst colleagues, when the area of learning causing difficulty is thoroughly understood, and when the teacher invests time to research carefully the precise nature of the child's difficulties.

One of the challenges of teaching is to understand and help children whose progress in learning is unusually slow, uneven or effortful. In recent years some of the fiercest debates in education have been about how to teach children who, for one reason or another, show difficulty in learning in school. Debates, misunderstandings and arguments arise when there is a common urgency to 'do something' to facilitate children's learning but different questions are being asked about what to do and why. For example, compare the questions 'why is she unable to learn more easily?' and 'why does my teaching seem to have so little effect on her?', in terms of the implications about whether the lack of progress is the child's problem or the teacher's.

The uncertainties and disagreements about why certain children do not learn as well as others of the same age highlight the importance of being explicit about which aspects of children's learning are causing concern in school. Teachers may be aware of several overlapping difficulties in areas which go beyond the immediate demands on learning of the subjects in the school curriculum, and it can be hard to separate concerns about children's classroom behaviour from concerns about their learning. It is not easy to pin-point the central problems or causes of learning difficulties, and it has long been recognised that the identification and assessment of children with particular problems in learning is not a simple matter of carrying out a test of intelligence or attainment (Croll and Moses 1985). In identifying which children may need special help and deciding how to respond, teachers must integrate their day-to-day classroom impressions with the information emerging from regular assessments of the children's learning, all the while taking account of the ways in which the school context may itself be making it difficult for certain children to learn.

The first part of this chapter focuses on different perceptions and definitions of 'learning difficulties', referring to debates about whether attention should mainly be given to the child in question, the school context, or some sort of interaction between them. I will then go on to discuss teaching strategies which aim to enhance the achievement, participation and active learning of children whose progress is causing concern in school, before putting forward some ideas about the basis for making appropriate teaching decisions in an inevitably complex, urgent and sensitive situation.

Perceptions and definitions of 'learning difficulties'

Here are some examples of the ways in which trainee teachers have described children whose difficulty in learning compared to other pupils in the class had presented them with a 'teaching challenge'. The following quotes are taken from questionnaires completed a few months after the trainees' first professional placement in school:

'Andrea' writes: 'G. (Year 4, 8–9 years) was a poor reader with low confidence in written work. He needed confidence boosting as much if not more than academic help. … Difficulties appeared in most areas due to poor reading ability. He was artistic with lovely handwriting. Good at PE and games. … He received no special help and was just called 'slow' and 'lazy' and sometimes 'naughty.' … I responded by choosing his language work to word process for display so that he could see a successful finished product.'

'Cathy' writes: 'A. (Year 3, 7–8 years) was always very reluctant to commit his thoughts and ideas to paper and usually he would waste time, sharpen his pencil, look for his book, etc. When asked a question he would become uneasy and say that he 'didn't know' the answer. … A one-to-one, relaxed setting produced greatest results, particularly after he had got to know me a little. I found that representing his ideas through art was quite successful, instead of in the written form. ... Both the class teacher and the special needs teacher helped me by showing how patience, perseverance and a relaxed attitude helped in getting the best out of A.'

'Emma' writes: 'J. (Year 5, 9–10 years) had an inability to grasp the basic elements of the subject (maths). She seemed unable to understand what she was being required to do, despite being told in many different ways. The inability to comprehend the relationship between numbers made any maths teaching difficult. ... She was in the 'special needs' group in her class and a special needs teacher took the whole group for one morning per week.'

'Frankie' writes: 'The child I chose, M. (Year 5, 9–10 years), was a poor reader and was not terribly promising in other subjects, although his enthusiasm to try hard doubled in PE lessons. He had a very short concentration span and was frequently to be seen walking round the classroom rather than sitting at his own desk working. ... The surprising thing was that even though his concentration span was so short, during the whole class story he would sit everyday for about half an hour listening intently and answering questions afterwards. ... M. seemed to be crying out for help. He was desperate to please the teachers but he didn't seem to have any control over this. I really wanted to help him overcome his difficulties and although I couldn't do this completely I thought I could start him off.'

In these brief extracts we can see references to different aspects of the children's development, learning and behaviour, including their educational attainment, self-confidence, motivation, classroom behaviour, understanding, concentration, social relationships and responses to teaching. The observations and comments do not entirely define how the children are different or special, however. Most people – children and adults – have lapses of concentration at times, even to the extent of distracting other people. Sometimes learning may be slow compared to others, and it can be hard to grasp new ideas and express oneself well. The accounts provide a complex picture of children's learning difficulties in school and an equally complex indication of the related teaching challenges. They suggest that a child's learning difficulty is likely to mean more a problem in aspects of learning like remembering information, reading and developing other skills, knowledge and understanding. For these beginning teachers, the practical challenge of teaching children who show difficulty in learning seems to lie in the combination of different aspects of the children's learning and behaviour, and in the severity, persistence and unusual character of these factors compared to other pupils of a similar age. However, teaching these children is not all about coping with difficulties: the trainee teachers recognise the children's strengths as well as weaknesses; they are accepting and optimistic about children's learning; and they allow themselves to be surprised when children respond positively in certain circumstances.

Describing and understanding learning difficulties: is it the child or the school context that needs attention?

In a review of research on learning difficulties, Skidmore (1999) refers to the following established approaches and explanations for children's difficulties in learning:

- *psychomedical* 'learning difficulties arise from deficits within the individual pupil'
- *organisational* 'learning difficulties arise from deficiencies in the ways in which schools are currently organised'
- *sociological* 'learning difficulties arise from the reproduction of structural inequalities in society'.

(Skidmore 1999:4)

So, in trying to understand and respond to children whose progress is causing concern in school, should we focus on the child, the teacher, the school situation, social values and expectations, or some sort of interaction between them? These positions are discussed in the next three sections.

Focusing on the child

The 'child-focused', psychomedical approach has been the framework for a large amount of research and critical discussion about the impact on learning of children's personal experiences and characteristics such as gender, race, motivation, intelligence, cognitive abilities, family background, emotional development, literacy, self-concept, personality, social skills and relationships, sensory and physical abilities and medical conditions (Varma 1993; Crozier 1997). Traditionally, the children's learning problems may be conceptualised as disorders, differences or delays in development, each of which holds assumptions about what could be expected of 'normal' learning for children of that age in that social context. This approach tends to be accompanied by the development of educational strategies for responding to what are seen as deficits or gaps in children's experience and abilities.

For most children whose progress causes concern in school, the problems are to do with experience and learning rather intrinsic intellectual weaknesses or deficits. The children's learning difficulties arise from problems in the activation and use of their knowledge and learning strategies in certain contexts. Dockrell and McShane (1993) express this in terms of the importance of the child's:

- knowledge base in different subject domains
- use of learning strategies
- metacognitive knowledge about the processes of learning
- metacognitive beliefs about the causes of success and failure in learning.

All of these aspects of learning develop as children grow up in a social context, and the implication is that children who are identified as having learning difficulties can be helped in one or more of these areas. So a teacher's immediate aims may be to use classroom strategies to enhance children's general knowledge, memory, motivation, listening skills or independence, for example, looking for signs of learning and progress in different curriculum areas.

Yet, these views about the educational needs of *most* children whose progress causes concern in school are countered by observations that certain children have persistent difficulties in learning, for example those identified as autistic or dyslexic. This leads many people to suggest that there *are* basic, often inherent, cognitive differences amongst children, which can result in significant discrepancies in learning and educational performance – as when excellent visual and spatial abilities may be combined with unusual problems in reading and spelling compared to other children of the same age. The associated conclusions are that special teaching approaches are necessary, either in special schools or units for children with the same type of problem or in a more flexible and better-resourced mainstream school setting. There are now many examples of teaching programmes and resources directed towards children with specific difficulties in literacy, for example, including the rapidly increasing use of information and communications technology to assist with the problems in basic skills and cognitive processes which can lead to serious obstacles to learning across the curriculum (McKeown 1999).

Terms such as 'dyslexia' are very broad, however, and they may incorporate a wide range of children with different problems and educational needs. The debates about the nature of specific learning difficulties continue and there is a large literature to search for information, opinion and evidence (e.g. Hulme and Snowling 1994; Pumfrey and Reason 1991; Wong 1996). In the end, one of the crucial issues from an educational point of view is whether the categorisation of children with learning difficulties is for administrative or educational purposes. From an educational perspective, many children with specific reading and spelling difficulties will respond to similar teaching strategies whatever the cause of their problems, but some children will benefit from additional, systematic help that is targeted towards their particular difficulty (e.g. those with a perceptual problem). Yet how can these children be identified and differentiated? As Singleton (1997) argues, there is a danger in relying on checklists and other types of sometimes rather crude screening to assess children's specific learning difficulties; the practicality of basic approaches to screening in school has to be balanced with accuracy in identifying children's individual differences and needs. Any assessment of children's reading difficulties, for example, would need to examine a variety of related cognitive abilities alongside relevant aspects of motivation and social experience, and this reduces the possibility of using neat categorisations in all cases. The move is now consistently towards developing an appropriately differentiated approach to assessment which can succeed in accurately identifying the profiles of the small minorities of children who could benefit from specific types of support in school and who would otherwise lose confidence and motivation when they persistently fail to respond to general teaching strategies.

Focusing on the context

An alternative approach to understanding children's learning difficulties focuses not on individual children's special needs but on the context of their learning. This approach, which may be at the organisational or sociological level, is often driven by a reaction to a school system which seems regularly to fail and exclude certain children, although, as discussed in this book, there are also strong psychological reasons for investigating children's learning and behaviour in the physical and social context as a matter of course. From an educational perspective, the school curriculum and teaching methods may be seen as inappropriate or ill-matched for children who show difficulties in learning, and some argue that this is because schools embody the broader inequalities of social and cultural values and practices which systematically discriminate against certain groups in society on the grounds of factors such as race, class and gender (Tomlinson 1982).

The contextual perspective on learning difficulties calls for solutions which go beyond individual children's learning and behaviour. The focus, rather, is on understanding the ways in which mainstream schools can increase access and support for individual pupils or, more radically, develop the whole curriculum so that the expectations and opportunities for learning include all the pupils in school as a matter of course (Carpenter *et al.* 1996; Ainscow 1999). Much of the writing on inclusive education focuses on developing the school as an organisation which has the responsibility and skills to teach pupils in all their diversity. Dyson and Millward (1997:58), for example, identify the ways in which inclusive mainstream schools can support the work of individual class teachers by means of whole-school policies, teamwork, curriculum development, and the co-ordinated use of alternative places where children can learn. This can be understood as part of the general need for schools to do more to recognise and respond to children as individuals.

Focusing on the child in context

As Skidmore (1999:4) points out, there are problems in reducing the causes of learning difficulties to 'factors within the individual or the school or society at large'. We have seen above that these different factors are indeed relevant to understanding children's progress, but it is important to avoid the danger of over-simplifying and over-generalising at any level. Attempts to focus on the child *in* context reflect a growing theoretical understanding of the nature of children's learning difficulties and special educational needs in terms of interacting biological, psychological and social factors (Norwich

1990; Clark *et al.* 1998). For example, research has shown how the experience and educational implications of having a genetic condition like Down's syndrome includes the impact of other people's attitudes on social relationships and educational opportunities as well as the range of medical and developmental effects which vary between individuals (Stratford and Gunn 1996).

With this 'bio-psycho-social' perspective, the identification of children's learning difficulties in school has to involve consideration of how factors like the curriculum, teaching strategies and school routines and relationships affect children in different ways over a period of time. The aim would be to understand and respond to the *educationally relevant* individual differences which can create persistent obstacles to children's learning in different contexts, without stereotyping the educational implications of factors like IQ score or difficult social circumstances. A key aspect of this process is to give due weight to the interpretations and intentions of the people involved. For example, Hart (1996) contrasts the traditional 'diagnostic' and 'differential' thinking, which focuses on the child's personal problems and educational needs, with what she calls 'innovative thinking' about the responses of individual children and groups of pupils who share characteristics like limited literacy.

> Innovative thinking seeks out new possibilities for responding to the situation 'through a probing analysis of our existing thinking and understandings ... in such a way as to generate new insight into what might be done, beyond what is currently being done or tried, to support and enhance the child's learning.'

> (Hart 1996:111)

Hart argues that teachers can extend their thinking and understanding of children's learning in the school context by using classroom observation and professional knowledge as a basis for 'five interpretive moves' which question:

- the influence of the school and classroom learning environment on children's responses
- the alternative ways of understanding children's responses
- the child's reasons for responding in certain ways
- the meaning and impact of feelings aroused in working with the child
- the other information which is needed before making a judgement about what is happening for the child as a learner in school and deciding how to respond as a teacher.

This approach suggests that teachers who are adept at going beyond the labels and stereotypes which become attached to certain children are able to combine a detailed understanding of individual pupils with a broader insight into child development and the general processes of teaching and learning in Primary schools. This knowledge and understanding will do much to support the use of positive and effective teaching strategies for children whose progress in learning is causing concern. Some examples are given in the next section.

Strategies for teaching children whose progress in learning is causing concern: enhancing achievement, participation and active learning

One of the striking impressions one gains from hearing about teachers' strategies for teaching children with difficulties in learning is the variety of approaches which are used – often within the same lesson. When teachers describe the ways in which they try to help children, it becomes clear that different teaching strategies are woven together in the classroom, focusing variously on children's attainments, independence, self-confidence, cognition and learning, motivations, emotions, social relationships, working habits and general ability to follow the routines of schoolwork and school life. These areas can be broadly grouped into 'working' and 'learning'.

Children's classroom 'work' is to engage in the social, physical and mental activity which initiates and supports the development of knowledge, skill and understanding within and beyond the school curriculum. Primary class teachers will often focus on children's working as a means of monitoring their progress in learning. If a teacher is confident about the potential educational value of a classroom activity, then learning objectives for children 'to know… ', 'to be able to… ' or 'to understand… ' may be informally monitored through the children's participation and responsiveness in classroom activities. As long as children involve themselves in the work and make progress over a period of time, the evaluation of their learning may be impressionistic from lesson to lesson in the ordinary school day. It is only when work is marked and when other systematic and formal assessments are carried out at regular intervals that more explicit attention is paid to the evidence of the children's growing knowledge, understanding and skill which has been gained through their experiences.

For children identified as having learning difficulties, however, the main concerns can be precisely that they do not participate successfully in the active experience that leads to learning. They may not understand what to do in lessons or easily involve themselves in classroom activities. Their engagement in work can be superficial and fragmentary, so that there are only weak connections between their activity, their experience and the development of their knowledge, skill and understanding. The problem is not just that children may not complete classroom tasks, for there could be many reasons for this which do not indicate unusual or persistent difficulties in learning. The concerns in the longer term are to do with whether the children *know how* to work and learn, whether they *want* to and whether they are *able* to. Figure 14.1 gives some examples of how teachers may respond to these different concerns, illustrated by trainee teachers' descriptions of strategies which they have used, observed or discussed with more experienced

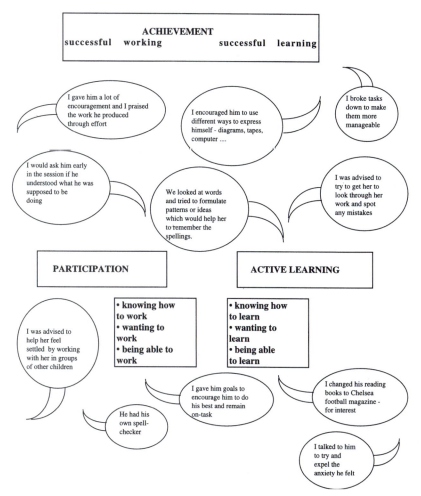

Figure 14.1 Examples of teaching strategies intended to support children's working and learning, and help them to develop knowledge, understanding and skill

teachers. These strategies form part of the everyday repertoire of strategies which teachers use with children. The quotes are taken from the question-naires about the 'teaching challenges' mentioned at the start of this chapter.

In Figure 14.1 we see examples of many different approaches which aim to help children to work and learn independently, confidently and successfully. These approaches focus in different ways on the outcomes and the processes of working and learning and the psychological conditions which enable chil-dren to make progress.

The outcomes of working and learning: completion and success

The teacher uses strategies of target-setting, differentiation and assessment to set appropriate work for the children, to help them to complete it successfully and to demonstrate their learning. This involves adapting the organisation of learning in the classroom, the content, structure or pace of the curriculum, and the type of support given to individual children during lessons.

The processes of working and learning: 'knowing how to'

The teacher aims to develop children's awareness and use of appropriate learning strategies. This involves helping children to understand what to do in lessons, to select relevant resources for learning, to structure their activity and to use their knowledge and mental strategies flexibly for processes like problem solving, memory, imagination and communication.

The psychological conditions of working and learning: 'wanting to' and 'being able to'

The teacher aims to:

- enhance children's motivation by keeping them 'on-task' through feedback and positive reinforcement, and by providing opportunities to engage in activities which are interesting, meaningful and purposeful
- support emotional growth in order to help children who are unable to learn because they are disengaged, distracted or overwhelmed with feelings of insecurity, anxiety and fear. The aim is to enable children to experience the feelings of security and self-confidence which allow the social interaction, exploration, risk-taking and decision-making which are essential for learning
- enable children to learn with the help of technology, which supports their physical, social and intellectual inclusion in school (cf. Blamires 1999).

In broad terms, the aims of these different teaching approaches and strategies are to help children to gain certain skills, knowledge and understanding, to engage in activities which will lead to further learning, and to become more motivated and able to learn independently in the future. The key areas are *achievement, participation* and *active learning*. Figure 14.2 shows how these facets of successful learning can be influenced by certain contextual and personal factors, which are displayed around the outside of the diagram.

Children may not have problems in all the facets of learning shown in Figure 14.2; that is, achievement, participation and active learning. The main problems can lie in the connections between them. For example, a child may complete a story without recognising or valuing her achievement;

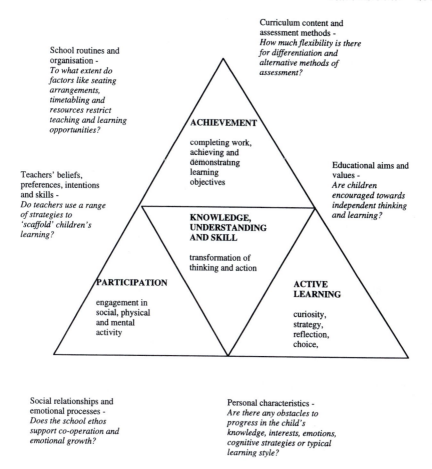

Figure 14.2 Facets of successful learning, and the potential influence of personal and contextual factors

she may engage in collaborative story-writing without adding to her understanding of narrative structure; or she may follow an interest in writing about football without producing a finished story.

It is the psychological connections between different aspects of successful working and learning which allow the teacher some flexibility in using different teaching strategies to help children. For example, consider the question of motivation:

> 'I made sure that I praised him when he had done a really good piece of writing.'

> 'By chance I found out that he was particularly interested in, and very skilled in, maps and mapwork. I thus tried to base a lot of the work I did with him, either on his own or in groups, on maps.'

'Using videos, books with lots of visual resources and art, all seemed to interest him more.'

In these examples, the principles connecting motivation and learning are that:

- giving praise about the specific strengths of a piece of work provides children with feedback about the learning objectives, so they understand better what to do next time
- responding to a child's personal interests and well-developed skills in one domain, e.g. maps, will help him not only to enjoy and attend better to his work, but also to learn effectively by making cognitive connections with his personal 'expert' knowledge
- responding to children's preferences for the ways in which information is presented, e.g. pictures or words, supports the connection with their own mental representations of information, and the differences in learning style which can sometimes explain why certain children (with tendencies as 'visualisers' or 'verbalisers', for example) learn more successfully than others in certain contexts (Riding and Rayner 1998). Caviglioli (1999) gives an example of the successful use of the graphic technique of 'mind mapping' to help a child with Down's syndrome to represent his understanding of stories, which had seemed limited when faced with more traditional verbal comprehension questions. Caviglioli comments that 'any areas of study that he found confusing or too novel were transformed into 'graspable', visually organised categories. ... Mapping soon became a regular, indispensable and always reliable strategy to clarify the world'. (Caviglioli 1998:28)

Figure 14.3 shows some of the main psychological connections between achievement, participation and active learning. The model in Figure 14.3 is intended to express the dynamic ways in which progress in one area can affect another. Examples of this can be seen in the connections between three general approaches which are commonly used for children with difficulties in learning: *target-setting, scaffolding* and *teaching thinking* skills, discussed below. Just as achievement, active participation and reflection are connected, target-setting, scaffolding and teaching thinking may be understood as part of the same overall teaching process for children with learning difficulties, even though they are often presented separately and they can be seen to have different psychological roots in behaviourism, social constructivism and information-processing.

Target-setting and teaching to objectives

'I gave him goals to encourage him to do his best and remain on-task.'

Target-setting has become a key part of educational policy for local authorities, schools, teachers and individual pupils. Successful targets are said to be

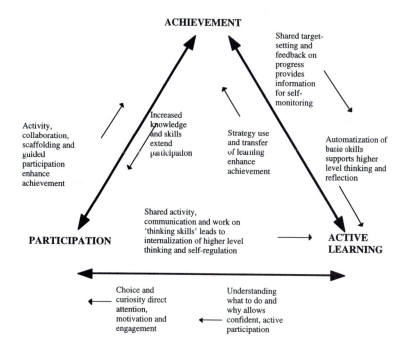

Figure 14.3 Psychological connections between achievement, participation and active learning

SMART: Specific, Measurable, Achievable, Realistic and Time-related (DfEE 1997:10). Target-setting is central to the individual education plans (IEPs) which are written for children with special educational needs, which often include targets like 'Jo will be able to count up to six objects by half-term'.

The psychological origins of target-setting for children's learning lie in behaviourism, which takes the view that learning is equivalent to an actual or potential change in observable behaviour, guided by feedback, prompts, reinforcement and other influences from the environment. Task analysis is used to break down the targeted behaviour or skill, as a basis for setting a sequence of objectives for individual children's learning. These behavioural objectives include the following features:

Behaviour   what the child will do
Conditions   the circumstances, materials, instructions, etc.
Criteria   the rate of success required before moving on to the next objective.

For example, 'When asked on three occasions during one lesson to "show me a red brick" from an array of up to 10 bricks of not more than three different colours, Ann will touch a red brick.'

The objectives may relate to different types of progress for individual children – eg. new learning, extension work, generalisation or the practice and reinforcement of familiar skills. The focus is on the outcomes of learning, not the process. The teaching strategies are not specified, but the child's progress is monitored and recorded, often visually in the form of charts and graphs.

The strengths and weaknesses of the behavioural approach and target-setting for children with learning difficulties are often debated (e.g. Farrell 1997). For example, the problems arising inofather than knowledge and understanding must be weighed against the value of gaining a clear sense of direction and visible signs of achievement and progress in relation to targets. Children who have targets set for them may adopt an unhelpfully passive role in learning, yet when children are actively involved in discussing learning targets and seeing the progress that they make, the increases in their self-esteem, motivation and understanding are very likely to enhance their participation and active learning.

Scaffolding and guided participation

'I scribed for him.'

This simple sentence provides a very powerful image of shared and purposeful activity. The child dictates what she or he wants to write and the teacher gets the words down on paper. Together they have produced a piece of writing.

Scaffolding is intrinsically purposeful in its focus on collaborative activity, and sometimes the help given by adults to children can also involve explicit attempts to push children further in their learning and development.

After PE he wanted us to dress him but we only gave verbal instructions.

The impression is that in this case the teacher is resisting what might be the simplest and quickest response (i.e. to dress the child) in favour of encouraging the child to be more independent and setting targets to achieve this.

Scaffolding is a response to the fact that children often need help to find their way through a problem, whether it is a self-contained activity like a jigsaw puzzle or a longer-term process like learning to read and write. More capable adults and peers can help children overcome uncertainty and learn how to achieve success:

> Pointing out, reminding, suggesting and praising all serve to orchestrate and structure the child's activities under the guidance of one who is more expert. ... By breaking complex tasks down into manageable, smaller problems, we help the child to detect regularities and patterns in his activity that he is unlikely to discover alone. We are also providing living examples of the way in which more expert people go about the task of regulating and managing activity in conditions of high uncertainty.
>
> (Wood 1998:98)

The roots of scaffolding lie in the social constructivist theories of Vygotsky and Bruner, who explain how these social acts of assistance are gradually internalised by the child to become the basis of self-regulated thinking and learning (Vygotsky 1978). Children not only gain expertise in the specific task, but they also learn how to learn and reason for themselves more generally. They take on the culturally developed forms of thinking and learning by internalising the language used during the shared social activity of problem-solving.

Wood points out that the traditional view of scaffolding identifies it as the means by which children are tutored to achieve specific outcomes in activities set up by adults. Yet most interactions between adults and children in life outside school are initiated by the child, and children have helpful contacts with many more people than one single adult tutor. Children also learn through observing other people without direct interaction. Wood offers Rogoff's (1990) term 'guided participation' as a more inclusive concept which expresses the ways in which children learn through engagement in daily activities like shopping and cooking when there is no explicit intention of teaching and learning. This view of learning can prompt us to examine the school curriculum for examples of guided participation in its broadest sense: do children with difficulties in learning have opportunities to initiate activities, learn collaboratively and share in the meaningful activities of school like running the office, showing visitors around, organising the class trip, and putting on the school play? Moreover, could children with difficulties in learning be better helped to immerse themselves in the deeply enjoyable, challenging, self-directed physical, intellectual and creative activities which actually transform the self – whether it is dancing, scientific investigation, writing poetry, or anything else (Csikszentmihalyi 1990)?

Teaching thinking skills and developing reflection on learning

Discussions of scaffolding and guided participation focus on the *means* of ensuring children's involvement and learning through shared activities. The teaching of thinking skills and reflection draws attention to the *cognitive* and *metacognitive* processes which are assumed to be involved. This approach takes account of psychological research on information-processing, including the processes of perception, memory, reasoning and decision-making and the connections between them. The focus is on the mental strategies which help to process information by 'organising information so that its complexity is reduced, and/or integrating information into the knowledge base that exists in the brain for later use' (Ashman and Conway 1997:43).

As discussed earlier in this chapter, it is the activation and use of learning strategies which can be a problem for many children with learning difficulties in school. So it is the concept of *metacognition* – the awareness and control of learning strategies – which is particularly important for children who cannot easily balance the interests and demands of classroom working with the processes and goals of classroom learning. Difficulties in learning can result from problems in predicting, planning, checking, self-monitoring and transferring learning in one context to another. Yet these problems can sometimes have a more fundamental source. For example, Adams (1994) argues with reference to reading that it is only when basic cognitive processes (e.g. decoding words) become automatic that children gain the ability to devote attention to the higher level thinking that focuses on the meaning of the text. So target-setting and systematic, intensive teaching for fluency in reading words can have a direct benefit for independent thinking, understanding and reflection on learning.

There are published 'thinking skills' programmes which are directed at the development of general learning processes and strategies, some in specific curriculum areas, but Ashman and Conway (1997:186) emphasise the central role of the teacher in making these programmes work in the ordinary classroom. It is important to remember that teachers teach 'thinking skills' informally every time they discuss learning with the children, or state the learning objectives at the beginning of a lesson, or model 'thinking' by talking out loud as they work out a problem, write the structure of a story on the board, or involve children in the assessment of their own learning.

Deciding how to intervene to help children with difficulties in learning

The impression that might be gained from this discussion of different teaching approaches is that a teacher should either 'do everything' or that any one teaching approach will work because it is ultimately connected in some way with children's achievement, participation and active learning. It can be difficult to identify exactly what successful teachers do in practice to help individual children make better progress and there is more than one route to effective teaching. Pijl and van den Bos (1998:114–5) write about 'decision making in uncertainty', which, they argue, is inevitable in the current absence of a solid, generalisable and educationally applicable theory of learning problems. They suggest that decision making in uncertainty requires the responsible use of our 'experience, available knowledge, our intuition and our common sense', supported by systematic procedures for the choice of certain approaches and the reporting and evaluation of the results.

Areas of knowledge which are relevant and useful for making teaching decisions include knowledge of learning, of the subject and of the children in their learning context.

Sharing professional knowledge of children's learning

A theoretical understanding of how children learn provides options and justifications for choosing certain teaching strategies, but the expertise and classroom practice of experienced teachers does not always make this knowledge explicit. For children whose progress is causing concern, it can be useful to draw more systematically on professional knowledge and understanding by developing the habit of adding a brief explanation which explains the significance of any one approach which seems to be of value over time. This might be a mental note or a conversation with colleagues, for example:

> 'I praise her work a lot … in the hope that this will enhance her self-esteem, so that she will take a few more risks next time and consider alternative options in her maths investigation.'

Or it can sometimes be directed towards the children:

> 'I'm going to display your work on the wall … so other people can read your exciting story. I hope that when you look at it you will remember what you achieved and write as well next time.'

Thinking through and explaining the connections to learning in this way can massively increase the power and justification of different teaching strategies, and by involving the children their own 'knowing how' is enhanced. The result is a more systematic, effective and potentially collaborative use of the range of teaching strategies which are already of known value for children's learning.

Using knowledge of the subject

Children's activities in school are all connected to learning *something* and the structure and content of different curriculum subjects has a significant effect on children's learning. Some subjects are very clearly made up of different components which have to link together in mind and action. For example, reading is a complex activity involving the decoding of print, the use of language, the understanding of meaning and the motivation to gain further knowledge and understanding about the world and human experience. To understand the problems of children with reading difficulties we have to understand the 'ingredients of literacy' in terms of the features of print, language and communication and the context of learning (Reason 1990). Part of this general understanding of the subject in question includes a knowledge of children's common misconceptions and mistakes at certain stages of learning (e.g. early reversals of 'b' and 'd', which are usually sorted out as reading and writing develop, but for some children may indicate a persistent, specific problem as time goes on).

Developing knowledge of the child in the context of learning

Here are some typical strategies:

> 'I held a reading interview with him by doing a miscue analysis which helped me to identify specific problems with various word endings, etc.'

'Having seen how the children reacted in two different situations (whole class and singly) I realised that you had to 'tackle' him from a certain angle.'

'I learned from the child herself about what she felt capable of doing.'

In developing different strategies to teach children with difficulties there is a strong connection between teaching and assessment in the learning context. Close observation of children's errors (e.g. 'miscue analysis') can give particularly useful insight not just into their cognitive understanding and skill but also into their attitudes to the task in hand (Arnold 1984). It is also important to take account of children's responses to teaching as part of the assessment process. The approaches of target-setting and scaffolding, discussed earlier, both incorporate this principle: the former in terms of 'curriculum-related assessment', in which children's progress is monitored in relation to a sequence of targets or objectives, and the latter in terms of 'dynamic assessment' or 'interactive assessment' which identify a child's ability to learn with help (Ashman and Conway 1997).

It should be recognised, however, that it is not easy to discover what is actually the most significant aspect of the child's experience of being a pupil with difficulties in learning in school. Teachers' impressions need to be complemented by an understanding of the children's views about their learning, gained from discussion and careful listening as well as the provision of opportunities for children to express their views in writing, drawing and play. Jones and Charlton (1996) and their co-authors emphasise this point in their book about the need for a 'partnership' which empowers pupils who have difficulties in school.

Conclusion: imagining the probable, the possible and the impossible

One of the intentions of this chapter has been to show how helpful and important it is for teachers to reflect on their thinking and actions, to share knowledge with others, to understand different perspectives and to follow the possibility of changing one's mind about children's difficulties in learning. All of these draw in some way on the power of the imagination in teaching. We need to imagine how things could be different for children whose progress is causing concern in school.

Imagining the probable

It is the growing knowledge of children's learning in context which allows achievable, realistic target-setting, and the confident, almost intuitive choice of strategies which are likely to be successful in scaffolding and guided participation for specific children.

Imagining the possible

It is the awareness of other possibilities which allows:

- understanding and empathy with the perceptions and feelings of the children and other adults involved
- consideration of what can be adapted within the given classroom and school routines and policies
- hypotheses about how to use knowledge of children in general and children who share particular characteristics to suggest possible teaching approaches (e.g. 'if research has shown that boys tend to … could this apply to Michael?')

Imagining the impossible

Perhaps most importantly, it is necessary to use the imagination to break down the assumptions which set up false barriers between children. Several researchers and writers have taken this creative leap and they have in turn influenced and inspired many other people. For example, Clarke and Clarke (1976) refused to believe that negative early experiences had to result in problems in later life. They were leaders in the field of thinking about young children's resilience to physical and psychological damage (Tizard and Varma 1992). Feuerstein (1980) challenged the concepts of fixed intellectual potential and 'cultural deprivation'. His programme of 'Instrumental Enrichment' for mediating children's learning and enhancing their cognitive performance has become a standard point of reference for the 'thinking skills' approach. Buckley *et al.* (1996) showed how by using a teaching approach which builds on their cognitive strengths, children with Down's syndrome can start to learn to read at an early age rather than being designated as 'ineducable'. Her approach is notable for the involvement of the children's parents as educators in their own right. Furthermore, it supports young people with Down's syndrome who are now working against prejudice to go to ordinary schools, to take examinations, to work for a living, to marry and generally to take responsibility for their lives.

   The title of this chapter reflects the fact that there is concern when children do not make easy progress in school, and it draws attention to the need to ask whose concern about which pupils triggers a response which may involve teaching that is different, extra or 'special' in some way? Where should efforts to enhance children's learning be directed? Educational success is important in our society and many people find it frustrating and hurtful to fail in school. It is not always obvious why children are having difficulty in learning, given that another child in apparently similar circumstances may be making rapid progress. The people involved, including the children themselves, often have differing concerns which reflect their own interests and values in the context of an educational system which, at the time of writing, is geared towards the achievement of common educational standards at certain ages.

The pressures for prioritising and decision-making in busy Primary class-rooms present a challenge to class teachers' emotions, skills and ingenuity. Yet certain approaches which are central to a teacher's day-to-day role can make a substantial difference to children's learning when they succeed in connecting the children's achievement, participation and active learning, as discussed in this chapter. Some of the familiar activities relating to assessment, planning, teaching and classroom organisation might be seen as simply part of the normal repertoire of good educational practice, but these approaches are fundamental to teaching children with difficulties in learning and they can help to generate useful new ideas, understanding and confidence in the possibility of making a difference.

The teaching of children with learning difficulties is a collaborative responsibility. The day-to-day work of individual class teachers needs to be put alongside ongoing efforts by the school staff team to develop the learning environment and the curriculum for pupils in all their diversity. We also see benefits when teachers from different schools make a combined professional response to influence the Special Educational Needs legislation and initiatives which have a significant impact on provision for individual children across the country (DoE 1994; DfEE 1998), and when teachers engage in their own research to contribute to the growing body of knowledge about educating children whose progress is causing concern.

Activities

A 'teaching challenge'

Think of a child who has presented you with a 'teaching challenge' because of their difficulties in learning compared to their peers in school. In which setting(s) and curriculum area(s) did the difficulties appear? In which did they not? What was the teaching challenge and how did you respond?

Write a short account of your experience of working with this child and then identify what else you would like to have known or done to help him or her. Then try to do the same from the child's perspective. How do these two accounts compare? Do the ideas relate mainly to the child's individual experience and characteristics, to factors in the school context or to some sort of relationship between them? How could the relevant aspects of the school context be changed to help the child to learn more successfully, from both your point of view and that of the child?

Task analysis and learning objectives

For the same child as in Activity 1, identify an area of learning which caused particular difficulty. Carry out a 'task analysis' to show the skills, knowledge and understanding involved in this area of learning. Write one or two targets for progress, and express these targets as specific and measurable learning objectives for the next half term.

How would you set about teaching to these objectives? How would you measure progress?

Increasing participation

Where are there opportunities within the day-to-day running of a Primary classroom to increase the active participation and engagement of children whose progress in learning is causing concern? Think particularly about the role of the class teacher and other adults, and about the involvement of the other children in the class.

Teaching about learning

Look again at the section in this chapter on teaching 'thinking skills' in the classroom, especially the role of the teacher in helping all children to think and talk about learning. What vocabulary, key questions and activities could help in bringing a greater awareness of learning processes into different curriculum areas, e.g. science, art, PE, English?

Further reading

Babbage, R., Byers, R. and Redding, H. (1999) *Approaches to Teaching and Learning: Including Pupils with Learning Difficulties*, London: Fulton.

Dockrell, J. and McShane, J. (1993) *Children's Learning Difficulties: A Cognitive Approach*, Oxford: Blackwell.

Farrell, P. (1997) *Teaching Pupils with Learning Difficulties: Strategies and Solutions*, London: Cassell.

Hart, S. (1996) *Beyond Special Needs: Enhancing children's learning through innovative thinking*, London: Paul Chapman.

Jones, K. and Charlton, T. (eds) (1996) *Overcoming Learning and Behaviour Difficulties: Partnership with Pupils*, London: Routledge.

References

Adams, M.J. (1994) 'Learning to read: modelling the reader versus modelling the learner', in C. Hulme and M. Snowling (eds) *Reading Development and Dyslexia*, London: Whurr.

Ainscow, M. (1999) *Understanding the Development of Inclusive Schools*, London: Falmer Press.

Arnold, H. (1984) *Making Sense of It*, Sevenoaks: Hodder and Stoughton.

Ashman, A.F. and Conway, R.N.F. (1997) *An Introduction to Cognitive Education: Theory and Applications*, London: Routledge.

Babbage, R., Byers, R. and Redding, H. (1999) *Approaches to Teaching and Learning: Including Pupils with Learning Difficulties*, London: Fulton.

Blamires, M. (ed.) (1999) *Enabling Technology for Inclusion*, London: Paul Chapman Publishing.

Buckley, S., Bird, G. and Byrne, A. (1996) 'Reading acquisition by young children', in B. Stratford and P. Gunn (eds) *New Approaches to Down's Syndrome*, London: Cassell.

Carpenter, B., Ashdown, R. and Bovair, K. (eds) (1996) *Enabling Access: effective teaching and learning for pupils with learning difficulties*, London: Fulton.

Caviglioli, O. (1999) 'Plains of the brain', *Special Children* 123, 25–29.

Clark, C., Dyson, A. and Millward, A. (eds) (1998) *Theorising Special Education*, London: Routledge.

Clarke, A.M. and Clarke, A.D.B. (eds) (1976) *Early Experience: myth and evidence*, London: Open Books.

Croll, P. and Moses, D. (1985) *One in Five: the assessment and incidence of special educational needs*, London: Routledge and Kegan Paul.

Crozier, W.R. (1997) *Individual Learners: personality differences in education*, London: Routledge.

Csikszentmihalyi, M. (1990) *Flow: The Psychology of Optimal Experience*, New York: Harper and Row.

DfEE (Department for Education and Employment) (1997) *From Targets to Action: guidance to support effective target-setting in schools*, London: DfEE.

DfEE (Department for Education and Employment) (1998) *Meeting Special Educational Needs: a programme of action* London: DfEE.

Dockrell, J. and McShane, J. (1993) *Children's Learning Difficulties: a cognitive approach*, Oxford: Blackwell.

DoE (Department of Education) (1994) *Code of Practice on the Identification and Assessment of Special Educational Needs*, London: Central Office of Information.

Dyson, A. and Millward, A. (1997) 'The reform of special education or the transformation of mainstream schools?', in S.J. Pijl, C.J.W. Meijer and S. Hegarty (eds) *Inclusive Education: a global agenda*, London: Routledge.

Farrell, P. (1997) *Teaching Pupils with Learning Difficulties: strategies and solutions*, London: Cassell.

Feuerstein, R. (1980) *Instrumental Enrichment*, Baltimore: University Park Press.

Hart, S. (1996) *Beyond Special Needs: enhancing children's learning through innovative thinking*, London: Paul Chapman.

Hulme, C. and Snowling, M. (eds) (1994) *Reading Development and Dyslexia*, London: Whurr.

Jones, K. and Charlton, T. (eds) (1996) *Overcoming Learning and Behaviour Difficulties: partnership with pupils*, London: Routledge.

McKeown, S. (1999) 'Supporting dyslexic learners', *Special Children* 123, 19–22.

Norwich, B. (1990) *Reappraising Special Needs Education*, London: Cassell.

Pijl, S. J. and van den Bos, K.P. (1998) 'Decision making in uncertainty', in C. Clark, A. Dyson and A. Millward (eds) (1998) *Theorising Special Education*, London: Routledge.

Pumfrey, P.D. and Reason, R. (1991) *Specific Learning Difficulties (Dyslexia): challenges and responses*, London: Routledge.

Reason, R. (1990) 'Reconciling different approaches to intervention', in P.D. Pumfrey and C.D. Elliott (eds) *Children's Difficulties in Reading, Spelling and Writing*, Basingstoke: Falmer.

Riding, R. and Rayner, S. (1998) *Cognitive Styles and Learning Strategies: understanding styles differences in learning and behaviour*, London: Fulton.

Rogoff, B. (1990) *Apprenticeship in Thinking: cognitive development in social context*, Oxford: Oxford University Press.

Singleton, C. (1997) 'Screening early literacy', in J.R. Beech and C. Singleton (eds) *The Psychological Assessment of Reading*, London: Routledge.

Skidmore, D. (1999) 'Continuities and developments in research into the education of pupils with learning difficulties', *British Journal of Educational Studies* 47 (1) 3–16.

Stratford, B. and Gunn, P. (eds) (1996) *New Approaches to Down's Syndrome*, London: Cassell.

Tizard, B. and Varma, V. (eds) (1992) *Vulnerability and Resilience in Human Development: a Festschrift for Ann and Alan Clarke*, London: Jessica Kingsley.

Tomlinson, S. (1982) *A Sociology of Special Education*, London: Routledge and Kegan Paul.

Varma, V. (ed.) (1993) *How and Why Children Fail*, London: Jessica Kingsley.

Vygotsky, L.S. (1978) *Mind in Society: the development of higher level psychological processes* (ed. M. Cole, V. John-Steiner, S. Scribner and E. Souberman) Cambridge: MA: Harvard University Press.

Wong, B.Y.L. (1996) *The ABCs of Learning Disabilities*, San Diego: Academic Press.

Wood, D. (1998) *How Children Think and Learn*, 2nd edition, Oxford: Blackwell.

15 Educating children with behaviour difficulties

Roland Chaplain

EDITOR'S SUMMARY

Children who present difficult behaviour are perhaps one of the most frequent causes of teacher stress and anxiety. This chapter begins by emphasising how important it is, as a consequence, to examine our own thoughts and feelings about such children before we proceed to attributing causal explanations of their behaviour which may be misguided and based on inadequate information. The crucial role of careful and systematic assessment is emphasised. The second half of the chapter reviews approaches to intervening effectively, based upon behavioural, humanistic and cognitive–behavioural approaches, together with advice about which approach will be appropriate in different circumstances.

Introduction

The subject of this chapter is children with behavioural difficulties; by behavioural difficulties, I mean social as opposed to academic behaviour but it is true to say that the two are not mutually exclusive. There are many studies which have established a correlation between academic performance and social behaviour, but little evidence exists to illustrate the direction of any causal links between them.

We have all observed (if not taught) children who behave in a way which we (as individuals or groups or both) find unacceptable. For example, the child in a supermarket who wants some Smarties but has been told by her harassed and embarrassed mother that she can not. The child proceeds to engage in a set of behaviours in order to get her own way. The technique, having a tantrum, can be very successful, resulting in mum buying the sweets, often with the words 'All right, you can have them provided you behave yourself for the rest of the day'. The child is probably most unlikely to improve her behaviour, as she has associated having a tantrum with getting a reward. This simple example illustrates a fundamental principle of a school of psychology known as behaviourist, very commonly used with difficult children and one to which we will return.

Having observed such behaviour, we usually go on to make evaluative judgements about the causes of such behaviour (e.g: who's to blame) a process known in social psychology as attribution theory. These evaluative judgements are based on two key features. The first is our existing knowledge of children and parenting and the second our interpretation of the current situation e.g., a problem child or an ineffective parent, or the situation (supermarket layout strategy). What is perhaps most interesting is how quickly we draw such conclusions based on very little factual information. We usually do not know what has preceded the behaviour nor how it related to other aspects of the child's behaviour nor of the interpersonal dynamics between those involved. Also, we are usually happy to draw our conclusions based on snippets of information. As professionals, teachers are required to make a large number of assessments and judgements about pupil behaviour (academic and social) on a regular basis. Indeed if a teacher were unable to do so one might say they were not doing their job – so it is important that they can make such judgements from an informed position.

Behavioural difficulties (or Emotional and Behavioural Difficulties as they are more usually referred to in the literature) are wide ranging and can include anything from serious disruption in a classroom to psychotic behaviour (although psychoses are fairly rare in children). For the purposes of this book we have treated emotional and behavioural difficulties separately when in fact there is a strong relationship between behaviour, social cognition and emotions: hence the terminology in Special Educational Needs combines the two. Providing an accurate definition has proved elusive for both government departments and specialists in the field. Many terms have been used to describe this 'group' of children, ranging from maladjusted to disturbed, depraved to deprived, emotionally damaged to dangerous. Children with these difficulties can find themselves the target of several human services at the same time, each of which may have a different and often conflicting perspective on the aetiology of the difficulties, how they should be assessed and what intervention is required to overcome them. In the rest of this chapter, I will suggest ways in which you might challenge and enhance your existing knowledge of children's behavioural difficulties. To do justice to the subject, however, will require you to consult some of the recommended reading.

Behavioural difficulties: causal explanations

Before reading this section complete both parts of Activity 1.

Activity 1

1 On your own make a list of what you consider to be behaviour problems exhibited by children. Now number them in order of severity starting with the worst possible behaviour and finishing with what you consider the least severe. If you are sharing this activity with fellow students or colleagues (which is preferable) compare the content of your list and your ratings of the severity of the behaviours. How similar are your results? Do you all come from similar backgrounds? Are you currently in similar situations?

2 Consider what you perceive to be the causes of behaviour problems and again make a list. Are some more unacceptable or blameworthy than others? Is for example, a child who has been abused and refuses to talk to anyone more responsible for their situation than a child who comes from a loving home and who continually assaults other children? Look at your list and indicate which of the causes of behaviour problems you have identified are within the control of the child and which are outside their control. For example, if you have listed brain damage at birth as a cause then this is not within the control of the child. How many of the causes you have identified are outside the control of the child? How many are outside the control of school? Discuss your findings with a colleague or colleagues.

What have your learned from this activity? People behave in particular ways which reflect the situation they are in. Behaviour in school is controlled by social and cultural expectations, so behaviour considered tolerable in one school would be completely unacceptable in another. Within schools the same is often the case: what is considered amusing banter by one teacher could be seen as insulting by another. Traditional (and many contemporary) accounts of behavioural difficulties focus on providing medical and para-medical descriptors of symptoms (and usually believed causes) of them, which often relate either to problems within the child (medical model) or problems in his or her environment (social or ecological model). So if a child continually disrupts a class, refuses to work, is offensive to teachers and other pupils, or breaks other people's property, it is likely that most teachers would work through a mixture of talking to or punishing him, or both, along with talking about him with other teachers and his parents. As a result of these endeavours a conclusion is likely to be drawn which either identifies the problem as being within the person, that is, he is a dysfunctional individual (an internal cause) or else the cause of the problem is seen as resulting from the situation (an external cause). Interestingly, even when the cause is considered to be the situation, it is seldom that teachers

Table 15.1 Some common explanations for children's behaviour problems

---

Explanations which are outside school control

Within-child factors: the child is sick or disturbed or wilful

Dysfunctional families: the child's family is problematic, with poor and ineffective child rearing, uncaring or abusive parents

Dysfunctional local community: the child comes from a problem neighbourhood that is socially and financially depressed, with high levels of crime

Problems within society: a general lack of respect for discipline, a non-caring society

Explanations which are within school control

Lack of resources in school: over-crowded classrooms, badly maintained buildings, lack of books and teaching materials

Poorly managed school: ineffective working relationships between school management, staff and pupils

Poor quality teaching: present or past teachers not establishing effective classroom management, ineffective interpersonal relationships between pupils and teachers

Unimaginative, inappropriate or over (or under) demanding curriculum

---

blame themselves or their schools for the difficulty, even though they are part of that situation. This tendency is not unique to teachers and is an example of what social psychologists call a 'self-serving bias', that is, the human tendency to attribute successes to ourselves and failures to others. Let me illustrate the thinking behind this with an example. Supposing a pupil, Damien, is verbally abusing his teacher Mrs Smith; Table 15.2 summarises possible explanations people (including Mrs Smith) might put forward for his behaviour.

Interpreting Table 15.2

Table 15.2 is based on Kelley's classic theory of covariation (Kelley 1967), an attribution theory in which he argued that people's understanding of their world develops through a causal analysis which resembles the way in which a scientist tests a hypothesis. This example demonstrates how Damien's behaviour (being verbally abusive to his teacher) could be explained by reference to something in the person (Damien), the entity or stimulus (Mrs Smith, his teacher) or the circumstances (e.g. problems at home, classroom organisation). Which of the perceived causal explanation is adopted (i.e. who or what is blamed) depends on the interaction of the three independent variables, i.e. consistency, distinctiveness and consensus.

Table 15.2 Patterns of covariance: illustrating how different causal explanations are generated about the same behaviour

Consistency	Distinctiveness	Consensus	Causal Explanation
High	*Low*	*Low*	*Person*
Damien is always verbally abusive to Mrs Smith	Damien is verbally abusive to most teachers	Other children are not verbally abusive to this teacher	There's something wrong with Damien: it's his fault
High	*High*	*High*	*Entity*
Damien is always verbally abusive to Mrs Smith	Damien is not usually verbally abusive to other teachers	Other pupils verbally abuse this teacher	There's something wrong with this teacher: it's her fault
Low	*High*	*Low*	*Circumstance*
Damien has not been verbally abusive to this teacher before	Damien isn't normally verbally abusive to teachers	Other children aren't cheeky to this teacher	It's because there's something different about the situation: a combination of problems

The first independent variable, consistency, relates to variations across people that is the degree to which the behaviour is consistent irrespective of the circumstances. In other words is Damien always (consistency is high) abusive towards Mrs Smith or is it a new development (consistency is low)?

The second variable, distinctiveness, relates to variations over entities (stimuli), in this case Damien's teacher(s). Does Damien behave this way towards all teachers or is it just reserved for Mrs Smith?

The third variable, consensus, relates to variations across people (in this example other pupils). Are other pupils also offensive to Mrs Smith or is the difficulty just between Mrs Smith and Damien?

Causal explanations of behaviour in this model, then, result from the inter-play (covariation) between the three independent variables, that is, the degree to which we perceive those under observation to score high or low on each variable. The selection of level (i.e. high or low) is influenced by the combination of existing knowledge of children's behaviour and knowledge of the current situation. The resultant causal explanation (the final column) reflects particular combinations of ratings (high or low) of the three variables.

You might ask, what does it matter? A great deal in fact, since the type of attribution you make as a teacher can have colossal effects on the consequences for the pupil. If you conclude that there is something wrong with Damien then you may call for additional help or ultimately the pupil may be statemented or even referred for medical attention. One might reasonably expect at both a moral and professional level, that subjecting a pupil to such

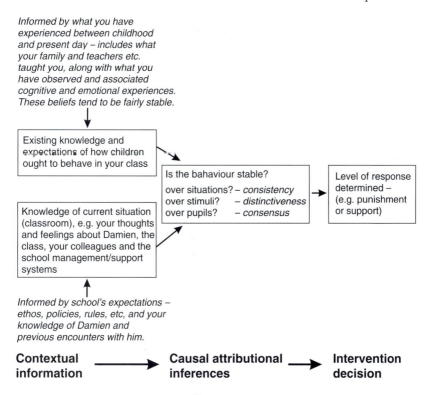

Figure 15.1 An attributional framework for intervention decisions for pupils exhibiting behaviour difficulties

extreme measures (or even embarking on the early processes) should require teachers to engage in deliberate and accurate analyses of behaviour. These analyses should incorporate other factors which might be influencing Damien's behaviour as well as the behaviour itself. Such additional factors will inevitably include school organisation and policy, curriculum demands and your own behaviour. Analysis of the latter can be overlooked but may reveal a series of ritualised sequences that you have both drifted into and which are exacerbating the difficulties. This process is summarised in the diagram (Figure 15.1) above. This figure illustrates the relationship between some of the factors which are central to the intervention decisions made about pupils. What you decide to do with Damien depends on your existing knowledge, beliefs and attitudes towards pupils which have built up over your lifetime; added to these are your thoughts and feelings about the current situation. From this you are likely to ascribe particular causal explanations for his behaviour. These explanations will in turn influence how you respond verbally and non-verbally to Damien and the subsequent intervention you recommend or implement. You might like to test this by looking at the following Case Study and then answering the accompanying questions.

Case Study: Identifying the problem

Imagine you are visiting a school where you will be soon be teaching. The teacher invites you to join her in your future classroom. The teacher is smart and friendly and appears very enthusiastic and well-organised. She has prepared a detailed timetable for you and gives you lots of information about the school. She introduces you to a group of pupils from the class who show you around the school. They are polite and well-behaved.

What are your thoughts and feelings about the school and your future class at this stage?

The teacher meets up with you and the head teacher with whom you have been chatting and offers to introduce you to the whole class. She tells you that they are all well-behaved and hard-working. As you walk in inevitably all eyes are focused on you. The children are generally dressed in sweatshirts adorned with the school logo. Most of the children smile when you walk in except for two boys who seem to be sniggering and are wearing Newcastle football shirts as opposed to school sweatshirts.

Make a note about your initial thoughts and feelings about the two boys.

How do you think they are likely to behave during your stay?

In what way might the physical state, reputation and ethos of the school affect your initial thoughts and expectations?

The teacher gives the children a piece of work to complete and then starts preparing some materials for a future lesson. As the lesson progresses you notice that the two boys do not appear to be doing the work that the teacher has set, and furthermore the teacher does not seem to be doing anything about it. A girl raises her hand to complain that one of the boys has poked her in the back with a pencil, the teacher tells her to get on with her work and to ignore them.

What are your thoughts and feelings about the teacher? Do you think she made the right decision? What would you have done, and why?

What are your thoughts and feelings about the dynamics of the classroom?

Would you want to ask the teacher about the situation, and if so what would you ask?

Are these boys out of control?

The teacher leaves the room leaving you alone. One of the boys leaves his seat and takes something from another pupil's desk. You tell him to sit down and he looks at you but does not do as you tell him.

What are your thoughts and feelings?

What do you do next?

Just then a second, much older teacher walks into the room and the boy rapidly returns to his seat and begins work along with everyone in the class. The second teacher has not said anything to the class. She checks through some papers on the desk and shortly afterwards leaves the room. The two boys then stand up and go over to the window again ignoring you when you tell them to sit down.

What are your thoughts and feelings about the second teacher? Why was she so effective?

What are your thoughts and feelings about the prospect of teaching this class?

What would you do next?

What have you learned from this activity?

A case study such as this may be criticised for lacking information and because to make the correct decisions requires more detail from which more accurate conclusions can be drawn. However, we often make fairly major decisions very quickly based on limited information, which result in unintended consequences, some of which can be quite devastating for the recipient. As a teacher you will be expected to make numerous decisions in your classroom based on limited information. However, it is important to spend time reviewing on what basis you are making your causal inferences. Much of our decision-making becomes routinised – so as to enable the brain to make sense of a fast-moving world – so it is essential to make sure that such decisions are appropriate, particularly where they involve a pupil's education or the surroundings in which they are educated.

Why is an understanding of causal explanations important?

It may seem at first reading that examining causal explanations has relatively little to do with assessing or intervening with behavioural difficulties. However, I would argue that decisions regarding assessment and intervention are very much influenced by these processes, and furthermore, failure to engage in deliberate analysis of our own attributions can be potentially disastrous for some young people. It is also salient to recognise that attributions can operate at a social level; in other words, social groups can often identify collective causal explanations, despite variance within the target group. A group of teachers in a school will often project a representation of why children behave in a particular way, which reflects a combination of their personal experience plus their knowledge of their situation (e.g. the local community, school management and organisation, school ethos, government and local management expectations, psycho-emotive state). Which explanation becomes generally accepted is usually dependent on the status of the individual(s) who initiate the process. As a student or newly qualified teacher you would usually hold relatively low status in the staffroom (compared with more experienced colleagues) and thus are less likely to influence the decision-making process until you are more fully socialised into the group.

Assessment

There are many psychological measures and profiling instruments available which claim to offer effective measurement of behaviour difficulties. (See for example Conners 1997; McGuire and Richman 1987; Rutter 1967.) However, before deciding which measure to use you should answer the following questions:

1   *Why do we want to assess the pupil?*
Whilst seemingly obvious, this question is often overlooked, sometimes because the process is being driven largely by emotions, as opposed to problem-solving processes. Take time to examine the situation (organisation, curriculum, classroom environment) in more detail. Has existing data been analysed in detail – what gaps exist?

2   *What behaviour do we want to assess?*
Academic or social behaviour (or both) and in what order? What are the possible consequences of our decision on what to assess?

3   *When would be the best time to assess the pupil?*
What part of the day or week, what type of lesson, when in relation to the decision to measure and how long should the process take? Consider what else is happening in the child's life at the time (e.g. family difficulties).

4   *How should we assess the pupil?*
How to assess the difficulty requires further attention both to what observations have already been made, and their relevance to the current situation. What tests or profiles are available and accessible to you which will measure the specific behaviour(s) you are interested in? If none exist will you construct your own? If you do so, how can you ensure they are valid and reliable?

5   *Where should the pupil be assessed?*
Many social behaviours that give teachers most cause for concern occur outside the classroom, in the playground or on the way to school for instance, so that measurement in the classroom may be of little value. On the other hand, where such behaviour occurs in a classroom you will usually want to clarify if it also occurs elsewhere and if so how often. It is not uncommon for teachers to rely on supplementary information from colleagues, but if this is unstructured it is of little use to someone

who wishes to change a pupil's behaviour in a considered way, it is merely hearsay. Where is there a suitable place to carry out the observations (noting safety and other needs)?

6   *Who should carry out the assessment?*
    How experienced are they as observers? How well do they know the pupil?

7   *What does the pupil think?*
    Taking account of the pupil's opinion is vital to the assessment process, since it is very unlikely you will effect behaviour change without their co-operation. Teachers are often surprised to discover how much pupils know of their difficulties and how much they want to resolve them. They often cannot do so, however, because both their behaviour and that of the teacher have become ritualised; adult and pupil engage in a sequence of behaviours as a matter of routine. I mention this because the solution to some of the difficulties that occur in schools can be found more readily in an analysis of the nature of the rituals (usually social interactions) in a classroom or school rather than in an analysis of 'problem' individuals (see Chaplain and Freeman 1998).

Don't forget it may take a little time before they are in a position to discuss the issue(s) in a calm and considered way – something which can seem less than appealing when a pupil's behaviour continues to be intolerable and is making your life a misery.

  Having addressed the above questions satisfactorily and decided if any more information is necessary, we can move on to the process of assessing the pupil. Figure 15.2 outlines an example of how to engage in such a process and should be seen as a generic approach which could be used at any stage of assessment.

Intervention

From the wide range of recognised approaches to helping children with behaviour difficulties, I have selected three popular alternatives by way of contrast. These are behavioural, humanistic and cognitive–behavioural approaches. Whilst there are a number of others, psychodynamic and gestalt for example, these tend to be utilised in special environments where all staff and organisational structures, often including living arrangements, are focused on that one approach. To highlight the distinctions between these perspectives I will briefly describe how each views human behaviour and illustrate how they might be used in school. It is impossible to do justice to these psychological techniques as part of a single chapter; if you wish to know more you should consult the recommended reading list.

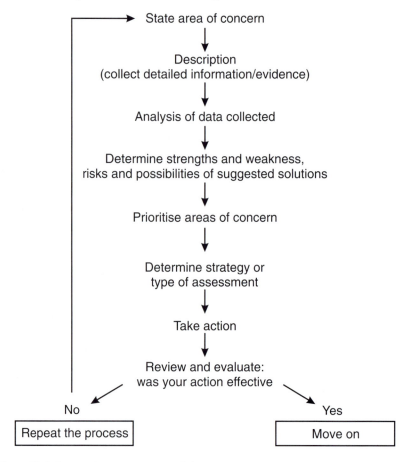

Figure 15.2 A generic assessment model

Behavioural approaches

These approaches originate from learning theories closely associated with psychologists such as Watson (1932) and Skinner (1974). Learning theory argues that all behaviour (including problematic) is ultimately controlled by environmental stimuli. In other words, an individual carries out a particular behaviour, is rewarded for doing so (wittingly or otherwise) and is therefore predisposed to repeat the behaviour. An example might be that a pupil mis- behaves during your maths lesson, you send him to see the head, who finds him something else to do as a 'punishment' (e.g. clean out the stock cup- board). However, the pupil enjoys the individual attention from the head and doing something other than maths, and so repeats the behaviour. You again refer him to the head who again 'punishes' him, and so on. You have started an interactive ritual (discussed earlier) which you can either work to overcome, or allow to continue, or even exacerbate. Behaviourists argue that in order to change behaviour (behaviour modification) you must follow a sequence of events:

1   Specify the behaviours as objectively as possible.
2   Determine what events precede the behaviour, the behaviour itself and what follows the behaviour.
3   Decide what behaviour you would consider more acceptable (i.e. to replace the undesirable behaviour since it is difficult to behave and misbehave at the same time).
4   Change what precedes the behaviour, the behaviour itself or what follows the behaviour – and reinforce the required behaviour.

The central feature of the process is making sure you describe what is happening in as detailed a way as possible. You will also notice that behaviourists are interested in the behaviour itself, as opposed to trying to find explanations in the past as to why it may now be occurring. It is often stated that behaviourists do not recognise thinking or indeed emotions, a premise which is not strictly true. Even earlier workers in the field such as the late B. F. Skinner acknowledged the existence of what he described as covert behaviours, in other words behaviour which could not be observed externally. Traditionally, however, behaviourists do believe that what really counts is what is happening and can be directly observed, and that energy should be directed to *unlearning* that which is unacceptable and replacing it with that which is.

Critics of this approach claim it is too mechanistic and directive in its views of and responses to human behaviour. Part of this criticism relates to the origins of research in the field which was mainly carried out on animals such as rats and pigeons. Despite this, however, all teachers engage in behaviour modification in some form or other, that is, they reward acceptable behaviour and punish or ignore unacceptable behaviour, which often works. However, using such techniques to modify very difficult behaviour requires attention to detailed analysis and recording and to hypothesis testing in a rigorous manner. Table 15.3 summarises and annotates the stages involved in behaviour modification. Study this and Activity 2 before reading on.

Humanistic approaches

Humanistic psychologists, like behaviourists, also believe in the importance of dealing with the present (as opposed to historical occurrences) but whilst behaviourists rely on structured analysis and intervention techniques, humanists place emphasis on the individual person and on building a caring relationship between adult and pupil. Humanists are strongly anti-technique and prefer to talk about attitudes and creating growth-promoting climates. A leading writer in this field was Carl Rogers (1961) who developed person-centred counselling. Humanistic psychologists argue that humans are basically good, capable of directing their own destinies (including their own

Table 15.3 Behaviour modification: the process

Sequence		What to do or what questions to consider
(a)	**The behaviour analysis stage**	
1	Define the behaviour difficulty	*Questions to consider:* Who's problem? Who's involved? Where does it take place?
2	Decide how to record the behaviour	*Some possibilities:* List each occurrence. Record at set times. Measure how long it persists.
3	Determine what sets the behaviour off	*Some possibilities:* Particular lessons. Particular teachers. Particular settings. The company of particular peers. Particular times or days of the week.
4	Determine what seems to keep it going	*Some possibilities:* Peers' actions. Teachers' actions. Classroom organisation/environment. Teaching/learning styles.
(b)	**The behaviour modification stage**	
5	Determine which behaviour(s) are to be responded to	Identify objectives from 3 or 4. If there are a number of behaviours causing concern then prioritise
6	Decide what behaviour you expect in place of the undesirable behaviour	State precisely what behaviour is required in place of the unacceptable behaviour
7	Determine what the pupils main interests are	Use this information to decide what to use as a reward for behaving acceptably (e.g. extra football practice, responsibility)
8	Decide how to respond	Change what sets the behaviour off (stimulus) Prevent the behaviour from being sustained (change or offer alternative reinforcer)
(c)	**The review stage**	
9	Determine accurately whether the behaviour has been modified as required	Re-run stage 2 and decide whether the frequency or intensity of the behaviour has reduced
10	If it has been successful	Either expect more from the pupil for the same level of reward, or reduce the amount of reward given
11	If it hasn't been successful	Re-run the process

Activity 2

This activity is one way of starting to use a problem-solving approach using the principles outlined above. Think of a class or a group of pupils or an individual whom you consider do not behave in an acceptable manner.

Set a starting date and observe and record their behaviour over a few weeks, in order to get a feel for how they 'normally' behave.

Establish what they are doing and in what sequence; they might for instance begin lessons very well and deteriorate towards the end or always take a while to settle down. Now consider what possible changes you might try; you could share your thoughts with a colleague or friend. Having considered the possibilities, decide on one new approach, for example, rearranging the seating or classroom layout or making a conscious effort to smile more or move around the room more regularly, finding something positive to say to each pupil.

Continue with this procedure for a week and record any changes. Talk to the pupils about how they feel. If there is no observable improvement go back to your list of possibilities and select another change or set of changes – but don't try changing too much at once. If there is an improvement in behaviour don't assume that it will be maintained for ever. You need to re-evaluate what is going on in a regular and systematic way, just as you evaluate the academic progress of your pupils and your teaching. Remember even the best-behaved classes will respond more and learn more effectively when you monitor the quality of your relationships and management style.

therapy) and are striving to 'self-actualise' (become everything they would wish to be). People become dysfunctional because they are prevented from achieving these goals. One central feature of this approach is the concept of the self. The self is a multifaceted construct made up of three basic elements:

- the ideal self (what you would wish to be)
- the actual self or self image (how you believe you are, based on your own self-perception plus how you feel 'significant others' (people important to you) see you
- the self esteem or self worth, the difference between the two.

Rogers argues that what is most important to those using this approach to help pupils is understanding the world as the individual pupil sees it, as opposed to how others see it. In the classroom this means that in order for you (the teacher) to understand why a child with behaviour difficulties behaves the way they do, you must first understand how she sees the world.

Whilst striving for self-actualisation we attempt to maintain a balance between self-regard (how we feel about ourselves) and how we feel we are regarded by others. Some individuals persecute themselves in order to be seen positively by others whilst other individuals are overly concerned with themselves to the exclusion of others. In between the two extremes is the majority of population. Rogers suggests that failure to maintain a balance between these two competing demands results in dysfunctional behaviour.

A humanistic approach to working with children who have behaviour difficulties has four core conditions.

1   *Empathy*   (not the same as sympathy) seeing the world through the eyes of the pupil, understanding their personal meanings
2   *Warmth*   a genuine warmth towards the pupil, which enables but doesn't stifle them (can be difficult with pupils who have caused considerable pain to other people in the school)
3   *Unconditional positive regard*   a genuine regard without strings attached. It represents an expression of sincere trust irrespective of what the individual has done (which doesn't mean that you approve of their behaviour)
4   *Congruence*   the degree to which you can be your real self, being genuine with the pupil.

These preconditions are linked to the overall requirement that the teacher or helper builds a close relationship with the pupil and by doing so can facilitate the pupil's awareness of, and trust in, self actualisation. The job of the teacher in this approach is not to direct what the pupil should be thinking or doing but rather to use the relationship to enable the pupil herself to explore her problems and those parts of herself which she usually keeps hidden from others, by entering the pupil's frame of reference. There are two basic inherent questions which the pupil is encouraged to explore: 'Who am I?' and 'How can I become myself?'

Critics of this approach suggest that it fails to help the pupil to face reality and is also less successful with severely disturbed individuals. Attempt Activity 3 before reading on.

Cognitive-behavioural approaches

For the behaviourist, thought or cognition has little to do with the learning process. In contrast, humanists argue that finding out what individuals think is more important than observing behaviour. For many years cognitivists and behaviourists were in opposite camps, each condemning the other's approach as either not scientific or as unimaginative. A third alternative came about with the development of cognitive-behavioural psychology. Cognitive-behavioural theories of learning apply a different interpretation to the stimulus-response relationship which is central to behaviourism. This approach recognises the ability of individuals to construct mental models which they then use to predict what might or might not happen. You might,

Activity 3

Central to humanistic approaches are good listening skills. Being a good listener requires attention to a range of issues some of which are verbal and others of which are non-verbal. Answer the following questions relating to the qualities you consider paramount to effective listening.

What do you consider to be the three most important verbal responses for a teacher to give when listening to a pupil?

What do you consider to be the three most important non-verbal responses for a teacher to give when listening to a pupil?

What do you consider to be the three most important aspects of a teacher's posture and gesture (e.g. hand and arm movements) that teachers should display when listening to a pupil?

What do you consider to be the ideal conditions in which to listen to what a pupil has to say?

Should these conditions be the same irrespective of what is being said?

What are the least satisfactory conditions in which to listen to a pupil?

What behaviours do you think best indicate that a person is interested in what you have to say?

How do you rate yourself alongside the qualities you consider valuable? Discuss your answers with a colleague. What implications do your conclusions have for your school (e.g. private space, uninterrupted time with pupils)?

What have you learned from this activity? See Table 15.4.

for instance, rehearse in your head what you will say to a badly behaved pupil before your encounter. In this process you usually try and consider the consequences of saying one thing or another, and what the pupil might say or do in response. The object here is to cope effectively and be prepared for the unexpected, trying to make a potentially unpredictable event more predictable and hence safe. This is an extension of behavioural approaches and one which treats thoughts as behaviours which will respond to restructuring using behavioural principles. Cognitive-behavioural psychology offers a more flexible approach to the learning process. Here individuals can build and modify mental models without the need for concrete experiences. It follows then that in order to understand an individual's behaviour we need to know something about their internal mental models of their world.

As an intervention strategy, unlike the humanistic approaches, the helper in cognitive-behavioural approaches is strongly active-directive and

Table 15.4 Some suggested rules for engaging in effective listening

Teacher behaviour

Being accessible – being available for pupils when *they* feel they need to talk. Select a non-threatening location in a neutral space where interruptions can be prevented. The corridor outside a classroom is not a good place.

Showing interest – looking interested in what the pupil has to say in a relaxed and welcoming manner. Leaning slightly forward indicates this as does gentle nodding of the head since it conveys interest and involvement. A smile is usually helpful, unless the pupil is deeply distressed.

Eye contact – look at the pupil when they are talking. Don't do this too much as staring is intimidating – nor too little as this suggests you are uncomfortable or uninterested.

Be on their level – make sure your head is at about the same level as the pupil since this helps the communication process. Having your head higher or lower than the person with whom you are communicating can make them feel uncomfortable.

Use verbal prompts to let the pupil know that you have received their message. Phrases such as 'I see ... ', 'Yes ... ', Go on ... ', 'Fancy that ... ' help to maintain the flow of the conversation.

challenges these models where they are producing dysfunctional behaviour. Cognitive-behavioural approaches encourage active prompting of the pupil in order to help them change. These approaches are associated with the work of Aaron Beck (1976) and Albert Ellis (1979). Whereas behaviourists highlight the relationship between an activating event (stimulus), and consequences (response), cognitive-behavioural approaches argue that it is irrational thinking (beliefs) about consequences which creates dysfunctional behaviour. To address this, cognitive-behaviourists use a combination of behaviour modification principles and procedures to change the beliefs that are creating difficulties for the pupil in the first place. For example, pupils who are depressed tend to view the world negatively, are self critical and expect to fail in social encounters and do themselves down if they are successful. A teacher/helper adopting a cognitive-behavioural approach would concentrate on helping the pupil to control the disturbing emotional reactions he is experiencing. By working with the pupil's distorted thinking the teacher or helper can prevent the pupil from driving himself into deeper difficulty. This involves directing the pupil towards more functional thinking and raising their *self-efficacy*, that is, their belief in their ability to succeed or achieve mastery at a task or tasks. The helper in a cognitive-behavioural relationship will use a combination of strategies to achieve this, including:

Activity 4

Whilst listening skills are important, becoming an effective helper also requires being aware of discrepancies between what someone says and their underlying intent or motives. People often say what they think you want to hear rather than what they really want to say and give out messages which go beyond what they are actually saying. This can be observed in the way they stand, their tone of voice, level of attention, etc., which can distort what is being communicated to the listener. Whilst one might expect this to lessen as relationships develop, this does not necessarily follow. To become an effective helper requires you to be sensitive to your pupils' underlying feelings and concerns. The following questions ask you to examine your beliefs about people's motivational intent. You are asked to identify verbal and non-verbal clues a person might give which indicate how they are feeling despite what they are actually saying.

Discuss your findings with a colleague; how alike were your findings?

	Verbal clue	*Non-verbal clue*
Friendliness	"Hi – pleased to meet you"	Smiling
Anger		
Fear		
Happiness		
Insolence		
Sadness		
Suspicion		
Shyness		

- direct questioning: 'What is the very worst that could happen?, 'How do you know that?'
- information giving: offering explanations and information to the pupil when the pupil has a misconception about a point of fact
- analogies: offering alternative perspectives to what the pupil is saying
- humour: highly recommended in this approach.

Whilst cognitive-behavioural helpers strive to be empathetic, genuine and unconditionally accept the pupil, as in humanistic approaches, they tend not to be unduly warm towards them. Undue warmth is seen as counter-productive from a long-term perspective, as pupils' dependency and approval might be inappropriately reinforced.

The behavioural component of the approach guides the pupil towards alternative strategies for coping with their lives. This involves the pupil in keeping a diary of his moods along with what he was thinking at the time. This diary is then used as a basis for challenging the false assumptions and logic of the pupil. To alter this dysfunctional thinking the pupil would then be provided with a programme of personal skills training drawn from a range of techniques, two common examples of which are social skills training and assertiveness training.

Social skills training

This involves breaking down social interactive processes into a number of skills which are taught in progressive steps. Social skills can range from simple behaviours such as eye contact to more sophisticated social strategies such as interviewing techniques which are made up of a number of integrated individual social skills.

For example, a teacher helping a pupil who tended to become aggressive when going into new situations might start by teaching (modelling) effective behaviours when meeting people for the first time. This would include verbal (what to say in different circumstances) and non-verbal behaviours (including posture, gesture, eye contact). The pupil would then rehearse these behaviours and behaviour sequences in safe conditions before being given 'homework' tasks away from the helper. A homework task might be attending a party and trying out the behaviours which would then be reported back to the teacher for evaluation before moving on to new scenarios. The method is similar to that used in classrom teaching.

Assertiveness training

This aims at communicating effectively where self respect and respect for others are both maintained. People's behaviour in social situations can be graded on a continuum ranging from aggressive to submissive, with assertiveness somewhere between the two.

- *Aggressive* individuals tend to try and get what they want irrespective of the feelings of others; their goal is conflict.
- *Passive* individuals tend to put other people's thoughts and wants before their own. They tend to agree with the demands of others in order to keep the peace; their goal is avoidance.
- *Assertive* individuals are open, honest and clear in their responses to other people, in which self-respect and respect for others is maintained. Their goal is open honest and appropriate verbal and non-verbal behaviour.

For example, pupils who exhibit behaviour difficulties, in particular aggressiveness, often lack the ability to express positive or negative feelings clearly, or lack social sensitivity of the thoughts and feelings of those on the receiving end of their behaviour. They may experience anxiety about expressing themselves even when they know what they want to say. Similar methods to those used in social skills training are used, such as behaviour rehearsal, modelling and role play. One objective of assertiveness training is to encourage the pupil to make specific direct rather than generalised comments or behaviours, e.g. *generalised*: 'I hate f***ing maths' and refusing to work; *specific*: 'I find it hard to understand these sums, could you help me?' The pupil is encouraged to examine both their verbal and non-verbal behaviours. Many people fail to be assertive because of the negative labels they carry or feel constrained by conforming to stereotypes. To bring about effective change requires the pupil to challenge (with help) their own irrational and ritualised thinking and behaviours and to learn effective rational alternatives. They may have come to believe since early childhood that they can satisfy their immediate wants by being aggressive. It is important, therefore, to make sure that the alternative thinking and behaviour you advise is going to pay dividends. In the early stages it is best to set agreed, achievable and short-term targets and gradually extend expectations.

Most of these techniques involve, at some point, role play or rehearsal techniques which are designed to allow the pupil to boost their morale by creating a sense of mastery which they then apply to 'real situations'.

Cognitive-behavioural approaches are hard headed, practically oriented and rational approaches which seek to replace dysfunctional thoughts with more resourceful ones. As with all approaches outlined, the objective is to empower the pupil to function more effectively. They differ in their approach because of the differences in the psychological perspective from which they are derived. The process offers a wider approach than that of behaviour modification but can require greater input. However, results can be very impressive.

Helping children: selecting the 'right' approach

As I pointed out earlier, there are many different ways of responding to the needs of children with behaviour difficulties. Which is most effective? Each has its own appeal and each has a record of success. Which you should opt for depends on a number of factors including your personal perspective on children's development, your personal expectations of how children should behave in your class and your knowledge of a particular approach. At the same time you will be required to operate within a specific context, namely your school, which in turn responds to the needs of the local community, under the auspices of government regulation and guidance. These wider constraints dictate, at one level, whether or not the pupil in your care is eligible for specialist intervention and what form this will take. In some areas there are external specialist support services and units; in others the resources are concentrated within each school. Thus, before embarking on a particular strategy it is important to ensure that the techniques you plan to adopt fall within the approval of parents, school policy and official guidance. Some interventions require the whole ethos of the school to be in support for them to be effective, so attempting to use them in isolation is likely to undermine their effectiveness. You should also take the time to read widely about what each approach offers and what preconditions are required, how much support you will need and what level of training (if any) is required to administer them before embarking on a particular approach. Make a point of contacting the local Behaviour Support Team (if you have one), Schools Psychological Service, Child Guidance Departments and Clinical Psychologists (who specialise in children) and find out what methods they use and what support they can offer.

Summary

In this chapter I have introduced a number of ways of understanding and helping pupils who are experiencing behaviour difficulties. Whilst the approaches reviewed are intended for this purpose many of their underlying principles are as valid to general teaching as they are when working with extreme children. The opening section focussed on the essential need to examine our own thinking as teachers regarding the nature and origins of behaviour difficulties. The traditional approach of locating the problem within the child still persists, often as part of our implicit understanding of children's behaviour and development. This approach can lead to the drawing of conclusions prematurely, before analysing and considering the evidence in detail. Whilst this process is part of the way we, as humans, make sense of our world, we need to take care when engaging in such a process if the unwitting consequences are the restriction of a child's freedom and a limitation of his or her education through unnecessary or inappropriate intervention.

Further reading

For more detailed information on issues discussed in this chapter

Chaplain, R. (1995) *Pupil Behaviour*, Cambridge: Pearson.

Chaplain, R. and Freeman, A. (1994) *Caring Under Pressure*, London: Fulton.

Chaplain, R. and Freeman, A. (1996) *Stress and Coping*, Cambridge: Pearson.

Chaplain, R. and Freeman, A. (1998) *Coping with Difficult Children* Cambridge: Pearson.

Chazan, M., Laing, A. and Davies, D. (1994) *Emotional and Behavioural Difficulties in Middle Childhood*, London: Falmer.

For more specific information on ways of helping pupils with behavioural difficulties

General texts

Geldard, K. and Geldard, D. (1997) *Couselling Children*, London: Sage.
Sharp, S. and Cowie, H. (1998) *Counselling and Supporting Children in Distress*, London: Sage.

Behavioural approaches

Domjan, M. (1996) *The Essentials of Conditioning and Learning*, California: Brooks/Cole.
Leslie, J. (1996) *Principles of Behavioral Analysis*, Amsterdam: Harwood.
O'Sullivan, G. (1996) 'Behavioural Therapy', in Dryden, W. (ed.) *Handbook of Individual Therapy*, London: Sage.
Presland, J. (1993) 'Behavioural Approaches', in T. Charlton and K. David (eds) *Managing Misbehaviour*, London: Routledge.
Wheldall, K. and Merrett, F. (1989) 'Packages for training teachers in classroom behaviour management: BATPACK, BATSAC and the Positive Teaching Packages'. *Support for Learning* 3, 86–92.

Humanistic approaches

Mearns, D. (1997) *Person-Centred Counselling Training*, London: Sage.
Mearns, D. and Thorne, B. (1999) *Person-Centred Counselling in Action*, 2nd edition, London: Sage.
Rennie, D. (1997) *Person-Centred Counselling: an experiential approach*, London: Sage.
Visser, J. (1983) 'The Humanistic Approach', in G. Upton (ed.), *Educating Children with Behaviour Problems*, Cardiff: University of Cardiff Press.

Cognitive-behavioural approaches

Dryden, W. (1999) *Rational Emotive Therapy in Action*, London: Sage.
Scott, M., Strading, S. and Dryden, W. (1995) *Developing Cognitive-behavioural Counselling*, London: Sage.
Wallen, S., Digiuseppe, R. and Dryden, W. (1992) *A Practitioner's Guide to Rational-Emotive Therapy* 2nd Ed., New York: Oxford University Press.

References

Beck, A. (1976) *Cognitive Therapy and the Emotional Disorders*, New York: New American Library.
Chaplain, R. and Freeman, A. (1998) *Coping with Difficult Children*, Cambridge: Pearson.
Conners, C.K. (1997) *Conners' Rating Scales (Revised)*, NFER: Nelson.
Ellis, A. (1979) 'The rational-emotive approach to counselling', in Burk, Jr. H. M. and Stefflre, B. (eds.) *Theories of Counselling*, New York: McGraw-Hill.
Kelley, H.H (1967) 'Attribution Theory in Social Psychology', in D. Levine (ed.) *Nebraska Symposium on Motivation*, Lincoln: University of Nebraska Press.

McGuire, J. and Richman, N. (1987) *Pre-School Behaviour Checklist*, NFER-Nelson.

Rogers, C. (1961) *On Becoming a Person: a therapist's view of psychotherapy*, London: Constable.

Rutter, M. (1967) 'A children's behaviour questionnaire for completion by teachers', *Journal of Child Psychology and Psychiatry* 8, 1, 1–11.

Skinner, B.F. (1974) *About Behaviorism*, New York: Knopf.

Watson, J.B. (1932) *Behaviorism*, Revised Ed., Chicago: University of Chicago Press.

16 Teaching children with emotional difficulties

Isobel Urquhart

EDITOR'S SUMMARY

This final chapter deals with perhaps one of the most difficult and personally challenging aspect of the teacher's work. Children with emotional difficulties are inevitably uncomfortable to live with in the close confines of a Primary classroom. The painful emotions they experience also act as a powerful barrier to learning in its widest sense.

The chapter deals with the range and sources of children's emotional difficulties and explores in particular the role of early attachments. Attachment theory, beginning with the work of John Bowlby and developed by Ainsworth and others, has proved to be a powerful tool in analysing and understanding the needs of children with emotional difficulties.

The means by which a secure emotional base is established, or not, are explored and the consequences for the young child in relation to self-concept, social relationships, autonomy and independence, problem-solving, perseverance, resilience, symbolic play and learning are clearly set out.

The final part of the chapter reviews strategies by which teachers may help insecure children feel safe and learn to explore their environment, experience success and take risks with confidence. These strategies include emotional holding, circle time and the use of children's own stories.

Introduction

Teaching children who experience emotional difficulties is an important part of our primary function as teachers: to help children learn. Learning is understood here in the widest sense, to include learning to get along with other people, or being able to modify a poor self-concept, staying on task, trying hard and remembering. Evidence suggests that cognition is intimately bound up with emotional development, and therefore emotional difficulties are of central concern in terms of children's ability to achieve educationally (Greenhalgh 1994; Sroufe 1995; Migone and Liotti 1998; Lincoln 1998). This chapter explores aspects of children's emotional development which help us understand how some children's powerful and difficult feelings prevent them from thriving in the school environment and may cause teachers a degree of emotional perplexity and frustration.

Range of emotional difficulties

It is difficult to define exactly the range of feelings and behaviour that define children with emotional difficulties (Lincoln 1998). Children with emotional difficulties often exhibit attitudes, behaviour, thoughts and feelings which suggest a pronounced emotional *resistance* to learning (Barrett and Varma 1996). Faced with situations that arouse their anxieties, children may adopt defensive measures to protect them from experiencing painful feelings which they fear will be overpowering. For children with emotional difficulties, reactions to these painful feelings go beyond 'sporadic naughtiness or moodiness' (DoE 1994). At the heart of their difficulties, children have often experienced profound hurt, and this may often have been in relation to adults close to them.

In school, therefore, children may:

- appear preoccupied
- find it difficult to form or sustain healthy friendships
- find it hard to get involved in work
- find it hard to take in ideas or make links between different things they know
- effectively sabotage their involvement in the class work (e.g. Danny deliberately falls off his chair, hides under the table, pulling other chairs in around him. He refuses to come out, saying he is in his castle)
- become tearful or throw tantrums, have headaches, tummy aches, sore throats.

These strategies for defending oneself against experiencing painful feelings appear to the child as effective ways to cope with troubling situations – in the immediate situation, they work as distractions, or dampers, or screens – but actually they prevent further development.

Sources of emotional difficulties

Many children with emotional difficulties have lived with high levels of anxiety and unhappiness because of circumstances outside school. Some children have been frightened or confused by events around them. Some have been abused physically, sexually or emotionally, or have been neglected. Children may live with parents who are themselves in emotional difficulty or are very ill. Some experience significant losses during childhood, e.g. move home, experience bereavements or multiple separations, endure lengthy absences of parents through imprisonment, or have arrived in a country that does nothing to make immigration easy. Children may have had frequent moves from foster home to foster home, or have experienced numerous exclusions and interruptions from schooling.

It is wrong, however, to lay the blame solely on the child experiencing emotional difficulties or on their parents, a response that denies the major contribution to individual development made by social and economic circumstances. Indeed, developmental theories such as attachment theory make strong links with the social circumstances children experience. Social differences, directly or indirectly, have been repeatedly found to predict, for example, security of attachment, with social advantage usually associated with secure attachment (Fonagy 1998).

Not all children's emotional difficulties are explicable in terms of these kinds of social factors, however. Some relate more to very early relationships and experiences that are not easily accessible to conscious thought. In favourable conditions, however, children in emotional difficulty can sometimes show us that, behind an inexplicably aggressive and hostile attitude, or an exasperating level of stupid behaviour, they are experiencing serious levels of fear, hurt and anxiety that inhibit their learning and social development. Understanding that these children are often attempting to avoid situations where their feelings are just too painful or frightening to think about helps teachers to understand both their own and the children's emotional reactions in the classroom, and thus to respond more effectively.

We are all prey to emotional difficulties at times. We know ourselves how feelings and levels of anxiety are aroused, modified or otherwise influenced by factors within particular social and learning contexts. The implication for teachers is that any particular classroom event, such as a particular teaching style, or how transitions are handled, or even who a child is asked to work with, can make things feel more or less threatening for a child. More positively, there are practical changes we can make to improve these factors. Such preventative action can contribute towards giving children a chance to feel safer and more contained, and so have the emotional space to learn and relate to others in a better way. Emotional difficulties are experienced in the context of relationships (or the failure of relationships), including how our own feelings are involved in our perceptions of the children we teach (Salzberger-Wittenberg *et al.* 1983; Hanko 1985; Decker *et al.* 1999). It is important, therefore, for teachers to be aware of how feelings that are aroused in us by children with emotional difficulties influence how we relate to them and the decisions we make on their behalf.

The role of early attachments

In this chapter, I intend to focus the discussion of children's emotional difficulties in terms of their early attachment experiences. Attachment theory does not pretend to be a comprehensive explanation of children's emotional difficulties. However, it is a powerful explanation of how early experiences may make some children particularly vulnerable to emotional difficulties in later life. For teachers, an understanding of the power and importance of the dynamic of attachment – the need to feel safe, and the need to explore – can help in understanding why children are emotionally distressed and how the school environment can be both a source of that distress but also a new chance to create more positive attachments and eventually learn more effectively (Barrett and Trevitt 1991).

Attachment theory also relates to the idea that social interaction is the basis of 'all higher functions and their relationships.' (Wertsch 1985). From birth, children communicate and establish meanings within the relationship they form with their care-givers and these become shared understandings between people. These meanings are *emotionally* experienced and communicated. Attachment theory is an example of this: attachments formed between infants and care-givers are constructed emotionally but are also conditional on the intersubjective development of cognitive processes (Sroufe 1995). Furthermore, attachment behaviour is designed to control the behaviour of the care-giver – getting and maintaining the proximity of the care-giver – which implies a cognitive capacity to understand the care-giver as having goals for her actions and to alter their own behaviour in order to achieve proximity or explore the environment.

Attachment theory, therefore, is a durable and powerful tool for understanding the source of some children's emotional difficulties and is currently concerned in describing the links between emotional development and cognitive learning (Sroufe 1995, Meins 1997). It offers the teacher an explanatory system which may help in understanding the emotional and learning needs of children with emotional difficulties. Teachers can use the theory to provide children with the kind of relationship and learning environment that sensitively recognises and supports their need both for security and for exploration and autonomy, e.g. in planning, differentiation of the curriculum, classroom organisation. It provides a framework within which teachers can make sense of children's troubling behaviour. Understanding that children with emotional difficulties may communicate their early attachment feelings indirectly through their behaviour can help us respond in a way that does not confirm early anxieties, and this is essential if children are to make changes in how they feel about themselves, other people and the learning environment (Barrett and Varma 1996).

Attachment theory

> Attachment: an affectional tie that one person or animal forms between himself and another specific one – a tie that binds them together in space and endures over time.
>
> (Ainsworth and Bell 1991:78).

John Bowlby (1907–1990) first suggested the importance of attachment behaviour in children's emotional development. He used the term to describe a universal and innate care-seeking need for relationship, which is accompanied by a number of attachment behaviours designed to ensure the proximity (closeness) of a care-giver. This bond is experienced emotionally by an infant, and separation from the care-giver causes feelings of anxiety, unhappiness and loss. Babies exhibit attachment behaviours designed to re-establish the proximity of the care-giver, at which point the attachment behaviour will usually subside, and the baby appears soothed and comforted by the proximity of the care-giver. Attachment behaviours in infants and very young children take the form of crying, calling out, watching the care-giver, smiling at her or his reappearance, or lifting up their arms to be picked up. Attachment behaviours, however, continue throughout life and could include more complex behaviours such as feeling homesick, for example. In older children and adults, the separation anxiety that triggers attachment behaviour may be experienced as feelings of anxiety, loss, and yearning. Much of what is called 'attention-seeking' behaviour in schools might more usefully be described as attachment-seeking behaviour. However, if early experiences of seeking attachments have not been positive, children's later development may be complicated by defensive measures designed to protect the child from painful memories of disappointed attempts to establish warm, caring proximity with the care-giver. When a baby's care-seeking behaviour meets a consistently care-giving response, Bowlby argued that a 'secure attachment' would form. If there are problems in the interaction between seeker and care-giver, then an insecure attachment may develop.

Secure and insecure attachments and Ainsworth's strange situation

Ainsworth's early studies of mothers and children (Ainsworth 1991; Ainsworth and Wittig 1991) led her to maintain that infants' responses to separations and reunions with their mothers indicated differences in the quality of their attachment relationship. She devised a laboratory test that reproduced a natural situation – mothers leaving their babies for a few minutes – which would assess different patterns of attachment. In the Strange Situation, the one-year-old infant is subjected to two very brief separations from the main care-giver, followed by reunions. Thus, the baby is induced into seeking proximity to and maintaining contact with the mother.

- Mother and baby are introduced into a room with two chairs and some toys.
- Mother and baby remain alone, and the baby is free to explore (3 minutes).
- A stranger enters the room, sits down, talks to the mother and then tries to engage the baby in play (3 minutes).
- The mother leaves, and the stranger and the baby remain alone (3 minutes).
- First reunion: the mother returns and the stranger leaves unobtrusively. The mother settles the baby if necessary, and then tries to withdraw to her chair (3 minutes).
- The mother then leaves. The baby remains alone for up to 3 minutes, although if the mother feels the baby is overly distressed, this can be cut short.
- The stranger returns and tries to settle the baby if necessary, and then withdraws to her chair (up to 3 minutes, but cut short if the baby is distressed).
- Second reunion. The mother returns and the stranger leaves unobtrusively. The mother settles the baby and tries to withdraw to her chair (3 minutes).

Following extensive replication studies, Ainsworth *et al.* (1978) were able to classify attachments into three categories, which were augmented with a fourth category by Main and Solomon in 1986.

Babies who showed signs of an insecure–avoidant attachment

- avoid close proximity with their mothers; show little sign of being distressed when separated from them
- avoid their mothers when they come back into the room
- attend more to inanimate objects rather than interpersonal events
- are watchful of their mothers; rather inhibited in their play
- suppress signs of distress; avoid proximity.

Babies who showed signs of a secure attachment

- show a moderate amount of separation anxiety when parted from their care-giver.
- greet their mother with smiles or physical activity on her return
- are easily comforted if they need it; will then return to happy play – showing excitement or contentment in their activity
- show a ready ability to explore the environment with confidence and curiosity.

Babies who showed signs of an insecure–ambivalent attachment (also known as insecure–resistant)

- are highly distressed by mother's leaving
- are difficult to console when she returns
- seek contact with the care-giver but, at the same time, squirm and turn their heads away, or go stiff and lean away, or bat away toys that are offered to them

- continue to alternate between angry rejection and clinging behaviour towards the mother
- are inhibited from playing in an exploratory manner.

Babies who showed signs of an insecure–disorganised attachment

- are difficult to classify; manifest no obvious pattern of behaviours on reunion
- manifest behaviours often described as 'frozen', or 'scared stiff' and are disorganised in response
- the care-giver may herself be frightened (Main and Hesse 1990)
- may be linked to abuse or maternal depression (Meins 1997)
- There is some evidence that the mothers may be somehow unpredictably frightening

(Marrone 1998).

A secure base

If early attachment behaviour meets with sensitive and timely responses, young children can use their mother or main care-giver as a 'secure base' from which to explore the world. Whenever the experience of separation becomes too great, the securely attached child has confidence that the attachment figure remains available and will provide a supportive and safe base to which to return.

For example, one- to two-year-old children return to their mother between bouts of exploration; they may bring her a ball they have been playing with, or try to attract her attention with some talk-like sounds or by looking at something and getting the mother to look at it too. In contrast, insecurely attached children have conflicting and anxious feelings because they simultaneously seek attachment *and* have bad memories of what happens *when* they seek it. They do not feel fully at ease either with the proximity of their attachment figures, or with their absence. They therefore find themselves experiencing anxiety or painful conflicts of emotion when separated from their base: e.g. when trying to form new relationships, or in experiencing a form of separation-anxiety as they try to learn. Their energies focus on maintaining proximity or on sustaining protective defences against feeling anxious. Their capacity to explore can be impaired.

Although the exploratory tendency has an obvious physical dimension as the baby learns to walk and physically move away from its carers, this dynamic of a need for a safe place of certainty, on the one hand, and an opportunity to be adventurous, exploratory and autonomous, on the other, influences how children develop cognitively as well as emotionally (Bretherton *et al.* 1990; Main 1991; Trevarthen 1998). The return to security and the push to explore is a mental imperative as well as a physical process.

Non-verbal social interactions are the start of a process which leads to higher cognitive functions such as language development, but seem to begin in early attachment responses to proximity-seeking and proximity-retaining activities initiated by the baby (Bruner 1975). These kinds of interactions enable the baby to construct a mental model of their external experience and of him or herself in relation to the care-giver and the environment. Bowlby coined this mental representation the 'internal working model'.

The internal working model

The internal working model is a mental representation of the attachment experience and influences the subsequent development of important cognitive components such as memory and the capacity to learn (Main 1991).

> Interactions provide the organism with mental representations which make up models of the working properties, characteristics and behaviour of the attachment figure, the self, others, and the world.
>
> (Cassidy 1990:114)

The child's early repeated experiences of attachment form a pattern of events which eventually become mental representations. Young children develop a memory of the availability of the attachment figure. Good memories of the reliability of the care-giver allow a child to feel greater confidence that separation is finite and therefore endurable, and so the infant becomes more able to explore its environment and remain separate for longer from the care-giver. Consequently, the child develops an increasing degree of autonomy and confidence.

However, early mental representations of insecurely attached children exert a more determining influence on subsequent attachment experiences. Because the early representations of insecurely attached children also include the need to defend themselves against conflicting feelings such as anxiety and anger with the attachment figure for perceived abandonment, together with a continuing innate desire for proximity, anxieties continue to be aroused by new situations, rather than being modified by new experience, and continue to be dealt with defensively.

Self concept

Securely attached children seem to develop a more positive global self concept and sense of self-efficacy than insecurely attached children (Cassidy 1990). If a child experiences neglect, confusion, or rejection in his or her early attachment relationship, there is little in this experience to make the child feel valued or worthwhile to the care-giver – and thus the child may develop, as part of this representation of self in relationship, a sense of worthlessness (Cassidy 1990). This representation of a lack of self-worth then influences children's expectations about themselves in further encounters with people and with learning and this may be evident in the school environment.

Children may experience profound anxieties not only about the form of relationship it is safe or desirable to have with an adult stranger but also about the challenges of making friends with other children.

The internal working model and possession of a secure base may also affect learning, since learning inevitably faces children with risk and uncertainty and separation from the familiarity of their existing mental representations. Children who feel less in control of the dynamic of safety and exploration are unlikely to take risks or embrace new experience with enthusiasm or excitement, and will find setbacks more distressing. Poor self-concept will exacerbate how they approach learning and what they expect of themselves in learning tasks. For example, some insecure children will be wary and watchful about the impact of their achievements upon significant attachment figures and will take few risks, preferring to repeat skills and learning they already understand and can do. While they appear emotionally in control, a fear of rejection may nevertheless make them avoid moving, mentally or physically, from certainty.

Bowlby (1988) noted that avoidantly attached children seemed to 'lack a narrative of their own life'. They did not derive from their attachment experiences a sense of personal agency in the world. Such children may appear unable to take responsibility for their own learning, or adopt or keep to a plan that helps them learn. In situations that make them feel unsafe, children may behave defensively, adopting avoiding and sabotaging behaviours. They may respond with hostility or become tearful or panicky or feel they can't think.

New learning and new experiences that take them away from what they know can make some children feel very anxious since separation from the comforting certainties of the care-giver was very distressing for them, but they can also feel very angry with the instigator of new learning who is perceived to have failed keep them safe and to have rejected their needs. Children may react with hostility and reject efforts to encourage them or show them warmth.

Secure attachment and exploratory behaviour in learning

This dynamic between a safe base and the capacity to move out from the safe base in order to explore seems to have the greatest importance in the child's subsequent development. Securely attached children do not need to spend their mental and emotional energies establishing a secure base. They can contemplate the unfamiliar, the strange and the new, and expect to be effective in those environments. They experience themselves as competent, and experience the urge to know and explore optimistically, leading to further favourable experiences.

Learning necessarily involves an encounter with what is not yet known, and our attachment disposition influences how exciting or terrifying this exploration into the unknown is likely to feel. Learning usually feels good for securely attached children; they are more likely to be enthusiastic about trying out new skills, more flexible, resourceful and tolerant of frustration, more persistent in task completion and problem-solving, better at symbolic play (Meins 1997). However, it feels threatening to insecurely attached children, and may elicit the defensive responses that characterise their insecure attachment experiences.

The beneficial correlations of secure attachment

This formulation is derived from Marrone (1998) and Meins (1997).

Social relationships

Securely attached children:
- relate well to peers throughout childhood
- are more confident with new people.

Insecurely attached children:
- experience conflicting feelings in forming relationships
- may be identified as easy victims by bullies and lack emotional resilience
- may become victimisers: develop aggressive behaviour as a defence against feelings of vulnerability which they cannot tolerate in themselves or others
- find it hard to trust others.

Autonomy and independence

Securely attached children:
- develop positive attitudes to autonomy and independence
- are confident to express their feelings, experience sadness and loss without emotional collapse.

Insecurely attached children:
- tend to react emotionally to events
- may be more clinging, needing the proximity of teachers to go on with work.

Problem-solving and task completion

Securely attached children:
- complete tasks and approach problem-solving more effectively.

Insecurely attached children:
- give up easily with challenging tasks
- find it hard to tolerate delays in achieving success.

Symbolic play

Symbolic play is the ability to pretend that one object is something entirely different or to imagine a pretend object in the absence of anything. In the early years from three to seven it holds great significance for intellectual development. As children use objects to 'stand for' something other than their everyday use, as when they turn a pile of Lego bricks into pirates' stew (see below), they create their own 'zone of proximal development'. In this exploratory zone, children construct their learning about real life events, and develop further mental control and understanding over them. Thus Andy and Serafino in the scene below rehearse in symbolic form their understanding of cooking and looking after the baby, as well as exploring what it means to be a pirate.

SERAFINO: I'm Captain Blood!

ANDY: I'm Captain Hook – you're not Captain Blood he's asleep.

SERAFINO: Come on we're walking the plank!

ANDY: You have to jump. Here's some treasure – I captured it.

SERAFINO: Yeah we're pirates we can have two people playing pirates. We have to bury the treasure. I'm cooking dinner – I'm cooking soup.

ANDY: We could have roast pig stew roast pig stew roast pig stew.

SERAFINO: I am a *(inaudible)* let's go for a picnic. I'll look after Jess *(puts cat in baby basket from dressing-up box)*.

ANDY: I'm cooking the picnic on the radiator *(stirs round a saucepan full of Lego bricks, plastic food, etc.)*.

SERAFINO: Put that near the oven to keep it warm. We could put it on here that would be a good idea then I'm going to be a shark.

ANDY: You're the red shark – we could both be sharks … *Quick!* Quick! The red sharks! *(the boys 'swim' around on the carpet. A group of girls (E., P. and L.) see that the pirate ship is unoccupied and move there.)*

SERAFINO: *(roars to the girls)* You're surrounded by sharks!
(The girls move around the kitchen area, putting on costumes.)

E: Hot spicy food on you! *(to the sharks who are shouting and trying to invade the cardboard walls of the ship)* We're going off on a journey – the sharks are coming with us – we're there! – Let's go and find the treasure!

Securely attached children:
- are more able to engage in symbolic play, especially when it represents co-operative interpersonal interactions, such as family situations in the play corner, or acting out a story.

Insecurely attached children:
- are more tentative and inhibited in using play in an exploratory way.

Symbolic play and the capacity to think

Differences in the capacity for symbolic play between securely and insecurely attached children relate to the 'ways cognitive competencies interact with social competencies.' (Slade 1987; Fonagy *et al.* 1995). Repeatedly, researchers have shown that effective learning before schooling takes place when mothers (it is usually mothers) interact with their babies in a 'contingent' way to ensure successful learning (Meins 1997). Research demonstrates that particular styles of maternal interaction in play situations influences children's abilities to play symbolically, and thus offers a way for attachment theorists to compare differences in attachment relationships with the main caregiver to differences in capacity to engage in symbolic play (Meins 1997). Those mothers who are attuned to their babies' needs, who match their own behaviour to their empathic understanding of what their babies need in the way of help (i.e. the kinds of mothers who enable secure attachments), make the most helpful kinds of response. Children internalise these social interaction processes which then become part of their own cognitive functioning. Attachment theory contributes to this argument the fact that the process is not only social but also is embedded in an affective (i.e. emotional) relationship, and that it begins very much earlier. This means that older children may genuinely be unable to verbalise or think about why they feel the way they do, because some of the crucial experience that impacts on how they feel now occurred so early that it is inaccessible to conscious thought. Similarly, defences designed to protect them from painful feelings of anxiety and frustration may also have been first experienced and formed pre-verbally.

Persistence and Resilience

Securely attached children:
- have a more resilient and robust sense of selfhood which spurs the individual to persist with challenging circumstances.

Insecurely attached children:
- exhibit low self-esteem and lack of resilience in challenging circumstances, give up easily or are unable to regulate their feelings

Classroom responses

This section examines classroom responses in terms of the attachment dynamic of feeling safe, and exploring the environment. It focuses on the primary function of teachers to help children learn, and emphasises preventative approaches, looking at how teachers form relationships with children in the classroom and how they plan and teach their lessons.

Feeling safe

Safe to form relationships

Children with emotional difficulties often come to school having experienced countless failures in their relationships with other people. The experience of unreciprocated attempts to form relationships in their first attachments has been unbearable and so children use various ways to block off their awareness of feelings that seem so powerful, dangerous and persecutory. As teachers, we have first to accept that these feelings are very real. Our role is to help children turn these powerful feelings into a capacity to think about them and subsequently be able to regulate them. Once children gain some control over their feelings, they are better able to turn their attention to their learning. We help children manage their feelings partly by demonstrating in our own response to difficult feelings, that it *is* possible to think and talk about those emotions rather than act them out defensively. We also help by providing a safe environment in which to begin to turn those feelings into thoughts that can be managed better.

Defences against the development of feelings

A defence is a psychological barrier which functions to protect the personality from the fear of threat or anxiety, and to keep the conflict which it masks out of consciousness. Emotional defences manifest themselves as various forms of behaviour which serve to keep the child at an emotional distance from other people.

(Greenhalgh 1994:49)

The problem is that 'emotional defences' prevent further development: they deter the development of thought and inhibit the child from responding resourcefully or creatively to their feelings.

Projection of painful feelings

Projection is an emotional defence that is used to deal with emotions that are so unbearable we cannot allow ourselves even to be conscious of them. We try to get rid of the feeling so it does not seem to be ours any more, but is situated outside ourselves. Children who project their difficult feelings split them off from their conscious awareness and cause other people to feel them instead. It is also a primitive pre-verbal way of letting others know about one's feelings. Nevertheless, the children who project their feelings genuinely perceive those unpleasant feelings as emanating from the other person. Similarly, the recipient of a projection may experience the feeling as their own rather than as a projection from someone else.

Teachers will inevitably sometimes be the recipients of children's projections. By paying close attention to our own feelings as projected communications of how a child may be feeling, teachers can learn something of the emotional conflicts that are troubling the child. Teachers may feel hurt, angry, anxious, incompetent or stupid because these feelings are being 'projected' by children. We may then find ourselves reacting to those feelings, e.g. feeling panic that we are not in control of the situation, or depressed and useless because we cannot help a child learn, or angry and frustrated at a child's rejecting behaviour. These may feel like our spontaneous responses to the situation, but taking time to reflect before we react may give us time to turn those feelings into reflective thoughts and an understanding about why we might be feeling those emotions. For example, noticing her own feelings of exasperation and impatience with Sally, forever writing 'Onc ther woz a princes ... ' and then throwing it away, a teacher may be better able to empathise with Sally's own sense of frustration at how difficult it is to get things right, and be perfect like a princess.

By learning to understand children's behaviour as a communication and expression of their feelings, we can avoid acting out our own defences against difficult feelings. If children see, by our reactions, that *we* also cannot tolerate experiencing difficult feelings, they may conclude that those feelings really are intolerable and overpowering, and thus their belief is confirmed that they are best got rid of (i.e. projected). Children's projections do often trigger in us our own most vulnerable feelings, and this can explain the exhaustion, disappointment or frustration we can feel when working with children with emotional difficulties. Understanding this can help us to sustain some personal resilience and to contain our own difficult feelings rather than expressing them back to children.

Being a container

Bion (1962, 1970) described the 'containing' function of the mother as the capacity to contain disturbing feelings coming from the baby, make sense of them and reintroduce them to the child at a time and in a form that was manageable for the child. For example, a mother may feel some anguish when her baby cries, but also understands that the baby is communicating a need that can be thought about and can communicate this understanding through her response: picking up and cuddling her baby, for example. Such an empathic response is precisely what the securely attached baby experiences. Teachers who are able to hold in their consciousness the meaning of the child's behaviour thus act as a 'container' by understanding the child's feelings and responding in a thought-about way that communicates to the child that difficult feelings can be 'lived with, thought about and understood' (Greenhalgh 1994).

The goal for the child is to learn that they do not have to project their difficult feelings because they themselves can now tolerate and hold within themselves the experience of painful feelings. However, this process is not easy to begin because a child has to *trust* that it is safe not to use the usual defences against experiencing precisely those difficult feelings of anguish and anxiety. By acting as containers, teachers provide an emotionally holding environment which provides firm, consistent boundaries, a secure, accepting relationship and a safe environment until such time that a child can develop enough trust to risk lowering his or her defences. That is, care-givers provide an emotionally holding environment which holds and contains the infants' disturbing feelings until they can manage those feelings themselves in the development of the internal working model. In schools, teachers can similarly work towards providing an emotionally holding environment. Teachers' capacity to understand children's unconscious communications, and to act as a container for projected feelings, is part of that holding function.

Emotional holding and creating a secure base

Ward (1998) describes emotional holding as including the following elements.

- The provision of appropriate boundaries for behaviour and the expression of strong feelings, so that emotions can be expressed but do not get out of hand.
- A conscious intention to remain human and flexible at times when things go wrong; e.g. to think about rather than just react to the situation, to retain a capacity to be tolerant so that children can feel that our response, however firm, is the result of our genuine concern for them as individuals, and derives from our concern to look after them as well as our class and ourselves. Without this ability to weigh up the particular situation and the child's needs, we are likely to create a situation in which we are more concerned with controlling behaviour than containing and holding the child's feelings. This is likely to be experienced as threatening and may therefore lead to more anxiety (and ever more defensive behaviours) in the child.
- The planning and scaffolding of learning tasks so that children can both experience and learn to tolerate a manageable level of risk and anxiety, but are not left feeling unsure about their ability to achieve the task or what they have to do
- Being very clear and unambiguous in our communications with children, clarifying and resolving misunderstandings as soon as possible.

Providing an emotionally holding environment creates a second secure base in which children can begin to trust themselves and others enough so that learning can take place.

Building a secure attachment with a teacher

Teachers do spend a great deal of time with children and usually form strong, positive relationships with them that reflect some of the characteristics of secure attachments. The warmth of that trusting relationship with a teacher is at the heart of children's learning and emotional development. We can help children with emotional difficulties, therefore, by getting to know them well enough to empathise with how they are feeling in the classroom and school contexts. However annoying and disruptive it is to have Danny build a castle in the middle of the classroom, teachers can also find the empathy and emotional space to think about what it means to Danny to build himself a fortress against learning.

There will inevitably be echoes of the child's early attachments in the way a child relates to his or her teacher. Teachers know, for example, that some children will sometimes call them mum or dad by mistake. Less positively, some children with emotional difficulties may relate to the teacher suspiciously, or anxiously, influenced by previous experiences of disappointing and unsatisfying attachment relationships. Offering a relationship to such children which is as reliable and consistent as can be achieved in busy classrooms, understanding the child's unconscious communications and providing clear boundaries, and modelling to children our own resilience in the face of difficult feelings, we may be able to give children in emotional difficulty an experience which 'keeps him [or her] safe, sets limits and helps him [or her] to manage his frustration and distress' until he or she gains enough good experiences for the insecure internal working model to adapt (Barrett and Trevitt 1991).

Core conditions

> Self-esteem can only be enhanced in a relationship, as it is only with another person that one can feel noticed, understood, taken seriously and respected.
>
> (Decker *et al.* 1999:20)

For a positive self to develop, people need relationships characterised by three 'core conditions': empathy, a valuing acceptance and respect for the other person, and a willingness to be real and genuine (congruent) in our response to that other person (Rogers 1978). In such a relationship a person can develop sufficient trust to risk lowering their defences and allowing new developments to occur. Teachers can use these ideals to work towards forming positive relationships with children with emotional difficulties. By *empathising* with the child, we can remain sensitive to the feelings behind the children's behaviour and our words and actions will be better matched to the children's emotional needs. By *being real*, by not hiding behind our own defensive behaviour, and by verbalising feelings at appropriate times, we can show the child that experiencing anxiety and anger may not be as disastrous as they fear. By *'staying with'* the child – i.e. not rejecting or giving up on a child, but sustaining an attitude of unconditional regard, in which we continue to value the individual, even when we are quite clear we do not accept the behaviour – we communicate a sense of belief in the child's worth.

Finding ways to express these core conditions and to form a relationship which pays attention, understands, takes seriously and respects the child is particularly important – and particularly difficult to remember – at the point where children fail, whether as learners or as social beings. However, evidence suggests that teachers who do offer this kind of relationship not only are more effective in boosting self-esteem, but also facilitate better learning achievements and effective classroom management (Aspy and Roebuck 1977).

We can try to be as real with children as is appropriate to our professional role, not getting too pompous, nor trying to be foolproof in all circumstances. The relief children experience, for example, when the teacher is able to admit to her own ignorance, is very powerful, and can allow children to admit in themselves to that most dreaded of all emotions: the fear of being stupid.

Circle time

Circle time is a group listening activity that draws on the ideas described above. It uses a variety of approaches including games and group problem-solving to mobilise peer bonding and build friendship groups (Mosley 1999) (see Figure 16.1). Used with careful preparation and a sensitive understanding of the process, circle time can be very effective in building trust and raising self-esteem. In a weekly session lasting about half an hour, children experience being part of a trusted group, where their feelings, views and unique strengths are explicitly acknowledged and respected. The teacher creates a safe, holding environment in which every child has equal worth and develops the skills needed to make positive relationships. Children learn how to take responsibility for their own feelings and needs, as well as developing the emotional space to explore and take care of others' feelings. Once the group is established, it functions as a place in which it is safe for feelings to be explored and taken seriously. Circle time thus encourages children with emotional difficulties to think and talk about difficult feelings and thus to regulate them better. In doing so, they develop a greater sense of autonomy and a more positive self-concept.

Stories and feelings

A story written, shared and remembered can also be like a container.
(Greenwood 1999:66)

Narrative – the capacity to tell a story – can be thought of as a primary act of mind related to an innate desire to make an ongoing coherent meaning from our lived experience. We tell ourselves about our lives as stories and, in doing so, we create ourselves as human subjects. Naturally, the story we tell ourselves about ourselves also takes account of how we feel about ourselves, and the feelings we have about the events and relationships that form our life.

In children's made-up stories, fictional narrative enables children to distance the emotional threats in the material they play out, or write or talk about. In a story, difficult feelings can be expressed and become more bearable because they are projected into other worlds and other characters. Children who are anxious no longer have to spend energy worrying about,

Figure 16.1 Circle time: 'We are passing the smile round', by Becky, aged 6.

or keeping from their conscious awareness, the anguish they feel, since the difficult feelings in the story are constructed as 'not theirs', and so they are freer to acknowledge, tolerate and explore them. The fiction itself has a containing function. Where children – often with writing difficulties – tell their stories to adult scribes, there is the additional factor that the scribe also acts as a container, someone able to tolerate the expression of angry, destructive feelings, for example, without making the child feel naughty, or dangerous, or stupid. Children who:

> … can't remember, can't articulate, or can't face talking about their preoccupations can thus communicate them through stories and characters, and have a feeling that such difficulties are understandable.
>
> (Greenwood 1999:84)

In Dawn's narratives, both in the fictional stories she dictated, and in her spoken narratives about her own life, she explored what it felt like to be a compliant, helpless and bullied little girl (Urquhart 1994; Urquhart 1999). In her fictional stories, Dawn moves, over time, from dictating a story in which her happiness depended on a magic man who made her wishes come true to a story about a girl who was the netball captain and who initiated the adventures that she and the other girls would have. A similar movement from dependency to something more adventurous occurred in her spoken narratives. She begins by telling the scribe about how she was *so* helpful to her mother, her Nan, and her neighbours that she was known as Darling Dawn to everyone. But in her last session, Dawn confides with a sense of delighted dis-covery that she does not really want to be Darling Dawn all the time.

Jedd substitutes a benevolent and loving father in his dictated fictional sto-ries for the real life narrative he told about the frightening, violent men who had come to stay with him. Only in his fiction could Jedd bear to think about what it might be like to want a kind dad who came home after a long absence and took care of his family.

The combination of writing dictated stories with the opportunity to slip in and out of autobiographical narrative has proved very effective with children with emotional difficulties. There is something very special about the presence of an understanding adult who scribes the child's words, who, in between writ-ing down the words, is open to talking and relating warmly to the child. Expe-rience and story interweave in a dialogue in which new meanings are spoken aloud, played with and become available to children who find it very difficult to explore new possibilities. Jedd's usual hostile, frozen inability to make new meanings – 'it's all agony and pain, miss', – his inability to think about the part of him that longed for affectionate relationship, was lowered just a little in these sessions. Sensing that the scribe could accept his communications meant he could go on to tell (and thus think about) the story of the loving father. Although we are right not to simplistically interpret children through their fic-tions, we can communicate our understanding of the meanings of the fiction by responding in kind, within the metaphor that the fiction sets up. So the scribe said to Jedd, 'What a nice Dad!' rather than talking about Jedd's feelings or real life experiences. It was clear that for Dawn and Jedd the scribe's accep-tance of their communications at a symbolic level enabled symbolic thought and communication to develop and for a context to develop in which they could begin to think about their own experience in a different way (Fox 1993; Smith 1994;Urquhart 1994). The capacity to symbolise is related to the devel-opment of a secure attachment, and thus dictated story writing created a secure base in which symbolisation could develop.

The language–experience approach from which dictated stories derives does not question, modify or interpret children's dictated words. Richard's story explored – in extremely gruesome and repetitive episodes of murder and bloodletting – his terrors of disintegration and lack of containment (Urquhart 1994). To acknowledge implicitly by scribing them that these *are* the terrible feelings that Richard is feeling did not imply that they were con-doned. But if we censor the relatively contained and distanced expression of those feelings in stories, how or where can Richard contemplate them? How is he to gain some mastery over them by turning them from behaviour into something that he can internalise and think about?

Teachers often make children's dictated stories into books for the child's own reading, affirming the worth and significance of the child's narrative (Smith 1994). The books should be carefully made and substantial, able to stand up to frequent use. Making their stories into something physically attractive and durable demonstrates respect for the real substance of their stories, as well as for the work and the feelings that went into making the story. The making of the book conveys an important message to children about the containment and valuing of their communications. When it is 'all inside the firm covers of the book', and private to the child to read again or not as he or she likes, there often follows a period of obsessive reading over and over again, and then a discarding of the book. Intriguingly this suggests that children internalise aspects of their own fictions, and when they have done so, no longer need the artefact. Thus:

> ...an individual child can use her work as a means to contain and keep together her mind and her sense of self, investing the work with significance beyond its intrinsic meaning and purpose.
>
> (Best 1998:183)

Exploration and learning

Once children feel relatively safe and have developed some trust, they have more cognitive space for attention and reflective and exploratory thought (Fonagy *et al.* 1995). Children with emotional difficulties need to experience genuine success in learning.

Competence and success: the development of an academic self-concept

The learning process can seem very frightening and full of dread, arousing for some children feelings of being useless and stupid, being unable to think, being unacceptable to others and helpless, shamed, hopeless or panicked when exposed to the unknown. Insecurely attached children divert much of their mental energies into making themselves feel safe. They may do this by inflexibly trying to relate to new experiences in old ways which do not allow new learning, or by diverting their attention away from the threatening experiences of learning completely. They may cling, as to a plank in a shipwreck, to their existing representations about self, the learning and other people, even when their internal working model does not work very well for them. For example, Sally's story, 'Onc ther woz a princes ...' never varied. The princess could be called into existence, but she could not move or act in the story world, just as Sally, a 'frozen' child, could not.

Taking risks and feeling stupid

Most of us can remember times when we have felt stupid, and can reflect on how we managed that experience. Feeling stupid may lead to panic, or feeling very dependent on someone else whom we hope knows what they are doing – and then resenting them if they don't know everything when we need them to. We may feel overwhelmed and collapse in despair at our inability to grasp anything at all about the matter. Or, we may distract ourselves with more enjoyable activities or wander off into a daydream.

And yet some experience of challenge and risk is needed in order for any learning to occur and for the learner to experience their competence and capacity for autonomy. With children with emotional difficulties, teachers have to be especially careful to manage the balance:

> ... between the amount of risk experienced in an activity and the amount of anxiety which might be experienced by a learner.
>
> (Greenhalgh 1994:231)

Teachers usually meet individual needs through differentiation. As we have seen, the capacity to think, to make meaning out of their experience, can be difficult for children with emotional difficulties, and it is the teacher's ability to do this thinking for them, through the time spent planning, differentiating, preparing and scaffolding learning tasks for children, i.e. by holding their needs in mind, that creates an environment in which it is safe to learn.

Conclusion

If teachers are to work in this way with their own feelings and with the relationships they form with children, schools must also look to their own organisational structures. How might a school provide a holding environment for the teachers and their difficult feelings? How can it provide time and a safe way for teachers to share the vicissitudes and the learning involved in working with difficult children? Some schools set up times when teachers can meet and talk about their experiences with individual children (Hanko 1995).

Ultimately, our responses to children with emotional difficulties, whether as individual teachers or school communities, involve our fundamental values and ideals about why we choose to be teachers in the first place, and what kinds of places we want schools to be. Teaching children with emotional difficulties can create significant but rarely publicly acknowledged dilemmas for teachers as they try to fulfil their obligations towards government and national policies while simultaneously trying to respond effectively to individuals with emotional needs: the sad, the confused, the angry and the humiliated children who sometimes appear in our classrooms.

Activities

Planning for autonomy and success

Plan a typical activity for a class of Primary aged children.
How will you plan for the 'anxiety-risk' ratio through scaffolding the task towards a successful outcome, developing children's autonomy, grouping, etc.?

> **Scribing stories**
>
> Over two or three days offer to scribe a story for a child who has emotional difficulties. When you have scribed the story or stories, make a small but sturdy book for the child to keep. Observe how the child responds to the offer to scribe, what kind of relationship forms between you and the child, and the way the stories are dictated and responded to by the author. Does the story seem to give the child a way to talk about difficult feelings?

Further reading

Barrett, M. and Trevitt, J. (1991) *Attachment Behaviour and the School Child – An Introduction to Educational Therapy*. London: Routledge.

Barrett, M. and Varma, V. (eds) (1996) *Educational Therapy in Clinic and Classroom*, Whurr.

Decker, S. *et al.* (1999) *Taking Children Seriously*, London: Cassell.

Garton, A. (1992) *Social Interaction and the Development of Language and Cognition*, Hillsdale: Erlbaum.

Greenhalgh, P. (1994) *Emotional Growth and Learning*, London: Routledge.

References

Ainsworth, M. D. S. (1991) 'The development of infant–mother interaction among the Ganda', in Parkes, C.M., Stevenson-Hinde, J. and Marris, P. (eds) *Attachment across the Life Cycle*, London: Routledge.

Ainsworth, M. D. S. and Bell, S. M. (1970) 'Attachment, exploration and separation: illustrated by the behaviour of one-year-olds in a strange situation', in *Child Development* 41, 49–67.

Ainsworth, M.D.S. and Bell, S.M. (1991) 'Some contemporary patterns in the feeding situation', in Parkes, C.M., Stevenson-Hinde, J. and Marris, P. (eds) *Attachment accross the Life Cycle*, London: Routledge.

Ainsworth, M.D.S., Blehar, M.C., Waters, E. and Wall, S. (1978) *Patterns of Attachment: a psychological study of the Strange Situation*, Erlbaum.

Ainsworth, M.D.S., and Wittig, B.A. (1991) 'Attachment and the exploratory behaviour of one-year-olds in a strange situation' in Parkes, C.M., Stevenson-Hinde, J. and Marris, P. (eds) *Attachment accross the Life Cycle*, London: Routledge.

Aspey, D.N. and Roebuck, F.N. (1977) *Kids Don't Learn From Teachers They Don't Like*, Amherst, Mass.: Human Resource Development Press.

Barrett, M. and Trevitt, J. (1991) *Attachment Behaviour and the School Child – An Introduction to Educational Therapy*, London: Routledge.

Barrett, M. and Varma, V. (eds) (1996) *Educational Therapy in Clinic and Classroom*, London: Whurr.

Best, D. (1998) 'Therapeutic work in an educational setting.' In Ward, A. with McMahon, L (eds) *Intuition is Not Enough: matching learning with practice in therapeutic child care*, London: Routledge.

Bion, W. (1962) *Learning from Experience*, London: Heinemann.

Bion, W. (1970) *Attention and Interpretation*, London: Tavistock.

Bowlby, J. (1951) *Maternal Care and Mental Health*, HMSO. Abridged: (1965) *Child Care and the Growth of Love*. 2nd edition. London: Penguin.

Bowlby, J. (1958) 'The nature of the child's tie to his mother', *International Journal of Psycho-Analysis* 39, 350–73.

Bowlby, J. (1973) *Attachment and loss: Vol. 2. Separation*, New York: Basic Books.

Bowlby, J. (1988) *A Secure Base: Clinical applications of Attachment Theory*, London: Routledge.

Bretherton, I., Ridgeway, D. and Cassidy, J. (1990) 'Assessing Internal Working Models of the Attachment Relationship: an Attachment Story Completion Task for 3 year olds', in M.T. Greenberg, *et al.* (eds) *Attachment in the Pre-school Years*, Chicago: University of Chicago Press.

Bruner, J.S. (1975) 'From Communication to Language, a psychological perspective' *Cognition* 3, 255–87.

Bruner, J. (1986) *Actual Minds, Possible Worlds*, Cambridge, MA: Harvard University Press.

Bruner, J. (1992) *Acts of Meaning*, Cambridge, MA: Harvard University Press.

Cassidy, J. (1990) 'Theoretical and Methodological Considerations in the Study of Attachment and the Self in Young Children', in M.T.Greenberg, *et al.* (eds) *Attachment in the Pre-school Years*, Chicago: University of Chicago Press.

Decker, S. et al. (eds) (1999) *Taking Children Seriously*, London: Cassell.

DoE (Department of Education) (1994) *The Education of Children with Emotional and Behavioural Difficulties*, Circular 9/94, DoE: London.

Fonagy, P., Steele, M., Steele, H., Moran, G. and Higgit, A. (1991) 'The capacity for understanding mental states: the reflective self in parent and child and its significance for security of attachment', *Infant Mental Health Journal* 13, 201–218.

Fonagy, P., Steele, M., Steele, H., Leigh, T., Kennedy, R., Mattoon, G. and Target, M. (1995) 'Attachment, the Reflective Self and Borderline States: the predictive specificity of the Adult Attachment Interview and pathological emotional development', in Marrone, M. *Attachment and Interaction*, London: Jessica Kingsley.

Fonagy, P. (1998) 'Early Influences on Development and Social Inequalities', paper for Sir Donald Acheson's Independent Inquiry into Inequalities in Health. (http//:cf.psychoanalysis.net/fonpap.htm)

Fox, C. (1993) *At the Very Edge of the Forest*, London: Cassell.

Garton, A. (1992) *Social Interaction and the Development of Language and Cognition*, Hillsdale: Erlbaum.

Greenhalgh, P. (1994) *Emotional Growth and Learning*, London: Routledge.

Greenwood, A. (1999) 'Stories and writing', in Decker, S. et al. (eds) (1999) *Taking Children Seriously*, London: Cassell.

Hanko, G. (1985) *Special Needs in Ordinary Classrooms*, 3rd edition. Oxford: Blackwell.

Lincoln, P. (1998) *Developing a National Policy for Children with Emotional and Behavioural Difficulties*, A report by the Sub-Group on Emotional and Behavioural Difficulties to the National Advisory Group on Special Educational Needs (www.ngfl.gov.uk)

Main, M. and Solomon, J. (1986) 'Discovery of an insecure disorganised/disoriented attachement pattern: procedures, findings and implications for the classification of behaviour'. In Yogman, M. and Brazelton, T.B. (eds) *Affective Development in Infancy*, Norwood, N.J.: Ablex.

Main, M. and Hesse, E. (1990) 'Interview-based assessments of a parent's unresolved trauma related to "infant D" attachment status: linking parental states of mind to infant behavior observed in a stressful situation', in Greenberg, M.T., Cicchetti, D. and Cummings, E.M. (eds) *Attachment in the Pre-School Years. Theory, Research aind Intervention*, Chicago: University of Chicago Press.

Main, M. (1991) 'Metacognitive knowledge, metacognitive monitoring and singular (coherent) vs. multiple (incoherent) model of attachment: findings and directions for future research', in Parkes, C. M., *et al.* (eds) *Attachment across the Life Cycle*, London: Routledge.

Marrone, M. (1998) *Attachment and Interaction*, London: Jessica Kingsley.

Meins, E. (1997) *Security of Attachment and the Social Development of Cognition*, London: Psychology Press.

Migone, P. and Liotti, G. (1998) 'Psychoanalysis and Cognitive-Evolutionary Psychology: an attempt at integration', *International Journal of Psycho-Analysis* 79, 1071–95.

Mosley, J. (1999) 'Circle Time: a whole class peer support model', in Decker, S. *et al.* (eds) *Taking Children Seriously*, London: Cassell.

Rogers, C. (1978) *Carl Rogers on Personal Power*, London: Constable.

Rogers, C. (ed.) (1983) *Freedom to Learn in the Eighties*, New York: Merrill.

Salzberger-Wittenberg, I., Henty, G. and Osborne, E. (1983) *The Emotional Experience of Learning and Teaching*, London: Routledge.

Slade, A. (1987) 'Quality of attachment and early symbolic play', *Developmental Psychology* 23, 83.

Smith, B. (1994) *Through Writing to Reading*, London: Routledge.

Sroufe, L. A. (1995) *Emotional Development. The Organisation of Emotional Life in the Early Years*, Cambridge: Cambridge University Press.

Trevarthen, C. (1998) *Children with Autism*, London: Jessica Kingsley.

Trevarthen, C., Aitken, K., Papoudi, D. and Robarts, J. (1996) *Children with Autism: diagnosis and interventions to meet their needs*, London: Jessica Kingsley.

Urquhart, I. (1994) 'Telling Stories: dictating stories to an adult and its relation to psychotherapeutic practice', unpublished dissertation. (Anglia Polytechnic University).

Urquhart, I. (1999) '"And they lived happily ever after ... not really!" Working with children's dictated texts', in Anderson, H. and Styles, M. (eds) *Teaching through Texts*, London: Routledge.

Ward, A. with McMahon, L. (eds) (1998) *Intuition is not Enough: matching learning with practice in therapeutic child care*, London: Routledge.

Wertsch, J. V. (1985) *Vygotsky and the social formation of mind*, Cambridge, MA: Harvard University Press.

Index